British Science Fiction
Film and Television

CRITICAL EXPLORATIONS IN SCIENCE FICTION AND FANTASY
(a series edited by Donald E. Palumbo and C.W. Sullivan III)

1 *Worlds Apart? Dualism and Transgression in Contemporary Female Dystopias* (Dunja M. Mohr, 2005)

2 *Tolkien and Shakespeare: Essays on Shared Themes and Language* (ed. Janet Brennan Croft, 2007)

3 *Culture, Identities and Technology in the* Star Wars *Films: Essays on the Two Trilogies* (ed. Carl Silvio, Tony M. Vinci, 2007)

4 *The Influence of* Star Trek *on Television, Film and Culture* (ed. Lincoln Geraghty, 2008)

5 *Hugo Gernsback and the Century of Science Fiction* (Gary Westfahl, 2007)

6 *One Earth, One People: The Mythopoeic Fantasy Series of Ursula K. Le Guin, Lloyd Alexander, Madeleine L'Engle and Orson Scott Card* (Marek Oziewicz, 2008)

7 *The Evolution of Tolkien's Mythology: A Study of the History of Middle-earth* (Elizabeth A. Whittingham, 2008)

8 *H. Beam Piper: A Biography* (John F. Carr, 2008)

9 *Dreams and Nightmares: Science and Technology in Myth and Fiction* (Mordecai Roshwald, 2008)

10 Lilith *in a New Light: Essays on the George MacDonald Fantasy Novel* (ed. Lucas H. Harriman, 2008)

11 *Feminist Narrative and the Supernatural: The Function of Fantastic Devices in Seven Recent Novels* (Katherine J. Weese, 2008)

12 *The Science of Fiction and the Fiction of Science: Collected Essays on SF Storytelling and the Gnostic Imagination* (Frank McConnell, ed. Gary Westfahl, 2009)

13 *Kim Stanley Robinson Maps the Unimaginable: Critical Essays* (ed. William J. Burling, 2009)

14 *The Inter-Galactic Playground: A Critical Study of Children's and Teens' Science Fiction* (Farah Mendlesohn, 2009)

15 *Science Fiction from Québec: A Postcolonial Study* (Amy J. Ransom, 2009)

16 *Science Fiction and the Two Cultures: Essays on Bridging the Gap Between the Sciences and the Humanities* (ed. Gary Westfahl, George Slusser, 2009)

17 *Stephen R. Donaldson and the Modern Epic Vision: A Critical Study of the "Chronicles of Thomas Covenant" Novels* (Christine Barkley, 2009)

18 *Ursula K. Le Guin's Journey to Post-Feminism* (Amy M. Clarke, 2010)

19 *Portals of Power: Magical Agency and Transformation in Literary Fantasy* (Lori M. Campbell, 2010)

20 *The Animal Fable in Science Fiction and Fantasy* (Bruce Shaw, 2010)

21 *Illuminating Torchwood: Essays on Narrative, Character and Sexuality in the BBC Series* (ed. Andrew Ireland, 2010)

22 *Comics as a Nexus of Cultures: Essays on the Interplay of Media, Disciplines and International Perspectives* (ed. Mark Berninger, Jochen Ecke, Gideon Haberkorn, 2010)

23 *The Anatomy of Utopia: Narration, Estrangement and Ambiguity in More, Wells, Huxley and Clarke* (Károly Pintér, 2010)

24 *The Anticipation Novelists of 1950s French Science Fiction* (Bradford Lyau, 2010)

25 *The* Twilight *Mystique: Critical Essays on the Novels and Films* (ed. Amy M. Clarke, Marijane Osborn, 2010)

26 *The Mythic Fantasy of Robert Holdstock: Critical Essays on the Fiction* (ed. Donald E. Morse, Kálmán Matolcsy, 2011)

27 *Science Fiction and the Prediction of the Future: Essays on Foresight and Fallacy* (ed. Gary Westfahl, Wong Kin Yuen, Amy Kit-sze Chan, 2011)

28 *Apocalypse in Australian Fiction and Film: A Critical Study* (Roslyn Weaver, 2011)

29 *British Science Fiction Film and Television: Critical Essays.* (ed. Tobias Hochscherf, James Leggott, 2011)

30 *Cult Telefantasy Series: A Critical Analysis of* The Prisoner, Twin Peaks, The X-Files, Buffy the Vampire Slayer, Lost, Heroes, Doctor Who *and* Star Trek (Sue Short, 2011)

31 *The Postnational Fantasy: Postcolonialism, Cosmopolitics and Science Fiction* (ed. Masood Ashraf Raja, Jason W. Ellis, Swaralipi Nandi, 2011)

British Science Fiction Film and Television

Critical Essays

Edited by TOBIAS HOCHSCHERF and JAMES LEGGOTT

CRITICAL EXPLORATIONS IN SCIENCE FICTION AND FANTASY, 29
Donald E. Palumbo *and* C.W. Sullivan III, *series editors*

McFarland & Company, Inc., Publishers
Jefferson, North Carolina, and London

LIBRARY OF CONGRESS CATALOGUING-IN-PUBLICATION DATA

British science fiction film and television : critical essays / edited by Tobias Hochscherf and James Leggott.
    [Donald Palumbo and C.W. Sullivan III, series editors]
      p.   cm. — (Critical explorations in science fiction and fantasy ; 29)
    Includes bibliographical references and index.

ISBN 978-0-7864-4621-6
softcover : 50# alkaline paper ∞

1. Science fiction films — Great Britain — History and criticism. 2. Science fiction television programs — Great Britain — History and criticism. I. Hochscherf, Tobias, 1976– II. Leggott, James.
PN1995.9.S26B655   2011
791.43'6150941—dc22   2010053788

BRITISH LIBRARY CATALOGUING DATA ARE AVAILABLE

© 2011 Tobias Hochscherf and James Leggott. All rights reserved

No part of this book may be reproduced or transmitted in any form or by any means, electronic or mechanical, including photocopying or recording, or by any information storage and retrieval system, without permission in writing from the publisher.

Front cover: *from left* Antonia Ellis and Gabrielle Drake in *UFO* (ITV) UK, 1970-1971 (Photofest); Space craft © 2011 Shutterstock

Manufactured in the United States of America

McFarland & Company, Inc., Publishers
  Box 611, Jefferson, North Carolina 28640
    www.mcfarlandpub.com

Acknowledgments

We are grateful for the support of the School of Arts and Social Sciences at Northumbria University. Thanks are due to all the contributors for their enthusiasm and patience, and to the following for their valuable assistance: Peter Hutchings, Michael Johnson, Karen Leggott (convener of the finest *Doctor Who* parties this side of Gallifrey), David Longhorn, and Alison Peirse. We would also like to thank the series editor Donald E. Palumbo for his valuable encouragement and comments from the early stages of a proposal outline to the final manuscript. We would also like to express our gratitude to Ken Dvorak, who has made us feel welcome whenever we were attending conferences in the United States.

We are grateful for being granted permission to include two revised versions of previously published material. A version of Peter Wright's chapter was originally published as "Intertextuality, Generic Shift and Ideological Transformation in the Internationalising of *Doctor Who*" in *Foundation: The International Review of Science Fiction*, 33.92 (Autumn 2004), 64–90. I.Q. Hunter's chapter is a revised version of "*A Clockwork Orange*, Exploitation and the Art Film," in *Recycling Culture(s)*, ed. by Sara Martin (Newcastle upon Tyne: Cambridge Scholars Publishing, 2008), pp. 11–20.

Table of Contents

Acknowledgments ... vii

Introduction: British Science Fiction Beyond the TARDIS
   TOBIAS HOCHSCHERF *and* JAMES LEGGOTT ... 1

1. H.G. Wells and Science Fiction Cinema
   JAMES CHAPMAN ... 11

2. Aftermaths: Post-Apocalyptic Imagery
   CHRISTIAN HOFFSTADT *and* DOMINIK SCHREY ... 28

3. The BBC Versus "Science Fiction": The Collision of Transnational Genre and National Identity in Television of the Early 1950s
   DEREK JOHNSTON ... 40

4. Hammer Horror and Science Fiction
   DAVID SIMMONS ... 50

5. Robert Fuest and *The Final Programme*: Science Fiction and the Question of Style
   MICHAEL DU PLESSIS ... 60

6. "Anything Can Happen in the Next Half-Hour": Gerry Anderson's Transnational Science Fiction
   JONATHAN BIGNELL ... 73

7. Tracking *UFO*: Format, Text and Context
   PETER HUTCHINGS ... 85

8. *A Clockwork Orange*, Exploitation and the Art Film
   I.Q. HUNTER ... 96

9. Visions of an English Dystopia: History, Technology and the Rural Landscape in *The Tripods*
   LINCOLN GERAGHTY ... 104

10. The Future of History in Dennis Potter's *Cold Lazarus*
   CHRISTINE SPRENGLER   117

11. Expatriate! Expatriate! *Doctor Who: The Movie* and Commercial Negotiation of a Multiple Text
   PETER WRIGHT   128

12. Invasion of the Brit-Snatchers: National Identity in Contemporary Science Fiction Cinema
   AIDAN POWER   143

13. A Cosy Catastrophe: Genre, National Cinema, and Fan Responses to *28 Days Later*
   BRIGID CHERRY   156

14. Desiring the Doctor: Identity, Gender and Genre in Online Fandom
   REBECCA WILLIAMS   167

15. Invaders from Space, Time Travel and Omnisexuality: The Multi-Layered Narrative of *Torchwood*
   LEE BARRON   178

Chapter Notes   193
Select Bibliography   213
About the Contributors   217
Index   221

Introduction
British Science Fiction Beyond the TARDIS*

TOBIAS HOCHSCHERF and
JAMES LEGGOTT

In the third episode of the 2010 series of *Doctor Who* (BBC, 1963–1989, 2005–), the Time Lord (played by Matt Smith) is summoned by Winston Churchill to the Cabinet War Rooms.[1] The Blitz is in full swing, but the Prime Minister has a secret weapon against the Nazi bombardment. The Doctor is incredulous when this is revealed to be none other than a Dalek, his oldest and deadliest enemy, now reduced to apparent servitude as part of the war effort. This unlikely plot development was extraordinarily resonant for British viewers. The Daleks were not merely the most iconic villains of this long-running BBC television program, cropping up regularly in storylines and in spin-off movies, but they had been deeply embedded in the collective consciousness since their first appearance on the show in December 1963. So in this particular episode ("Victory of the Daleks") their newfound status as khaki-clad soldiers and general dogsbodies is not only anxiety-inducing for the hero, who rightly assumes a deviant plan, but it is also the source of great pleasure for the audience, many of whom are likely to be cognizant of how the Daleks had originally been conceived and interpreted as Nazi-like baddies. The Daleks' trademark vocal commands, formerly staccato barks of boast and threat ("Exterminate!") that had given generations of children cause to hide behind their sofas, were now showing a greater sensitivity to the English psyche. In a disarming, and faintly comic encounter, the Doctor is asked by his greatest nemesis if he would "care for some tea?"

---

*The TARDIS (Time and Relative Dimension in Space) is the spacecraft and time machine used by the hero of *Doctor Who*. Famously bigger on the inside than the outside, and able to blend chameleon-like with its surroundings, the TARDIS has been an icon of British popular culture for nearly fifty years.

At the time of this episode's original transmission, one did not have to look far for extratextual evidence of the elevated status of the Daleks, and *Doctor Who* more generally, within the British popular imagination. The television listings magazine *Radio Times* celebrated the broadcast on 17 April 2010 by issuing three variations for purchase, each with a differently colored Dalek adorning the cover. This was partially an acknowledgment of the new design modifications introduced within "Victory of the Daleks," innovations that were very much in keeping with the show's highly successful strategy of constant regeneration. But the color coding and "Vote Dalek" slogan on the *Radio Times* covers were also an opportune reference to the general election campaign being waged at the time (with the red, blue and yellow Daleks representing, respectively, the Labor, Conservative and Liberal Democrat parties). Indeed, the 2010 run of *Doctor Who* coincided neatly with the fall of the long-running Labor Party and the election of a new Coalition government (a Liberal/Conservative alliance), and commentary on both phenomena occasionally found parallels and connections, particularly where *Doctor Who* storylines involved political manoeuvring.[2] In the same issue of *Radio Times*, Gordon Brown, the soon-to-be-disposed Prime Minister, was quizzed about his cultural interests, and claimed that his favorite incarnation of the Doctor had been the previous one, David Tennant (who had recently contributed a voice-over to a campaign film by the Labour Party).[3] This was not to suggest that the popularity of *Doctor Who* had rubbed off on the election campaign. The viewing figures for BBC news programs of the time were well below those of Britain's most popular science fiction series, which gathered an average of 7.65 million viewers in the United Kingdom during April and May 2010.[4]

At the same time, debate was swirling around the show's place within the BBC's public service remit and — even more significantly — its generic categorization. In his BAFTA Television Lecture in June 2010, the actor and writer Stephen Fry argued that the BBC had become overcome with "infantilism," in prioritizing childrens' shows such as *Doctor Who* (which he likened to "chicken nuggets") at the expense of quality, adult-oriented drama.[5] Meanwhile, the respected fantasy author Terry Pratchett made the claim that, whatever its other merits, *Doctor Who* had serious failings as science fiction, not least its tendency to replace logical plot developments with speedy *deus ex machina* resolutions, fast dialogue and "makeitupasyougalongeum."[6]

Either way, the political, generic and institutional ramifications of *Doctor Who* were being thrashed out quite publicly, and not just within the rapidly expanding field of academic scholarship on the program and its various spin-offs.[7] Whether or not the noise around *Doctor Who* was drowning out other developments in British science fiction film and television was a more troubling question. A notable trend of early twenty-first century television had been for remakes of (or returns to) iconic or influential programs from previous decades. Examples included a live version of *The Quatermass Experiment* in 2005 (based upon the 1953 BBC original written by Nigel Kneale and produced by Rudolph

Cartier), followed quickly in the next year by a remake of *A for Andromeda* (BBC, 1961), both broadcast on BBC4. Between 2008 and 2010 there were two series of an updated version of Terry Nation's *Survivors* (BBC, 1975–1977), yet another adaptation of John Wyndham's novel *Day of the Triffids* (1951) — existing already as a 1962 film and a 1981 BBC serial — and a trans–Atlantic-funded revision of *The Prisoner* (ITC, 1967–1968), Patrick McGoohan's cult drama. The decade also witnessed the reunion of the cast and creative team of the space sitcom *Red Dwarf* (BBC, 1988–1999) for a poorly received 2009 mini-series, and a movie version of *The Hitchhiker's Guide to the Galaxy* (Garth Jennings, 2005), based upon the Douglas Adams property that had evolved from a 1970s radio show into a television comedy (BBC, 1981) and a series of books. Rumors also persisted of forthcoming remake of Terry Nation's cheaply made yet fondly remembered *Blake's 7* (BBC, 1978–1981).

This tendency for television reboots, remakes and updates demonstrated some confidence, on the part of producers, in the nostalgic/cult appeal and continuing relevance of key titles from the British science fiction canon. Then again, the immediate cross-generational success of the revamped *Doctor Who* franchise in 2005 may well have accelerated a lazy trend for familiar (and in some cases, internationally exportable) titles. The revised versions of *Survivors* and *Day of the Triffids* suggested that post-apocalyptic scenarios — one of the hallmarks of British science fiction culture — had continuing potency in an era of epidemics, terrorist threat and ecological anxiety. They also exploited the warm reception given to Danny Boyle's "zombie" catastrophe thriller *28 Days Later* (2002), arguably the most significant and influential British science fiction film of recent memory. But it was less easy to locate fresh formats and stories that did not self-consciously rework titles from British (or American) traditions, although the first decade of the twenty-first century did witness a scattering of science fiction activity on British television, including the scientific conspiracy drama *Eleventh Hour* (ITV, 2006), some comedies in the *Red Dwarf* vein such as *Hyperdrive* (BBC, 2006–2007), and programs like *Misfits* (Channel Four, 2009–), *No Heroics* (ITV, 2008–2009) and *Being Human* (BBC, 2008–) that offered a distinctly British take on trends in international telefantasy. Setting aside the *Doctor Who* franchise, for many the greatest enrichment of the British science fiction canon came from the existential police drama *Life on Mars* (BBC, 2006–2007) and its sequel *Ashes to Ashes* (BBC, 2008–2010); the series finale of the latter happened to be broadcast on the same weekend as the ending of the American series *Lost* (U.S., ABC, 2004–2010), a similarly "disguised" work of science fiction, leading observers to relate their comparable conclusions to differences in British and American broadcasting.

Scholarship on British film and television culture has only just begun to grapple with the issues that science fiction raises about national specificity, generic identification, authorship and political significance. In his introduction to an edited collection on British science fiction cinema published in 1999, I.Q. Hunter argued that it was "largely unknown, its origins and purpose still a total mystery."[8] The subsequent decade would continue a tradition of sporadic British entries to the canon. The most prominent examples, aside from a small cluster of catastrophe stories that included *28 Days Later* and *Children of Men* (U.K./Japan/U.S., Alfonso Cuarón, 2006), were films such as Danny Boyle's *Sunshine* (2007) and Duncan Jones's *Moon* (2009), both philosophically inclined space films that did not seem particularly British in terms of their casting. For all the contributions made by British writers to the international evolution of science fiction — from H.G. Wells to J.G. Ballard — the British science fiction film remained for many a wretched thing, hamstrung at times by a reputation for being cheap, Americanized or overly dependent on established television formats and personalities. Although a handful of notable exceptions like *High Treason, The Tunnel* (both Maurice Elvey, 1929 and 1935) and *Things to Come* (William Cameron Menzies, 1936) had been respectfully canonized, and others such as Stanley Kubrick's *2001: A Space Odyssey* (U.K./U.S., 1968) and *A Clockwork Orange* (U.K./U.S., 1971) — the subject of a chapter in this volume by I.Q. Hunter — and Nic Roeg's *The Man Who Fell to Earth* (1976) safely folded within the *oeuvres* of their respective auteurs, the majority of British science fiction cinema had indeed escaped rigorous critical scrutiny. Snobbery or squeamishness may have had a part to play, as well as the fact that discussions of British contributions to fantasy cinema had tended to pursue instead the exportability and indigenous coherence of horror (such as the work of the Hammer studio, discussed in this book in a chapter by David Simmons).

Advocates of British science fiction cinema may argue that it is "more diverse, more responsive to the cultural moment" than often assumed, and that it has "more to offer than has been commonly been acknowledged, having produced a numbers of films that can stand with the best of the genre."[9] Britain has also been recognized as having produced some of the earliest examples of the genre, via scientific-themed "trick" films such as *The X-Ray Fiend* and *Making Sausages* (both George Albert Smith, 1897).[10] But its intermittency and lack of popular success — in the main — at least goes some way to explaining its relative academic neglect. Such disdain may also have been rooted in a sense of inferiority in comparison with the supposed sophistication of continental European science fiction cinema, which has produced the likes of Fritz Lang's *Die Frau im Mond / Girl in the Moon* and *Metropolis* (Germany 1929 and 1927), Jean-Luc Godard's *Alphaville, une étrange aventure de Lemmy Caution* (France, 1965), François Truffaut's *Fahrenheit 451* (France, 1966) and Andrei Tarkovsky's *Solaris* (USSR, 1972).

British science fiction television has also traditionally been an under-researched area, despite the many examples of programs being fondly remembered by viewers in the U.K. and beyond. The minimal presence of science fiction television within many accounts of British television culture can again be explained by its perceived cheapness or inferiority to Hollywood equivalents. Once again, it has been the texts with authorial prestige — such as Peter Watkins's *The War Game* (BBC, 1965) and Nigel Kneale's highly influential work — including the *Quatermass* serials of the 1950s and the seminal *The Year of the Sex Olympics* (BBC 1968) — that have received the most scholarly attention, while the privileged place of *Doctor*

Who (first broadcast in 1963) can be as much explained by way of its sheer longevity as its usefulness, for example, in comparative studies of science fiction fans.[11]

John R. Cook and Peter Wright have argued that the budgetary constraints of British science fiction television, in contrast to special-effects-laden outings on the big screen, has resulted in a more ideas-led approach that, at its best, can exploit the intimacy of the viewing experience so as to mediate the dreams and anxieties of its audiences.[12] Like British science fiction cinema, its eclecticism is a challenge to the scholar, yet Cook and Wright, in common with other commentators on the genre, identify a number of characteristic elements, including a kind of "realist" impulse that emerges through a tendency for dystopian or post-apocalyptic scenarios, or through darkly satirical humor. Above all, British science fiction television programs dare to "dream of other possibilities beyond their immediate present," thus constituting a "distinctive mode of cultural criticism."[13]

Just as Hunter's *British Science Fiction Cinema* represented the first scholarly work entirely on the subject, so Cook and Wright's *British Science Fiction Television: A Hitchhiker's Guide*—a survey of key programs and program-makers from the 1950s to the present—went some way to rescuing the genre from an academic black hole. The significance of these two anthologies in establishing a foundation for the field cannot be overstated, but in taking a (predominantly) text-led and canonical route through the field, they have cleared the path for approaches that are more conceptually specific. Emerging work on British science fiction has been attentive, for example, to questions of generic classification, authorship, historiography, cultdom, audiences, music and institutional context. So, despite the inclusion of chapters that deal with some of the most significant contributions to the genre, our collection eschews any claim to being a comprehensive survey of British science fiction culture. Although it seeks to convey the evolution of a rich and interesting tradition, this book has been conceived as a contrapuntal companion to existing overviews, moving in an egalitarian fashion between texts and authors that are canonical and those that might be considered peripheral or even unsuccessful.

This collection also rests upon a conviction that a specifically national contribution to a popular genre demands contextualization as much as advocacy. To this end, and in different ways, our contributors are all concerned with situating texts, personnel or impulses within their broader contexts, be they institutional, generic, cultural, political or literary. Furthermore, in bringing the discussion of film and television together, this volume chimes with the developing tendency in science fiction studies to make connections across media forms, as exemplified by the establishment in 2009 of the journal *Science Fiction Film and Television*. This was also the apparent logic behind the BBC's celebratory "Science Fiction Britannica" season in 2006, which included a three-part documentary, *The Martians and Us*, exploring the contribution of British writers to the national and international development of the genre. But such intertextuality runs far deeper, in fact, and the complex cross-fertilization between science fiction and popular culture has long been acknowledged by fans and cultural observers. For example, the science-fiction comic book hero of 1950s Britain, Dan Dare (with a circulation of up to a million), cannot be convincingly separated from literary, cinematic and televisual traditions that inform the series' myths and values that are traditionally associated with Britishness as James Chapman has convincingly argued.[14] In a 2008 article for the U.K. magazine *SFX,* to use a more recent example, David Quantick made a compelling argument for the involvement of pop artists such as Gary Numan and the Human League, and comics such as *2000AD,* in the shaping of an indigenous culture of British science fiction.[15]

At the same time, this desire to pin down the peculiarly "British" quality of science fiction emerging from the U.K. might be said to be problematically regressive, out of step with the more nuanced way that audiences actually consume media texts. Moreover, the idea of the national as a critically useful concept has of late been challenged within cultural studies in general, and film and television studies in particular, with persuasive claims for transnationalism or internationalism as more fruitful paradigms for an understanding of global screen culture. Introducing such concepts to the field of popular genre raises further complications, as generic production has tended to be synonymous with Hollywood, or at least a stylistic and narrative approach that aspires towards Hollywood convention. It is surely significant that recent critical work on science fiction film and television has often transcended the issue of national specificity, bringing together U.S. and U.K. (and sometimes international) examples so as to demonstrate their interdependence.[16]

In this regard, a collection on the theme of British science fiction film and television might seem to be an outdated act of ghettoization, or even of jingoism. However, rather than ignoring the fashion for the troubling of the "national" within contemporary critical thinking, this anthology aspires to contribute to an ongoing conversation about the interrelationship of genre and national identity. Our contention is that the popularity of British science fiction films and television programs can be attributed in part to their ability to constantly reinvent the genre, incorporating impulses from literature, popular culture, politics, philosophy, and scientific thought. The contributions here by academics from various countries and academic disciplines collectively support a case for British science fiction as a cultural phenomenon that exceeds the realm of individual media and narrowly defined notions of the nation. First and foremost, this collection seeks to advance an understanding of how a popular genre can be fruitfully conceptualized, as well as to account for its continuing success. It follows a broadly chronological structure, thus generating a narrative that charts the journey from the late nineteenth century fiction of H.G. Wells to the complexly hybrid texts of the early twenty-first century such as *Torchwood* (BBC, 2006–). However, it is also focused conceptually around three key issues, each a response to important developments with media and cultural studies, and all prompted by the rationale that British science fiction — whether on the small or big screen — demands a methodology appropriate to its formal and aesthetic richness.

Beyond the Nation

Building upon a recent tendency in film and television studies to query narrow definitions of national media cultures, a number of the chapters recognize a specifically British strain of science fiction, but also acknowledge that this exists within international or transnational contexts. In this respect, the scrutiny of individual authors, producers and texts draws attention to wider debates around the intermingling of different cultural traditions. The chapters by James Chapman, Derek Johnston and Jonathan Bignell capture key historical moments in the development of British science fiction culture: the literary influence of H.G. Wells, the arrival of indigenous science fiction television in the 1950s, and the international aspirations of Gerry Anderson in the 1960s. In each case, British traditions have been in conversation (sometimes contentiously) with other influences. In his discussion of the BBC's relationship with science fiction in the 1950s, Johnston describes how the importation of American science fiction into Britain, and the BBC's response to this, accelerated debates around taste as well as terminology. And in relation to Gerry Anderson's glossy productions for children, Bignell contemplates a complex negotiation between British and American impulses at the levels of production, representation, aesthetics and reception. Two texts from the mid–1990s raise issues of cultural imperialism for Christine Sprengler and Peter Wright. In relation to *Cold Lazarus* (Channel Four, 1996), Sprengler identifies how the celebrated author Dennis Potter deployed the science fiction genre — for the first and only time — as a means to critique the post-war Americanization of British culture. Wright's chapter on the ill-fated *Doctor Who* movie of 1996 warns against the simplistic categorization of this one-off film as a straightforwardly "Americanized" product in favor of a more nuanced assessment of its international, intertextual strategies. The contributions by Aidan Power and Brigid Cherry on more recent cinema similarly recognize the international context in which films are produced, distributed and made meaningful. Power queries the "Britishness" of *28 Days Later, Children of Men* and *V for Vendetta* (U.K./U.S./Germany, James McTeigue, 2006), while Cherry uses a case-study of fan responses to *28 Days Later* to interrogate the importance of nationality to the way the film has been judged and interpreted. All of these chapters thus establish a transnational framework for an understanding of the production and reception of British science fiction film and television.

Beyond the Author

A great deal of film and television scholarship is concerned with the achievements and influence of key creative personnel, and British science fiction studies has given due attention to important figures such as Nigel Kneale and Terry

Nation. However, a recurring question throughout these pages is the extent to which the notion of the "author"—defined variously by contributors here as the writer, director, producer or studio—can be fruitful for an understanding of popular genre. There is, of course, a forceful argument for the diminished function of the auteur working within a genre with its very own codes and conventions. However, this is a problem confronted directly by many of the contributors here. Michael du Plessis's chapter pays attention to Robert Fuest, a hitherto neglected figure who had a major influence upon the look of science fiction in film and television, and David Simmons makes a case for the importance of the science fiction films produced by Hammer, a studio better known for its horror productions. Peter Hutchings, I.Q. Hunter and Christine Sprengler argue for the necessity of placing authored texts—associated respectively with Gerry Anderson, Stanley Kubrick and Dennis Potter—within broader generic, cultural and social contexts.

Beyond Genre

Many of our contributors demonstrate how British science fiction film and television has consistently drawn upon a range of literary and cultural traditions. James Chapman examines the impact of the writer H.G. Wells on the development of science fiction cinema, and assesses the faithfulness of adaptations of his work to his original vision. Through an exploration of Robert Fuest's work for film and television, Michael du Plessis identifies connections between science fiction and Pop Art in the 1960s, and also identifies Fuest's *The Final Programme* (1973)— based upon a novel by Michael Moorcock—as a rare visualization of work associated with the so-called New Wave of British science fiction writing of the 1960s onwards. Christian Hoffstadt and Dominik Schrey focus upon how British cinema and television has found inspiration in a tradition of catastrophic or post-apocalyptic story-telling, whilst Lincoln Geraghty situates *The Tripods* (BBC, 1984– 1985), based upon children's novels by John Christopher, within wider political debates around heritage. Using the examples of *Torchwood* and the updated *Doctor Who* series, Lee Barron and Rebecca Williams stress the importance of locating texts within their contemporary media and cultural landscape, by paying close attention to the dynamics of reception, representation and celebrity in the twenty-first century. Williams also argues that the widespread appeal of *Doctor Who* to a female audience is particularly striking, given common assumptions about science fiction being the preserve of the male fan. These chapters thus recognize the importance of generic hybridity and cross-media influence in the development of British science fiction, and they illuminate the value of a cross-disciplinary approach to genre studies.

An Alien Nation?

In bringing together writers with an established publication record in the broad terrain of British media culture with up-and-coming researchers from various fields, this book aspires to open up fresh perspectives on the subject of British science fiction film and television. Far from operating schematically, the three core themes of genre, nationality and authorship are merely leitmotifs to guide and intrigue the reader. And far from being discrete case-studies of disconnected moments, the fifteen chapters strike up a dialogue with each other about British science fiction history and analysis. In other words, the book's conceptual boundaries are as loose, and as open to imaginative leaps, as the genre under scrutiny. Indeed, a recurrent theme of this collection is the resistance of a great deal of British science fiction to straightforward categorization or even comprehension. A handful of the chapters deal with programs and films that have widely been perceived as artistic, critical or generic "failures": see, for example, du Plessis on the elusive *The Final Programme*, Geraghty on *The Tripods*, cancelled after two series, Wright on the *Doctor Who* movie, which failed to reboot the franchise in the 1990s, and Sprengler on Dennis Potter's *Cold Lazarus*, the recipient of overwhelmingly negative reviews at the time. The chapters by Barron on *Torchwood*, Hunter on *A Clockwork Orange*, and by Bignell and Hutchings on the programs of Gerry Anderson, are particularly attentive to the way their case studies challenge the various boundaries commonly placed around texts by producers, critics and audiences — whether through challenging the distinction between child and adult-oriented programming, or through absorbing influences from a host of genres and traditions. But these are merely emblematical of a characteristic *awkwardness* in British science fiction culture, a propensity for hybridity, complexity and sheer strangeness that beguiles the fan and scholar alike.

The contributors to this collection are not afraid to wrestle with these peculiarities. Nor are they unwilling to offer defense, praise, criticism or interpretations that go against the critical grain. Daleks and tea-drinking may well provide an apt beginning for a discussion of British science film and television, but the remainder of this book surely proves that these are only part of the story.

1

H.G. Wells and Science Fiction Cinema

JAMES CHAPMAN

A common criticism of science fiction in the cinema is that it lacks the intellectual depth and complexity of science fiction in literature. In 1959, for example, Richard Hodgens felt that while science fiction literature was amongst "the most original and thoughtful contemporary fiction," in cinema the genre "has so far been unoriginal and limited."[1] A similar point is made by Barry Keith Grant, arguing that the formal properties of film, particularly its visual spectacle, "have been at the root of the genre's general failure to express fully the ideas and concepts found in the best science fiction literature."[2] This is hardly surprising. The film industry has always been more comfortable with narrative and spectacle than with ideas and philosophy. This point was recognized by H.G. Wells. In his preface to the published screenplay of the 1936 film *Things to Come* (William Cameron Menzies)— which he adapted himself from his book *The Shape of Things to Come*— Wells wrote: "*The Shape of Things to Come* (1933) is essentially a *discussion* of social and political forces and possibilities, and a film is no place for argument. The conclusions of that book therefore are taken for granted and a new story has been invented to display them."[3]

The genre of film adaptations of Wells's work provides an excellent case study of the relationship between science fiction literature and science fiction cinema. Wells was a prolific author — he wrote over a hundred books including fiction, essays, history and sociology — and his work has inspired numerous films. In his survey of Wellsian film adaptations, Don G. Smith identifies a total of forty-three theatrically released films based, either directly or indirectly, on Wells's fiction between 1909 and 1997.[4] This figure includes adaptations of his social realist fiction, including *The Wheels of Chance* (Harold M. Shaw, 1922), *Kipps* (Harold M. Shaw, 1921; Carol Reed, 1941) *The History of Mr. Polly* (Anthony Pelissier, 1949) and *The Passionate Friends* (Maurice Elvey, 1922; David Lean, 1949). It is Wells's science fiction, however, that has proved most attractive to the film industry. There have been major films of *The Time Machine* (U.S., George Pal, 1960; U.S., Simon Wells, 2002) and *The War of the Worlds* (U.S., Byron Haskin, 1953; U.S., Steven Spielberg, 2005). *The Invisible Man* had already inspired several short silent films before the definitive version by James Whale in 1933 (U.S.). There have been three acknowledged versions of *The Island of Doctor Moreau* (as *Island of Lost Souls*: U.S., Erle C. Kenton, 1932; U.S., Don Taylor, 1977; U.S., John Frankenheimer, 1996), and several unacknowledged versions.[5] There have also been films of *The Man Who Could Work Miracles* (Lothar Mendes, 1937), *The First Men in the Moon* (Bruce Gordon and J.L.V. Leigh, 1919; Nathan Juran, 1964), *The Food of the Gods* (U.S., Bert I. Gordon, 1976) and *Empire of the Ants* (U.S., Bert I. Gordon, 1977). To this list we may also add no fewer than four television series called *The Invisible Man* (ATV, 1958–1959; U.S., NBC, 1975; BBC, 1984; U.S., U.S. Network, 2000) and one called *The War of the Worlds* (U.S., Hometown Films, 1988–1989).[6]

The most striking point that emerges from the pattern of Wellsian adaptations is that the cinema has, overwhelmingly, preferred Wells's early fiction to his later speculative work. Most of the major Wellsian films are based on stories he published between 1895 and 1904: *The Time Machine* (1895), *The Island of Doctor Moreau* (1896), *The Invisible Man* (1897), *The War of the Worlds* (1898), *The First Men in the Moon* (1901) and *The Food of the Gods* (1904). This was the period when Wells popularized the novel of "scientific romance," which combined vigorous story-telling with a degree of philosophical reflection on the relationship between science and humanity. Later in his career, following the First World War, Wells switched from novels to weighty historical tomes and political treatises, including *The Outline of History* (1920), *The Salvaging of Civilization* (1921), *The Open Conspiracy* (1928), *The Work, Wealth and Happiness of Mankind* (1932) and *The Shape of Things to Come* (1933). These represented Wells's attempt to draw lessons from the war and to lay down a manifesto for political and economic organization in order to avoid another world catastrophe. However, only one of his later books, *The Shape of Things to Come*, has ever been made into a film. Wells, for his own part, recognized that his fame rested on his early "romances." "To many young people nowadays I am just the author of the *Invisible Man*," he said in his autobiography in 1934, adding "a tale that, thanks largely to the excellent film recently produced by James Whale, is still read as much as it ever was."[7]

To appreciate Wells's contribution to the history of science fiction his work needs to be understood in its historical contexts. Wells's literary career began in the late Victorian era and extended until the end of the Second World War, publishing his last book, the uncharacteristically pessimistic *Mind at the End of Its Tether*, in 1945. Wells was a "man of his times" whose writing both reflected and informed public discourse on a range of topics. He was a Darwinist — Wells had studied biology under Darwin's disciple Thomas Huxley at the Normal School of Science (later Imperial College of Science and Technology) in the 1880s — and evolutionary theory informs several of his works including *The Time Machine* and *The Island of Doctor Moreau*. He was also a socialist: Wells joined the Fabian Society in 1903 and in the 1920s he stood (unsuccessfully) as a parliamentary candidate for the Labour Party. In 1905 he wrote *A Modern Utopia*, the first of many books combining fiction and politics. He was an advocate of sexual equality and women's rights, as demonstrated in his novel *Ann Veronica* (1909) whose protagonist represented the Edwardian "new woman." In later life Wells was not only a famous author but a major public figure. He met two U.S. presidents, Theodore Roosevelt and Franklin D. Roosevelt, and two Soviet leaders, Lenin and Stalin. He published hundreds of pieces of political journalism and in the 1930s he became a regular contributor to "Talks" programs on the BBC.

Although Wells has often been described as the father of science fiction— American science fiction author Robert Silverberg, for example, calls him "the father of us all"— this is a claim that requires some qualification.[8] The term "science fiction" itself did not enter into common usage until Hugo Gernsback founded the magazine *Amazing Stories* in 1926. Wells was more properly a purveyor of "scientific romance," a term that brings together a range of narratives including invention stories, tales of the future, pseudo-scientific fantasy, lost world sagas and the "*voyages imaginaires*" of authors like Jules Verne. Wells's achievement was not so much that he created a genre but rather that he synthesized everything that had gone before. Wells provided paradigmatic examples of some of the major templates of modern science fiction: time travel (*The Time Machine*), alien invasion (*The War of the Worlds*), eugenics (*The Island of Doctor Moreau*), scientific discovery (*The Invisible Man*), space travel (*The First Men in the Moon*) and future war (*The War in the Air* [1908]).[9]

Wells's writing demonstrates two of the distinguishing characteristics of science fiction. The first is its predictive quality. In particular his "future war" stories predicted with uncanny accuracy how technological developments would shape modern warfare. Wells envisaged the use of armored tanks (in his short story "The Land Ironclads" in 1903) and the development of strategic air power (*The War in the Air*). The "heat rays" of the Martians in *The War of the Worlds* (Wells was the first writer to use the term) anticipate laser technology. His most celebrated prediction was a weapon that he described as an "atomic bomb" (*The World Set Free*, 1914). Later he predicted the outbreak of the Second World War to within a year (*The Shape of Things to Come*). His fertile scientific imagination also produced devices that anticipate television and video (*When the Sleeper Wakes*, 1899) and a global information storage and retrieval system that predates the World Wide Web (*The World Brain*, 1938).

The other distinguishing feature of Wells's fiction is its social relevance. Wells was one of the first writers to recognize the potential of science fiction to function as a commentary on the present and as a warning for mankind. *The Time Machine*, for example, can be read as an allegory of historical process and even as a Marxist critique of the suppression of the working-classes by an intellectual elite. *The Island of Doctor Moreau* is a metaphor for the bestial and animalistic qualities within us all. *The Invisible Man* is a parable of the power of science to corrupt humanity. And *The War of the Worlds* is, quite explicitly, a critique of white European imperialism as Wells posits a nightmarish scenario in which late Victorian England is violently colonized by an invasive alien power.

It has been argued that there is an affinity between Wells's fiction and cinema. One does not need to subscribe to the fashionable cult of Deleuze to recognize that cinema is posited on the manipulation of time and the image. Evidence of the proto-filmic quality of Wells's writing is to be found in its motifs of temporal displacement (*The Time Machine*) and optical processes (*The Invisible Man*). It is significant in this regard that *The Time Machine* was published in 1895, the same year that the Lumière brothers unveiled their Cinématographe in Paris and the Skladanowsky brothers projected their Bioskop in Berlin. Following publication of *The Time Machine*, the pioneer British cinematographer R.W. Paul approached Wells with a view to collaboration. Paul and Wells patented a device called the Theatroscope, described as "a novel form of exhibition whereby the spectators have presented to their view scenes which are supposed to occur in the future or past, while they are given the sensation of voyaging upon a machine through time."[10] The project remained unrealized, but it demonstrates the affinity between Wells's fiction and early cinema.

It is significant, too, that one of the earliest film genres was the optical trick-effect film, using techniques such as dissolves, double exposures and stop-motion to make objects appear and disappear before the camera. Wells provided the inspiration for a number of early optical trick-effect films, including Georges Méliès's *Le Voyage dans la lune / A Trip to the Moon* (France, 1902) — which drew upon both Jules Verne's *From the Earth to the Moon* (1865) and Wells's *The First Men in the Moon* — and Charles Pathé's *L'Invisible Voleur / The Invisible Thief* (France, 1909). Méliès was the first pioneer to understand the potential of cinema for fantasy, and parallels were drawn at the time with both Verne and Wells. The British distributor of Méliès's *A la Conquête du Pole / The Conquest of the Pole* (France, 1912), for example, described him as "the H.G. Wells of picturedom."[11] The first films to credit Wells as a source were the American Mutoscope and Biograph Company's *The Invisible Fluid* (Wallace McCutcheon, 1908) — which judging from descriptions in trade catalogs had rather less to do with Wells's *The Invisible Man* than the Pathé film had done — and Charles Urban's *The Airship Destroyer* (Walter R. Booth,1909), which was described as "an actual motion picture prediction of the ideas of Rudyard Kipling, H.G. Wells, Jules Verne, and other powerful writers of imaginative fiction."[12]

Although he was disappointed with most of the film adaptations of his work that he lived to see — *The Invisible Man* was the one exception — Wells maintained a keen interest in the medium. "I was and am still interested in the film as a means of expression rather than entertainment," he recorded in his diary in 1935.[13] Unlike many of his contemporaries in the literary arts, who regarded film as vulgar and low-brow, Wells recognized its potential as a vehicle for education and social improvement. He was an active member of the intellectual film culture that emerged in Britain during the 1920s. He was a founding member of the Film Society in London in 1925, alongside such figures as George Bernard Shaw, the critics Ivor Montagu and Iris Barry, film directors Anthony Asquith and Adrian Brunel, actor Ivor Novello, and theater director John Strachey. The biologist Julian Huxley, with whom Wells collaborated on *The Science of Life* (1930), an encyclopedia of biology, was also a member.[14] In 1927 Wells wrote the scenario for a film entitled *The Peace of the World* promoting his idea of a world state. The project collapsed when the producer, Edward Godal, went bankrupt, but a revised version of the scenario was published as *The King Who Was a King* in 1929.[15] Wells also provided the stories for three short comedy films produced by Ivor Montagu and Adrian Brunel in 1928 — *Bluebottles, Daydreams* and *The Tonic* — starring Elsa Lanchester and her husband Charles Laughton.[16]

Wells's fullest involvement with the film industry, however, was via his collaboration with Alexander Korda in the 1930s. Korda, an Anglophile Hungarian émigré, had established himself as a major force in the British film industry with *The Private Life of Henry VIII* (Alexander Korda) in 1933. The success of that film had prompted Korda to embark upon an ambitious production program with a cycle of expensive films including *The Scarlet Pimpernel* (Harold Young, 1934), *Catherine the Great* (Paul Czinner, 1934), *The Ghost Goes West* (René Clair, 1935), *Rembrandt* (Alexander Korda, 1936), *Knight Without Armour* (Jacques Feyder, 1937) and an unfinished film of *I, Claudius*. Korda was prepared to take economic and aesthetic risks in his quest to produce films that could compete in the international market with the best Hollywood had to offer. He produced two films from Wells sources, *Things to Come* in 1936 and *The Man Who Could Work Miracles* in 1937. Wells was credited with writing the scenario for both films, though in fact he had little input into *The Man Who Could Work Miracles* which was entirely the work of Korda's regular collaborator Lajos Biró.

Wells was very much involved, however, in the production of *Things to Come*, which at a cost of over £250,000 was the most expensive British film to that point. The expense was due to the scale of the sets representing the city of the future and the extensive use of models and special effects. The trade press reported that the film employed "every resource and discovery of modern film technique."[17] Korda assembled a top-drawer production team including William Cameron Menzies, the leading Hollywood production designer, to direct the film, his own brother Vincent Korda as art director, cinematographer Georges Périnal and composer Arthur Bliss whose score, with its famous march depicting the outbreak of war, is generally regarded as the first major landmark of British film music. The finished film is a visual and aural *tour de force* — sequences such as the montage of the rebuilding of Everytown were, unusually, edited to fit the music rather than *vice versa* — and at the level of production design it ranks as one of the greatest technical achievements of British cinema. If the film is somewhat uneven as a narrative this may be due to the various competing creative agencies involved in its production: Korda, Menzies, Bliss and, not least, Wells himself.[18]

Wells had been promised that he would be consulted at every level of the production and that the film would be a faithful translation of his ideas. Publically, at least, he praised Korda and expressed his satisfaction with the finished film. In an interview for *Film Weekly* he said: "Alexander Korda offered to make a film which was, as far as humanly possible, exactly as I dictated [...] The film has emerged spiritually correct, despite the fact that it now embodies many alterations suggested by Alexander Korda, William Cameron Menzies, and a score of other people."[19] Privately, however, Wells regarded the film as "a huge disappointment." Menzies, he averred, was "an incompetent director" who "had no grasp of my ideas." His own participation in the film had been "ineffective." Wells felt that "I did not take Korda's measure soon enough or secure an influence over him soon enough [...] I grew tired of writing stuff into the treatment that was afterwards mishandled or cut out again." He thought the film had failed in his intention to educate the public and feared that it "would damage my prestige, perhaps irreparably."[20]

Yet, for all his dissatisfaction with the finished film, it bears Wells's *imprimatur* to a very significant extent. The structure of the film is recognizable from Wells's first treatment, entitled *Whither Mankind?*[21] This maps out the narrative and most of the specific incidents of the film. It opens in Everytown at Christmas 1940 where the principal characters (John Cabal, Edward Harding and "Pipper" Passworthy) are introduced discussing the possibility of war. War breaks out and Everytown is subjected to heavy aerial bombardment followed by a gas attack. Cabal, a pilot, shoots down an enemy airman who, fatally wounded, gives his gas mask to a little girl. The war continues, through a montage of newspaper banners, until 1968, when we are reintroduced to Harding, a doctor, trying to find a cure for the pestilence known as the Wandering Sickness "which is destroying mankind." Everytown is now ruled by a petty dictator known as The Boss. In 1975 Cabal arrives back in Everytown, representing the World Transport Board (which in the film becomes the rather more impressive-sounding "Wings Over the World"), an organization that comprises "we who are all that is left of the old technical services, the old engineers and industrial machinists." Cabal subdues the Boss and his men with peace gas. Wells then describes the rebuilding of Everytown. In 2054 Cabal's descendant, Oswald Cabal, is President of the Council. He and Raymond Passworthy discuss the Space Gun that is about to fire the first human beings to the Moon. An artist, Theotocopoulos, opposes the launch. He rouses a mob to destroy the Space Gun but is too late. The treatment ends with Cabal pontificating: "If we are no more than animals we must love and suffer and pass and mutter no more than all the other animals do or have done. It is that — or this? All the universe or nothingness. Which will it be, Passworthy?"

Things to Come is a distinctively Wellsian vision of the future. Two themes stand out in particular. The first is pacifism. Wells, like many of his generation, had been profoundly affected by the First World War. He abhorred war on both moral and rational grounds. The theme of the futility of war is powerfully expressed in the film. This is the purpose of the incident that Wells's treatment describes as "The Episode of the Two Aviators." Cabal shoots down an enemy plane and then comforts the dying pilot while asking rhetorically: "Why does it have to come to this? God, why do we have to murder each other?" When a small girl wanders across the battlefield, the pilot hands her his gas mask and muses: "I dropped the gas on her. Maybe I've killed her father and mother. Maybe I've killed her whole family. And then I go and give up my mask to save her. That's funny. That's a joke." To this extent *Things to Come* can be seen as an expression of the *zeitgeist*. In the mid–1930s there were many indicators that public opinion in Britain was strongly anti-war. In 1933 the Oxford Union passed its famous motion that "This House will in no circumstance fight for King and Country" and an independent anti-war candidate, John Wilmott, won the East Fulham by-election; in 1934 the Peace Pledge Union was founded; in 1935 ten million people signed a "Peace Ballot" calling for a reduction of armaments; and in 1936 a group of documentary filmmakers produced the short film *Peace of Britain* urging people to write to their MPs (Members of Parliament) to oppose the National Government's rearmament program.

As well as expressing his revulsion against war, however, *Things to Come* also affirms Wells's faith in scientific and technological progress. Most commentators have focused on its vivid representation of the destructive potential of air power — the sequence of the bombing of Everytown has been seen as an anticipation of the *Luftwaffe*'s Blitz of London in 1940 — but just as technology has the power to destroy it also has the power to reconstruct. *Things to Come* promotes the idea of a technocracy — rule by a scientific elite (represented by John Cabal) who use their knowledge for the betterment of mankind. Cabal represents "the brotherhood of efficiency, the free masonry of science. We're the last trustees of civilization when everything else has failed." This is contrasted with the fascistic tribalism of The Boss (Ralph Richardson, who played the role as a caricature of Mussolini) and, later, with the reactionary philistinism of Theotocopoulos (Cedric Hardwicke). The last third of the film is a celebration of technology as great machines undertake the mammoth task of reconstruction and a new Everytown emerges from the rubble. *Things to Come* offers an essentially utopian vision of the future in which technology is equated with scientific progress and with aesthetic beauty. As a child says to her grandfather at the start of the final segment: "They keep on inventing things and making life lovelier and lovelier."

Things to Come was released in February 1936 and was generally well received by the critics, who rhapsodized about its technical qualities and visual spectacle even if they sometimes had reservations about the stilted acting. *Kinematograph Weekly*, for example, declared: "Technically the production is the greatest thing that has ever happened in the history of the kinema, and histrionically it yields to none, in spite of the fact that acting is forced to play second fiddle to stagecraft." The *Monthly Film Bulletin* found it "a film which because of its conception and technical achievements demands to be seen and deserves careful and discriminating attention." The *Morning Post* thought it "incomparably the greatest achievement of filmcraft to date, and in scope and sincerity sets a mark for film producers to aim at for many years to come." C. A. Lejeune in the *Observer* declared that "for the first time in its story, the cinema has replaced the pulpit, the stage, or even the printed word as the forum of the popular orator." The *Inquirer* called it "a triumph both of Cinema art and of the creative genius of H.G. Wells." A dissenting note was sounded, however, by Alistair Cooke in the *Listener*, who thought it "well meant but not very shrewd." He conceded that it was "as visually exciting a film as ever came out of a British or any other studio," but felt it was let down by "bad acting, dialogue [and] psychology."[22] As with so many visionary films it was not a popular success. According to Michael Korda, Alexander Korda's nephew:

> *Things to Come* opened to what may well have been the best reviews ever to be received by an English film — and became an instant box-office failure. Audiences either found the destruction of London [sic] by foreign bombers too absurd or too terrifyingly real to sit through, and Wells's vision of the future seemed to most people cold and inhuman. The film did poorly in the United States, where, as one distributor said, "Nobody is going to believe that the world is going to be saved by a bunch of people with British accents."[23]

Other reasons for the film's commercial failure may have been its unconventional narrative structure and its lack of star names. Or it may have been that science fiction was box-office poison in the 1930s: other science fiction films on both sides of the Atlantic, such as Fox's *Just Imagine* (U.S., David Butler, 1930) and Gaumont-British's *The Tunnel* (Maurice Elvey, 1935), had shared a similar fate.

In retrospect, however, *Things to Come* stands out as one of the most important science fiction films ever made. Its power resides less in the accuracy or otherwise of its speculation about the future — Wells predicted the outbreak of the Second World War but not its outcome — than in its relationship to ideological currents in the 1930s.[24] *The Man Who Could Work Miracles*, which followed *Things to Come* into production and was released one year later, has often been overlooked.[25] It is not "pure" science fiction in the sense of speculating about the future or depending upon technological hardware but rather a fantasy in which the plot hinges upon celestial intervention. Yet it is very much a companion piece to *Things to Come*, employing several members of the same cast and crew. The director on this occasion was the German-born Lothar Mendes, whom Wells thought "a far worse director even than Menzies," though the finished film, he accepted, "emerged as a more coherent work of art altogether than its predecessor."[26] It is a less portentous film than *Things to Come* and a more humorous one, due mainly to a charming performance from Roland Young as the bemused "little man" who finds he has the power to work miracles and tries to set the world to rights.

The Man Who Could Work Miracles is an extension of Wells's short story of the same title. It is a political fable. George McWhirter Fotheringay, a middle-aged draper's assistant (recalling Wells's own background in a department store that he also drew upon in *The History of Mr. Polly*) finds that he is able to work miracles ("something contrarywise to the course of nature done by an act of will"). His gift, unbeknown to him, is an experiment by the gods to test whether human beings ("such silly little creatures") have the potential to develop to a higher intellectual and moral level ("If they had power they would be no better"). Fotheringay is initially content to use his new-found powers for parlor tricks such as turning lamps upside down and pulling rabbits out of hats. After seeing the shop tidy itself, his boss Grigsby offers him a stake in the firm if he will use his powers to benefit the business ("There isn't a competitor in the business we couldn't down by sheer rapidity and economy"), while a philanthropist, Maydig, urges him to benefit mankind ("Why not banish disease from the face of the earth? Do in one swoop what science and medicine have been trying to do little by little — a world without disease!"). The film therefore rehearses a debate between capitalism and philanthropy, anticipating another fable of the "little man" pitted against corporate interests, Ealing's *The Man in the White Suit* (Alexander Mackendrick, 1951). Fotheringay brings together all the world's leaders in an ultimately vain attempt to create a new world order: when he tries to prove the extent of his power by stopping the Earth turning in space, the vast pantheon he has created collapses and the gods conclude that mankind is not yet ready for such power. The sequence of the collapsing pantheon provides a spectacular climax to a film otherwise characterized by an air of whimsical fantasy.

Both *Things to Come* and *The Man Who Could Work Miracles* were promoted heavily on the strength of Wells's name. The 1930s have been characterized as "the Wellsian decade" in science fiction cinema.[27] The two Korda films had been preceded by Hollywood films of *The Invisible Man* and *The Island of Doctor Moreau*, though the latter film, titled *Island of Lost Souls*, was banned by the British Board of Film Censors and was not shown in Britain until the 1960s.[28] *The Invisible Man* (1933) and *Island of Lost Souls* (1932) were both part of the horror cycle of the early 1930s following the success of *Dracula* (U.S., Tod Browning, 1931) and *Frankenstein* (U.S., James Whale, 1931). Universal Pictures bought *The Invisible Man* as a vehicle for *Frankenstein*'s star Boris Karloff and director James Whale. When Karloff declined the role on the grounds that he would not appear on screen until the end of the film, Claude Rains was cast instead. R.C. Sheriff, author of *Journey's End* (1930), filmed by Whale as an early talking picture, was brought in to rewrite the script following the best efforts of a dozen studio hacks. Sheriff simply went back to the source, recognizing that the novel "could be adapted chapter by chapter, almost as Wells had written it."[29]

The Invisible Man is unequivocally the best of all Wellsian adaptations and a superb example of the efficacy of the studio system. It remains true to the book, locating the action in a quaintly realized studio representation of an English village (Universal's much re-used set from *All Quiet on the Western Front* [U.S., Lewis

Milestone, 1930], which had also seen service in *Frankenstein*). Whale's direction is fluid and economical, the cinematography expressionist and moody. The film benefits from Whale's decision to treat the material as a macabre comedy — an approach he would take to an even more grotesque extreme in *Bride of Frankenstein* (U.S., 1935) — and from the quality of the special effects by John P. Fulton. The film achieves moments of inspired surreal imagery such as the policeman being flung about by an invisible force and the shot of a pair of trousers skipping down a country lane singing "Here we go gathering nuts in May."

Whale's film reproduces many of the quasi-cinematic effects described in the novel, including Griffin removing his bandages, cigarettes lighting themselves and furniture moving itself. Fulton employed a range of technical devices — double exposures, superimpositions, wires and dummies — that locate *The Invisible Man* in the lineage of "trick" films extending back to early cinema. Keith Williams has argued that in affording prominence to optical effects, the film demonstrates an "ambiguous" and "potentially subversive" relationship with the supposed transparency of film narration as institutionalized in classical Hollywood.[30] It is ironic that in a mode of production that privileged "invisible" story-telling, invisibility itself becomes a form of spectacle that draws attention to the artifice and trickery involved.

Other than the addition of a largely irrelevant romantic interest — a device that would become a recurring feature of Wellsian adaptations — *The Invisible Man* makes one very significant change from the book. Wells's Griffin is not a mad scientist but a rational, highly intelligent man frustrated by the conventional, dull-witted minds around him. He discovers invisibility through "a general principle of pigments and refraction" and concludes that his superior intellect and difference from others make it necessary to "establish a Reign of Terror ... take some town ... terrify and dominate it." The film's Griffin, however, has achieved invisibility through experimenting with a drug, monocaine, whose side effect is insanity. He becomes a megalomaniac whose ambition is "power to rule — to make the world grovel at my feet." Griffin's dying words in the film — "I meddled in things that man must leave alone" — inserts a moral message that may have been added to appease the Hays Office's censors.

Island of Lost Souls certainly did run foul of the censors, and not only in Britain. It was one of those films — other examples included *The Mask of Fu Manchu* (U.S., Charles Brabin, 1932) and *King Kong* (U.S., Merian C. Cooper and Ernest B. Schoedsack, 1933) — released before the institution of the Production Code Administration that had to be cut retrospectively in order to comply with its regulations. The PCA refused its seal of approval when Paramount wanted to reissue the film in 1935 and only allowed it in 1941 when the studio agreed to cuts that would "eliminate from the picture the suggestion that Moreau considers himself on a par with God as creator, and reduce him to the status of a scientist conducting bio-anthrophological experiments."[31]

Although visually it is a less stylish film than *The Invisible Man*, *Island of*

Lost Souls, directed by Erle C. Kenton from a screenplay by science fiction author Philip Wylie (*When Worlds Collide*), is nevertheless a powerful adaptation of Wells's novel.[32] Charles Laughton delivers a characteristically barnstorming performance as the vivisectionist conducting experiments on animals that turn them into ape-like creatures ("Man is the present climax of a long process of organic revolution. All animal life is tending towards a human form.") In contrast to the rational scientist of the book, however, Moreau is characterized is a sadist with delusions of godhood ("Do you know what it means to feel like God?"). There are other changes, including the requisite love interest for the hero, here called Edward Parker. Another is the "Panther Woman" listed amongst the cast in the opening credits. This turns out to be Lota, whom Moreau introduces to Parker as an experiment to find out if she is "capable of mating, loving and having children." The suggestion of perverse sexuality — also, incidentally, a feature of *The Mask of Fu Manchu* and *King Kong*—probably helps explain the film's problematic status with various censors.

If the 1930s had been "the Wellsian decade," the 1940s in contrast was a barren time for science fiction cinema. With the exception of a series of "sequels" to *The Invisible Man* that bore little relation to Wells there were no further Hollywood films, while British cinema turned to Wells's realist novels, producing films of *Kipps*, *The Passionate Friends* and *The History of Mr. Polly* that fitted the critical project of creating a "quality" cinema during the 1940s.[33] When Wells and science fiction returned to the cinema in the 1950s, it was through the agency of another Hungarian émigré, this time in Hollywood, George Pal. Pal produced the "Puppetoon" cartoons for Paramount during the 1940s before turning to feature films in the early 1950s. He was at the forefront of the science fiction boom of the 1950s: *Destination Moon* (U.S., Irving Pichel, 1950) and *When Worlds Collide* (U.S., Rudolph Maté, 1951) both won Academy Awards for their special effects. Paramount owned the rights to *The War of the Worlds*, which the studio had bought for Cecil B. De Mille in 1925. Now the property was handed to Pal with a then record budget (for an science fiction film) of $2 million. *The War of the Worlds*, which again won an Academy Award for its special effects, exemplified the cinema of spectacle that represented Hollywood's response to the threat of television in the 1950s.

The principal inspiration for *The War of the Worlds* was not Wells but Welles: Orson Welles. In 1938 Welles had produced an adaptation of the book for his "Mercury Theatre on the Air." Welles and his co-writer Howard Koch relocated the story to America and updated it in such a way that some listeners were panicked into thinking that Martians had indeed landed in New Jersey. The notoriety of the radio broadcast interested Hollywood — Welles was recruited by RKO to make *Citizen Kane* (U.S., 1941) — but the Second World War intervened and it was not until the 1950s that a film adaptation came to fruition. *The War of the Worlds* met the ideological agenda of the U.S. film industry during the 1950s when a cycle of invasion narratives — including *The Thing* (Christian Nyby, 1951),

Invaders from Mars (William Cameron Menzies, 1953) and *Invasion of the Body Snatchers* (Don Siegel, 1956) — reflected the anxieties of the early Cold War.[34] The ideological context of the Cold War is essential to understanding the changes that screenwriter Barré Lyndon and director Byron Haskin imposed.

Pal's *The War of the Worlds* is set in the present (1953) and relocated to California. It turns Wells's unnamed narrator into scientist Clayton Forrester and introduces a love interest in the form of student Sylvia. A voice-over narration (by Sir Cedric Hardwicke) adapts Wells's famous opening ("No-one would have believed in the middle of the twentieth century that human affairs were being watched keenly and closely by intelligences greater than ours") and as in the novel the invading Martian war machines prove invulnerable to conventional weapons. Even the atomic bomb is unable to halt their progress. As in the book the Martians are eventually overcome not by human resistance but through their vulnerability to common bacteria. Unlike the book, however, an overtly religious dimension is overlaid onto this outcome. The film's conclusion privileges a passing comment by Wells's narrator: "After all that man could do had failed, the Martians were destroyed and humanity saved by the littlest creatures that God in His wisdom had put upon this earth." This locates the film squarely within the context of American Cold War propaganda that invoked religion as a defining characteristic of American life: "Communists don't have a god, but we do."[35] The fact that the film reunites the romantic couple in a church would further seem to affirm the importance of Christian values as "a necessary condition for planetary survival."[36]

Pal was also responsible for the next major Wellsian film, *The Time Machine* (1960), which he produced and directed for MGM. This was the first film adaptation, though the BBC had broadcast a one-hour live television production in 1949. *The Time Machine* won yet another Academy Award for special effects and deserved another for art direction, being the first Wellsian science fiction film set in the Victorian period. The time machine itself is a genuine Heath Robinson contraption, a marvelously antique device of levers and dials that anticipates the "steampunk" aesthetic associated with later "retro" science fiction. Pal "foregrounds the novella's implicit analogy between Time Traveller and film spectator by numerous devices."[37] The journey forward through time is represented by point of view shots from the traveler's perspective as he sits in a cinema-style seat. The effect of time rolling forward is created through a montage of flicker effects, animation and accelerated motion reminiscent of early cinema.[38]

One of the consequences of keeping *The Time Machine* in period (it starts in 1900), however, is that some of the future of Wells's novel had become the past for the audiences of 1960. These "historical future" incidents are dealt with briefly as the protagonist, here called George (Rod Taylor), stops in 1917 and 1940 — observing the effects of the two world wars — and again in 1966 where he witnesses the destruction of London in an atomic missile attack ("The labour of centuries gone in an instant!"). Disillusioned by war and destruction, George travels into the distant future, finally arriving in 802,701, where he discovers two groups of humans, the surface-dwelling Eloi and the subterranean Morlocks, are the survivors of the centuries-old war between East and West. At this point David Duncan's screenplay eschews the Wellsian subtext of a class war between intellectuals and labor in favor of a simple action-adventure narrative that casts the Eloi as beatniks of the future and the Morlocks as sub-human mutations — a characteristic theme of 1950s science fiction cinema. Duncan also adds a love interest between George and the Eloi Weena that is not in the book.

The Time Machine, then, was more interested in the potential of Wells for spectacle than in his philosophical ideas. The same is true of *The First Men in the Moon* (1964), which was also influenced by the "retro" look of *The Time Machine*. *The First Men in the Moon* was one of a cycle of fantasy films produced by Charles H. Schneer to showcase the stop-motion special effects of his producing partner Ray Harryhausen.[39] It was directed by genre veteran Nathan Juran and written by Nigel Kneale, the British writer of the acclaimed *Quatermass* serials of the 1950s.[40] For Wells the novel had been a means of exploring, through the Selenites, the idea of a controlled scientific society. This theme is entirely absent from the film, which treats the story as a comedy adventure, with a delightful performance from Lionel Jeffries as the eccentric scientist who discovers an anti-gravity substance that he uses for a trip to the Moon. The tone is set by the opening sequence in which a United Nations landing on the Moon discovers a Union Jack and a note claiming the territory for Her Majesty Queen Victoria — an ironic reminder that, whereas Wells was writing at the height of British imperialism, the film was made during a period of decolonization.

Following *The First Men in the Moon* there were no Wellsian science fiction films for a decade, though Wellsian influences can be detected in such diverse genre films as *Fantastic Voyage* (U.S., Richard Fleischer, 1966), *Quatermass and the Pit* (Roy Ward Baker, 1967), *Planet of the Apes* (U.S., Franklin J. Schnaffer, 1968), *No Blade of Grass* (U.S., Cornel Wilde, 1970) and even Woody Allen's *Sleeper* (U.S., 1973) which bears a superficial resemblance to *When the Sleeper Wakes* (1910). In the mid–1970s, however, American International Pictures produced a Wellsian triptych: *The Food of the Gods, Empire of the Ants,* and *The Island of Dr. Moreau*. AIP specialized in low-budget horror and exploitation fare, and both *The Food of the Gods*, a monster movie bearing little resemblance to its nominal source, and *Empire of the Ants*, less a Wellsian adaptation than a remake of the altogether superior *Them!* (U.S., Gordon Douglas, 1954), belong squarely to this lineage, but *The Island of Dr. Moreau*, directed by Don Taylor, is a legitimate adaptation that suggests some level of cultural ambition.

The Island of Dr. Moreau is a handsome-looking film — glossy color cinematography, a sun-drenched location in the U.S. Virgin Islands — with a handsome cast led by Michael York (as the hero figure, here called Andrew Braddock) and former model Barbara Carrera as the obligatory love interest (a young woman rescued from prostitution by Moreau). This Moreau is no sadist in the Laughton manner but is characterized instead as a misguided idealist who sets out, initially, with humanitarian aims: "To reach for the control of heredity — think what we can do for humanity — the pain we can ease, deformities we can avoid — the possibilities are endless." However, he crosses the boundary of ethical behavior when he injects Braddock with a serum that turns him into a part-animal, the reason being to understand why his experiments always regress to an animalistic state. The film suggests that Moreau himself has regressed morally, declaring: "If we are to study nature, we must become as remorseless as nature." In most key respects it is a faithful adaptation that attempts to provide psychologically plausible characterizations.

The same cannot be said of the next version of *The Island of Dr. Moreau* (1996). This was produced by New Line Cinema, another horror specialist (best known for the *Nightmare on Elm Street* series), and is chiefly notable for the casting of Marlon Brando as Moreau, who appears in bizarre white make-up and adopts the effete English accent that he had employed for his Fletcher Christian in *Mutiny on the Bounty* (U.S., Lewis Milestone, 1962). Moreau's aim here is "to create a perfect human race" and to assert the mastery of scientific knowledge over superstition ("I have seen the devil in my microscope and I have chained him"). Brando's performance is matched in its eccentricity by Val Kilmer's as his sidekick Montgomery, here portrayed as a dope-smoking hedonist. *The Island of Dr. Moreau* is structurally flawed — Brando is killed after barely an hour — and its narrative is often incoherent with *non sequiturs* and sequences that appear to have been cut. The film is a blot on the *curriculum vitae* of its director, John Frankenheimer, and it deservedly went straight-to-video on its release.

The most authentic Wellsian adaptation to date was made not for the cinema but for television. *The Invisible Man* (1984) was produced for the BBC as a six-part serial by Barry Letts (a former producer of the science fiction-adventure series *Doctor Who* [BBC, 1963–1989, 2005–], itself partly inspired by *The Time Machine*). It is an extremely faithful adaptation that maintains the philosophical content of the novel as well as showcasing trick effects. With its claustrophobic interiors and intense conversation-based sequences between Griffin and Dr. Kemp, *The Invisible Man* is particularly well suited to the studio-bound intimacy of the small screen. One reviewer remarked that "James Andrew Hall's adaptation conveyed the real essence of Wells's story and Brian Lighthill's direction placed it firmly in its Victorian context."[41] It demonstrated that television was capable of producing authentic and literate science fiction adaptations without the need for cinema-style spectacle.

In the early twenty-first century, however, Hollywood has once again turned to Wells as a vehicle for showcasing state-of-the-art special effects technologies. *The Time Machine* (2002) and *War of the Worlds* (2005) both demonstrate the trend within the contemporary blockbuster to privilege spectacle over narrative — a trend that has sometimes been seen as a return to the "cinema of attractions" that dominated during the first decade of cinema before the narrative film became dominant.[42] They also exemplify the tendency towards a sense of self-awareness regarding their source materials and a postmodern strategy of pastiche and quotation. *The Time Machine*, for example, consciously refers to its own place in the lineage of Wells adaptations by mentioning Wells himself as author of the novel *The Time Machine* "later turned into a film by George Pal and a stage musical by Andrew Lloyd Webber." This is a meta-fictional device characteristic of much modern science fiction that mixes real and fictional characters. Nicholas Mayer's film *Time After Time* (U.S., 1979), for instance, had posited the notion that the "real" Herbert George Wells had invented a time machine in which he pursued Jack the Ripper to modern San Francisco.[43] The promotional materials for *The Time Machine*, furthermore, made much of the fact that its director, Simon Wells, was Wells's great-grandson, thereby adding an additional layer of intertextuality to the film.[44]

John Logan's screenplay for *The Time Machine* is a highly imaginative reworking of Wells's story. It creates a more personal psychological motivation for its hero than the mere intellectual curiosity of Wells's protagonist. Alexander Hartdegen is a young mathematics professor at Columbia University at the end of the nineteenth century. After his fiancée Emma is shot by an armed robber, Hartdegen creates a time machine in order to go back in time to save her. This he does, only to see her run down and killed by a motor car. Hartdegen realizes that he cannot change the outcome of the past and travels into the future in an attempt to find out why. He stops in 2037, where he visits the Fifth Avenue Library and discovers that he was presumed to have died in 1903. He witnesses the near-destruction of New York when the Moon explodes — environmental catastrophe being the early twenty-first century equivalent of nuclear war. As with the Pal film, the distant future section is the least successful part as Hartdegen resorts to conventional action-hero stereotype in saving Mara (Samantha Mumba) from a fate worse than death at the hands of the Uber-Morlock (Jeremy Irons). The conclusion differs radically from the novel: rather than returning to his own time, Hartdegen sacrifices his time machine to destroy the Morlocks and remains in the future.

The Time Machine failed to be the box-office blockbuster that its makers had wanted, but *War of the Worlds*, which grossed $592 million worldwide, certainly was. *War of the Worlds* was directed by Steven Spielberg and has clear parallels with his other science fiction films such as *Close Encounters of the Third Kind* (U.S., 1978) and *Jurassic Park* (U.S., 1993) in that it balances the outright spectacle with a narrative that centers on the break-up and restitution of the family. The screenplay by Josh Friedman and David Koepp turns Wells's educated scientist into the emphatically blue-collar Ray Ferrier, and, as in *Jurassic Park*, in which Koepp also had a hand, the cataclysmic events are really just a background story to a personal drama in which an extreme situation forces a protagonist who is awkward with children to develop into a responsible father. Otherwise, *War of the Worlds* is an updated version of the story that makes references both to the 1938 radio production (setting the action in New Jersey) and to the 1953 film (featuring cameo appearances by its stars Gene Barry and Ann Robinson). At the same time, however, the film does not lose sight of its original source: the alien tripods, the effects of the heat ray and the "red weed" all appear as Wells described them, while Spielberg includes an important episode missing from the Pal film, turning Wells's disillusioned artilleryman into the deranged survivalist Ogilvy.

Spielberg's *War of the Worlds* is also alert to the subtext of Wells's novel. Wells had set out to show the British what it would be like to be on the receiving end of colonialism rather than its perpetrators. Spielberg seems to be showing American audiences what it feels like to be invaded. *War of the Worlds* consciously invokes the recent memory of the terrorist attacks on the World Trade Center and the Pentagon on 11 September 2001. When the attack begins, the immediate response of Ray's son Robbie is: "Is it terrorists?" As Kim Newman pointed out, however, the subtext of the film is not 9/11 but the Iraq War:

> If Wells' Martians echo European imperialists in far-flung corners of the globe, then Spielberg's invaders — in their carapace-like machines, ignoring the native peoples except to imprison them and subject them to meaningless privations, so incapable of understanding the climate of the land they have conquered that a plan brewing for "a million years" is undone because they did not take elementary precautions against disease — stand less for Al-Qaeda or Saddam Hussein than for George W. Bush's America at work in Iraq.[45]

Thus a narrative originally conceived as a cautionary tale for *fin-de-siècle* Victorian Britain was turned into an allegory of early twenty-first century American imperialism.[46]

The success of *War of the Worlds* suggests that Wells remained potent "box office" at the start of the twenty-first century. The question that needs to be asked, however, is to what extent the film industry has remained faithful to Wells's ideas and vision? Wellsian purists tend to think that Wells has not been well served by the film industry, in particular that the intellectual content of his work has been dumbed down or overlooked entirely in favor of sensation and spectacle. Don G. Smith, for example, contends that "the cinema has probably betrayed Wells more than any other important author."[47] It is certainly true that there have been some very poor Wellsian film adaptations, just as there have been many poor science fiction films. But there have also been some very good films that, whatever their literal departures from the source texts, retain their "Wellsian" elements, including *The Invisible Man* (Whale), *Island of Lost Souls* (Kenton), *The Time Machine* (Pal) and *War of the Worlds* (Spielberg). *Things to Come*, despite his own reservations, retains the essence of Wells's social and political outlook. I would argue that, far from "betraying" Wells, the cinema has kept his legacy alive long after the author's death. Wells has exerted a significant influence on the history of science fiction cinema, establishing two of the major narrative templates, time travel and alien invasion, that have been amongst the most oft-filmed subjects.[48] The film industry has adapted Wells to meet its own cultural and ideological needs, ranging from the visionary utopia of the 1930s and the Cold War propaganda of the 1950s to the postmodern cultural anxieties of the present. There is, however, a more fundamental parallel between Wells and the film industry. Wells maintained, for most of his career, an underlying faith in human and technological progress. He was, essentially, a utopian who believed that science and intellect could be harnessed for the good of mankind. The film industry — the "dream factory" that has been the most potent modern purveyor of fantasy and myth — has also tended to prefer utopian outcomes. The most popular films at the box office have always been those that have offered hope and optimism rather than despair and dismay. Perhaps science fiction cinema and science fiction literature are not so far removed after all.

2

Aftermaths
Post-Apocalyptic Imagery

CHRISTIAN HOFFSTADT *and*
DOMINIK SCHREY

Repeatedly, British science fiction has been addressed as being particularly interested in catastrophes and secular apocalypse. In fact, some of the best-known works of British science fiction — literary, filmic and televisual — are post-apocalyptic fictions in the broadest sense of the term: they pay equal or more attention to the life *after* the apocalypse rather than to the spectacle of the apocalypse itself. The paradoxical notion of narratives exceeding the end of the world or even beginning after the end is mitigated by Bill McGuire who distinguishes different apocalyptic scenarios — with one of his categories being called "the end of the world *as we know it*."[1] This appendix recalls the fact that the Greek word *apokálypsis* translates as "lifting the veil" or "revelation." In the Christian tradition the apocalypse is understood as the foreseeable and necessarily tragic end of all history that nevertheless has a cathartic or purifying function. It is at the same time the ultimate aim of mankind and the threshold between this world and the hereafter. Thus, the notion of an "after the apocalypse" has always been part of the concept — though only in the literature of the early nineteenth century does this "after" begin to shift away from the notion of purgatory and paradise towards the more profane image of a post-cataclysmic world in ruins. Depictions of a possible life after the collapse of society and the devastation of the urban environment became particularly popular during the Cold War when there was an innate fear of a nuclear holocaust. In particular, British science fiction film and television, deeply rooted in the tradition of dystopian literature, has attended to the topic and provided some of the most realistic and frightening post-apocalyptic settings.

This chapter seeks to identify these lines of tradition and follow them to present day fictions where the threat of nuclear extinction has been replaced by figurations of new fears. After an initial survey of the roots of British post-apocalyptic fiction we will take a closer look at the strange fascination "doom and gloom" scenarios hold for the viewer. Subsequently, we will examine the history of British science fiction in film and television and discuss the changing nature of works with post-apocalyptic themes, concluding with a discussion of the increasing tendency towards internationalization in recent British dystopian science fiction films. Although science fiction — including modern post-apocalyptic fiction — is an international phenomenon, and the market is dominated by American productions, there have always been certain national peculiarities regarding styles, motifs and subject matter. However, it is not the purpose of this chapter to conceive the essence of British science fiction as a whole, but to trace one of its most persistent thematic traditions to the present day and to determine which elements vary in the course of time and which stay consistent.

The Literary Origins of British Post-Apocalyptic Fiction

British science fiction is known for its strong socio-critical tradition, deriving from an indigenous political and utopian history of ideas. The aesthetics of technical spectacle play only a minor role in comparison to the issue of social cohesion. According to Isaac Asimov, science fiction is a literary genre primarily concerned with the impact of scientific progress on humanity. In opposition to that, so-called social science fiction, or "social fiction," is sociologically-minded, neglecting the "science" element and prioritizing social aspects instead: "social fiction is that branch of literature which moralizes about a current society through the device of dealing with a fictitious society."[2] British post-apocalypse scenarios are in the vast majority of cases such social fictions. They are often more realistic and pessimistic than their American equivalents, and they frequently deploy dystopian visions of the future to make statements about contemporary culture and society.

Besides Plato's *Republic*, Thomas More's *Utopia*, published in 1516, offers the best-known utopian concept. It initiated a literary and philosophical genre of ideal social concepts, most of them designed as institutionalized cities. Several critically acclaimed novels of twentieth century Britain — e.g. Aldous Huxley's *Brave New World* (1932) and George Orwell's *Nineteen Eighty-Four* (1949) — stand evidently in the tradition of More. According to Susan Sontag, "science fiction films also project a utopian fantasy. In the classic models of utopian thinking [...] society had worked out a perfect consensus. In these societies reasonableness had achieved an unbreakable supremacy over the emotions."[3] The reason and order utopian thinking tries to constitute can in effect turn out to neglect emotion and humanity.

There are thus two sides to utopian thought. The utopian concept critiques contemporary society, but sometimes it also installs elements of dictatorship to straighten out these deficiencies. If these negative elements seem to dominate, we talk about *dystopia*. Accordingly, the classical idea of dystopian society always contains "a utopian core, but a defeated one; the protagonist's rebellion against the totalitarian system."[4] What most of these dystopias — as well as the positive utopias — address is the lack of freedom of action, governance of thought, etc. Post-apocalyptic settings in science fiction seem to extrapolate the ethical questions raised by the genres of science and utopian fiction. Thus, a clear distinction between the concepts of utopia, dystopia, and even science fiction is increasingly difficult — and in many cases indeed obsolete.[5]

Mary Shelley's *The Last Man* (1826) is an early example of a dystopian vision and often regarded as the first work of modern post-apocalyptic fiction. This three-volume novel describes the aftermath of a global pandemic that carried off the greatest part of mankind. Another early instance is the 1885 novel *After London* by Richard Jefferies, following a group of survivors of a similarly devastating, yet unspecified catastrophe. A few years later, just before the end of the century, H.G. Wells published *The Time Machine* (1895) which was not only the first of his seminal "scientific romances," but is also generally considered to be one of the key texts to shape the genre of science fiction (see James Chapman's chapter in this book for a detailed discussion of H.G. Wells and the cinema). The novel is about a nameless time-traveler who visits the year 802,701 where he finds a humanity that has split into two different species, the effeminate Eloi and the cannibalistic Morlock. But what is more interesting in this context is what happens after the actual adventure. The protagonist gradually directs his machine further and further into the future, attracted by the incredible idea of being able to see the end of the planet Earth. Although the scene he witnesses is bleak and hostile, the time traveler feels disturbingly intrigued by the sight of the dying world — he is "drawn on by the mystery of the earth's fate, watching with a strange fascination the sun grow larger and duller in the westward sky, and the life of the old earth ebb away."[6] The allure of apocalyptic settings is rarely addressed so explicitly.

Wells postpones the date of the apocalypse into a future so remote that the reader does not have to feel concerned or even alarmed. However, in many of Wells's later works the end comes somewhat sooner. In his 1897 short story titled *The Star* a huge celestial body nearly hits Earth, causing devastating ecological consequences and the almost complete perishing of mankind. Only one year later, in *The War of the Worlds*, Wells described the invasion of earth by a technically superior alien race, destroying every human in their path and burning down all major cities with their colossal tripod fighting machines. Eventually the alien attack is stopped — not by human resistance but ironically by an ally nobody reckoned with: pathogenic germs to which the Martian invaders have no immunity. What had been the cause for the end of mankind in Shelley's *The Last Man* has now become its last hope. In later fictions diseases would become mankind's nemesis again, though with one important difference: after the Second World

War they are principally the result of experiments gone terribly wrong. They are thus no longer a natural disaster but a man-made one, and reflect fears of an uncontrollable military-industrial complex.

A Strange Fascination

Global pandemics, asteroids hitting earth and alien invasions are certainly among the most popular fictional causes for the end of the world — at least until the 1950s when the fear of a nuclear holocaust began to supersede all other scenarios for at least the next two decades.[7] The specific nature of the apocalyptic event or catastrophe is an important part of all post-apocalyptic fiction, as it determines the way in which human life and society are organized thereafter (e.g. hiding in underground shelters, living as wandering nomads, or rebuilding the destroyed cities and starting all over again). In spite of these obvious differences, there are also some common patterns to be observed: above all, the fact that mankind is usually not completely extinct but civilization and social order have collapsed, so the fictions can center on the efforts of re-establishing these. As a result, most post-apocalyptic fictions do not think of the apocalypse as the end of time or worldly reality itself, but rather as the end of an era, which is at the same time the beginning of a new one. Although the overall tone of most post-apocalyptic fiction tends to be dark and pessimistic, there are only very few works that abstain completely from the figure of hope inherent to such new beginnings,[8] the British docudramas depicting the aftermath of nuclear war being an important exception.

The end of the world as we know it is often implicitly depicted as a cathartic effect, as nature's righteous payback or "divine" punishment for mankind's undiscerning behavior. The exodus from ruined cities — the symbols of civilization — to rural areas is thus a common topos, especially in British science fiction. Martha Bartter demonstrates in her analysis of post-nuclear war fictions that the "resulting 'return to wilderness,' despite its horrifying cause, shows up [...] as secretly desirable."[9] The cities, or what is left of them, are in almost every case forbidden, inaccessible, or at least very dangerous places as they are infested with rats and wild dogs, contaminated with radiation or germs, or even populated by ravenous zombies. While in post-apocalyptic films this is certainly at least partly due to simple economic facts like the lower production costs of shooting in deserted rural areas, gravel pits and the like, there seems to be something true about this notion nonetheless, as there are no comparable restrictions for literature where similar scenarios can be found.

In "The Imagination of Disaster," an influential essay on the science fiction films of the 1950s and 1960s, Susan Sontag addresses the already mentioned "strange fascination" that is evoked by scenarios of the downfall of civilization as represented by the destruction of cities:

> The lure of such generalised disaster as a fantasy is that it releases one from normal obligations. The trump card of the end-of-the-world movies [...] is that great scene with New York or London or Tokyo discovered empty, its entire population annihilated. [...] Another kind of satisfaction these films supply is extreme moral simplification — that is to say, a morally acceptable fantasy where one can give outlet to cruel or at least amoral feelings.[10]

Sontag regards the "aesthetics of destruction" as a core element inherent to all forms of science fiction film: the bigger the budget, the greater the "thrill of watching all those expensive sets tumbling down."[11] According to Sontag, disaster fictions are able to normalize the psychologically unbearable by neutralizing the world. The audience is able to gain a prospective imaginative experience about the possible cataclysm of mankind, merging the unthinkable terror of modern threats to mankind and the "terrible beauty" of doom and gloom scenarios.

While these psychological reasons Sontag describes still appear to be appropriate, the genre itself has changed. In most of the British post-apocalyptic films under analysis here, the "peculiar beauties to be found in wreaking havoc, making a mess"[12] play only a minor role. In almost all cases, the annihilation of civilization has already taken place before the beginning of the story or is merely insinuated, rather than explicitly shown. In his discussion of a vast amount of post-apocalyptic films, Mick Broderick thus notices "a discernable shift away from an imagination of disaster toward one of survival."[13] This seems to be especially true for British science fiction which has traditionally put more emphasis on the depiction of society as a fragile structure than on spectacle or individual heroism.

Sontag also deprives the science fiction film in general of any form of social criticism, disregarding the potential for alarm inherent within post-apocalyptic fiction, as stressed by David Dowling, who argues that "nuclear disaster fictions attempt to hasten not the horror but the enlightenment, and thus — paradoxically — to put off the day. They help us to know ourselves by giving us a new perspective on ourselves, capitalizing on the nuclear threat to "defamiliarize" ourselves, a strategy which Frederic Jameson argues is common to all fiction but more spectacularly to speculative and science fiction. We can then engage in restructuring our own experience and our own future in the present and out of the womb of the future."[14]

A Short History of British Post-Apocalyptic Film and Television Series

While there are a few surveys on British disaster science fiction in literature,[15] a corresponding analysis of film history is yet to be written. The following overview is not meant to fill this gap, but to give an overview of the changing scenarios of British post-apocalyptic film, focusing on a few outstanding examples.

One of the earliest and best-known feature-length British science fiction films is *Things to Come* (William Cameron Menzies, 1936), an adaptation of H.G. Wells's novel *The Shape of Things to Come* (1933). This early film already features some post-apocalyptic elements, as it portrays a devastating global war that causes a technological and social regression to medieval standards. In the not so distant future of the year 1970, society has collapsed after a devastating war and a terrible plague following it. Local warlords are still fighting each other, drawing on the few modern weapons still available. But this near-complete downfall of humanity turns out to be the necessary precondition for a new start — as so often, the end of the world *as we know it* is at the same time the beginning of a new world *as we desire it*. Wells's bleak scenario is only a transition to the utopian notion of a unified world led by scientists instead of politicians, and therefore the film's ending is fairly optimistic. However, from a present day point of view, the solution offered by Wells would clearly be viewed with horror, as many of its pivotal features are obviously prone to ideas associated with fascism.[16] Here, again, the fluidity between utopia and dystopia becomes apparent.

Internationally, the dominant subject and motivation of post-apocalyptic fiction in the first decades after the Second World War was without doubt the fear of nuclear holocaust. As Susan Sontag states, "in the middle of the twentieth century it became obvious that from now on to the end of human history, every person would spend his or her individual life under the threat not only of individual death, which is certain, but of something almost insupportable psychologically — collective incineration and extinction which could come at any time, virtually without warning."[17] Great Britain joined the "nuclear club" in 1952 by conducting its first tests. Ever since then the public imagination and cultural imagery of the atomic threat have been a constant factor in British science fiction. The insular status so crucial to the self-conception of Britain not only lost its strategic relevance, but now no other nation contained so many nuclear targets per acre, as Peter Watkins's *The War Game* (BBC, 1965) made clear: "the uniqueness of the nuclear threat is that it posits a real possibility of the extinction of human life in totality and therefore is different in kind [...] from the other great threats that our imaginations have confronted."[18]

Some films have found impressive metaphors (e.g. gigantic monsters) for the threat of total extinction, others have addressed the subject explicitly. In the latter case, British examples have distinction for being painfully realistic and overtly pessimistic. In particular, the docudramas *The War Game* and *Threads* (BBC, 1984) and the animated feature film *When the Wind Blows* (Jimmy Murakami, 1986 after the graphic novel by Raymond Briggs) are extremely bleak. Indeed, as a result of its "realism," the BBC withheld *The War Game* from broadcasting for twenty years.[19] All three of these examples try to paint a realistic picture of the aftermath of nuclear war, without deluding the viewer that there will be much hope of a new beginning for mankind. The lessons they draw is that there is no refuge from nuclear war and its consequences.[20]

The highly symbolic last shot of *Threads* shows one of the protagonists giving birth to a heavily deformed stillborn baby, but the film freezes just in the moment when she opens her mouth to utter a desperate scream, which leaves the spectator with the unpleasant feeling of missing catharsis. Similarly oppressive is the ending of *When the Wind Blows*, depicting a naïve but likeable elderly couple that has survived a Soviet nuclear attack on Britain and is slowly dying from radiation sickness, while not even comprehending what is happening to them. Both are deeply confused about the seriousness of the impalpable threat of radioactive contamination, and the old woman keeps boasting that they survived the air raids of the Blitz, not at all understanding the new dimension of nuclear warfare. In contrast, her husband tries to thoroughly acquaint himself with the topic by studying the "Protect and Survive" brochures that were issued by the British government in the 1980s. But the advice given in these leaflets turns out to be as naïve as the couple's romantically glorified memories of the Second World War.

In the British post-nuclear settings of the Cold War era, the concept of governance is often reduced to absurdity through a demonstration of the total collapse of the state system. In contrast to its American counterpart *The Day After* (ABC, 1983), *The War Game* focuses more on the societal consequences of nuclear war: evacuation and shelter problems, missing food supplies, and anarchy and panic leading to self-administered justice. While the American film centers on a small group of individuals and their struggle for survival, the message of *The War Game* is obvious: what is important is not the survival of the individual, but the viability of the social infrastructure. Almost cynically, the population is reminded to hold "a box containing birth and marriage certificates, savings bank books and National Health Medical Cards" in safe custody for the case of nuclear emergency. Similarly to the near-grotesque — but equally authentic — governmental leaflets in *When the Wind Blows*, the instructions are revealed to be completely useless when it comes to an actual nuclear war, as within only a few days society collapses and anarchy breaks out. All three of the films addressing the immediate aftermath of a nuclear attack on Britain attempt to problematize the pervading myth of the Spirit of the Blitz, when the population supposedly stuck together in the face of imminent danger. Instead, these films suggest that not even the coercion of martial law could uphold society.

In comparison to these explicit depictions of post-nuclear worlds, other fictions that are post-apocalyptic in a broader sense nearly always appear to be optimistic, in offering at least a glimmer of hope to their otherwise bleak scenarios. *The Day of the Triffids* (Steve Sekely, 1962), a film based on the 1951 novel by the British author John Wyndham, is a good example. The majority of mankind has been blinded after having exposed their eyes to the spectacle of a colorful meteorite shower. At the same time, the "triffids," some sort of extraterrestrial carnivorous plants, begin to grow and spread enormously, feeding on the flesh of the — now helpless — humans. The idea is thus one of combining the topoi of alien invasion, natural catastrophe and global pandemic. An American submarine finally rescues the film's protagonists while an alcoholic marine biologist finds out that simple sea water liquidates the head-high weeds, implying that humanity has a good chance to eventually defeat the alien plants. The novel, as well as the later serialization for the BBC (1981), is less optimistic though, and stresses the collapse of society more strikingly (the two-part serialization broadcast by the BBC in 2009 was similarly bleak).

Nevertheless, the science fiction author and historian Brian Aldiss coined the term "cosy catastrophe" for works like *The Day of the Triffids*: "the essence of cosy catastrophe is that the hero should have a pretty good time (a girl, free suites at the Savoy, automobiles for the taking) while everyone else is dying off."[21] According to Christopher Priest, this applies to many of the British post-apocalyptic fictions that feature primarily middle-class characters lamenting "the collapse of law and order, the failure of communications, the looting of shopping precincts and the absence of the daily newspaper."[22] Aldiss also speculates on possible reasons for the popularity of imagined catastrophes in British science fiction: "either it was something to do with the collapse of the British Empire, or the back-to-nature movement, or a general feeling that industrialization had gone too far, or all three."[23]

Obviously in the tradition of the "cosy catastrophe" is *Survivors*, a successful television series devised by Terry Nation of *Doctor Who* fame and aired by the BBC in the years 1975 to 1978. The series tells the story of a group of British middle-class characters who survived a global pandemic caused by an accident in a Chinese laboratory that had unleashed a mutated virus killing more than ninety-five percent of the human race within only a few days. After a period of solitary wandering, the few survivors begin to form small groups, some of them trying to re-establish law and order (eventually ending in despotism), others still roaming as nomads living off the waning remnants of civilization, while the group the series focuses on tries to run a farm and live self-sufficiently.[24] Repeatedly, the series "returns to the question of proper government, with a problematic democracy fending off dictatorships of various sorts before finally attempting to unite the country through the self-consciously deceitful mythologizing of one of their number."[25]

Between 2008 and 2010 the BBC aired two series of a remake of *Survivors* that adjusted the setting and cast to the reality of contemporary British society by introducing characters from different cultural backgrounds. But the coziness of the original series is not at all reduced by these changes — quite the contrary is the case. The producers decided to focus more "on the hope and the humanity, otherwise it would be too depressing to make and to watch,"[26] as one of the actresses stated in an interview. By doing so, it could be argued, the series adapts to a more international — that is, American — mode of post-apocalyptic film-making, a tendency that can also be observed in other recent British disaster science fiction like *Doomsday* (Neil Marshall, 2008) that in a similar way diminishes the social aspects in favor of spectacular action elements.

Survivors is not the only British television serial featuring a post-apocalyptic world though. Aside from the serializations of *The Day of the Triffids*, a noteworthy example is the six-episode drama *The Last Train* (ITV, 1999), which follows a group of individuals who have been cryogenically frozen by accident shortly before a huge asteroid hits the earth, thawing years later to find a shattered world. Further post-apocalyptic serials include *The Changes* (BBC, 1975) and *The Tripods* (BBC, 1984–1985), both involving elements of the "cosy catastrophe" trope and reflecting on the notion of a forced return to pre-industrial times (see Lincoln Geraghty's chapter in this volume for a detailed discussion of *The Tripods*).

The 1970s also saw the release of the highly individual film *Zardoz* (John Boorman, 1974), starring Sean Connery as a barbaric "exterminator" in an unidentifiable wasteland that is later in the film revealed to be not a random fantasy world, but the future of our own civilization — in this respect, the film bears a striking resemblance to the American film *Planet of the Apes* (U.S., Franklin J. Schaffner, 1968). *Zardoz* is also one of the few films which play a special role in the British post-apocalyptic discourse in being difficult to categorize, making allusions to both popular and high culture. Other films standing outside the mainstream of post-apocalyptic filmmaking in Britain are *The Bed Sitting Room* (Richard Lester, 1969), a satirical, absurdist film set shortly after a nuclear war that had lasted less than three minutes, and *Memoirs of a Survivor* (David Gladwell, 1981), an adaptation of a novel by Doris Lessing set in a cataclysmic future after an unspecified catastrophe. Here, society has split into a conservative bourgeoisie and an anarchic young population living like nomads and without rules. While the former still live in their houses and only leave them to search for food, street riots are taking place on the outside. The protagonist is able to step into the virtual realm of a Victorian mansion of the past, and the film thus intertwines different registers of time and space, generating an enigmatic and oneiric atmosphere.

British Post-Apocalyptic Film After 1989

After the collapse of the Soviet Union and the end of the Cold War some theoreticians proclaimed — somewhat hastily — the end of the discourse of global catastrophe, arguing that post-apocalyptic filmmaking was therefore now anachronistic.[27] Indeed, depictions of global nuclear war and its aftermath became unpopular during the first half of the 1990s and the number of new post-apocalyptic films began to decline worldwide. Richard Stanley's *Hardware* (1990), a blend of Cyberpunk motifs and allusions to the *Mad Max* trilogy (Australia, 1979; 1980; Australia/U.S., 1985, George Miller),[28] is a straggler in this regard — but the silence was soon brought to an end by millenarianism. The scenarios of nuclear holocaust may have vanished, but the emotionally charged *fin de siècle* mood resulted in the return of some of the older motifs of post-apocalyptic fiction. In more recent films the apocalypse has been prompted by genetically engineered viruses, machines gone out of control, or natural catastrophes (that are in turn the effect of mankind's undiscerning behavior). In contrast to their American counterparts, contemporary British post-apocalyptic films concentrate primarily on global pandemics, albeit with a postmodern twist. Depictions of post-catastrophic society have become mixed with elements of other popular genres. Danny Boyle's *28 Days Later* (2002) and its sequel *28 Weeks Later* (U.K./Spain, Juan Carlos Fresnadillo, 2007) pay homage to the tradition of zombie horror, and the idiosyncratic *Doomsday* combines aspects of medieval and archaic fictions, Cyberpunk, the road movie and action film. In contrast, *Children of Men* (Alfonso Cuarón, 2006) plays with the conventions of post-apocalyptic film-making by featuring what could be called a "soft" apocalypse, as it resembles more of a slow fade-out than the conventional "big bang." In the year 2027, the last human born after 2008 has died, and with him dies the hope of mankind's survival, since for an unknown reason mankind is rendered unable to procreate. Although the film is a British/American co-production, it has a distinctly British quality to it, through its emphasis upon questions of political oppression (see Aidan Power's chapter in this volume for a detailed discussion of these films and issues of nationality, and Brigid Cherry's chapter for an analysis of fan responses to *28 Days Later*).

In general, British post-apocalypse cinema is characteristically more political than its American counterpart, although there are exceptions on both sides. The Thatcher era witnessed a number of films depicting totalitarian police states and anarchic, punk style movements, but the notion of order at the expense of democracy and, vice versa, individual freedom at the cost of brutal anarchy, is staged very explicitly in a number of films, including *Zardoz, Children of Men* and *Doomsday*. *28 Days Later* addresses the issue more implicitly by calling the relentless virus that turns harmless citizens into blood-thirsty zombies "rage," which calls for an allegorical reading: "[t]he creation of zombies in *28 Days Later* is linked to an utopian ideal, the elimination of rage; and the film can be read as a quest for a utopian space in a pastoral setting."[29] Thus, it seems inevitable that the film moves towards the return to an ideal nuclear family, although at the end of the film even this utopian concept is ambivalently presented. The three surviving protagonists escape to a remote cottage, laying out giant letters made of bed sheets on the meadow to contact the aircrafts observing the progression of the disease from a safe distance. The final letter of the message "HELLO" is still missing so that it seems to say "HELL." Nevertheless, the film obviously stands in the British tradition of the "cosy catastrophe" and even features some overt allusions to *The Day of the Triffids*. In a manner reminiscent of the latter story, the protagonist awakes in a deserted and ravaged hospital. London is eerily empty, and all humans seem to have vanished. But soon the protagonist runs into a group of zombies that have flocked together in a church. Ironically, the first monster to be killed is a former priest — being a believer evidently does not save him from being infected with the Rage virus. To refuse Christian models of salvation while at the same time playing with their symbolism is very typical for newer British post-apocalyptic fiction. Here, as in *The Day of the Triffids*, rescue comes from outside, as it is revealed that only Britain has been affected by the disease and the whole British isles have been put into quarantine.

28 Weeks Later starts with a retelling of the events of its prequel from a different perspective. After all the zombies have apparently died, American military forces escort the few survivors to a security zone established for this purpose in London. This heavily guarded area is not only meant to defend the survivors and returnees from the infected of the outside, but also to monitor them inside in case of another outbreak of the virus *within* the safe zone. Eventually, the virus cannot be held at bay, the technique of inward surveillance fails, and the disease spreads across the British borders — promising a further sequel with an even more international dimension.

In *Children of Men* the British isles as a whole function as the inner circle that has to be shielded. The film tells the story of the first pregnant woman for nearly two decades. Due to the fact that she is an illegal immigrant she has to be protected and brought out of totalitarian Britain, in order to give birth to her child. But unlike in the earlier *Threads,* the baby is in fact born alive, symbolizing a possible future. Near the end of the film, the cry of the new born baby even immediately stops the fighting between the official forces and different groups of revolutionaries over the political importance of the baby. The film's ending is thus reluctantly hopeful. Whilst the male protagonist dies, the mother and her baby seem to be rescued, although it still remains open if this is enough for humanity to survive.

The leitmotif of *Children of Men* is the tinnitus that is ringing in the protagonist's ears (and on the soundtrack) after explosions and gunshots. The annoying sound of the dying ear cells is euphemistically described as their "swan song": as a character warns, "once it's gone you'll never hear that frequency again — enjoy it while it lasts." The film as a whole is a meditation on this notion of an imminent end. An awareness of being the last generation on earth results in fatalism and chaos worldwide. Civil wars and terrorist attacks abound, even in Britain, the only nation where a totalitarian government has tried to uphold law and order. As the omnipresent commercials proclaim, "the world has collapsed — only Britain soldiers on!"

Once again, Britain's insular status is significant to these representations of post-catastrophe, but there are fundamental changes. While early post-apocalyptic visions like that of Wells's *The War of the Worlds* reflect the fear of an actual invasion by enemy troops, the Cold War scenarios emphasized how nuclear warfare might remove the safe thresholds that had been challenged by the German air raids of the Second World War. Today, now that the threat of nuclear warfare has diminished, following the collapse of the Soviet Union, Britain is conceived as an island once again — but now, the threat comes from the inside. Films like *28 Days Later, 28 Weeks later, Doomsday* and *Children of Men* all seem to reflect anxieties about a surveillance society. The utopian wish to control anger and violence — along with other aspects of human existence — had already been addressed in *Things to Come*, though as something to hope for, as the reversal of the apocalypse. In contrast to that, more recent British science fiction has suggested that this notion of utopia is itself the cause for the apocalypse, as it is compelled ultimately to turn into fascism. The fear of an *invasion* of the safe island has shifted into the desire for *evasion*: an urge to flee a confining society.

Children of Men in particular epitomizes an interesting new type of post-apocalyptic film, in combining elements of Hollywood story-telling — breathtaking action sequences, biblical allusions and a personalized hope for a new beginning — with emblematical components of the British tradition, such as a bleakness of tone, a concern with questions of political governance, and the representation of the countryside as an (endangered) utopian refuge. Generally, the most recent post-apocalyptic films have been adapted to an international or American taste. But instead of losing their specific cultural identity, they have adhered to some recurrent motifs and maintain a familiar atmosphere. Meanwhile, in an ironic twist, American post-apocalyptic science fiction film and television has taken inspiration from the stories of "cosy catastrophe" that were once a particularly British characteristic, as demonstrated, for instance, by the television series *Jericho* (U.S., CBS Paramount, 2006–2008).

3

The BBC Versus "Science Fiction"

The Collision of Transnational Genre and National Identity in Television of the Early 1950s

DEREK JOHNSTON

One of the first things that becomes clear in researching early British television science fiction is the difficulty of identifying productions as "science fiction," as very few were identified by that term in publicity or production material. This is the case even though the term existed in American magazines at least, spreading into novel publishing and film criticism and production throughout the period from the 1930s through the 1950s. This raises the question of why this term was not used by the BBC. In line with Jason Mittell's work on television genre, this chapter examines how the genre of "science fiction" developed in "broader cultural circulation,"[1] by investigating various media, including magazines and radio, together with commentaries and histories, both popular and academic, which illuminate this development. It uses this material to examine how the international development of a genre, science fiction, impacted on the production, promotion and development of science fiction drama on BBC television in the early to mid 1950s.

"Scientific Romance," "Science Fiction" and Matters of Definition

The BBC began producing television science fiction dramas in 1938, when Jan Bussell adapted and produced a version of Karel Čapek's *R.U.R.*, but there were no more than one such production a year until the 1950s. Yet, while all of these dramas are acknowledged now as "science fiction," or are at least recognizable as being "science fiction" because of the tropes that they contain, none of them were labeled as such at the time by the BBC. Instead, the preference was to associate these productions with the European "scientific romance" genre, labeling them "Wellsian fantasies" or similar. The BBC avoided the term "science fiction" not only with regard to television, but also in describing radio programs, with *Spaceways* (1952) described as "a story of the very near future,"[2] showing a very similar formulation to that used for *Journey Into Space* (1953–1956), which was described as "a tale of the future."[3] This choice of, and differentiation between, genre labels reflected concerns about Americanization and cultural hierarchies that were current during the period.

The first issue is to investigate if there is any actual differentiation between "scientific romance" and "science fiction," or whether they do refer to exactly the same genre. The scientific romance as a nameable genre emerged in British magazine writing in the late nineteenth century, referring to both speculative fiction and speculative non-fiction. This material was published in general interest rather than specialist magazines. While the label was applied to Wells's early, more fantastic fiction, he himself preferred the label of "Fantastic and Imaginative Romances" in lists of his works. However, in 1933 an omnibus edition was released of Wells's early novels under the title, apparently approved by the author, *The Scientific Romances of H.G. Wells*.[4]

The problem of differentiation between "scientific romance" and "science fiction" is reinforced by the publication of the same anthology in the U.S., retitled as *Seven Famous Science Fiction Novels*, to Wells's dislike. The term "science fiction" was first used by Hugo Gernsback in 1929 to refer to the kind of stories that he included in his pulp magazine *Amazing Stories*. Gernsback defined these stories as "the Jules Verne, H.G. Wells and Edgar Allan Poe type of story — a charming romance intermingled with scientific fact and prophetic vision."[5] So the people who were defining "science fiction" as a genre considered Wells, Verne, Poe and other acknowledged writers of "scientific romances" as writers of "science fiction." Which returns us to the question of whether there is an actual difference between the labels or not.

Arguably, the difference is in the associations of the two labels. Brian Stableford has suggested that "scientific romance"

> remains useful as a means of highlighting the clear distinction that existed between the British and American traditions of speculative fiction until the massive importation of American sf into Britain in the wake of World War II brought them together in irredeemable confusion.[6]

However, when studying material from the 1930s to 1950s it becomes clear that there is a shift in acceptance and usage of terms, and that the idea of "science fiction" and the associations with that label are different from those relating to "scientific romance," even though it is very difficult to be specific about those differences. Brian Attebury has suggested that there is a disjunction between the literary "scientific romance" and the magazine "science fiction," despite the connections drawn between the two by editors such as Gernsback. Attebury sees more connections to the "popular science and formula fiction parentage" of the magazine "science fiction" story than to the works of writers like Wells, Verne and Poe.[7]

Another key difference lies in the ghettoization of "science fiction," situating it as a thing apart, where "scientific romance" was more generally popular. As Attebery notes, there was a formulaic aspect to the magazine "science fiction" which helped to deny it wider literary respectability. However, the ghettoization was also driven by the writers and fans of the magazine "science fiction," as the distinctions between the categories of creator and consumer were broken down by the editors of the magazines through writing competitions and the promotion of interaction through their magazine letter columns. This interaction extended beyond the letter columns, developing not only into personal correspondences, but also into the formation of fan clubs and conventions, while some fans, including Joseph W. Campbell, Arthur C. Clarke and John Beynon Harris, better known as John Wyndham, became professional editors and writers themselves.

However, many of those who took up writing did not have the originality or skill of these individuals, and ultimately continued to reproduce the formulae of the stories that dominated the magazines. In this way, the fans separated themselves off from dominant culture, by recirculating their formulaic narratives, by creating their own clubs and societies which thereby excluded the dominant culture. This separation worked the other way as well; when more literary writers took up the ideas of "science fiction," or when more establishment figures considered the prototypes of modern "science fiction," the connections were rejected. As Arthur Koestler put it in a BBC Home Service talk:

> Swift's *Gulliver*, Huxley's *Brave New World*, Orwell's *Nineteen Eighty-Four* are great works of literature because in them the oddities of alien worlds serve merely as a background or pretext for a social message. In other words, they are literature precisely to the extent to which they are not science fiction, to which they are works of disciplined imagination and not of unlimited fantasy.[8]

These views clearly illustrate that the definition of "science fiction" as being culturally lacking in value was self-reinforcing: anything that was "good" art could not be science fiction, and anything that was "science fiction" could not be good art. Koestler applies the same limitations to other genre fiction, declaring that the detective novels of Georges Simenon, "become works of art precisely at the point where character and atmosphere become more important than the plot, where imagination triumphs over invention."[9] This differentiation between genre fiction as a whole and "art" is indicative of the conflict between popular and "high" culture that can be seen in a range of cultural discourses and events in the period.

By this stage of the 1950s, Koestler is talking about science fiction novels as well as magazine science fiction. David Pringle has claimed that, "it was in 1948–1949 that major publishers began to issue science fiction novels which were labeled as such. [...] In Britain, it took a little longer for the public to become aware of sf as a book-publishing category; nevertheless, "science fiction" seems to have become a widely-used term in the early 1950s."[10] This indicates one reason that the term "science fiction" was not as widely used as it might have been by the BBC in the early-to-mid 1950s. While the term had been in circulation and was known through the science fiction magazines and contacts with American culture (Orwell uses Gernsback's initial phrase "scientifiction" in his 1939 essay "Boy's Weeklies"),[11] it was not as widely accepted as it would become. The use of the phrase "science fiction" as a classification on book jackets would have helped to spread the term and increase familiarity with it amongst the general public. But it is significant that the novel which launched this category in Britain, according to David Pringle, was John Wyndham's *The Day of the Triffids* (1951), a novel which Christopher Priest has argued succeeded because Wyndham broke away from the American idiom in science fiction and instead wrote books which "are comedies of English manners,"[12] making them more appealing to the middle-class, middlebrow mass-market than to a narrower, more specific science fiction market.

Within this wider cultural conflict between "popular" and "high" culture there is an overarching conflict between American and European culture, in which America comes to represent the "popular" opposed to European "high" culture, which is emphasized by the way that the term "science fiction" was introduced into Britain. This ties in with questions of quality, and thereby matters of taste and class, alongside associations with different genres and media. The arrival of the term "science fiction" in Britain was not orchestrated, despite the effort that Gernsback and other editors had put into creating a label to identify their particular kind of stories in the crowded American fiction magazine market. Ships travelling from America to Britain in the interwar years were often ballasted with these pulp magazines, which were then sold through stores such as Woolworth's. In his critical study of science fiction, *New Maps of Hell*, Kingsley Amis remembered:

> I have been a devotee of science fiction ever since investigating, at the age of twelve or so, a bin in the neighbourhood Woolworth's with the label YANK MAGAZINES: Interesting Reading. Those stories of twenty-five years ago, of course, with their exploitation of violence and horror, were as far below the level of contemporary science fiction as the music of the B.B.C. Dance Orchestra (which provided another key epiphany of that period) was below that of Louis Armstrong's Hot Five; but the first coverful of many-eyed and -tentacled monsters was enough assurance for me, as it must have been for thousands of others, that this was the right kind of stuff. This strongly suggests, at least, that what attracts people to science fiction is not in the first place literary quality in the accustomed sense of that term.[13]

This memory shows that, in the mid 1930s, when Amis would have been "twelve or so," the association of American genre science fiction was definitely with spectacle and exploitation and, through the dump-bin distribution through cheap-and-cheerful Woolworth's, with the lower classes and lack of quality.

The Threat of the New World

This slick, attractive but all-surface spectacle was associated strongly throughout the period with American products. Worse, commentators saw these developments as signs of a growing encroachment of American values onto British ones. Richard Hoggart commented that British-produced comics were adopting a "new manner," including stories about "adventures in space-ships," which was "derived from the American 'strips' and differing from the older English ones as a slick milk-bar differs from an unimproved fish-and-chips shop."[14] Considering Hoggart's description of milk-bars as a hangout for juke-box girls and "boys aged between fifteen and twenty, with drape-suits, picture ties, and an American slouch,"[15] who, as "their clothes, their hair-styles, their facial expressions all indicate — are living in a myth-world compounded of a few simple elements which they take to be those of American life,"[16] he hardly sees this slickness and Americanization as beneficial.

Hoggart was not alone. Arthur Koestler saw the publication of a series of science fiction novels and the formation of the British Science Fiction Club in 1953 as a sign "that the new craze, a kind of cosmic jitterbug, has crossed the Atlantic."[17] Nigel Kneale claimed that his 1953 television serial *The Quatermass Experiment*, "was supposed to be something of a critique of science fiction of the time, those terrible American films that were full of flag-waving and dreadful, crude dialogue and exhibited a singular lack of imagination and a total lack of interest in the characters."[18] The serial was also not referred to as "science fiction" in its listings in the *Radio Times* or in its title sequence, with both describing the serial as "a thriller in six parts."

However, producer Rudolph Cartier did recognize that he was working in an established and recognizable genre when he wrote to the Air Ministry to request the loan of some pressure suits to add authenticity to the production, stating, "I am preparing a 'Science Fiction' Serial."[19] The associations that were held with relation to "Science fiction" (and note that Cartier put that label in quotation marks, as if to imply a lack of legitimacy) are made clear when Cartier notes that: "I am most anxious to lift this production above the level of strip-cartoons and magazine thrillers, and we have secured technical datae [sic] and scientific support from responsible quarters."[20] While science fiction has frequently turned to claims of scientific and technical accuracy as a legitimizing technique, the idea that authenticity was a key to lifting this television serial above the level of cheap and disposable fiction was clearly a strong one.

As well as being associated with cheap and superficial American cultural imports, the science fiction stories of the comics and magazines were associated with infantilism and lack of intelligence, with these associations being carried over into other appearances of the genre. These associations were not limited to science fiction, but to fantastic narratives in general. In a 1951 talk about comics on the Home Service, the Director of the Institute of Education at Nottingham University opined that:

These kinds of stories, both the old-fashioned and the new-fangled ones — deal with something that is not real. They deal with the past, or they deal with the future. They are romance, they are fantasy. They are the kind of romance, I agree, that appeals only to immature minds, to children and to young people, and to some adults who are perhaps not very intelligent.[21]

Similar language was used in relation to the perceived threat of American horror comics, although discussions about these comics revealed that the concern was not limited to those containing genre horror but also science fiction, stories including drug abuse, gangsterism, and other "objectionable" matters. And the fears were not just in relation to corruption of morals, but also to the mind becoming accustomed to not being challenged, a fear which extended to a number of media, as expressed by Dr. Horace King to the Commons in 1954:

> It may be that television, the film and the comic strip will win in the long run, and that mankind, which is just on the march towards literacy, may be allowed to slip back into a state in which there are more illiterates than literates. This conjures up for those with a belief in social democracy a more fearsome picture even than the horror comic itself, with comic strip election addresses and Frankenstein or Fascist legislation and legislators.[22]

King also noted that, "the horror comic transcends all class distinctions, all intelligence levels, all social and home conditions,"[23] emphasizing the perniciousness of the threat, which could find its way into even the best of homes, and bring anyone down to its immoral, illiterate level.

As Martin Barker has shown with regard to the British horror comics campaign, the fears that drove the campaign were those of a loss of English character and heritage: "Englishness, good manners, proper English language, fine literature. People who have these things know instinctively that anything else is harmful."[24] But more importantly the fear was that the spread of American culture in particular removed the possibility of a resurgent Britain spreading its own cultural empire across the world, instead of an industrial or military one. In other words, the effective American cultural imperialism meant the end of a new British imperial future and the need to accept that Britain was no longer Great, but subservient.

The BBC Versus "Science Fiction"

With this dominant narrative of anti–Americanism, and particularly the sort of Americanism spread by popular culture, it is little wonder that a public service broadcaster with the remit of informing, educating and entertaining would be averse to the use of terms associated with this form of popular culture. To have admitted that the BBC was broadcasting "science fiction" or "Westerns" would have been to admit to spreading this pernicious American cultural propaganda and undermining British culture. The one use of "science fiction" in the *Radio Times* in direct relation to a program before 1955 (the extent of my research) is an editorial heading given to two letters relating to the production *Mystery Story* in 1952. Neither letter uses the phrase "science fiction," although one does refer to "scientific-romances" and asks for more, as "they make a delightful change from the usual run of plays."[25] This follows the lead given by the listing for the play, which claims that: "Jules Verne and H.G. Wells would highly approve of the 'scientific-romantic' mystery here being carried to the nth degree, in a flurry of plot based on the Space-Time Continuum and the impenetrability of natural forces."[26] However, despite describing the play as a "'scientific-romantic' mystery," the listing also describes it as a "new American play,"[27] thereby complicating the associations of science fiction as American and scientific romance as European.

The 1953 play *Number Three* is associated with science fiction by the *Radio Times*, but not directly labeled as such. An article accompanying the broadcast notes that the play's author, Charles Irving, "has always been interested in science fiction and is a keen admirer of the great proponents of this art, from H.G. Wells to Ray Bradbury."[28] The same article notes that: "he thinks that 'detective' and 'scientific' fiction have one important thing in common — the quality of fantasy. 'Though the things they describe couldn't really happen,' he says, 'it is great fun to believe that they might.'"[29] As this play is a largely realist examination of the conflicts of interest and morals at a nuclear research station where researchers discover that their experiments in energy generation are wanted more for their potential use as a bomb, this association of the play with "fun" and "fantasy" seems to be a technique of disarming the serious issues contained within the drama in order to comfort the reader. It also seems at odds with another article on the production, which notes that: "the conflicts of characters and consciences, the ethical questions they ask themselves and each other, the human emotional problems that affect some of the answers, should result in stimulating and provocative television, with a tingling, high-tension climax."[30]

What the *Radio Times* is doing with these articles is similar to the strategy that Rick Altman identified in American film studios' promotion of their productions. "At every turn," he notes, "we find that Hollywood labours to identify its pictures with multiple genres, in order to benefit from the increased interest that this strategy inspires in diverse demographic groups."[31] By relating *Number Three* to "fun" and "fantasy" alongside "conflicts," "ethical questions" and "stimulating and provocative television," a number of potential appeals are identified for the production, maximizing the possible audience.

This avoidance of the genre term did ultimately come to an end. A 1955 article from the *Radio Times* promoting a forthcoming children's radio serial, *The Purple Comet*, uses the term "science fiction" twice, once capitalized and once uncapitalized but hyphenated, possibly indicating some lingering uncertainty over just how the phrase should be used. In the article, the author of the play still sees a need to offer up a sort of definition of the genre, indicating some concern that it may not be familiar to the audience:

> You've all read science fiction stories, I expect; in most of them an expedition of some sort is outward-bound through space to Mars, or Venus, or one of the nine [sic.] small or vast planets which, with our own Earth, endlessly circle the sun. That is all in the distant future. But why, in our own time, should there not be another sort of expedition? Coming to Earth — from somewhere *else*?[32]

One explanation for this need for definition may be that this column was printed under the heading "For the Children," suggesting that it not only was related to the children's programming for that week, but that it was also intended to be read by the children. In this case, it is not unreasonable to give some sort of expanded idea of what sort of story may be involved, except that this narrative sets out, like *Stranger from Space* (1951–1953) or *Quatermass II* (1955), to explicitly invert the explorer motif of science fiction in favor of the alien incursion motif.

Instead, the relationship of science fiction to narratives of exploration connects it to contemporary American science fiction rather than nineteenth century European scientific romance. This in turn connects to the idea of science fiction being a genre for the young and one which they circulate amongst themselves. This idea can be found in an article in the *Radio Times*, also from 1955, in which Dorothy Berry bemoans the way that her son, having started school, is no longer entertained by the narratives and activities which she draws from *Listen with Mother* (1950–1982), the radio children's program which she and her son used to listen to together.

> I had a perfectly good reason for continuing with *Listen With Mother*: it was to provide me with easy material for storytelling. But, alas, Hugh had been introduced to space fiction in the school playground. Being a kindly child he listened politely as I recounted the sagas of the bunnies and kittens. He even listened to the doings of all those sweet children, with their eternally good-tempered mummies and daddies, who always laughed so heartily when the little tots jumped in muddy puddles or fell into streams. But as I drew lamely to a close, he would say thoughtfully "What I can't understand is how the air-lock worked if the moon man left it at neutral ..." and I would know his mind was miles away in outer space.[33]

So science fiction was perceived as having a more modern appeal, and one that was spread by the children themselves; it was the children's own fiction, as opposed to that selected for them by their parents. Berry's comments also paint "space fiction" as being more concerned with logic and technology than the emotional narratives of anthropomorphized animals and small children in amusing scrapes presented by *Listen with Mother*. It is the modern fiction of the technological age, not the whimsy of the Edwardian nursery.

This in turn can be seen as connected to the fears around American genre fictions as things that would negatively influence British culture through the younger generation. This was not a new fear, as is illustrated by George Orwell's "Riding Down to Bangor" from 1946, in which he writes:

> English children are still Americanised by way of the films, but it would no longer be generally claimed that American books are the best ones for children. Who, without misgivings, would bring up a child on the coloured 'comics' in which sinister professors

manufacture atomic bombs in the underground laboratories while Superman whizzes through the clouds, the machine-gun bullets bouncing off his chest like peas, and platinum blondes are raped, or very nearly, by steel robots and fifty-foot dinosaurs? It is a far cry from Superman to the Bible and the woodpile.[34]

In this essay, Orwell is not only decrying the effects of these, as he perceives them, power fantasies on British children, but is also identifying this science fictional trend as a detrimental change in American literature for children. Orwell also recognizes a range of media influences that could be understood as damaging to British children, that they will receive the same Americanizing influences through the cinema as they will through their exposure to comics and the associated new style of American children's fiction that he is arguing against.

The BBC's reticence around the use of genre labels to describe programs for the young is not restricted to "science fiction"; another 1955 article describes the new children's serial *Lariat Boy* as "the first 'Wild Western' serial written for Children's Hour."[35] Throughout the article the terms "Wild Western" and "Western" are included in quotation marks, indicating a lack of legitimacy similar to that implied by Cartier's inclusion of the term "Science Fiction" in quotation marks in his letter to the Air Ministry quoted above. Even the mix of "Wild Western" and "Western" imply a degree of uncertainty and flux in the generic terminology, even though the term "Western" was used to describe a film genre as far back as the 1910s.[36] This suggests that the BBC, through the *Radio Times*, was still generally reticent about the use of popular genre terms at this stage.

Conclusions

This essay has ranged across a variety of subjects in order to examine the reasons why the BBC Television Service did not refer to productions as "science fiction." It has indicated how the history of the term, stemming as it did from American pulp magazines, is a key source of a prejudice against its use. The associations which grew out of this history also counted against it, especially in an intellectual and cultural atmosphere predisposed against the influences of American popular culture. When considered alongside the needs of the BBC to appeal widely, the reasons against using the term "science fiction" become clear. At the same time, it is clear that the BBC made little use of genre terms at this time, in part because the term "science fiction" was still making its way into general usage in Britain during this period. However, there was also a general feeling within British culture of the time that genre fictions were not only less "tasteful" than "high" culture, but that they were actively pernicious.

Nevertheless, it is also clear that genre science fiction did influence BBC television dramas. This was sometimes in a sense of trying to avoid particular associations, as with *The Quatermass Experiment* and its striving to avoid the pitfalls of lack of characterization or technical authenticity. At other times, the writers were untroubled by the association, as was the case with Charles Irving, because they were familiar with the genre and so could look beyond its negative connotations. Nevertheless, when the BBC Television Service adapted science fiction works, they were either canonical, as with Wells, Čapek and Orwell, or they were from established playwrights, or they were written expressly for television; none of the productions during this period were adapted from stories from the science fiction magazines. That would have brought the BBC far too close to the popular culture connections of the genre for its still largely middle-class audience.

4

Hammer Horror and Science Fiction

David Simmons

Though the last few years have witnessed a growing amount of critical discussion concerning the horror output of the Hammer film studio, there has been comparatively little analysis of the important part that science fiction and the scientific has played in its output.[1] Perhaps as a result of both the studio's predominance of overtly melodramatic horror productions and the need for dominant critical hegemonies to create convenient taxonomies, critics have chosen to ignore the science fiction content of many of the films released by the studio. This chapter aims to address this significant failing, arguing, through an analysis of Hammer's changing depictions of the Quatermass and Frankenstein figures, that the studio maintained a belief in the commercial viability of science fiction, with much of its most respected work drawing upon the genre's tropes and iconography. Indeed, I will make a case that Hammer's commitment to the genre only faltered entirely with the general decline of the studio during the 1970s, and that up to this point, the studio frequently infused some of its most successful films with science fiction content.

I take this more narrative and character-centric approach because to suggest any sense of a stylistic, visual or aural commonality between the many and varied science fiction films released by Hammer would seem misleading. From the more expressionistic trappings of Hammer's early *Quatermass* films, through the lurid visual excesses of the Frankenstein adaptations, up to the anachronistic futurism of *Moon Zero Two* (Roy Ward Baker, 1969), the films under discussion in this chapter at times appear so aesthetically disparate that they perhaps stand as a testament to the immense diversity of influences that inspired those at work for the studio over its fifty-odd years of production.

The ellipsis in critical discussion concerning Hammer and science fiction warrants further analysis, for there is a body of evidence to suggest that rather than being an unfortunate part of established knowledge on the subject, such an oversight has actually intensified as writers have increasingly sought to pigeonhole the studio's output. This act of critical contraction could be part of a concerted desire to present a more cohesive model, one that adheres more closely to a nostalgic, and inevitably incorrect, popular collective memory. Indeed, if we go back to some of the earliest scholarly discussion of the Hammer studio we discover that there is in fact a distinct if partial acknowledgement of the importance of science fiction in Hammer's films. This stance is exemplified most clearly in David Pirie's influential 1973 study *A Heritage of Horror: The English Gothic Cinema: 1946–1972* (revised as *A New Heritage of Horror: The English Gothic Cinema* in 2007), in which Pirie notes the interesting dynamic between horror and science fiction cinema in Britain. Never afraid to highlight the interstices of British genre cinema production, Pirie declares that "the entire British Horror film cycle was directly derived from the science fiction boom of the 1950s."[2] The author then proceeds to offer a nuanced discussion of the role of the overtly science fiction *Quatermass* films in Hammer's early success. Yet, despite this nascent recognition of the scientific content of some of Hammer's films, Pirie seems ambiguous in his appreciation. For, when discussing Hammer's other major science fiction franchise, the Frankenstein films, he seems at pains to dismiss the science fiction elements therein as "a mere pretext"[3] in favor of positioning the Frankenstein series in terms of a range of other genres such as the Gothic, horror, and the fairy tale.

The classificatory title of Pirie's study also points towards another pertinent issue when considering the relative absence of science fiction from critical discussions of Hammer: namely, the lack of a historical and critical tradition of British science fiction comparable to that possessed by the ostensibly more highbrow genre of the Gothic. For while critics such as Pirie were able to find a level of validity in discussing Hammer's horror output by situating it within the respected (literary) field of the Gothic as far back as the 1970s, it is only much more recently that authors including I.Q. Hunter[4] have been afforded a similar opportunity with the tentative formation of a "respectable" science fiction canon based on the writing of U.K. authors such as H.G. Wells, John Wyndham, and J.G. Ballard.

It is, of course, reasonable to suggest that Hammer's often particularly loose adaptations of the Frankenstein mythos are more accurately categorized as Gothic in nature. However, much of Pirie's basis for this hypothesis seems to rest on the favor he shows towards the director, Terence Fisher. While it may be true, as Pirie notes, that science fiction was "a field in which Fisher [...] declared himself uninterested,"[5] this statement does not mean that those films directed both by Fisher and others such as Jimmy Sangster and Roy Ward Baker do not hold a great deal of interesting science fiction content. After all, though Pirie suggests that Fisher consciously steers his early Hammer outing, *The Four Sided Triangle* (1953), away from science fiction, Pirie then proceeds to detail its use of overtly scientific tropes (laboratories, clones etc) to suggest that Fisher produces a substantial piece of work comparable to both George Langelaan's short story *The Fly* (1957) and Fisher's own later Frankenstein films. Pirie's writing seems to belong to a collection of work whose prominence may have been responsible for a collapsing of Fisher's work with that of Hammer,[6] meaning that subsequent critics have tended to concentrate on the Gothic output of the studio to the cost of all else. Moreover, Pirie's declaration that during Hammer's most successful period, "science fiction quickly became for a time the poor neighbour of horror,"[7] seems to have come to dominate critical discussion of Hammer's genre output, with the largest number of consequent volumes on the studio focussing almost exclusively on the horror films produced as a result of the huge success of *The Curse of Frankenstein* (Terence Fisher, 1957).

Hammer had made steps towards science fiction before the advent of *Curse of Frankenstein*, in the science fiction tinged *Dick Barton Strikes Back* (Godfrey Grayson, 1949), and 1953's co-production *Spaceways* (Terence Fisher), which tells the story of the first manned spaceflight. The most prominent of these Hammer ventures into science fiction is the studio's film adaptation of the smash hit BBC serial *The Quatermass Experiment* (1953). Much has already been written about this visionary television series and the creative brilliance of its creator, Nigel Kneale. Conversely, while Kneale's work has been held up as a bastion of great British science fiction, Hammer's adaptations are just as likely to be considered in discussions of the studio's Gothic output as they are in terms of science fiction. Given the cult of personality surrounding Kneale, such readings of these adaptations seem somewhat incongruous.

On a first viewing *The Quatermass Xperiment* (Val Guest, 1955) (the X was intended to reflect its salacious certification) seems to utilize many of the tropes of popular science fiction. The film tells the story of the rocket, *Quatermass 1*, as it crashes back to earth. The sole survivor of the craft is one Victor Carroon, who is seriously ill from an alien parasite with which he has become infected. As the parasite takes hold, Victor is slowly mutating into something inhuman. After tracking down Carroon to Westminster Abbey, Professor Bernard Quatermass, part of the team that originated the rocket program, must race to destroy the creature that Carroon has become. Filmed in a documentary style by director Val Guest, the film includes many of the trappings and motifs of popular science fiction: spaceships, invasion from outer space, biological change etc.

Though not directly linked to the Quatermass series, wishing to capitalize on *The Quatermass Xperiment*'s success, Hammer released its imitation follow-up vehicle, X *The Unknown* (Leslie Norman) in 1956. The film would utilize that other recurrent science fictional plot device of the 1950s: radiation. Similar in many ways to the more famous *The Blob* (U.S., Irwin S. Yeaworth Jr., 1958), the story concerns an apparently sentient creature made of radioactive mud. A team of scientists are called in to try and stop the creature, headed by the chief scientist at Lochmouth's Atomic Energy Establishment, Dr. Adam Royston. It is interesting to note that while Quatermass, as played by Brian Donlevy, is a brusque and dogged individual, the depiction of Dr. Royston as an eccentric yet appealing figure sets an early precedent for the heroic middle-aged, middle-class model of masculinity that would be developed and honed in later Hammer films, particularly in those roles played by Peter Cushing. Given that such characters were often intended to be vehicles for Hammer's "single-minded promotion of a bourgeois patriarchal individualism,"[8] it is perhaps not surprising that the benevolent scientist, rather than a character drawn from the excesses of the Gothic, should initiate the trend. Though we are not provided with much background on Royston, his age, dress (a knitted cap and overcoat), demeanor, and position of employment indicate that he conforms to Hammer's nascent intellectual, asexual, and patriarchal models of heroism.

The commercial viability of science fiction was such that Hammer returned to the overt genre trappings of the Quatermass series with *Quatermass 2* (Val Guest, 1957). This second Orwellian entry in the series was based on another script by Kneale. The film charts Quatermass's discovery of a plot to infect politicians with spores from fallen meteorites as a means of colonizing earth, and the subsequent race to launch a rocket to destroy these meteorites. Like *The Quatermass Xperiment* and *X The Unknown*, Hammer's second entry in the *Quatermass* series employs science fiction iconography and a range of genre tropes in such a seemingly overt manner that it appears nonsensical to suggest otherwise.

Though, in many respects, an excellent survey on the history of the British horror film, *English Gothic: A Century of Horror Cinema* (2000), by Jonathan Rigby, is at times guilty of marginalizing the science fiction content of the *Quatermass* films (and *X The Unknown*) in order to support its own critical taxonomy. For Rigby repeatedly repositions these films in terms of a Gothic *oeuvre*. In discussing the first film of the *Quatermass* series, Rigby suggests that "when first seen, Carroon the astronaut looks rather like a medieval knight-in-armour."[9] Despite noting that original responses from the trade press deemed the film "gripping science fiction,"[10] Rigby proposes that *X The Unknown*'s set pieces possess "an atmospheric chill more in keeping with Gothic horror than the sterile 'search and destroy' ethic of most 1950s science fiction."[11] Indeed, when Rigby is finished describing how much *Quatermass 2* "twists [...] stridently modern motifs into age-old Gothic shapes,"[12] it seems obvious that his thesis will not allow for a proper recognition of the science fiction aspects of *Quatermass*, *X The Unknown* and *Quatermass 2*.

Rigby provides a useful summation of his approach to the three films when he suggests that "the enduring power of Kneale's *Quatermass* stories derives from the way he dresses ancient terrors in space age clothing, resulting in the most Gothic kind of science fiction imaginable."[13] This desire to (re)interpret the films in terms of the Gothic implicitly suggests both a belief that this form is more valid as it pre-dates science fiction, and that science fiction is itself a derivative of, and therefore inferior to, the Gothic. This view is not surprising given Kneale's own dismissive comments about the genre: "I don't see myself as a science fiction writer, and I never have done," he said in 1989, "I find from my occasional sampling of science fiction that it's very disappointing and horribly overwritten."[14]

Such value judgments are of course highly subjective and indicate the complexities inherent in attempting to neatly categorize the often elusive films released by Hammer.

Continuing his chronological examination of national horror cinema, Rigby proceeds to discuss the critical and market forces that may have led Hammer to turn towards the more explicit Gothic excesses of *The Curse of Frankenstein*: "despite their supremacy in the field (of science fiction), Hammer were keenly aware that the science boom was approaching its sell-by date. One of the reviews of *The Quatermass Xperiment*, in the *Daily Sketch*, had referred to it as a 'poor man's Frankenstein.'"[15] Rigby's comments typify a commonplace critical tendency to elide the science fiction content of the Frankenstein films. They point towards a propensity to position those genre films that take place in a historically definable or imaginary past as Gothic and those that look forwards with futuristic locales and inventions as science fiction. Indeed, such a process of categorization would help, in part, to answer the problem as to why Hammer's *Quatermass* films are more frequently discussed in collections on science fiction in comparison to Hammer's adaptations of the Frankenstein story.

In *The Curse of Frankenstein* we join the amoral Victor Frankenstein as he is working on developing an artificial man out of body parts from cadavers. To finish his experiment Victor kills the renowned Professor Bernstein in order to use his brain. Victor believes this will imbue his creation with great intelligence. Unfortunately the brain is damaged before Victor has a chance to use it. As a result the creature proceeds to kill several of the local townsfolk. Eventually the creature returns to Victor's lab where it is shot and falls into a bath of acid. Now with no proof that it was the monster rather than he that is responsible for the murders, Victor is sentenced to execution.

Hammer's versions of Frankenstein primarily belong to the category of the Gothic and it would be churlish to try and argue that they do not; rather, I wish to take issue with the manner in which successive critics have ignored the science fiction content of these films, as if to imply that the two forms were mutually exclusive, when in fact science fiction and gothic horror are very often combined in the films released by Hammer. In *English Gothic*, Rigby recounts the words of *The Curse of Frankenstein* producer Anthony Hinds when discussing the crew's grasp of the source material: "Terry Fisher, Bernard Robinson, Jack Asher, Jim Needs [the editor] and I — were all brought up on the original Gothic horror tradition and I think we knew what it was all about."[16] Yet, given the proclivity to read Hammer's *The Curse of Frankenstein* as Gothic horror, it is interesting to remember not only that Mary Shelley's original *Frankenstein* (1831) is frequently cited as one of the first examples of science fiction, but also how particular emphasis in discussions of the novel as science fiction is given to the mad scientist character of Victor. As Roslynn D. Haynes notes in her exhaustive study of the subject, *From Faust to Strangelove: Representations of the Scientist in Western Literature* (1994), "one of the most enduring and influential images of the scientist in both literature and film has been that of Victor Frankenstein."[17] It is ironic therefore, that this focus on Victor is carried through to Hammer's adaptation, which in both trying to differentiate itself from the former Universal versions, and perhaps capitalize on the success of the scientific Quatermass (and Royston) figures, inarguably and successfully foregrounds the scientist above his monstrous creation. As Pirie notes, "the change of emphasis that Hammer had made in the Frankenstein myth — making the baron, rather than the monster, its central character — turned out to be fully justified in box office terms."[18]

This repositioning of the Victor character into a more central role than previous film adaptations may be said to demonstrate a continued belief in the commercial appeal of science fiction on the part of Hammer. Though, as Pirie points out, Victor is in many ways comparable to a nineteenth century dandy, the film also makes it clear that Victor is a radical who has devoted his life to scientific advancement in a period of staunch conservativeness. Indeed, Victor is defeated more by the repressive nature of the bourgeois society in which he operates, than by the monster itself. In this sense, "the character comes closest to being a victimized scientific pioneer in the tradition of Galileo or Freud."[19]

The remainder of the 1950s would see Hammer return to the Frankenstein story with *The Revenge of Frankenstein* (Terence Fisher, 1958) and make the science fiction tinged *The Man Who Could Cheat Death* (Terence Fisher, 1959). The former was a quick follow up to *Curse* and in terms of science fiction content is notable only for Cushing's refinement of the Victor character. *The Man Who Could Cheat Death*, a tale of a doctor whose pioneering work into gland surgery has lead to him murdering innocent victims in order to stay eternally youthful, testifies to Hammer's desire to marry the Gothic aesthetics of their successful Frankenstein and Dracula stories with many of the plot devices and motifs of science fiction, the result in this case being "an odd mish-mash of mad scientist flick and Gothic flannel."[20]

In 1959 Hammer released *Operation Universe* (Peter Bryan, 1959) a documentary narrated by Robert Beatty about atomic power. The film visits the research stations involved and shows an RAF officer getting information about an experimental rocket track. Though it is difficult to analyze this lost curio, its focus on the emergent uses of nuclear power demonstrates awareness on Hammer's part of the general interest in scientific progress that existed in the post-war cinema-going populace. The apparent belief in the commercial validity of science and science fiction would remain a constant in Hammer's output, peaking concurrently with the culmination of the space race in the mid to late 1960s.

With the advent of the 1960s, the success of Hammer's Frankenstein and Dracula films saw the studio's international partners place pressure on Hammer to produce more horror output. The first half of the decade saw the studio release no predominantly science fiction product, favoring instead the sort of Gothic material it knew it could sell to overseas markets. The one exception to this is perhaps *The Damned* (Joesph Losey, 1963), based on a novel by H.L. Lawrence called *The Children of Light* (1960). More in keeping with Hammer's earlier 1950s science fiction films in both plot and tone (it was also filmed in black and white when the majority of Hammer films had moved to color), *The Damned* tells the story of an American, Simon Wells, who, on the run from a crazed biker gang, discovers a secret scientific establishment in which radioactive children are kept trapped. Ironically, while critics tend to point out that director Joseph Losey was antipathetic towards science fiction as a genre, as John Oliver notes "*The Damned* is at its strongest when it focuses on [...] very science fiction themes."[21] Key to the film's discussion is the moral quandary posed by the children themselves. For though the children are perceived as mutants and pose a threat to those who come into contact with them, given the film's warnings about an imminent nuclear holocaust it is suggested that their condition may be the only means of survival for humanity. In its Orwellian condemnation of a corrupt bureaucracy the film echoes the thematic concerns of the earlier *Quatermass 2*. Furthermore, as Hearn and Barnes suggest, the film has proven hugely influential; its apocalyptic vision of a Britain ruled by Biker gangs being reprised in *A Clockwork Orange* (U.S./U.K., Stanley Kubrick, 1971), and its conspiracy melodrama discernible in a host of later genre work including *The X-Files* (U.S., Fox, 1993–2002).

The 1960s witnessed the production of three more Frankenstein films by Hammer. 1963's *The Evil of Frankenstein* (Freddie Francis) sees Victor rediscover his creature in a block of ice and de-thaw it only to find its brain is malfunctioning because it has been riddled with bullet wounds. To try and solve this problem Frankenstein hires a mesmerist by the name of Zoltan to revive the creature but Zoltan places the creature under his control and uses it to commit several murders. Though ostensibly less scientific in nature than previous entries in the series (the Zoltan elements of the plot seem to hark back to *The Cabinet of Dr. Caligari* [Germany, Robert Wiene, 1920]), there is evidence that those involved in its making were still aware of the continuing appeal of science fiction, not least director Freddie Francis, whose only proviso for being involved was "that he required a very substantive laboratory set to be built."[22] The film is also notable for the abrupt change in the character of Victor. Whereas, in previous films, Cushing had portrayed Victor as a Promethean overreacher, *The Evil of Frankenstein* arguably attempts to rewrite Frankenstein as a more sensitive figure. This effort to "make Hammer's horrors more compassionate"[23] was probably an attempt to placate the growing worries of the British Board of Film Censorship (BBFC), who had been closely watching Hammer's output since *Dracula* (Terence Fisher) in 1958. Increased self-censorship would have a significant effect on Hammer's future depictions of the figures of both Victor Frankenstein and Professor Quatermass. Yet, this sense of trepidation was not immediately perceptible in Hammer's next Frankenstein entry, *Frankenstein Created Woman* (Terence Fisher, 1967). The film, which tells of Victor resuscitating a beautiful murdered village girl but accidentally implanting her soul with that of her vengeful and murdered lover, revolves around the central character of Christina Kleve, played by Playboy playmate Susan

Denberg. Having had her more innocent soul replaced with that of her more violent boyfriend Hans, through "the spurious scientific contrivance of soul transplants,"[24] Christina becomes a kind of gender-confused Bavarian succubus, who entraps and murders those men responsible for the death of her fiancée. The film has often been acclaimed by critics because it marks a move away from the more physical science of previous films to a more existential focus. This repositioning is perhaps in keeping with a desire to produce films that would be of less concern to the BBFC, a fact that would seem to be supported by Cushing's revised portrayal of Victor as the hero of the piece.

Quatermass and the Pit (Roy Ward Baker, 1967) was Hammer's final return to Kneale's Quatermass figure. The film, which was once more loosely adapted from a BBC television series, can perhaps be considered as Hammer's last commercially successful science fiction film. Categorized by Rigby as "perhaps the most persuasive and disturbing of all science fiction/horror speculations,"[25] Hammer's third entry in the *Quatermass* series opens with the discovery of what seem to be prehistoric ape men by workmen digging near Hobbs End underground station. When a huge craft is exposed, Professor Quatermass is called in to investigate. The alien contents of the craft lead Quatermass to believe that ancient man was genetically altered by Martians and returned to earth as a colony by proxy. Subsequent events suggest that the drilling has unleashed an extraterrestrial force that drives those with inherited Martian instincts into a frenzy of destruction. Director Roy Ward Baker's film replaces Brian Donlevy in the role of Quatermass with the Hammer stalwart Andrew Keir who gives a performance that is much closer to Andre Morell's original small screen take on the character as "a caring middle-class scientist."[26] Ironically, given Peter Cushing's association with the model in critical discussion, Keir's version of Quatermass represents the epitome of Hammer's own middle-class, middle-aged ideal.

In addition to the film's Cold War topicality, *Quatermass and the Pit* presents the viewer with an interesting, almost meta-fictional element to its plot. Given Hammer's symbiotic utilization of both science fiction and horror content in many of its more interesting films up to this point, it seems noteworthy that *Quatermass and the Pit* is the story of a scientist who uses a newly formulated scientific theorem to effectively explain away the vast majority of human superstition, taking in every staple of the Gothic horror genre from gargoyles to Satan. This plot machination aptly reflects a growing incompatibility between the differing genre elements of Hammer's films, partially brought about by the increasing budgetary demands required to produce visually credible science fiction. This would soon become much more of an issue for Hammer with the release of a wave of blockbuster genre films such as *2001: A Space Odyssey* (U.K./U.S., Stanley Kubrick, 1968) and *Planet of the Apes* (U.S., Franklin J. Schaffner, 1968). Though Hammer's paltry budgets meant that realistically it could not hope to compete with the lavish releases of the Hollywood studios, it would only learn this lesson by misguidedly attempting to emulate their success.

In contrast to the more overt science fiction content of *Quatermass*, lies *Frankenstein Must Be Destroyed* (Terence Fisher, 1969). A particularly gruesome film, *Frankenstein Must Be Destroyed*, sees a fugitive Victor create a new monster by transplanting the brain of an old colleague into a new body with disastrous results. Coming across as a defiant reversal of Hammer's more graphically moderate films of the time, before the misjudged *The Horror of Frankenstein* (Jimmy Sangster, 1970), this fifth entry is perhaps the closest to Shelley's original novel in terms of character dynamics. Duly, the once semi-heroic Victor now engages in murder, blackmail and rape while the monster is arguably the most sympathetic he has ever been. Though the film seems to shift audience sympathies away from the scientist to his creation, Victor's seemingly humanitarian opinion of his actually barbaric brain transplantation techniques implicitly hints at a more complex discussion over scientific and medical progress versus morality that permeates the film.

Moon Zero Two represents Hammer's most high profile attempt to produce a popular science fiction film during the 1960s. The film, a kind of low-budget space western reminiscent of some of Gerry Anderson's later television series, was intended to capitalize on widespread interest in the moon landings and the success of Stanley Kubrick's *2001: A Space Odyssey*, but turned out to be a huge commercial failure. After an entertaining cartoon credits sequence featuring fighting spacemen, we are introduced to the hero of the film, Bill Kemp, pilot of the Moon 02 as he reaches Moon City. While there Kemp meets the industrialist J.J. Hubbard who offers to give him a new ship should he successfully (and illegally) pilot an asteroid made of sapphire to a spot on the Moon designated by Hubbard. Kemp agrees, but later discovers that Hubbard plans to build super-powered rockets which will enable him to colonize Mercury and the moons of Jupiter.

Unsurprisingly, the film's patchy special effects pale in comparison to those of *2001*. Particularly bad are the space suits that the characters wear and the Moon Bug they travel around in. Though Hammer managed to acquire extra funding from Warner Bros / Seven Arts, as the comments of director Roy Ward Baker suggest, this money was not enough: "It was hopeless [...] we tried to fly people on wires and all this kind of stuff but you need elaborate technical apparatus which requires large, silent studios [...] it never got to work."[27] The tone of the film is also somewhat uneven with a distinct lack of action for a Hammer film. Strangely, the apparent seriousness of the film's recreation of life in space (including factors such as low gravity, outer space mechanics, and the risks of living inside a pressurized dome) are at odds with its camp 1960s envisioning of the future (Moonopoly, Go-go girls et al.). The dismal performance of the film (which had been intended to spawn a franchise) seems to have led Hammer away from science fiction, with none of its remaining films incorporating the trappings of the genre to any significant degree. It is perhaps ironic, considering both the seriousness of other contemporary science fiction films, and the imminent explosion in camp (see Michael du Plessis's chapter in this book), that the studio's decision to replace the moral complexities of its earlier science fiction work with a more conventional western plot was rejected by British audiences who "took the moon rather more seriously than Hammer had anticipated."[28]

By the time 1974's *Frankenstein and the Monster from Hell* (Terence Fisher) came around, Hammer was struggling, both financially and artistically. It is therefore significant that the studio made the film at all. As Jonathan Rigby notes, "Michael Carreras only just succeeded in convincing Paramount to fund the film."[29] While it would be stretching the truth to suggest that the film demonstrates Hammer's persistent interest in science fiction it is more likely that it merely expounds the studio's continuing reliance on the Frankenstein name to find a popular audience (many critics have proposed that the film was also intended as a favor to director Terence Fisher, whose last project it was). While it does contain some superficial examination of the kind explored in previous films — at one point a judge declares "if we cannot trust even our so-called enlightened men of science, who are we to trust?"— like the facile *The Horror of Frankenstein*, one cannot help but feel that *Frankenstein and the Monster from Hell* leaps back too eagerly into the Gothic excesses of its forefathers, removing any moral complexity in favor of lurid melodrama.

Despite being burned with its later dalliances with the genre, Hammer continued to be involved with science fiction in the form of its television series. While the first series, *Hammer House of Horror* (ITV, 1980), was primarily devoted to stories of horror, occasional episodes of the second series and the later *Hammer House of Mystery and Suspense* (ITV, 1984–1986), dealt with science fiction inflected stories. Notable amongst these are "Last Video and Testament," in which an aging electronics wizard uses his knowledge to terrorize his unfaithful wife and her lover, and "Child's Play," where a family find themselves the playthings of alien children.

While previous scholarship on the subject has tended to collapse the distinctions between Hammer and some of its more critically respected directors, often producing valuable if narrow accounts of the genre in the process, my approach in this chapter has been to try to offer a more holistic reassessment of the studio's output. For, though Hammer will be most frequently remembered for its unique brand of melodramatic horror, it is important not to forget that the company also contributed greatly to the development of British science fiction cinema. By adapting the commercial appeal of the form to tell its own stories and extol its own ideologies, Hammer's body of science fiction work stands as a significant reminder of national cultural history.

5

Robert Fuest and *The Final Programme*
Science Fiction and the Question of Style

MICHAEL DU PLESSIS

Robert Fuest's film *The Final Programme* (1973) adapted to the screen Michael Moorcock's novel of the same name and remains perhaps the only attempt to provide a cinematic equivalent to what the British New Wave was doing in literary science fiction. As such, the film merits a serious reconsideration, while Fuest himself deserves critical recognition as auteur. Not only *The Final Programme*, but also Fuest's work as television director on the 1968–1969 series of *The Avengers* and his two *Phibes* films with Vincent Price, *The Abominable Dr. Phibes* (1971) and *Dr. Phibes Rises Again* (1972), demonstrates an engagement with the styles, modes, and concerns of the New Wave, as well as with British strands of Pop Art. How Pop Art and the New Wave together came to signify "style" in the 1960s and early 1970s is part of the story that we see in Fuest's work, which manifests an almost tautological association with stylishness, so that his style becomes "style" itself. Indeed, so strongly marked does the issue of style become in Fuest that his work poses the question of camp: style for the sake of style. Theories of the auteur have offered a way of understanding film like painting or the novel, as the product of a single aesthetic vision, a single style, despite its technological reproducibility and its assembly-line production.[1] "Stylish" is, indeed, one of the most common descriptions of Fuest's film work.[2] Fuest's work manifests style as such, style for style's sake. This concern with style as such in an age of technological reproducibility brings to mind the critic Susan Sontag's assertion in 1964 that "camp is the modern dandyism," because it solves the problem of "how to be a dandy in an age of mass culture."[3] A dandy in mass culture, Fuest links Pop, New Wave, and camp: his film and television work record how British visual culture of the 1960s and early 1970s drew upon science fiction itself as style rather than genre. The result was that science fiction became transformed from a genre, narrowly defined, to a style or mode. *The Final Programme* constitutes a fascinating moment in that much larger transformation.

Fuest began his career as a copywriter, but, in 1961, became an art director for the first season of a new television show, *The Avengers* (ABC, 1961–1969). He returned as art director for one episode, the fortieth, in the second season (1962): the style of this show is fairly unremarkable, especially by the standards of the later *Avengers*. However, in 1968, Fuest directed a film called *Just Like a Woman* that led to his being hailed, at least in one review, as "the High Priest of Pop Art."[4]

In 1968, too, Fuest returned to *The Avengers*, now in its sixth season (1968–1969), as director. *The Avengers* itself had, at this point, established a very close association with a particular kind of British style and stylishness, often considered "Pop" or "mod" within the frame of genre-defying espionage fantasy.[5] What style achieves here, as a signifier of its own signified, is to erase or at least displace genre meanings, particularly those of espionage and science fiction, so that Cold War weaponry and military gadgetry make way for pure capitalist commodity camp. Camp, it seems, was always an open secret of *The Avengers*: commenting on the same 1968 season, newspaper critic Julian Critchley asserted that this season was "camp as a row of tents which is how we like it nowadays."[6]

When this season came to an end, Fuest, with Brian Clemens and Albert Fennell, two producers (and in the case of Clemens, a writer) of the series, made a feature film, the psychological thriller, *And Soon the Darkness* (1969). Fuest was director and writer, with Clemens as co-writer and producer. Fuest was then approached by American International Pictures to make a film of *Wuthering Heights*, "[p]lanned as a prestige release by AIP."[7] His version, released in the U.K. in 1970, with Timothy Dalton and Anna Calder-Marshall as Heathcliff and Cathy, sets the events in a brooding eighteenth century Yorkshire and stresses what is only elliptically implied in the novel, namely, that Heathcliff and Cathy are not only raised as brother and sister, but that they are, indeed, half-siblings related by blood. The poster for the film, in saturated and acidic violets and lilacs, shows a close-up of Cathy and Heathcliff that looms spectrally large above an isolated house. In its "unnatural" coloring as well as its tagline, the poster emphasizes the Gothic link between desire, transgression, and fear: the poster proclaims the film to be "the power, the passion, the terror of Emily Bronte's [sic] unforgettable love story."[8]

From this kind of "prestige" Gothic of *Wuthering Heights*, Fuest's next two films, *The Abominable Dr. Phibes* (U.K./U.S., 1971) and *Dr. Phibes Rises Again* (U.K./U.S., 1972), both for AIP, consolidated Fuest's place as a director who fused Pop and camp in a way that received both commercial and critical recognition. Writing about the success of *The Abominable Dr. Phibes*, James Robert Parrish and Steven Whitney remark: "the film seemed to receive acclaim from every corner of the country. Willard van Dyke, then director of films at the Museum of Modern

Art in New York, requested the movie be screened at that venerable institution, and *Newsweek* magazine reported it received 'unexpected cultural kudos' at the museum."[9] A wide range of contemporary reviews named the mode that dare not speak its name. *The New York Times* complained that "the tone of steamroller camp flattens the fun," while *Variety* tried to sum up the film as "anachronistic period horror musical camp fantasy, loaded with comedic gore of the kind that packs theatres and drives child psychologists up the wall." The *Philadelphia Inquirer* went so far as to imagine the film winning a camp Oscar (or an Oscar for camp?), noting that "this camp horror movie reaches a pinnacle of absurd glory [...] they should strike off a magenta Oscar for this one" and the film's "art-deco camp ambience" is the aspect that critics universally remark on.[10]

One might well wonder whether MOMA's screening of *The Abominable Doctor Phibes* was not, in a way, a means of celebrating Pop Art. Certainly in their linkage of high art, and literary allusiveness to lowbrow farce, *Grand Guignol*, and elements of science fantasy, the *Phibes* films consolidated what had seemed, perhaps, like incompatible aspects of Fuest's eclectic film and television career. After the two *Phibes* films, then, Fuest's decision to film Moorcock's novel *The Final Programme* should be understood as more than an extension of his film style to the genre of science fiction. Instead, the stylistic concerns of Fuest's filmmaking resonated with the significant mutations that British science fiction, acting in response to Pop Art, among other changes, had undergone in the 1960s and early 1970s.

After *The Final Programme*, Fuest made a supernatural horror film, *The Devil's Rain* (1975), in the U.S. He returned to television with *The New Avengers* (ITC, 1976–1977), of which he directed two episodes in 1976, before returning to the U.S. where, for most of the 1980s, he directed episodes and films for television, including an adaptation of Edgar Allan Poe's *The Gold Bug* (ABC, 1980) and a sequel to *The Stepford Wives*, made for NBC-TV, called *The Revenge of the Stepford Wives* (1981). It is, however, on the body of films and television work made in a very short period of time, 1968 to 1973, that Fuest's reputation rests.

The British New Wave

Since the New Wave is central to understanding both Fuest's context and his innovation, it is important to recall what it was and how it came about. In 1964 a young writer named Michael Moorcock was offered the chance to take over the moribund British science fiction magazine *New Worlds*. He and J.G. Ballard assembled a dummy issue as a sample, and a May/June issue (number 142) of *New Worlds* appeared in May of that same year. For Moorcock, the editorship of *New Worlds* offered the chance of renewing not just the magazine but transforming the genre too:

5. Robert Fuest and The Final Programme (Plessis)   63

> [The proposed magazine] would be on art paper, to take good quality illustrations; it would be the size of, say, *Playboy* so that it would get good display space on the newsstands; it would specialize in experimental work by writers like [William] Burroughs and artists like [Eduardo] Paolozzi, but it would be "popular," it would seek to publicize such experimenters; it would publish all those writers who had become demoralized by a lack of sympathetic publishers and by baffled critics; it would attempt a cross-fertilization of popular sf [sic], science and the work of the literary and artistic avant-garde.[11]

So successful was this conjunction of high and mass culture that, with the help of Brian Aldiss, *New Worlds* even received an Arts Council grant in 1967. The magazine continued up to issue 201 in March 1971 and thereafter continued intermittently as *New Worlds Quarterly*, appearing as ten paperback books from 1971 until 1976.[12]

It is therefore possible to regard British engagements with mass culture, understood to be signally "American" (and with science fiction as one part of that mass culture), as operating still within the milieu of high cultural production while drawing on mass culture. Such might be the example, perhaps, of the Independent Group (IG), a loose collection of artists, architects, and critics who met at the Institute for Contemporary Art (ICA) in the 1950s and 1960s, and who consolidated a Pop aesthetic. By contrast, *New Worlds* might appear at first to operate within mass culture as a popular fan magazine, but with ambitions toward high culture. In fact, the relations are much more complicated.[13] A key figure in the IG, Eduardo Paolozzi, also contributed to *New Worlds*. Ballard, who claimed to have been galvanized by the IG and who later had installations at the ICA and the New Arts Laboratory, was an editor and central contributor.[14] A piece like Christopher Finch's "Language Mechanism," a review of Paolozzi's visual work in relation to the language philosophy of Ludwig Wittgenstein, is not anomalous in the milieu Moorcock strove to establish.[15]

One effect of the intermingling of high and mass culture that *New Worlds* effected is that, as Colin Greenland observes, "sf [sic] passes out of fandom's walled city and into general circulation."[16] He adds that the genre becomes, as we have seen for the IG, raw material for an aesthetic mode:

> Earlier, unsophisticated fictions in the tradition now appear to have a mythological force unsuspected by their authors. The imagery is suitably cheap and glossy, uncontaminated by official authorisation, ready to be dismantled and reconstructed by artists and theorists who have lost faith in orthodox models.[17]

Such dismantling and reconstruction of earlier, "unsophisticated" genre material is key to Fuest's approach as well, and forms a significant intersection with his adaptation of Moorcock's novel. Near the beginning of his book on the British New Wave, Greenland cites[18] the American literary and cultural critic Leslie Fiedler, who claims that in the course of the 1960s, "quite serious writers [...] emulate the modes of Science Fiction [sic]."[19]

Michael Moorcock and the Jerry Cornelius Tetralogy

In 1973, the same year that Fuest released his film adaptation of the first Jerry Cornelius novel, *The Final Programme*, Brian Aldiss wrote about Moorcock's creation: "in Cornelius, the worlds of Ronald Firbank and Ian Fleming meet. Cornelius embodies many aspects of the present day projected into an art deco international future, with Ladbroke Grove as important a destination as Alpha Centaurus was."[20] What is striking about Aldiss's formulation is what is striking about Moorcock's tetralogy as well: its imagination of the future is a projection of the past as a camp style. The future will be retro, the tetralogy has already told us — Cold War espionage, displaced, could become the exquisite high camp of Ronald Firbank.[21]

Tellingly, the Cornelius tetralogy — which consists of *The Final Programme* (1969), *A Cure for Cancer* (1971), *The English Assassin* (1972), and *The Condition of Muzak* (1977) — ends in the title of its last volume, with a parodic iteration, a dying fall, one might say, of Walter Pater's famous late Victorian epigram: "all art constantly aspires to the condition of music."[22] Musical structure and analogy pervade the tetralogy. Moorcock notes in the pretextual matter to *A Cure for Cancer* that "like the other books in the tetralogy (like the tetralogy itself), it is developed in something approximating sonata form: Introduction; Development (1 and 2); Recapitulation; Coda."[23] However, these multiple iterations occur as diminishment. No longer aspiring to music, art turns into muzak, mundane commodity for a mundane commodity world. Moorcock even glosses the term as the very last sentence of the four volumes: "Muzak is a trade name for piped music used in restaurants, supermarkets, bars and other public places."[24]

Not only art but personal identity is subject to multiple iterations and objectification. So, in the introduction to the 1977 U.S. edition of the tetralogy, John Clute describes Jerry Cornelius as:

> a sexually ambivalent, amoral (but exceedingly oral), portmanteau anti-hero who was part saint and part devil, an instant myth of the pop sixties whose taste in music, clothes, cars, drugs, wombs, technology and apotheosis all seemed to make him an authentic emblem of Swinging London and (more narrowly) of the New Wave in sf [sic] which Moorcock had instigated by giving space to its writers in his magazines, which soon became notorious. As did its mascot.[25]

Clute continues by noting that Moorcock offered Cornelius as a figure that exceeded conventional authorial control: "Moorcock encouraged his fellow writers to use Cornelius as a template in stories of their own."[26] Commenting on Cornelius and the New Wave in 2003, Moorcock writes: "we rejected conventional modernism as well as the conventions of commercial science fiction, hoping to discover methods which would help us deal more effectively in our fiction with the events and idiosyncrasies of modern life. Jerry Cornelius was my response."[27] He then adds a fascinating qualification: "Not so much a character, as [M. John] Harrison pointed out, as a technique."[28]

This perception of character not as essence and identity but as strategy and technique permeates the novels of the tetralogy which are radically non-linear and disjunctive. In *The Final Programme*, the most conventional of the set, we encounter Jerry Cornelius, a non-affiliated secret agent armed with a needle gun, a Nobel Prize–winning author of speculative texts on time and space with titles such as *Time-Search Through the Declining West, Toward the Ultimate Paradox*, and *The Ethical Simulation*, dressed in his "usual black car coat, dark trousers, and high heels," driving a 1936 Duesenberg limousine.[29] While such details may appear to shape a conventionally novelistic "character" here they effectively only offer coordinates in a welter of shifting signs and contexts.

We find out that Jerry is in love with his sister, Catherine, who resembles him.[30] His half-brother, Frank, appears in all the novels as Jerry's antagonist. Here, he keeps Catherine drugged in their (dead) father's "fake Le Corbusier château."[31] The description of the château resonates with my concerns with period styles, so its description is worth quoting here: "a large six-storey building with that quaint, dated appearance that all the 'futuristic' buildings of the twenties and thirties had. To boot, this château had a dash of German expressionism in its architecture."[32] This is wonderfully characteristic of Moorcock's own style: the wit of the fake Le Corbusier château, the comment on the datedness of future visions, the suggestion of menace in its eclecticism — both Le Corbusier-functional and Expressionist-menacing. Armed with state-of-the-art Cold War psychological weaponry, the château serves some of the purposes of castles in fairytales and the Gothic.

On a quest to free Catherine from the castle and obtain a microfilm of his father's calculations and the Newman manuscript, a supposedly visionary text written by an American astronaut, Jerry is drugged by Frank and kills Catherine by mistake:

He had killed her.
In agony, he began to caress her stiff.[33]

This inadvertent sororicide, the correlative of Jerry and Catherine's incestuous love, echoes throughout the tetralogy, in which the Catherine-Jerry-Frank relationship is permeated and saturated, less as a conventional novelistic set of circumstances than as a set of shifting possibilities — sometimes Catherine is briefly, Eurydice-like, returned from the dead, at others, she is still alive. In fact, the tetralogy ends with Catherine, alive and pregnant by Jerry, and with their mother, an increasingly looming presence after the first novel, dead.

Whatever else may be at play here, it becomes evident that Moorcock is indeed utilizing the characters as techniques, as mobile ciphers that can be reinscribed in an endless variety of narrative possibilities, so that "character" never entirely closes off a narrative option as it does in all realist fiction. Moreover,

Moorcock is constructing a myth out of the archaic taboos of incest and murder to present in the tetralogy a mythopoeic combinatory for an age skeptical of narrative in general and myth in particular. (We can contemplate the significance of the initials J.C. at our discretion as a meaning we may or may not decide to activate.)

This novel introduces Miss Brunner, a computer programmer, who is ambiguously ally and adversary of Jerry's. She has the power to absorb not only the energy of her lovers, but their entire bodies. The program on which Miss Brunner is working involves condensing the sum total of human knowledge into one comprehensive equation with the corresponding issue of how to download this equation into a human brain: this is the eponymous "final program."[34] The problem of downloading the equation can only be solved, as the name of the super-computer, DUEL, punningly indicates, by feeding the program into dual separate human brains. The aim transforms itself, so that it is not just knowledge but the production of "an all-purpose human being"[35] that is at stake:

> A human being equipped with total knowledge, hermaphrodite in every respect — self-fertilizing and this self-regenerating — and this immortal, re-creating itself over and over again, retaining its knowledge and adding to it. In short, ladies and gentleman, we are creating a being that our ancestors would have called a god![36]

As this description indicates, the "final program" here is something like a perfect cybernetic loop. Miss Brunner and Jerry Cornelius become this dual unified being, Cornelius Brunner. It is "hermaphrodite and beautiful,"[37] an intersexed giant that forthwith leads the people of an economically collapsing Europe into a literally lemming-like plunge into the Black Sea: "within six hours, only one head [remains] above water. Naturally it [is] the head of Cornelius Brunner."[38] The novel ends with Cornelius Brunner blowing up the patriarchal château and "[striding]" toward what "it" (the pronoun the text uses) calls a "tasty world ... A very tasty world."[39] If the "final program" is the perfect cybernetic loop figured, in the Cornelius-Brunner duel/dual, its function as the title, also, of the text we are reading is neither negligible nor coincidental — it evokes a non-coincidence in which this is and is not "the final program." Thus, entropy and noise enter the perfect loop: as the subtitle of the third novel in the tetralogy, *The English Assassin*, has it, we are reading "A Romance of Entropy."

Moreover, the narrative of/about/as information has displaced the quest for the Newman manuscript. The quest for the astronaut's manuscript does eventually turn up the text which consists of 203 pages neatly covered with the word "ha."[40] The conventional trajectory towards "outer space" in science fiction is a derisory dead end; the true "New Man" is the "all-purpose human being." Information technology displaces space exploration just as narrative itself becomes code.

The novel still communicates a vivid, liberating force in its multiple permutations of sex, gender, and sexuality. These begin in the very first section when we find that after their metaphysical discussion, Jerry and the Brahmin physicist Professor Hira casually later "that night [lie] in bed together, talking and smiling."[41] A few chapters later Jerry thinks:

The true aristocracy that would rule the seventies were out in force: the queers and the lesbians and the bisexuals, already half-aware of their great destiny which would be realized when the central ambivalence of sex would become totally recognized and the terms *male* and *female* would become all but meaningless. Here they were. As he wandered, he was surrounded by all the possible replacements for sex, one or several of which would be the main driving force for the humanity of circa 2000 — light, color, music, the pin tables, the pill dispensers, the gun ranges — scarcely substitutes for sex anymore, but natural replacements.[42]

If the rest of the tetralogy fuses tabloid snippets with art nouveau and art deco, this vision anchors some of that stylistic camp in a vision of truly immaterial sex. Likewise, the permeability of erotic relationships, sexes, genders, and sexualities (Brunner is male, for example in *A Cure for Cancer*) model in a sense the "all-purpose human being" for whom there is no identity, only situations.

The combinatory possibilities of features, identities, and structures replicate the collage aesthetic that determines the novels, to such an extent that Mooorcock's acknowledgements at the beginning of *A Cure for Cancer* state:

> Parts of this novel originally appeared in *Fate, Prediction, Record Mirror, New Worlds, Billboard, Headquarters, Detective, True Life Confessions, The Village Voice, Guns and Ammo, Scientific American, Time, Interavia, Motorcycle Mechanics, TV and Movie Play, Man's Magazine, Screen and TV Album, New Man, Silver Screen, Titbits, The Observer, Reveille, The Plain Truth, Science Horizons, Daily Sketch, Vogue* and other British and American magazines to whom acknowledgements are gratefully made.[43]

Likewise, the appendix to *The Condition of Muzak* declares: "the captions to chapters in this novel are advertisements and headlines taken from the following sources, most of them published 1975–1976: *Jane's Weapons Systems, Interavia, Official Detective, Crime Detective, True Detective, Official UFO, Guns and Ammo, Titbits, Weekend, Guardian, Daily Mirror, Horology Magazine*."[44] Authorship itself, Moorcock suggests, is a matter of programming: combining and cutting is style. Indeed, given that Umberto Eco had a few years earlier faulted the James Bond books for being conglomerations of styles and modes and genres that had been homogenized into an illusory unity (one might say formal as well as ideological), one might consider what Moorcock achieves with secret agent and science fiction here to be a kind of drastic decomposition and disassembling.[45]

Robert Fuest's The Final Programme

While Fuest's *The Final Programme* has typically been dismissed by critics, the film strikingly continues the director's own signature concerns with visual styles.[46] There are many elements of Pop, for example in the collage-like juxtaposition of Jerry's gleaming black vintage limousine with the highway overpasses, or of the signifiers of place (of nation, even) and tradition with the detritus of a mechanized consumer society: Nelson's Column and St. Paul's façade appear next to piles of cars, as though heritage and automobile graveyard are simply adjacent.

In some frames, Fuest's cinematography creates similar Pop collages. Thus, we see Catherine's photograph in a black and white oval attached to the rearview mirror of Jerry's car in a point of view shot that shows him driving and pouring himself a whiskey from a Bell's bottle (here, less early product placement than a Pop citation of commodity label). In the car, as well, a shot of the floor reveals it to be littered with chocolate digestive biscuits, a variety of pills and pharmaceutical objects, and gleaming pink and gold beads, to create a Pop effect, in which the mundane, the technological, and the commodity fuse. Jerry's own trademark, the needle gun, appears in the film, notably during the shootout with Frank that leads to Catherine's death, as well as Jerry and Frank's final shootout. Along with the black limousine, the gun evokes the glamorous technologies of speed and death, with the "super-fetishism" that art historian Hal Foster has identified in the work of British Pop artists such as Richard Hamilton.[47]

A long sequence in the film takes place in a pinball arcade. The pinball machine, with its lurid colors, flashing lights, and allure of juvenile delinquency, itself constituted a highly over-determined Pop artifact on its own, but Fuest's design has the pinball arcade itself be in the shape of a giant pinball machine, complete with young women in silvery white bikinis inside large clear plastic spheres for pinballs. Drum majorettes in red, white and blue uniforms and a Harlequin (inside another large plastic sphere) add to the quality of assemblage. As emphasis, Fuest uses costume jewelry, on both the turbaned fortuneteller and on Miss Dazzle who appear in this scene.[48] In this setting, Jerry's ostensible purpose — to buy napalm from the assassin Shades — becomes only another exercise in consumption: Shades reminds him that the napalm will not be available the next day, because "shops are shut on Sundays." A similar banality about military technology has occurred in an earlier scene: Jerry visits Major "Wrong Way" Lindberg, who rattles off a long catalog of available weaponry. Everything is on the verge of turning commodity: weapons, people, images. In this way, the film evokes the collage techniques of Moorcock's tetralogy.

The briefly glimpsed Harlequin in this sequence recalls how much popular traditions of entertainment pervade Moorcock's tetralogy, so that everything from music hall and popular song to pantomime (one source, perhaps, for the myriad instances of drag and transvestism in the novels) to, directly, the Harlequinade (particularly pervasive in the final volume). Here Fuest differs from Moorcock: when Jerry meets Miss Brunner at a restaurant, the wrestlers in a ring of white paint evoke the end, in commodity-spectacle, of popular entertainment rather than any continuity with theatrical traditions.[49]

Two other visual styles deserve mention: the presence of industrial imagery in the way the film visualizes the computer technology at the core of its delineation of a weaponized information era introduces another visual style, for here Fuest relies on what one might call the ready-made or found object of industrial imagery — generators, dials, coils, meters, blinking buttons, wavering needles, in olive greens and primary colors, in large cubes or beams. Likewise, Fuest's very theatrical use of black spaces as visible "spaces off" in some scenes (when Jerry is in hospital or in the restaurant), as though we were seeing the actual studio in which filming is taking place, past the set as such, is both an inventive response to a very tight budget and a way of drawing attention to the high degree of artifice in the characters and their world, as well as in the film's representation.

Typically, Fuest uses art deco and some art nouveau (central in the *Phibes* films) to mark in visual terms a *mise-en-scène* of camp. From the geometries of the vintage car to the geometric zigzag pattern on Miss Dazzle's sequined dress, "retro" stylistic elements appear as citations. The Cornelius family home combines art deco with early 1970s modern: a room is furnished primarily in white with a stylized stencil of pink lotus flowers and blue butterflies that quotes the work of Scottish Arts and Crafts designer Charles Rennie Mackintosh. Catherine's bedroom is all deco pastels and angular or semi-circular shapes, from its vanity to the bed and carpet. There are two statuettes of female figures in this room, one a gilt deco piece, the other a bronze art nouveau. Catherine's bedside table, a jumble of mirrors, syringes, and capsules, connects the Pop with the revivalist citing of late nineteenth and early twentieth century styles. Not only Catherine, but Miss Brunner, whose dresses and skirts with their intricate geometric pleating make a deco statuette at points, gets linked to these artifacts and styles. When Miss Brunner appears in a white pleated shift prior to making love with Jerry and their ultimate fusion, she raises her arms hieratically in the manner, precisely, of a deco statuette. It is tempting to speculate about the extent to which this kind of deco is a cinematic science fiction tradition that extends all the way back to Fritz Lang's female android in *Metropolis* (Germany, 1927).

So self-conscious a film as *The Final Programme* invites a reading of itself as meta-cinema. Major Lindberg, the Harlequin, Miss Brunner, and the fused Cornelius-Brunner at the end all look into camera, an instance of cinematic self-reflexivity, as though they acknowledge the presence of both camera and spectators. Cornelius-Brunner does this most explicitly by verbally addressing the audience with "See you around, sweetheart," the film's final words, and an example of the film's ubiquitous camp.[50] The use of "psychedelic" effects, such as flashing lights, filters and color development in sharp pinks and purples during Jerry's attack on the Cornelius château, and the slow motion and multiple simultaneous exposures, combined with "trippy" solarization and color printing (more acid yellows and purples), during the love-making and fusion of Miss Brunner and Jerry, communicate, hyperbolically, the effects of the cinematic apparatus. In the latter sequence, the exaggerated visual effects not only recount the transformation, they further underscore a contemporary 1960s and 1970s sense that sex and sexuality are a "trip."

Jerry's gaze is identified a number of times with the camera. At the end of the first scene of the film, Jerry leaves by helicopter and the camera flies with him. When he drives his car, we get his point of view through the windshield, as well as through the windshield of small plane, a little later. When Cornelius-Brunner emerges from the pyramid in which the fusion of the "final program" has taken place, we again see with the point of view of Cornelius-Brunner, so that we get a slightly out-of-focus tracking view of the destroyed lab, until the camera-point of view encounters Miss Brunner's sometime lover, Dmitri, who asks, as focus returns, "so you are the new Messiah?" A counter-shot now reveals Cornelius-Brunner, who replies: "I'm not sure." What emerges from this linkage of Jerry's look with the camera is a connection between the self and the apparatus, whether it be the machinery of the final program or the cinema, as well as with the technologies of sexuality and sex. In a parallel, when Miss Brunner vampirically absorbs her lovers, the camera in the film registers a slight quiver, as though the limits of identity were indeed only a visual effect.

While the film is not nearly as expansive or as generous in its recognition of multiple sexualities and genders, a scene in which Miss Brunner seduces her assistant, Jenny, is remarkable in how it plays with the look. Jerry looks at the two women, but does so at one remove, indirectly, in an ornate mirror, so that he is looking at a scene which is in actuality behind him. We in our turn see Jerry, both "real" and reflected, as well as what he sees in the mirror. These are all instances of meta-cinema in *The Final Programme*, and tellingly, they are part of the film's deployment of the technology of sexuality and gender. Together, these instances add up to something more than just self-reflexivity, for they implicate "modern" gendered and sexed selfhood in visual technologies, such as the cinema. Meta-cinema's self-reflexivity mirrors, too, the reflexivity of camp, which I have described earlier as style for style's sake. Here we have cinema for cinema's sake.

The eponymous program itself appears initially via a missing microfilm. When Miss Brunner obtains the film and projects it, it works as a series of still images: we see a series of hieroglyphs and geometric patterns that, on the one hand, do the diegetic work of plausibly resembling some arcane computer program of the future, while on the other, providing a kind of visual meta-text and meta-comment about the combinatory possibilities of identity and sex in the film. The sequence of patterns fill the screen for a few moments, echoing the art deco motifs and resonating with some Pop Art of the time, notably the graphic work of Paolozzi, in its exploration of hieroglyphs and industrial design fused as a kind of iconic language for new mythologies.[51] The first image in the sequence shows a gilt sun surrounded by a pattern of red circles, blue triangles and gold squares. The second image shows a stylized human head with a brain in cross section, like a textbook illustration, with a slightly different arrangement of the same shapes in the same colors. The next shows a blue triangle with the letter F in it, a gold triangle with C in it and a red square with a J in it at the bottom of the screen. The fourth and final screen shows simply the red circle with J from the previous image and with all the other elements erased, as though Frank, Catherine, and Jerry were indeed elements in a program of which Jerry is both solution and synthesis. In a sense, this is a film within the film: reduced to hieroglyphs, the images tell of the absorption of Frank and Catherine into Jerry as Jerry becomes "the all-purpose human being" of Moorcock's novel.[52]

5. Robert Fuest and The Final Programme (Plessis) 71

The sibling incest of Jerry and Catherine recalls the incest that Fuest gave center stage in his *Wuthering Heights*: the coincidence of "Catherine" as a name can hardly be a coincidence. For example, Harry Andrews, cast in *The Final Programme* as the loyal retainer who tries to let Jerry and Catherine escape Frank, plays the role of Mr. Earnshaw, the patriarch from whose extramarital relationship Heathcliff originates, in Fuest's *Wuthering Heights*. The triangular sibling relation of Jerry, Catherine, and Frank recalls the Heathcliff, Catherine, and Lindley triangle, as well.

In a way typical of late nineteenth century "decadent" fantasies of sex and gender, this fusion through incest of brother and sister parallels the fusion of male and female in intersexed, androgynous, or bisexual selfhood, here achieved via the final program.[53] Perhaps the stylized pseudo-Egyptian glyphs in the château are more than ornamental, since they evoke fantasies of dynastic incest in ancient Egypt, as well as of the lotus as an Egyptian symbol of life and rebirth. The diagram of the microfilm joins science fiction with alchemy, for the schemas resemble both imagined binary programs and alchemical drawings; the union of opposites and completion of the Great Work in alchemy is figured by the hermaphrodite.[54] Moorcock invokes this figure when Jerry, drugged, kills Catherine by accident: "he thought he saw a creature bending over them both — a creature without a navel, hermaphrodite and sweetly smiling [...]."[55]

A last hermaphrodite appears in the film's poster. Apparently designed by British Pop artist Allen Jones, the poster forms an integral part of the network of meanings I have been tracing here, and serves as summary and summa of the film.[56] On a background of canary yellow, it shows a strongly frieze-like, narrow vertical figure in hieratic three-quarter profile. The figure is itself divided bilaterally down its middle, so that the left half appears as male, or as Jerry. This half sports his signature black double-breasted jacket and black trousers, has black curly hair and a black glove. The more distant right side (the figure is facing right) is female, with one exaggeratedly high heel, and a bare hand, which nonetheless holds Jerry's trademark needle gun (we may note that the gun resembles exactly the design of the gun in the film). The right-side half has emphatically outlined breasts in its white dress. A shadow behind the female side adds ambiguity, as its silhouette stresses the "female" breast and teasingly adds a cigarette that the "real" figure does not appear to have. Indeed, bifurcated at its crotch, the doubled, bi-sexed figure sets in motion a play of fetishes at key points in the figure and image, from single high heel shoe at the bottom of the image (above the title of the film) to the hand holding the comic-book phallic gun in middle by way of the shadowy cigarette near the very top. The tagline for the film, "The end — or the beginning?," is split by the gun into "The end-" and "or the beginning" in the poster. An additional fetish focuses on the image of the body itself, because we see two breasts and not just one on the female side, which would have followed some logic of bilateral male versus female. The double breasts constitute a visual pun, no doubt, on the double-breasted jacket Jerry wears. The face area, however, is entirely undefined and rudimentary, not a marker of identity in this program of shifting fetish combinations. Machinic and geometric, the figure and overall design are both highly retro in that they recall art deco explicitly, yet with soft outlines, as though the program that is conjugated here were indeed a fusion not only of male and female, machine and human, but also a fusion of commodity fetishism with sexual fetishism in an elegant triumph of the commodity-spectacle.[57]

A similar moment of camp triumph occurs at the end of the film which departs significantly from the novel. Cornelius-Brunner, in Fuest's version, is a hairy creature at once swishy and shambling, and not at all the alluringly lethal intersexed machine-commodity of Jones's poster. While the end of Fuest's film may at first seem like a reductively camp take on Moorcock's ending with all the complexity sacrificed for a rather facile punch-line, in its own way, this ending serves as a witty riposte to the hazy, self-serving mysticism of Stanley Kubrick's *2001: A Space Odyssey* (U.K./U.S., 1968): no star child orbiting Earth here. As the proposed alternative title for the U.S. makes clear, these are *The Last Days of Man on Earth*, with a camp emphasis on the false generic "man."

Fuest's film and television work offers an intriguing case study in thinking about the limits and possibilities of genre, as well as the limits and possibilities of auteurism and how "camp" and "style" historically briefly became synonymous. More than a quaint relic, curious anomaly, or a minor cult object, *The Final Programme* stands as a reminder of a time when it seemed that science fiction and the avant-garde, mass and high cultures could converge. Thus, Fuest's film connects, beyond a national filmmaking tradition, to other international Pop films of the 1960s and early 1970s, such as Mario Bava's *Danger: Diabolik* (Italy/France, 1968), Roger Vadim's *Barbarella* (France/Italy, 1968), Joseph Losey's *Modesty Blaise* (1966), Elio Petri's *The Tenth Victim* (Italy/France,1965), and even Stanley Kubrick's *A Clockwork Orange* (U.S./U.K., 1971); the latter for which Allen Jones designed the notorious fetish furniture in the shape of *trompe l'oeil* female mannequins dressed in fetish gear. But *The Final Programme* has links to a particularly British tradition of theatrical dystopianism that we see in films like Derek Jarman's *Jubilee* (1977), which featured Jenny Runacre, Fuest's Miss Brunner, in a dual role, and Terry Gilliam's *Brazil* (1985). Of its successors, perhaps *The Rocky Horror Picture* (U.K./U.S., Jim Sharman, 1975) did the most to consolidate camp, commodity culture, and science fiction played for all its theatricality. Finally, rather than considering the film as a failed adaptation of Moorcock's novel, we might imagine Fuest's work as another iteration of the Cornelius myth in what Moorcock has often claimed as the "multiverse" that his fiction constructs.[58] More significantly, like his other film and television work in the genre of science fiction, Fuest's *The Final Programme* makes style matter as it offers a camp critique. If this is a "comic apocalypse," to echo Moorcock's phrase, making sexual ambiguity a commodity, a consumer choice among others, it announces, in a way that transforms genre and gender expectations, "the last days of *man* on earth."[59]

6

"Anything Can Happen in the Next Half-Hour"
Gerry Anderson's Transnational Science Fiction

JONATHAN BIGNELL

Gerry Anderson's puppet series of the 1960s have hybrid identities in relation to their medial, geographical, and production histories.[1] This chapter ranges over his science fiction series from *Supercar* (ATV/ITC, 1961) to *Joe 90* (ATV/ITC, 1968–1969), arguing that Anderson's television science fiction in that period crossed many kinds of boundary and border. Anderson's television series were a compromise between his desire to make films for adults versus an available market for children's television programs, and aimed to appeal to a cross-generational family audience. They were made on film, using novel effects, for a U.K. television production culture that still relied largely on live and videotaped production. While commissioned by British ITV companies, the programs had notable success in the U.S., achieving national networked screening as well as syndication, and they were designed to be transatlantic products. The transnational hero teams and security organizations featured in the series supported this internationalism, and simultaneously negotiated between the cultural meanings of Britishness and Americanness. By discussing their means of production, the aesthetic and narrative features of the programs, their institutional contexts, and their international distribution, this chapter argues that Anderson's series suggest ways of rethinking the boundaries of British science fiction television in the 1960s.

Filmed Television and the Drive to Export

Gerry Anderson began his career as a film editor, and when seeking to move into film production and direction, his first break was to be invited to make a puppet series for British television, based on the work of the writer Roberta Leigh. *The Adventures of Twizzle* (1957) was made for the Rediffusion company that supplied programs for the commercial Independent Television network, and featured the adventures of a group of lost toys. Anderson formed the production company AP Films with former colleagues Arthur Provis, Reg Hill, John Read and Sylvia Thamm (later to become Anderson's wife) to produce the series in the small Islet Park film studio. His second project, *Torchy the Battery Boy* (1960) featured the clockwork toy Torchy, equipped with a battery-powered light on his hat, who traveled in his space rocket to Topsy-Turvy Land where its forgotten and mal-treated toys came alive. In the same year APF made *Four Feather Falls* for the Granada ITV company, cementing Anderson's association with puppetry for television, in which Sherrif Tex Tucker policed a Kansas town assisted by his talking dog and horse. The company's base moved to larger premises in the town of Slough, west of London, where specific facilities for puppet production and special effects filming were gradually developed.

Anderson's subsequent science fiction series were made with the backing of the television mogul Lew Grade, who ran the ITV company Associated Television (ATV) and whose Incorporated Television Company (ITC) was at the forefront of program export to the U.S.[2] Grade made programs for the ATV region and also for supply to the national ITV network, thus covering the majority of their costs, but his ITC distribution arm also sold programs to the U.S. and other overseas markets to increase their profitability. ATV/ITC's first success was the co-production of *The Adventures of Robin Hood*, a filmed drama series broadcast in Britain and also sold to CBS in 1955. Further ATV/ITC live-action costume series and spy adventures such as *The Avengers* (1961–1969) and *The Prisoner* (1967–1968) followed, paralleling Hollywood's television production strategy of domestic production at marginal profit, then overseas sale at much greater profit. Grade's export achievement was recognized by an award from the Queen in 1967, and his backing for Anderson's puppet science fiction needs to be understood in this economic context. By the end of the 1960s, ITC had sold *Supercar, Fireball XL5* (1962), *Stingray* (1964–1965), *Thunderbirds* (1965–1966), *Captain Scarlet and the Mysterons* (1967–1968) and *Joe 90* to U.S. syndication or to U.S. networks, as well as selling them to the British ITV network, and 60 percent of Anderson's revenue derived from sales to U.S. television.[3]

The association with Grade rescued APF, which was close to financial collapse in 1960, and according to Anderson, *Supercar* also saved ITC, which had suffered a drop in overseas sales success at that time.[4] Anderson successfully pitched *Supercar* to Grade, and the first of its thirty-nine episodes was aired in the U.K. in January 1961. ITC's experience in export sales led to a syndication deal that saw *Supercar* broadcast in the U.S. in the autumn of 1962 on over a hundred stations. Supercar could drive, fly, travel underwater, and go into space, piloted by the series protagonist Mike Mercury, assisted by its inventors Professor Popkiss and Doctor Beaker, ten-year-old Jimmy, and Mitch the monkey. The series was set in the present day, but APF's increasing specialization in special effects led to further futuristic and technological premises for its series. *Fireball XL5* (1962) was set in 2063, when Steve Zodiac piloted the eponymous flagship of the World Space Patrol, based in galaxy sector 25. The crew was the space doctor Venus, Professor Matthew Matic, the transparent robot Robert and their alien pet Zoonie. *Fireball* was the first British children's program networked in the U.S., screened by NBC in 1962.[5] In that year, Grade bought APF from Anderson, and the company began to operate from larger studios. There they made *Stingray*, set in 2064, in which WASP (the World Aquanaut Security Patrol) sent its flagship submarine Stingray to combat the alien technology of the underwater kingdom of Titanica, led by Titan, and his agent X20. Stingray, based at the Marineville military installation run by Commander Shore, was captained by Troy Tempest, assisted by "Phones" Sheridan and the underwater woman Marina whom they had rescued. The series was sold by ITC for U.S. syndication, and led to a further commission from Grade for a more ambitious format.

Thunderbirds was APF's first fifty-minute episode series, enabling more complex storylines, more characters, and more effects. It was set in 2065 and featured the Tracy family leading the International Rescue organization from their secret Pacific island base. Each Tracy son piloted one of the vehicles, invented by "Brains" Hackenbacker, that specialized in air, space, underwater or ground travel and had rescue capabilities. The Tracys were assisted by their manservant Kyrano and his daughter TinTin, the British agent Lady Penelope Creighton-Ward, and her chauffeur Parker. A mismanaged bidding war between U.S. networks meant that *Thunderbirds* was syndicated, not networked, in America, and was therefore cancelled while its second series was in production.[6] APF was renamed Century 21 Productions and continued with *Captain Scarlet*, which began with a landing on Mars in 2068 by the Earth security organization Spectrum. Captains Scarlet and Black mistakenly destroyed a Mysteron city, triggering Mysteron revenge attacks against Earth. The Mysterons killed and duplicated Scarlet and Black in indestructible form, Black becoming a Mysteron agent and Scarlet leading Spectrum's operations from Cloudbase, its airborne military and communications center. *Captain Scarlet* was syndicated in the U.S., as was the next project, *Joe 90*. The series protagonist was the adopted nine-year-old son of the scientist Professor McClaine. Joe and his father worked for WIN (the World Intelligence Network) and could transfer the brain patterns of selected individuals into Joe's special eyeglasses from the BIG RAT (Brain Impulse Galvanoscope Record And Transfer). Thus Joe was able to undertake secret missions, such as stealing a Russian fighter plane in the first episode, or piloting a World Army tank to prevent a rogue state from activating a military base. In 1968, the company was working at MGM's Borehamwood studios, and later at Pinewood near London, as its Slough facilities wound down and were closed by 1970. Anderson's last puppet series in the 1960s was *The Secret Service* (1969), blending live action with puppets in a contemporary setting, but Grade regarded the series as unsuitable for sale to U.S. television because of the nonsense dialogue voiced by British comedian Stanley Unwin, who played the main character.[7] Anderson moved into live action science fiction thereafter, never equaling the success of his earlier work (see Peter Hutchings's chapter on *UFO* [Century 21/ITC, 1969–1970]).

The production organization of these projects was a concrete instance of negotiation between British and American production norms. Each series was shot on film, paralleling the industrial practices developed in Hollywood, in contrast to the "as-if-live" videotaping of British series such as *Doctor Who* (BBC, 1963–1989, 2005–) in the same period. The series were designed for U.S. sales, as well as broadcast on the British commercial television network. Filmed drama was the most common program form among U.S. imports to the U.K., because it comprised the majority of primetime U.S. network programming, but regulation and self-imposed quotas restricted U.S. imports to about fifteen percent of programs on any one channel. Pressure to sell British programs to the U.S. tended to regularize U.K.–produced program duration to match U.S. episode lengths of about twenty-five or fifty minutes that were standardized to accommodate commercials. Thus U.K. productions with export potential, like U.S. imports, had segmented episode forms, and avoided serial storyline development so that episodes could exploit a stable format. This meant that a robust production system could be established at the Slough studios, in which numerous contributors could work on the separate tasks required for complex puppet and set construction, and special effects. With the production of *Stingray*, it became necessary for two crews to work simultaneously on the filming of episodes and the industrial organization of the studio enabled the manufacture of duplicate sets of puppets and the operation of two parallel soundstages. The same system had to be adopted to make *Thunderbirds*, for which two episodes were shot simultaneously so that the first series of twenty-six episodes could be completed within one year. With around a hundred effects sequences per episode, *Thunderbirds* demanded the integration of parallel film units and elaborate production planning. Anderson's programs resembled American ones in structure, medium of shooting and studio organization, so that they could be assimilated into U.S. scheduling patterns, could exploit technologies such as high-speed film for effects sequences, and efficiently group teams of different specialists together in one place.

Anderson's name became a signifier for this industrial enterprise, standing for a science fiction style, a mode of production using puppets for filmed series, and a brand that ITC could develop as part of its export strategy. The AP Films and Century 21 Productions brands linked the programs, and the company devised the new brand Supermarionation for *Supercar* to express its innovations in puppetry, supplemented by the impressive-sounding Videcolor (for *Stingray*) and VistaVision (in *Thunderbirds*) that signaled the studio's emphasis on visual spectacle. The studio's series were designed to reward sustained viewing and involvement, through the creation of distinctive visual styles of action and spectacle, and characters and storylines. Each filmed series was made in one studio facility, so consistency could become an aspect of their distinctiveness, and *mise-en-scène* was highly significant in its literal meaning of where and how the drama was staged. The studio was a specific but hybrid place: a site in Slough that made television using film, a U.K. production company that adopted Hollywood-style industrial organization, and a company that made British programs for U.S. export.

The company used voice actors who were American or Canadian, as well as British. The exodus of performers and other personnel to Britain following U.S. anti–Communist hysteria in the 1950s, and in the 1960s as a result of political resistance to the Vietnam War, created a pool of talent that could be deployed in British programs. Canadians working in Britain often masqueraded as Americans for voice work, and could be employed more easily than Americans because they did not need work permits. Canada is a member of the Commonwealth with strong historical connections with Britain, and Canadian citizens could be engaged at short notice and without extensive paperwork. For these practical reasons, awareness of American production techniques, forms, and styles was available to Anderson, who regularly visited the United States,[8] and transatlantic voices could be used in his series to enhance their exportability. For example, in *Supercar* the heroic, square-jawed pilot Mike Mercury was voiced by the Canadian Graydon Gould, and Canadian actor Paul Maxwell voiced Steve Zodiac of *Fireball* and various characters in *Captain Scarlet*. The Canadian-born Shane Rimmer voiced *Thunderbirds'* Virgil Tracy and also appeared in *Captain Scarlet* and *Joe 90*. Key puppet characters were also designed to resemble American film actors, or international stars appearing in U.S. films. *Supercar*'s antagonist Masterspy was based on the portly Sydney Greenstreet, and his henchman Zarin sounded like Peter Lorre, thus recalling these actors' pairing in *The Maltese Falcon* (U.S., John Huston, 1941). The Lorre characterization was reprised for Agent X20 in *Stingray*, where Troy Tempest was based on the film star James Garner.[9] Tempest's mute companion Marina seems modeled on Ursula Andress, seen in *Dr. No* (Terence Young, 1962), and Commander Shore's daughter Atlanta facially resembled Lois Maxwell, the Canadian actress who voiced her and who appeared in the James Bond films as M's secretary, Miss Moneypenny. Captain Scarlet was intended to signal coolness and sophistication, by the resemblance to Cary Grant in both the puppet's facial features and in his voice (supplied by the British actor Francis Matthews). In *Thunderbirds*, Jeff Tracy's sons Scott, Virgil, Alan, Gordon, and John were named for the first U.S. astronauts.[10] The transatlantic appeal of Anderson's science fiction series depended not only on their U.S.–influenced formats and modes of production, but also on aesthetic features of image and sound that signaled U.S. popular cultural icons, and more broadly a set of shared international references.

Science Fictional Worlds

The science fictional worlds of Anderson's series were conceived as an opportunity for the visual revelation of machines and physical action. This emphasis is clear from their opening credit sequences, in which vehicles and technologies were prominently featured. *Supercar* began with shots of the vehicle flying through the clouds, and *Thunderbirds* with images of the five main rescue craft, moments of the action in the episode to come, and images of the Tracy boys and Lady Penelope in front of the vehicles associated with them. The *Thunderbirds* opening ran for a lengthy one-and-a-half minutes, and similarly in *Joe 90* an even longer two-minute sequence showed the operation of the BIG RAT computer, and the spinning spherical apparatus within which Joe sat as brain patterns were transferred to him. Within the episodes, storylines were constructed around moments which foregrounded spectacular effects. These frequently involved the explosive destruction of model buildings and vehicles, but alongside these short-duration highlights, longer sequences of effects work offered engagement with technologies in operation. Anderson explained: "Because we had characters who couldn't stand properly without their knees sagging, and characters who had no expression, it was very difficult to play a love scene and impossible to have a fight. And so it seemed the way to go was anything that was fast moving and had excitement, so it seemed science fiction was the best option."[11] The most sustained example was the launch sequences for the Thunderbirds, motivated by the requirement for multiple types of rescue intervention from the air, underwater, or in space. Thunderbird 1's launch from beneath a retracting swimming pool, or Thunderbird 2's along a palm-lined runway and inclined ramp, were also preceded by lengthy scenes of their pilots being transferred by elevators, hydraulic platforms, and chutes into the vehicles. The focus on vehicles was initially motivated by Anderson's dissatisfaction with puppets' ability to walk convincingly, leading to vehicular movement wherever possible.[12] But extended visual sequences of technologies in action could be re-used, notably the launch sequences, and their duration and repetition made them the most memorable aspects of the episodes' narratives. Visual style and generic identity, rapidly defined early in each program, and repeated in effects and model sequences within them, became unifying mechanisms holding each series' format together.

The earlier series were filmed in monochrome, but the fact that U.S. television had been broadcasting in color since 1954 meant that the settings and design of Anderson's programs were quickly conceived with color in mind. In Britain, the minority channel BBC2 did not broadcast in color until 1967, and the main channels BBC1 and ITV did not do so until 1969. *Stingray* was the first British children's series made entirely in color, because it was designed to appeal to the American market, but had to be screened on British television in black and white, as did each of the later series on first showing. Viewing the color series, it is striking how much strong colors establish visual signatures for them, for example in the bright red colors of the laboratory in *Joe 90*. Color also differentiated key vehicles, such as the red Thunderbird 3, the yellow Thunderbird 4 and Lady Penelope's pink Rolls Royce car. The emphasis on *mise-en-scène* associated with models and effects was enhanced by depth of color and visual detail, and shooting on 35 mm film could achieve this much better than the electronic video cameras and magnetic tape available in Britain in the 1960s.[13] The Slough studios could mount elaborate lighting above the soundstages, and were equipped with overhead gantries above the sets used for puppet action, on which the puppeteers worked. Shallow water tanks were built, surrounded by cycloramas for model sequences featuring ships, or for the establishing shots of *Thunderbirds'* Tracy Island. A narrow vertical aquarium was built in front of the underwater sets for *Stingray* so that cameras could shoot through it, placing the submarine behind small tropical fish inside the tank and thus suggesting that it was immersed in water.[14] Extended long shots situated the vehicles and buildings in a large space that determined scale, and drew attention to the precise creation of a futuristic *mise-en-scène*. In key action sequences there were more mobile and rapidly cut sequences for pursuit and combat. Because of the production system using single film cameras, each shot could be individually lit and its camera positions planned to exploit point of view. Planned and consistent visual signatures set the Anderson brand in place as much as the consistent narrative tropes of good versus evil, or the use of futuristic machines. Patterns of setting characterized by scale and technological complexity worked with patterns of pacing in editing technique to establish recognizable stylistic motifs that were shared across Anderson's series. Music also became an important linking and branding mechanism, when the composer Barry Gray joined Anderson's team and contributed distinctive, military-style musical themes that combined traditional orchestral instruments with futuristic, electronic instruments.

Making programs for children using the devalued mode of the puppet series, Anderson was able to experiment with formats in which interesting ideas and novel production techniques could be tried out. As early as *The Adventures of Twizzle* in 1957, APF developed video assist so that the production crew could see what the film camera was recording,[15] and for *Torchy the Battery Boy*, puppets had moving mouths and eyes for the first time. Fiberglass puppet heads were first introduced in *Four Feather Falls* and APF invented electronic lip-synch to precisely match a pre-recorded voice track to the solenoids activating the puppets' mouths.[16] Back projection in puppetry was pioneered for *Supercar*'s title sequence, and for *Thunderbirds* a rolling road was created to permit extended sequences of vehicle movement. Proportionately sized puppets were introduced in *Captain Scarlet and the Mysterons* when more sophisticated solenoids permitted smaller puppet heads. While the aim of these innovations was to increase realism, the program formats were sufficiently distanced from realist conventions to develop an open fictional world in which fantastic and spectacular events could occur, and programs were also structured to allow considerable interpretive action by the viewer to fill in logical gaps or unexplained features of that fictional world. These characteristics also provided the basis for the programs to become "cult" successes, because the science fictional qualities of their narrative worlds left room for sustained involvement, repeated viewing, and intense attention.

This fictional world became the foundation on which fan culture and consumer products associated with Anderson's series were built. In Britain in the 1950–1970 period, the concept of "cult TV" scarcely existed, and the self-identity of the fan, the producer category of the "niche" audience, and the academic analysis of fandom, became current only from the 1970s. Anderson's series were early examples of product exploitation in British television, with a product range including comics, toy vehicles, dress-up costumes, LP records, confectionary, badges and sheet music.[17] APF established Century 21 Merchandising, Century 21 Toys and Century 21 Music to produce products associated with its programs, and the significance of that exploitation of its intellectual property led to the renaming of APF as Century 21 Productions in 1965, after the success of *Thunderbirds* merchandise. Commercial activities beyond television production raised and maintained individual programs' profile, supported the brand identity of Anderson's work, gained income from merchandising agreements, and promoted viewer interaction with and loyalty to the program. While Anderson's work centered on television, its financing substantially rested on products in other media to support production costs, notably the weekly comic-book *TV Century 21* that featured strips based on each Anderson series, alongside popular British and American programs such as *The Munsters* (U.S., CBS, 1964–1966), *Get Smart* (U.S., NBC/CBS, 1965–1970), and the Daleks from *Doctor Who*.[18]

The puppet series were conceived, scheduled, and advertised to address child audiences, but in the 1960s, British households would normally have only one television set, usually positioned in the main living room. There would be negotiations and arguments between family members over which program to watch, and an expectation that any program up to 9:00 P.M. (when scheduling for adults began) could be watched collectively by all the family. Anderson's puppet adventures were planned to provide possibilities of fantasy and imagination that could entertain both child and adult audiences, and bring them together in shared experiences of engagement with the program. A promotional brochure for *Joe 90* claimed, for example, that this was "fantasy adventure that will soon have every boy *and his Dad* playing JOE 90" (emphasis in the original).[19] The limits on individual action, uncertainties of social role, and ever-present threats of war and environmental degradation which both adult and child audiences experienced in the 1960s, were present in Anderson's series in a coded form. These problems were both granted spectacular power, but also symbolically tamed within the narrative structure, where repeated tropes of environmental and technological danger were given reassuring and spectacular resolutions. The fearful and other were brought into the domestic viewing experience by the program, but were also tamed by the text, and by the home viewing context. Part of that context was the peripheral culture of play and consumption related to the program's imagery, characters, and themes. The emergence of the program as "cult," and the growth of merchandise, was significantly dependent on the visual aesthetic discussed above, and a collective and domestic viewing context that also included other texts and products. Inasmuch as they concretize and express social meanings for children, toys are totemic objects around which children's difference from adults can be organized, and which can represent aspects of the child, or aspects of the world around the child that he or she can manipulate during play.[20] Playing with the toys extended the possible meanings of the characters and machines, as either representations of the child's own desires, or as representations of those forces outside him or her with which the child had to negotiate.

Anderson's series not only took part in how television functions as a homely medium that links the domestic space to the world beyond, but also had specific characteristics that reflected on the dualisms of familiar and alien, safety and danger. The home, and the demands of growing up away from it, were a consistent theme in Anderson's series because of the presence of a base or home as a place of safety and familiarity, and the pseudo-parental relationship between figures of authority and child characters, or characters in a subordinate power-position. One of the ways that the programs could address their audience of both children and adults was by building storylines that dealt with the mutually defining roles of child and adult, and with overlaps or slippages between those roles. The protagonist of *Supercar* was accompanied by a child, and an animal, *Fireball* featured the often-inept robot Robbie and the alien Zoonie in child-like roles, and the premise of *Joe 90* was that a boy could masquerade as an adult with the aid of technology. In contrast to the bleaker visions of the future that he finds in a majority of British science fiction programs of this period, John R. Cook places Anderson's work, and *Joe 90* in particular, among a group of series that "mediated in their different ways the utopian hopes and dreams of a new Aquarian order of enlightenment and rationality led by the young."[21]

Transnational Politics and Culture

By the mid–1960s, many adventure series, especially those produced for ITC, were deliberately international in setting and appeal, marketing both British pop culture and also the spatial mobility that British people began to aspire to, as affordable air travel and foreign holidays became accessible to them. Such programs also alluded to the internationalized exoticism of the James Bond cycle that began with *Dr. No*, and that contributed to the popularity of filmed action-adventure television programs like *The Saint* (ITC, 1962–1969), *The Avengers*, and Anderson's live-action series *The Protectors* (ITC, 1972–1974).[22] In *Thunderbirds*, for example, the Britishness of Lady Penelope and Parker were attractions to both British and U.S. audiences in the surrounding context of the American Tracy family, and drew on the cultural meaning of "cool Britannia." Anderson recalled, "I thought, 'I've got to do something for the home audience. Now, we British can laugh at ourselves, so therefore we had Penelope and Parker as this comedy team. And in America they love the British aristocracy too.'"[23] Sylvia Anderson scripted Lady Penelope with "not only the daring and panache of a secret agent but also the poise of a cool and beautiful aristocrat," and costume ideas for the puppet were based on Sylvia's interest in the Carnaby Street fashions of 1960s London.[24]

For British audiences of the 1960s, the cultural meanings of the U.S. were contradictory, with consumer capitalism associated with energy, progress, and entrepreneurialism, but also acquisitiveness, and the replacement of British imperial power by a new order of cultural imperialism emblematized by American products. The modernity represented by American youth culture and the ideology of opportunity, could also entail disrespect for tradition, loss of national specificity, and cultural colonization. The plurality of these meanings could be mapped onto the aesthetics of the American-influenced programs that Anderson made. As Steve Neale's work demonstrates,[25] for contemporaneous commentators the adventure series associated with ATV/ITC were seen as both high and low in quality, and as both British and American in character, so these transnational programs could be mobilized in conflicting and ambiguous ways. Bernard Sendall, for example, reports the London *Evening Standard*'s comment of 30 April 1960 that ITV was a "dull routine of cowboys, crime, murders, pop singers and half-wit quiz games,"[26] demonstrating that although ITV was regularly watched by some two-thirds of the British public, condemnation of the channel referred to program genres associated with the U.S. as evidence of its poor quality. In the context of the Cold War, and the U.S.'s rise to become the dominant superpower, Anderson's programs negotiated the place of Britain and Britishness in a changing world.

Anderson's puppet science fiction series represented a world in which British and American characters (and subsidiary characters from other non–Communist nations) work together. He commented: "we had the United Nations and I imagined that the world would come together and there would be a world government."[27] *Supercar* and *Thunderbirds* feature non-state organizations that cooperate with apparently benevolent worldwide authorities. *Fireball XL5* introduced the pan-galactic authority of the World Space Patrol, and in *Stingray*, *Captain Scarlet*, and *Joe 90* the main characters work for a specific arm of a transnational government resembling the United Nations. This political context was rarely addressed directly in the series, and worked to de-specify storylines so that they became conflicts between forces of order or security versus disorder or disruption. Such a generalized model of transnational organizations combating specific temporary threats, usually projected into the future, also made the series less anchored to the place of their production, and easier to export beyond the U.K. But this loose backstory nevertheless supported the assumption that American military and economic might underwrote the security of the fictional world, and that American isolationism or exceptionalism had been replaced by participation in a world system. It was this participation and leadership that was being argued for by political elites in the U.S. in the 1960s,[28] to advance U.S. economic interests in a stable, free-market capitalist environment that would include the Western

Hemisphere, the British Empire and Commonwealth, and the Far East. In line with the Truman "Doctrine" of 1947, Anderson's series imagined a Free World that the protagonists helped to secure.

The protagonists of *Supercar* and *Thunderbirds* had repeated personalized conflicts with villains who were apparently outside geopolitical conflict. These evil masterminds acted as freelance agents who threatened to disrupt the status quo, and ideological conflict was assumed rather than expressed. Despite the villain's elaborate plans, the protagonists' superior technologies, self-sacrificing heroism, and collaboration with each other always defeated him. The combined British, European, and American team in *Supercar*, for example, was based in Black Rock, Nevada, and traveled widely to combat Masterspy's and Zarin's attempts to steal the car's secrets. There were hints of Cold War conflict, especially in Masterspy's repeated address to "friend Zarin," suggesting the Soviet appellation "comrade," and in the episode "Island Incident," for example, Mercury learned that the president of a small Pacific island had turned it into a police state. The president's brother asked the team to return him home in Supercar to unseat the president, which they accomplished successfully. In *Thunderbirds* the recurring villain was The Hood, who acted as a freelance agent seeking to sell International Rescue technologies to the highest bidder. But in "Edge of Impact" he was under the command of "General X," and his Oriental appearance, hypnotic powers over his brother Kyrano, and his overweening arrogance, associated him with the James Bond villains of the period, and pervasive fears of China as a "third force" antagonistic to the West. *Fireball XL5* introduced Anderson's more usual premise of a world security organization, operating to keep the galaxy safe from threats that were embodied in alien antagonists. Similarly in *Stingray*, the fish-like Titanicans are non-human, but their militarism and aggression associated them with representations of the Soviet threat in Cold War fictions. The Mysterons of *Captain Scarlet* replaced humans with precise copies who they controlled, paralleling the body-snatching metaphor for Communist infiltration that was common in 1950s American science fiction, and again assumed a state of continual Cold War between humans and an alien civilization. The first episode saw Scarlet foil an attempt to assassinate the World President, and in "Winged Assassin," the Mysterons targeted the leader of the United Asian Republic. *Joe 90* began with an unusually precise reference to the 1960s context, in which Joe was tasked with stealing a Russian fighter plane that threatened to disrupt the balance of an arms race between governments. In the later episodes "International Concerto," "Business Holiday," "Arctic Adventure," and "The Professional," Joe foiled threats from East European agents, and governments referred to as "the Eastern Alliance." Across the 1960s puppet series, British, American, and allied characters and organizations, supported the hegemony of a Free World that pointed towards a future, hybrid, Western identity.

American television's production methods, personnel, and attitudes to the audience have been adopted, yet also resisted, by British television culture, and this was exemplified by Anderson's science fiction series. U.S. television was a model for British television practices, and also a stigmatized other against which domestic producers and audiences defined a contrasting identity. This complex negotiation, involving the carving out of a new sense of cultural specificity, took place in the context of relatively successful attempts to sell British programming to U.S. broadcasters in the 1960s. Television was both reflective of ideas of national identity, and a means for imagining new kinds of national and transnational community. This tension was evident not only in the specific forms of television within national broadcasting contexts, but also in patterns of television import and export. In Anderson's puppet science fiction, the boundaries between Britishness and Americanness shifted in dynamic ways, in relation to production, representation, and reception. Science fiction television for children is an interesting location for examining these issues of identity, difference, and hybridity. The genre entails the imagining of different kinds of otherness, including speculations about the future, homely, familiar environments as well as external threatening ones, and national and transnational identities. In television for children, science fiction programs such as Anderson's have provided scope for experimentation and speculation about each of these issues, partly because of their ambivalent position in hierarchies of cultural value.

7

Tracking *UFO*
Format, Text and Context

Peter Hutchings

Beyond Cult

Much like its menacing alien spacecraft, the British television series *UFO* (Century 21/ITC, 1969–1970) hovers enigmatically, its precise identity and purpose not immediately apparent. This might seem a surprising response to a show that has in recent years been placed firmly as a cult product, marketable in nostalgic terms but at the same time not meant to be taken too seriously. Yet this is not how the series was positioned originally, and returning it to that point of origin can cast an interesting new light on the relation between science fiction material of this kind and televisual formats.

Key to *UFO*'s "cult-ness" is a sense of the excess it projects, of stylistic imperatives that threaten to diminish or in some instances completely overwhelm any dramatic content, with this most obviously manifest in the bold designs that characterized all of its producer Gerry Anderson's 1960s television programs. That earlier work had come in the form of puppet shows, notable among which were *Thunderbirds* (ATV/ITC, 1965–1966), *Captain Scarlet and the Mysterons* (ATV/ITC, 1967–1968) and *Joe 90* (ATV/ITC, 1968–1969). (For a discussion of these shows, see the chapter by Jonathan Bignell in this volume.) By contrast, *UFO* was a live action series, Anderson's first, but it offered a comparable *mélange* of shiny, sleek surfaces, hopelessly impractical costumes, and elaborately technological vehicles and weapon systems. To give just a few examples, this was the show in which the women serving on Moonbase inexplicably sported purple hair (which reverted to their natural color when back on Earth), where the effectiveness of the visually impressive space-bound interceptors was severely limited by the fact that there were only three of them and they carried just one missile each (meaning that the aliens only had to send four UFOs to evade this first line of defense, although admittedly it took most of the series for them to work this out), where a submarine could rapidly, if improbably, convert into an aeroplane, and where episodes would often cut to banks of flashing computer lights as a way of indicating urgency with no accompanying sense of what these computers were actually doing. Couple this with Barry Gray's funky organ-based main theme and a fondness for forced acronyms also evident in Anderson's earlier work — in this case, the secret organization fighting the aliens is known as SHADO, which stands for Supreme Headquarters Alien Defence Organisation[1] — and you have an Andersonian world that, while reveling in its own visual and aural excess, also conveyed in its loving attention to technology and organizational efficiency what Bill Osgerby has called "forward-looking modernity."[2] From a contemporary perspective, the fact that the show was set in the early 1980s has since helped to bestow a retrospective layer of absurdity inasmuch as *UFO* now comes over as a set of generally inaccurate predictions about its future and our past, sealed off from the present day as a cultural museum piece replete not just with some dodgy fashion designs and hair styles but also some decidedly non–PC attitudes. Of such elements and conventions are cult objects made.

In the face of this, this chapter will argue that there is more to *UFO* than its present cult status suggests and that locating the program back in its original production context reveals complexities and ambiguities in part to do with its relation to a broader social and cultural milieu but deriving more particularly from the program's unusual format and production history. Indeed, some of the issues that arise from this way of looking at *UFO* are pertinent to a wider understanding of television series-based drama inasmuch as they require some reflection on the role of textual analysis in understanding this kind of program, on how to relate individual episodes to an overarching format, and on the location of text-based meaning within this. In the case of *UFO*, such is the disparity between its episodes in terms of both story content and characterization — with, for example, some not featuring unidentified flying objects or aliens at all — that it is hard to base any textual analysis around the idea that these episodes, and details within them, illustrate a general format which itself can be used to define the overall meaning and significance of the show. Even those design and stylistic elements so important to cult appropriations of the show can perform different functions — ranging from the reassuring repetition of familiar sites and events (e. g. the launching of the interceptors from Moonbase) to an altogether more discomforting play with audience expectations. It follows that one needs to work with a sense of the series' fractured structure and the relation of this both to a production history that included an unplanned six-month hiatus and extensive cast and crew changes and to a production context in which the nature of the show's address to particular audiences was not always as clear or as cohesive as it might have been. *UFO* emerges from this as a series that is of intrinsic interest and value — as much for its ambiguities as for its clarities — but which at the same time manages to convey in all its complexity and awkwardness some of the difficulties in grasping precisely what makes a television series distinctive in textual terms.

The Many Contexts of UFO

Standing in a somewhat uneasy relationship with the idea of *UFO* as either a cult period piece or an optimistic embracing of the modern is a sense, not just in the small amount of critical material addressing the program but in fan responses to it as well, that it offers some dark and potentially disturbing elements. This quality is usually seen as bound up with the moment of its production. From this perspective, one way of locating *UFO* historically is to view it as a zeitgeist expression of a late 1960s and early 1970s social disillusionment in which the youthful idealism of the 1960s was beginning to turn nasty, with this publicly manifest in such events as the 1969 Altamont free concert, in which a fan was stabbed to death in front of the stage, and the murders committed by the followers of Charles Manson, which also took place in 1969. More generally, the 1970s was characterized by economic troubles and political and social unrest, both in Great Britain and internationally, with this — retrospectively at least — providing a context within which to make sense of *UFO*.

In his account of Anderson's work for his own Century 21 company, Bill Osgerby argues along these lines: "characterised by an atmosphere of unease and ambiguity, the Century 21 productions of the late Sixties and Seventies dramatised at a symbolic level the wider sense of crisis and the collapse of social and political certainties."[3] Osgerby goes on to find intimations of "the serious themes of anxiety and mistrust" in Anderson's puppet show *Captain Scarlet and the Mysterons*, in which aliens provoked by a human attack on them kill off humans and replace them with "mysteron" substitutes, but locates the fullest expression of these themes in *UFO* itself. John R. Cook also finds elements of negativity in *UFO*, elements that it shares with a range of other British science fiction television programs from the late 1960s and 1970s. However, for Cook, *UFO* offers a far from cohesive experience in this respect: "yet what might at first seem a dark proto *X-Files* [(Fox, 1993–2002)] [...] narrative of government secrecy in the face of an alien threat is at the same time mediated by the sheer seduction of its late–1960s' vision of the imminent technological utopia to come, as exemplified by its striking sets, props and costumes."[4]

This use of popular cultural product as a barometer of social change is not unproblematic, especially in its potential both for historical over-generalization and for a lack of appropriate consideration of the levels of mediation that intervene between broad social trends and particular cultural artifacts. Nevertheless, dystopian and apocalyptic elements clearly do become a notable feature of popular entertainment in Britain, America and elsewhere during the late 1960s and 1970s — manifesting, albeit in different ways, in for example, horror, crime, a cycle of disaster narratives, and science fiction — with *UFO* fitting into this.[5] However, *UFO*'s generic identity as a piece of science fiction also, potentially, aligns it with other contemporaneous developments in the genre, developments that lead away from a sense of the program as irretrievably dark, cheerfully utopian, or somewhere in between.

In her study of science fiction cinema, Christine Cornea has identified two generic trends pertinent to *UFO*. The first involves an enhanced realism in the representation of space travel that reflected the growing public awareness of the reality of space travel during the 1960s, with a key text here clearly Stanley Kubrick's *2001: A Space Odyssey* (U.K./U.S., 1968). As Cornea puts it, "it certainly seems plausible that the 1960s was a time when science fiction and science fact became remarkably intertwined, sometimes blurred, particularly within the context of an American national preoccupation with the story of the Space Race."[6] *UFO*'s vision of the future turns out to be in essence a slightly tweaked version of the late 1960s present, with many of its designs or props emulating contemporaneous trends (not surprisingly given that some were purchased from what was commercially available at the time). One might argue that this was in part due to budgetary restraints but it is a quality that accords with other science fiction product of the period and it also connects with an increasing emphasis on realism evident in Anderson's 1960s puppet shows.[7] The extent to which this limits any future-utopian elements remains unclear, yet it is the case that *UFO* presented to its original audiences a future that, for all those more outré elements so beloved by the cultists, was largely rooted in the present day.[8] It is arguably only in retrospect, as we move away from the moment of the show's production, that this future starts to look both dated and, paradoxically perhaps, increasingly futuristic.

Another trend identified by Cornea, especially in relation to a science fiction New Wave literary movement (see Michael du Plessis's chapter in this volume), was an increasing concern with intense subjective states, especially as accessed via hallucinogenic drugs (and again *2001: A Space Odyssey* seems an obvious cinematic example, especially in its climactic Star Gate sequence).[9] In line with this, a preoccupation with extreme subjective states of consciousness does emerge periodically throughout *UFO*, especially in its later episodes. However, the extent to which this entails a subscription to the counterculutral values associated with some of the more mind-bending science fiction of the period only really becomes evident through a closer look at those particular episodes. Indeed a closer look at the program itself, and why and how it got made, arguably helps in finding a way through some of the tensions and apparent contradictions — between realism and fantasy, puppets and live action, and discourses of the 1960s and 1970s — thrown up by any attempt to contextualize it as a unified whole. A good starting point for this is the man who, for all the extensive networks of collaborators involved in the production of *UFO*, has more claim than any other to be its author — its producer (and occasional director) Gerry Anderson.

Anderson has never bothered to hide his disappointment over his association with puppet-based television series designed primarily for children.[10] His desire to move beyond what he clearly perceived as a relatively lowly area was manifested in the hyperbolic "Supermarionation" label that he applied to most of his shows, a term designed to enhance their status as more than just puppet projects, as well as in the development of increasingly realistic puppets and in attempts to inculcate cinematic qualities in the programs' *mise-en-scène*, especially after they moved into color with *Stingray* in 1964. The logical outcome of such ambition was the production of a live-action feature film aimed primarily at adults, which Anderson duly managed in 1969 with *Doppelganger* (directed by Robert Parrish and known in the U.S. as *Journey to the Far Side of the Sun*).[11] This film is important to the genesis of *UFO* for a number of reasons. Firstly, it established for Lew Grade, head of ITC and responsible for the commissioning of *UFO*, that Anderson could handle live-action drama. Secondly, many of its cast and crew, along with props, costumes and some musical cues, ended up featuring in *UFO*. Thirdly, a certain awkward quality in the film's tone also seems to have seeped into *UFO*.

Doppelganger combined *Thunderbirds*-style model-based action and explosions with a downbeat narrative in which a replica of Earth is discovered on the far side of the Sun and where the astronaut hero dies at the end in an unsuccessful attempt to return to his own planet. *UFO* would also offer spectacular and stylish elements that would not have been out of place in one of Anderson's child-orientated science fiction puppet series (and indeed might be seen as an expression of an authorial signature or style linking together a series of programs) that sometimes sat uneasily with the more adult-centered explorations of emotional and sexual relationships that were also a prominent feature of the show.[12] Indeed, both American and British television networks, which were more accustomed to Anderson's earlier work, struggled to categorize and place this new program. Anderson himself has recalled the dismay that greeted "Confetti Check A-OK," an episode of *UFO* that focused on the marriage breakdown of one of its main characters, while the controversial episode "The Long Sleep," which featured a drugs theme, was during the series' early transmissions often shifted to a late night slot or not screened at all.[13]

As if to illustrate this sense of *UFO* attempting to connect with a more mature audience while still holding onto the commercially viable Anderson hardware, the show's lively opening credit sequence was comprised mainly of moments of action involving space interceptors, attack submarines and alien spacecraft but had as its opening image an unnerving close-up of what appears to be a contact lens (actually an eye shield, we discover in the first episode) being removed from the eye of a dying alien, with blood-soaked bandages clearly in evidence in the shot.[14] The show's closing credits — involving a slow, moody trawl through space to a discordant musical theme — also sought to project a sense of something altogether more serious than audiences might have been accustomed to from their science fiction television programs, not least those produced by Gerry Anderson.

Identified?

UFO ran for one season of twenty-six episodes. Principal photography commenced in April 1969, with the production based at MGM Borehamwood studios.

However, the studios were closed down by a financially troubled MGM at the end of the year, with only seventeen episodes of *UFO* completed. The production was relocated to Pinewood Studios but had to wait for studio space to become available. Principal photography began again in June 1970 and was completed in September. This unusual seventeen-month production period created both problems and opportunities. In particular, some members of the regular cast were not available for the second batch of episodes—most notably George Sewell who played SHADO's second-in-command Alec Freeman and Gabrielle Drake who played purple-haired Moonbase commander Gay Ellis. Having noted this, a certain instability in the cast line-up had become evident prior to the production hiatus—for example, Harry Baird (interceptor pilot Mark Bradley) left after only four episodes as a result of dissatisfaction with the terms of his contract (although thanks to some recycling of footage he would make brief appearances in later episodes) and the dancer-turned-actor Peter Gordeno (Skydiver Captain Peter Carlin) left after eight episodes out of fear of being typecast. Other regulars or semi-regulars joined later in the series—Michael Billington as dashing Colonel Paul Foster in the third episode and Vladek Sheybal as Dr. Doug Jackson in the fourth. Additions and departures of this kind were facilitated by the show's large cast and the dispersal of its drama across several locations, which meant that characters could drop in and out of the series. It is still striking though that this was a series in which only one actor, Ed Bishop (as Commander Ed Straker, the chief of SHADO) appeared in all of its episodes.

Perhaps the most significant addition to the post-hiatus *UFO* was behind the camera, however, with David Tomblin joining as writer and director and Terence Feely as writer. Significantly, both had been creative influences on the cult television series *The Prisoner* (ITC, 1967–68), Tomblin as a writer, director and producer, Feely as a writer, with each a partner in the company that had made the series. It is certainly the case that the five episodes of *UFO* on which one or other worked—and especially "The Cat with Ten Lives," "Timelash" and "The Long Sleep"—offered pronounced hallucinogenic and self-reflexive elements that had also been evident in *The Prisoner*. Indeed, the second batch of episodes generally can be seen as refocusing the show's themes to the extent that it functions as a kind of second season (although *UFO* was not premiered until shooting on all twenty-six episodes had been completed).

It seems from that that, in some of its aspects at least, *UFO* offers a decidedly fragmented experience, the pinning down of which in anything other than stylistic terms is far from straightforward. It is worth considering in this respect the first episode, which was entitled "Identified" and which was directed by Gerry Anderson himself. "Identified" is clearly designed as a showcase for the program format. The aliens are introduced in it and their motivation explained—they are coming to Earth to steal human organs, which they then transplant into their own enfeebled bodies—and we are also given what in effect is a tour of SHADO and its hardware, including its film studio headquarters, Moonbase and the Skydiver submarine. The sexual politics of the episode are, especially from today's perspective, both striking and problematic, with a woman — Lieutenant Gay Ellis — in charge of Moonbase, but with women defined consistently as sexual objects, not just by the male characters but also by some voyeuristic sequences involving women, including Ellis, partially stripping off or walking around in their underwear. This quality has led John R. Cook to comment thus on the series: "hence while this is a depicted future of greater freedom and equality between the sexes, it is also a veritable sexual playground. Its world of gadgets, super-vehicles and pneumatic, available women in the workplace, commanded over by identity-inviting male heroes such as Ed Straker, is ultimately a late–1960s' male liberatory fantasy."[15]

This is all very well as a description of the first episode but it is worth noting that, especially in terms of gender representation, "Identified" is not typical of the series as a whole. While it would be hard to make any claim for *UFO* as wholly progressive in terms of gender, the extremes of voyeurism evident in "Identified" do not recur in later episodes. In addition, the sexually predatory attitudes of some of the male characters are either changed or clarified. Straker is presented as an aloof, distant figure, with many episodes turning on his emotional isolation. His second-in-command, Alec Freeman, might be shown in the first episode hitting on a woman and using sexualized language elsewhere, but thereafter he becomes an altogether more sensitive figure, in effect acting as Straker's conscience and showing little or no sexual interest in women. The kind of male fantasy figure described by Cook is actually embodied most in the series by the more priapic character Paul Foster, who does not show up until the third episode to be filmed. Interestingly, Foster was a belated replacement for another character intended for inclusion in "Identified." Originally the Moonbase commander was to be a male but, reportedly because of difficulties with the actor cast in the role, this character was written out during filming, with the Gay Ellis character subsequently receiving an impromptu promotion.[16]

Another possible reason for the sexual content of "Identified," along with what for the time was a surprising level of violent and gory imagery, was the aforementioned desire to separate out the program from Anderson's earlier shows by constructing a more adult-centered address. Indeed, the series as a whole seems driven by the need to distinguish itself from more family-orientated science fiction fare, with this informing the types of stories that it tells.

If one takes the first batch of *UFO*'s seventeen episodes as an example one finds only six episodes that take as their main subject an alien/SHADO conflict — "Identified," "Survival," "The Dalotek Affair," "Flight Path," "ESP" and "Kill Straker." Of these, "Survival" — which depicts a growing mutual understanding between Foster and an alien — clearly seeks to undermine any simplistic sense of the alien as conventional Other, while "ESP" and "Kill Straker" introduce a theme of mind control which would become important later in the series and which further complicates the nature of the alien's identity, and "Flight Path" spends as much time exploring a marital relationship as it does uncovering an alien conspiracy. The more common story structures for these seventeen episodes involve either juxtaposing an alien-centered narrative thread with another narrative thread that is not itself science fiction-based or marginalizing or removing entirely any alien-centered elements. In other words, the show's strategy for rendering itself adult entertainment is to contain, limit or diminish its generic science fiction elements, with this — perhaps justifiably given Anderson's own history and the state of British science fiction television at this time — guided by the assumption that such elements were not likely to be taken seriously.

One approach under this rubric is to have an alien blunder into and disrupt story material that in itself has nothing to do with extraterrestrials. So in "The Square Triangle" an alien and subsequently SHADO become accidentally involved in a wife's attempt to murder her husband. More poignantly, in "A Question of Priorities" Straker has to chose between using SHADO equipment to save his dying son's life and using that same equipment to track down a defecting alien (and chooses the latter). More common is a concern to explore the workings of SHADO as an institution that has both militaristic and corporate qualities, with a particular focus on tensions between emotional expression and operational efficiency. Indeed, "The Computer Affair," which was the second episode to be filmed, takes this as its explicit subject, dealing with a SHADO investigation into whether the unacknowledged desire of two Moonbase operatives for each other impaired their judgment in an encounter with a UFO.[17] In fact, standing in contrast with what John Cook has identified as a liberatory theme in *UFO* is the notion that sexual abstinence and repression is a necessary prerequisite for a SHADO operative — in "The Responsibility Seat," for example, in which Straker seems attracted sexually to a woman only ultimately to reject her (a decision made easier by the fact that she turns out to be an industrial spy). In similar vein, "Subsmash" depicts SHADO operatives working together efficiently in a downed submarine only through repressing their own emotions. In all these cases, the UFOs are incidental, of interest in terms of the drama they provoke rather than in themselves.

Other episodes focus more on the struggles involved in running SHADO as a kind of corporate enterprise. The conflict in "Conflict" turns out not to be an alien-human conflict at all but rather one between different strata of SHADO management, while the drama of "Close Up" is drawn from the difficulties involved in setting up and managing an ambitious intelligence-gathering project. The imagery in these and other episodes of men in suits standing in offices smoking cigars and drinking whisky while planning their next stratagem is arguably more reminiscent of business-centered television dramas such as *The Power Game* (ATV, 1965–1969) or *The Brothers* (BBC, 1972–1976) than it is of science fiction. The similarly company-themed "Exposed," which introduces Paul Foster, takes the form of a conspiracy narrative, with Foster exposing the mysterious SHADO organization only to find that in so doing he has been recruited into it, while

"Ordeal" has him being kidnapped by aliens only to reveal bathetically — in a plot twist borrowed from an episode of *Captain Scarlet and the Mysterons* — that the whole thing, aliens included, was a sauna-induced hallucination. The logical culmination of this is to have completely alien-free episodes, and *UFO* duly obliges with "Court Martial," which like "The Responsibility Seat" deals with SHADO internal security, and, most strikingly, "Confetti Check A-OK," which flashes back to the setting up of SHADO and the associated break-up of Straker's marriage. As already noted, this episode proved unpopular with some of the series' distributors but it also stands as a clear testament to Anderson's ambitions for *UFO* to be something different and serious.

Seeing *UFO* in this way makes it easier to grasp what changes are made in the second batch of nine episodes, for what these do is redirect the series back to science fiction-themed material, in particular connecting it to the more adult-centered preoccupation with extreme subjective and hallucinogenic states of being that has been identified by Cornea as a distinctive generic theme of the period. Key to six of the episodes — namely "The Cat with Ten Lives," "Destruction," "Mindbender," "The Long Sleep," "The Man Who Came Back" and "The Psychobombs" — is the idea of mind control, while "Timelash" also addresses different states of consciousness through showing SHADO personnel trapped in a temporal distortion by the aliens. "The Cat with Ten Lives," "Mindbender" and "The Long Sleep" all contain weird, hallucinogenic imagery (which in the case of the last named is quite literally the result of ingesting recreational drugs), with "Mindbender" also offering some remarkable self-reflexivity by having Straker hallucinating that he is an actor working on a television series, while the trippy "The Cat with Ten Lives," which features an alien-controlled cat, remains by general consent the series' strangest episode. Admittedly, "The Man Who Came Back" and "The Psychobombs" are more conventional than this but they too offer what for the series was a new sense of human personality as something that could readily be effaced by radical technologies. (By contrast, "The Sound of Silence" and "Reflections in the Water" were more like the first batch of seventeen, although not without some surreal imagery, not least in "Reflections in the Water" in which Straker and his associates confront alien doubles of themselves). This change in emphasis was accompanied by a more speculative approach to the nature and motivation of the aliens, for while the organ snatching theme continues, Dr. Jackson considers in "The Cat With Ten Lives" the possibility that the enemy aliens might not be humanoid but are instead imprinting themselves on humanoid forms; in other words, the red-suited aliens who have been the enemy thus far in the series might not be the real aliens at all. This fascination with what can be perceived as potentially countercultural material in no way translates into unqualified support for any youth-based countercultural movement, however. Indeed, as was very much the case with *The Prisoner*, altered states of consciousness tend to be associated with repression and domination.[18] This is most obvious in the controversial "The Long Sleep" episode in which two hippie-like characters encounter some aliens while tripping on drugs and where drug use leads inexorably to death.

What Do We Really Know About UFOs?

Amidst all the action of "Identified," *UFO*'s premiere episode, Commander Straker poses the questions "What do we really know about UFOs? What are they? Where do they come from? What do they want?" It is striking how much the series does not answer these questions, either out of provocative design or in reaction to unpredictable production-based contingencies, and indeed how much the possibility of any answers seems to recede as the series progresses. Even the discovery in "Identified" of the aliens' organ-grabbing raids is accompanied by Straker's "there may be other reasons."

UFO did not make it to a second season, so the prospect evident in its last few episodes of a different kind of science fiction show emerging was never realized. In any event, the impact of the second batch of episodes was limited in many markets, especially the British, by the fact that episodes were often shown out of the order recommended by ITC. Indeed, the jumbling of episodes and the different schedule times allotted them across the regional independent television network in the U.K. throughout 1970 and 1971 was arguably one of the reasons why *UFO* was eventually deemed insufficiently successful to merit its being re-commissioned. The series was also syndicated in the U.S. in 1972, which apparently prompted some discussion of a possible second season, although this came to nothing.[19] Despite this, returning *UFO* to its production context does uncover a complex textual identity that manifests in different ways across a body of episodes. Broad judgments about the series based on a few episodes are likely to miss its peculiar quality (although to be fair it is precisely this generalized sense of the show that was probably encouraged in its original transmissions). A more detailed and granular approach that considers all the episodes in terms of shifting relationships between individual texts and a format that itself was being re-engineered throughout the production process, is potentially more revealing so far as ascertaining the distinctiveness, and indeed the value, of the series.

It would be hard to present *UFO* as a series that is either typical or which exemplifies serial television production. In fact, it is not typical in some respects even of the work of its producer Gerry Anderson, whose next series, *Space 1999* (ITC, 1975–1977), although reformatted between its first and second seasons, generally adhered to a more predictable "alien of the week" format. However, the issues raised by *UFO* are relevant to a wider aesthetic appreciation of popular serial television dramas, where repetition from one episode to another might not necessarily be the order of the day and where a good part of a series' imaginative drive and creative energies might be found not in its original conception but rather in its ongoing development.

One thing is clear. No matter in what order *UFO*'s episodes fall, or how few one has seen, a sense of its underlying seriousness is inescapable. Most of its episodes conclude in downbeat fashion, with the climactic deaths of significant characters not uncommon. Episodes constantly assert that relentless sacrifice is required in the conflict with the aliens, and the Churchillian stoicism of the final lines of "Identified"—Straker's "Is this the end of the beginning?"—resonates throughout the series. That the series' serious and occasionally ponderous tone connects with a desire to distance itself from the science fiction genre, while at the same time obviously being a piece of science fiction, generates, as we have seen, both tensions and quite a few moments of awkwardness. This desire to be different is explicable by reference to the shape of its producer Gerry Anderson's career but arguably it also reflects the low critical status of British science fiction television in the late 1960s and early 1970s. Given this, it is ironic that *UFO* now tends to be viewed as a program primarily for children and cult fans. If nothing else, this chapter suggests that there is more to it than this.

8

A Clockwork Orange, Exploitation and the Art Film

I.Q. Hunter

Despite its "art house" trappings, Stanley Kubrick's *A Clockwork Orange* (U.K./U.S., 1971) was a big-budget exploitation film, a rich and troubling combination of high style and low, even trashy content.[1] Although an acknowledged classic of British science fiction, it splices a number of competing genres and modes, including the art movie, underground film, the juvenile delinquency movie, and even pornography.[2] But its most intriguing relationship is to the exploitation movie, and specifically to British science fiction, horror and sexploitation cycles of the 1960s and 1970s. Only two critics, Janet Staiger and Matthew Sweet, have dwelled on the film's debts and similarities to the exploitation film.[3] Most critics tend to locate it in a single, self-contained genre consisting entirely of masterpieces — that of the "Kubrick film"— and gloss over its provocative and deliberately shocking eclecticism.

The term "exploitation" deserves a little contextualization. Relating *A Clockwork Orange* to exploitation is not intended to demean the film as an artistic achievement. The film draws on exploitation as an aesthetic resource with the aim of unsettling audiences by confusing the categories of art and trash. "Exploitation" functions in film history as both a semi-generic description and a pejorative term, and there is an unavoidable element of vagueness in its use. Originally, "exploitation" referred to low-budget feature films which catered to a specific demographic, often to the pointed exclusion of other audiences, and which advertised sensational material unavailable in mainstream cinema. This meaning goes back to the so called "classical exploitation films" of the American cinema of the 1920s and 1930s, such as *Reefer Madness* (U.S., Louis Gasnier, 1936). Independent films dabbling in topics banned by the Production Code, they "relied on forbidden spectacle to differentiate themselves from classical Hollywood narrative films and conventional documentaries."[4] Crucially, these films adopted an educational and moralistic framework ("the square up"), which was intended not only to appease police and censors but also to legitimate the audience's curiosity. A considerably looser meaning of "exploitation" dates from the 1950s, when classical exploitation no longer existed as a distinctive and segregated mode of production. Exploitation came simply to denote a low-budget genre film that is blatantly gratuitous, prurient and very definitely *not* art. Most frequently these were horror, violent thrillers, science fiction and soft-core sex films, often parasitic on the success of mainstream movies and produced in cycles for targeted audiences such as teenagers, men, or black people in the case of blaxploitation action films. A number of these trashy movies have since attracted cult audiences for their aggressively unreconstructed pleasures. British exploitation cinema was somewhat hamstrung by censorship, but from nudist films and Hammer horror movies of the late 1950s to the numerous sex comedies of the 1970s, it emerged as a distinctive, unrespectable and energetic alternative to the recognized mainstream of British literary adaptations and realist dramas.

A Clockwork Orange can be aligned with exploitation because of its lurid subject matter and visceral appeal to sensation-seeking audiences. The first forty minutes of the film (which, I hazard, is what audiences most vividly remember about it) consist of breathlessly exhilarating violent set-pieces, after which the film slows considerably (the prison scenes, especially Alex's dehumanizing induction, are provokingly repetitive and turgid) as if punishing the audience for thrilling to Alex's fast-paced mayhem. Although ostensibly illustrating a philosophical debate about free will, the opening scenes celebrate the uniquely kinetic joys of violence on screen, much like the extended cartoonish brawls in the biker film *Hells Angels on Wheels* (U.S., Richard Rush, 1967).

But, aside from its violence (admittedly staged with considerable artifice and irony), *A Clockwork Orange* shares important themes with British exploitation films of the 1960s and 1970s, themes anticipated by Burgess's novel and reworked here in the guise of an art film. Alex, the film's anti-hero played by Malcolm McDowell, simultaneously embodies several iconic post-war British social demons—Teddy Boy (the key reference in Burgess's novel), skinhead, working-class lout, and long-haired layabout. Channelling both Mick Jagger and Robin Askwith, he is a malevolent variation on the working-class hedonists of sexploitation films such as *Cool It Carol!* (Peter Walker, 1970) and *Confessions of a Window Cleaner* (Val Guest, 1974), unleashed by permissiveness into new worlds of sexual possibility and consumerism.[5] *A Clockwork Orange* is ambivalent about working-class liberation, as Justin Smith notes: "it charts with uncanny perception the way in which the bourgeois radicalization and liberalization of 1968 had begun by the 1970s to permeate working-class culture, with potentially more dangerous effects and the palpable threat of an establishment backlash."[6] Gang "ultraviolence" was the focus, too, of numerous low-budget British horror and science fiction films, from *The Damned* (Joseph Losey, 1961) to *Psychomania* (Don Sharp, 1973), which also loosely allegorized class and generational antagonism and the dangerous pleasures of the Permissive Society.[7] *A Clockwork Orange*'s scenario of an older establishment revenging itself and eventually co-opting the rebellious young is played out in such horror films as *Frightmare* (Pete Walker, 1973) and *House of Whipcord* (Pete Walker, 1974), while its schematic depiction of oppressively rational authority pitted against the unruly and Dionysian echoes *Blood on Satan's Claw* (Piers Haggard, 1968) and anticipates *The Wicker Man* (Robin Hardy, 1973), among many British horror films representing a world divided into predators and victims, with middle-class normality besieged by its liberated Other.[8] This theme has recently been revived and updated with "chav" or "hoodie" horror films such as *Summer Scars* (Julian Richards, 2007), *Eden Lake* (James Watkins, 2008), *The Children* (Tom Shankland, 2008), *F* (Johannes Roberts, 2010) and *Cherry Tree Lane* (Paul Andrew Williams, 2010), which demonize the young while playing on fears of an uncontrollable underclass. (This clutch of films is arguably more conservative than Permissive-era predecessors such as *Horror Hospital* [Antony Balch, 1973], which sided with young rebels against decrepit authoritarianism.)

To take a wider view, *A Clockwork Orange* belonged to what John Fraser in 1974 called the Violation Film, an amorphous but useful term for a cycle "in which the principle *frisson* comes from the threatened gross invasion of the privacy of 'decent' people by violent men, an invasion in which rape as well as murder may be a real possibility."[9] Anticipated by *The Desperate Hours* (U.S., William Wyler, 1955), *Cape Fear* (U.S., J. Lee Thompson, 1962) and *Lady in a Cage* (U.S., Walter Grauman, 1964), the Violation Film coalesced as an international subgenre of thrillers and exploitation films in the late 1960s. Violent fare in Britain (*The Penthouse* [Peter Collinson, 1967], *Straw Dogs* [Sam Peckinpah, 1971], and *A Clockwork Orange*); the U.S. (*The Last House on the Left* [Wes Craven, 1971]); and Italy (*Late Night Trains* [Aldo Lado, 1975] and *House on the Edge of the Park* [Ruggero Deodato, 1980]) depicted a proletarian "return of the repressed" shattering middle-class indifference and complacency, in which the frequent threat of rape asserted working-class virility over middle-class repression. Loose variations on this scenario are played out in art house films such as *The Servant* (Joseph Losey, 1963), *Theorem* (Italy, Pier Paolo Pasolini, 1968), *Performance* (Donald Cammell and Nicolas Roeg, 1970), and *Brimstone and Treacle* (Richard Loncraine, 1982), *The Great Ecstasy of Robert Carmichael* (Thomas Clay, 2005) (perhaps, with *Bronson* [Nicholas Winding Refn, 2008], the closest imitation yet of *A Clockwork Orange*'s collision of art and exploitation), literary works such as Beryl Bainbridge's novel, *Injury Time* (1977) and Ian McEwan's *Saturday* (2005), as well as the "hoodie horror" films mentioned above. Fraser remarks that there is often a sense of educative rough justice meted out by the violators, who are somehow more real than their victims:

> The interior of the secluded house in *A Clockwork Orange* hinted at a somewhat artificial evasion of unpleasant social realities by the married couple, so that with the invasion by the three figures in masquerade costumes there was a feeling of appropriateness both in the ironic confrontation of quasi-doubles and in the implacable entry of those realities.[10]

To that extent the violation film is illuminated by Robin Wood's celebrated account of American horror films in the 1970s, such as *The Texas Chain Saw Massacre* (U.S., Tobe Hooper, 1974), in which, he argues, the audience covertly sympathises with the monster when it erupts within repressive normality, because it (like Alex rampaging through the first third of *A Clockwork Orange*) is free to transgress artificial taboos and bourgeois norms.[11]

It must be said that overlap between exploitation and the mainstream was not unusual in the period. Changes in censorship, the waning of the family film, and the need for films to appeal to young male audiences, which would become a keynote of the New Hollywood in the 1970s, meant that mainstream films from *Bonnie and Clyde* (U.S., Arthur Penn, 1967) and *The Wild Bunch* (U.S., Sam Peckinpah, 1969) to *Taxi Driver* (U.S., Martin Scorsese, 1976) increasingly drew on violent and sexual material hitherto restricted to exploitation.[12] Often underpinned by a Pop Art trash aesthetic, and directed by graduates of exploitation filmmaking, films such as *The Godfather* (U.S., Francis Ford Coppola, 1972), *The Exorcist* (U.S., William Friedkin, 1973) and *Jaws* (U.S., Steven Spielberg, 1975) muddied cultural boundaries with a confident insouciance we now think of as postmodern. The rise of the cult midnight movie in the late 1960s, with *Night of the Living Dead* (U.S., George A. Romero, 1968), *El Topo* (Mexico, Alejandro Jodorowsky, 1970), *Harold and Maude* (U.S., Hal Ashby, 1972) and *Pink Flamingos* (U.S., John Waters, 1972), institutionalized this confusion of high and low, art and trash, exploitation and its Other. Crass, sometimes pornographic, often violent and invariably sick, cult "midnight movies" were art-exploitation efforts indebted equally to Surrealism and underground film and to sexploitation, comic strips and the Bs. As Joan Hawkins remarks of cult films like *Andy Warhol's Dracula* (Italy/France, Paul Morrissey, 1974), they "promise *both* affect and 'something different'; they are films that defy the traditional genre labels by which we try to make sense of cinematic history and cultures, films that seem to have a stake in both high and low art."[13] In retrospect, *A Clockwork Orange* fits squarely and most comfortably into the emergent category of the cult film, insofar as it was transgressive, seductively quotable, anti-authoritarian, subculturally appealing, and invited appropriation by youthful cineastes.[14] Blurring registers and genres within a coherent auteurist vision was a mark of Kubrick's films. *2001: A Space Odyssey* (U.K./U.S., 1968), Kubrick's previous film, innovatively fused tropes from non-narrative experimental film with visionary hard science fiction, producing a "head film" equally consumable as high art symbolism and psychedelic lightshow. *A Clockwork Orange* gleefully mashes up austere political fable with arousingly choreographed brutality and a good deal of homoerotic high camp — something else it shared with the first wave of cult films.[15] As Gabbard and Sharma note, this strategy invigorates the art movie tradition of ambiguity and subjectivity with dissonant elements of trash culture. The film appeals to young audiences as well as recapturing some of the shock value of early modernist art:

> Working at the very end of [the art movie] tradition, Kubrick was perhaps trying to *reinvent* the art cinema with *A Clockwork Orange*, most prominently with the film's music and its depiction of violence. The sensation of shock, so important to the avant-garde and modernism from Surrealism to the Nouveau Roman—both in cinema and in the other arts—is an integral part of Kubrick's project, even as he foregrounds the music of High Romanticism.[16]

Like other cutting edge artists of the 1960s and 1970s (Warhol, Godard, Ballard), Kubrick valued the salutary shocks that derived from indifferently combining sex, violence and philosophical complexity.

This ambiguous conflation of art and trash worried censors and critics, unsure how to deal with a film both rabble-rousing and intellectually rigorous (a quality *A Clockwork Orange* shares with that other key British cult film and disquieting commentary on exploitation, *Peeping Tom* [Michael Powell, 1960]). As with *The Devils* (Ken Russell, 1970) and *Straw Dogs*, with which *A Clockwork Orange* was invariably linked, it was hard to reconcile the film's impeccable artistic credentials and seriousness of purpose with the celebratory manner in which it staged rape and violence. Since the 1950s, especially in the U.S., "art house" (or in the U.K., "continental film") had been a euphemism for sexy *frissons*, but *A Clockwork Orange* was not a straightforward art movie offering safe thrills for middle-class cineastes, who could be expected to cope with any amount of incendiary content. And while it shared the taboo-busting appeal of the exploitation film—as Jon Lewis notes, it "took audiences someplace they'd never been and showed them some things they'd never seen before"—it could not easily be dismissed as disreputable entertainment for the dangerous lower classes.[17] As Janet Staiger has explored at length, this uneasy distinction, between "good" art film and "bad" exploitation, was extremely important in the reception of *A Clockwork Orange*.[18] Gauging the film's location along the art / exploitation axis turned out to be crucial to its interpretation and to measuring its potential harm. Sympathetic critics argued that the film ironized the depiction of violence by presenting the fight scenes as stylized ballets and by counterpointing them with classical music and Alex's ingratiating voiceover. Such methods of distanciation denied viewers the pleasures of non-intellectual involvement and constructed them instead as ironic voyeurs, who registered the violence primarily as moments of "cinema" illustrative of the film's ideas. From this sympathetic point of view *A Clockwork Orange* was a film with a thesis, "about" violence rather than simply a "violent film" (a makeshift category invented in the late 1960s to cover a variety of brutal but generically diverse movies). As in "violent films" such as *The Wild Bunch, Soldier Blue* (U.S., Ralph Nelson, 1970), *Straw Dogs,* and even *2001,* violence was isolated as a general characteristic of and explanation for human social relations.[19] *A Clockwork Orange* staged a debate, with cold intellectual and aesthetic precision, about how to control "natural" violence (embodied in Alex) in order to drive home its moral that free will is preferable to state control of the individual.

This was certainly the position of the British Board of Film Censors (BBFC), whose secretary, Stephen Murphy, went to remarkable lengths, in replying to critics of the decision to release it uncut, to defend the film's artistic integrity and intellectual rigor and distinguish it from exploitation:

> The film is, in its stylized way, simply a vehicle for all kinds of speculation about the human spirit, and about the nature of Western society. Disturbed though we were by the first half of the film, which is basically a statement of some of the problems of violence, we were, nevertheless, satisfied by the end of the film that it could not be accused of exploitation: quite the contrary, it is a valuable contribution to the whole debate about violence.[20]

"Art" was what raised the film above mere exploitation and made the rapes and beatings, in all their vivid and involving detail, aesthetically essential. Art, too, was what made the film *safe*. Art films were understood to promote distance and intellectual contemplation whereas exploitation incited low, kinetic and wholly non-bourgeois responses — arousal, emotional engagement, corporeal thrills — and therefore, according to the BBFC at the time, had to be censored.

Hostile critics, by contrast, such as Pauline Kael and Andrew Sarris, accused Kubrick of cynically exploiting violence and sexual display.[21] They compared the film unfavorably with Anthony Burgess's source novel (1962) in which Nadsat, the idiolect spoken by Alex's "droogs," imposed a prophylactic imaginative distance between act and description. Kael went so far as to dismiss the film as resembling a porno violent science fiction comedy made by a strict German professor.[22] While *A Clockwork Orange* exhibited the canonical qualities of an art film — stylized, authored, self-reflexive, rather boring at times — its artiness could be seen as an elaborate "square up" intended to justify an obsessive focus on rape, voyeurism, and naked breasts. As Justin Smith remarks, the film "presents a prurient fascination for the female form as *other* [...]. The camera dwells upon the female body with a novice's raw mixture of abhorrence and lust."[23] Although Kubrick staged violence as ritualized theatrical performance, scenes such as the gang fight in the deserted casino and the Cat Lady's murder were undoubtedly exciting, balletic, bloodlessly aestheticized and cruelly funny.

To some extent these strictures repeat a complaint against cinema itself, which is, as Fredric Jameson put it, "essentially pornographic."[24] Film trembles always on the edge of exploitation because of the untameable immediacy of the visual. By focusing on the troublesome fault line between art and exploitation, the debate over *A Clockwork Orange* registered that such categories as art and exploitation, high and low, underground and mainstream were no longer mutually exclusive. The issue was especially complex and pressing in the early 1970s. Auteurism, the liberation of materials, the ambiguous aesthetic location of film, and the breakdown of traditional audiences made it much more difficult for mainstream critics and censors to separate out art and exploitation films, to anticipate audience responses, or to distinguish between "safe" art and mere but "dangerous" entertainment. Films like *A Clockwork Orange* and *Straw Dogs* cut across not just art and exploitation but also class based distinctions between different audiences. Art house audiences might be trusted to read *A Clockwork Orange* with the "correct" measure of ironic distance, but other more dangerous and vulnerable audiences, such as those for exploitation films, might thrill to and imitate its violence and anarchy. Yet, being young, male and working-class, the exploitation crowd was clearly a key target audience for this action filled romp about teen rebellion.

What is especially interesting about *A Clockwork Orange* is not so much the art / exploitation crossover but how it is thematicized in the film itself so as to render viewers (or at any rate some viewers) profoundly uneasy. In brief, *A Clockwork Orange* contemptuously refuses any distinction between art and trash, and seduces the audience with strategies drawn from both. Linda Ruth Williams has noted that Kubrick "long played with genre, emulating and exemplifying the pinnacles of trash genres through meticulously rendered works of cinema art."[25] *The Shining* (1980) coolly deconstructs Stephen King's pulp novel (1977) in order to produce an intricate open text, as much a commentary on as a contribution to the horror genre. *Eyes Wide Shut* (U.S., 1999) nostalgically updates erotic art cinema of the 1970s, from Buñuelian surrealism to the glossy soft-core of *The Story of O* (France, Just Jaeckin, 1975), within the contemporary format of the erotic thriller. As I have argued elsewhere, *A Clockwork Orange* deliberately lurks on the borders of pornography; its aesthetic is one of gratuitousness and prurience, kitsch, crudity and high art flourishes:

> Gratuitous erotic material and images of the commodification of sex are scattered throughout *A Clockwork Orange*, confounding the distinction between high art, trash and porn. Teenage girls suck phallic ice-lollies before engaging in high-speed sex with Alex (the result is a mini porn loop in itself); the camera lingers with icy voyeurism as the Cat Woman spreads her legs during yoga; there is an aimless shot of a topless nurse when Alex is in hospital; and, the film's most outrageous comment on the creative overlap between porn and great art, Alex commandeers Beethoven and the Bible as masturbation fodder. [...] A troubling combination of high style and low content, it foregrounds the exploitative elements and unsettles the boundaries between art as pure form (aesthetically redeeming violent content) and art as incitement (Alex jerking off to "Ode to Joy").[26]

Culture and art are presented as neither intrinsically good nor uplifting. Art cannot resist appropriation to perverse ends. Alex is an intelligent connoisseur of great music but art inspires in him only fantasies of rape and domination. The implication is that, as Vivian Sobchack puts it, "Art and Violence spring from the same source; they are both expressions of the individual, egotistic, vital, and non-institutionalized man."[27] One of the film's most important strategies is to contaminate innocent artistic material with unwanted associations — notably of violence. Art works become weapons (the Cat Lady is beaten to death with a bust of Beethoven and an enormous phallic sculpture), a Rossini overture is détourned to accompany a gang fight, while the song, "Singin' in the Rain," is defiled by Alex crooning it during a scene of beating and rape, so that its previous associations are overlaid with ones of violence (the same trick of contamination is used in

Reservoir Dogs (U.S., Quentin Tarantino, 1991), when an ear is cut off, unforgettably, to the accompaniment of "Stuck in the Middle with You"). The audience is conditioned (like F. Alexander) to associate "Singin' in the Rain" only with the rape for which it provided an opportunistic soundtrack. This parodies, of course, the accidental way in which Alex, during the Ludovico Treatment, inadvertently becomes allergic to his beloved Beethoven's Ninth Symphony. (It also reminds us that we are watching a film — the rape is not rape but a set-piece performance, like a number in a musical. Alex is a virtuoso performer, in his own life as in the film.) What is demonstrated is cinema's power to reshape audiences' minds; in watching the film, we are not contemplating art but rather undergoing the Treatment ourselves.

A Clockwork Orange was a crucial moment in the development of new viewing positions in the early 1970s, as certain audiences (such as cultists, emerging from what Robert Ray called the "ironic audience") started to cherish narrative incoherence, confusions of genre, and the ability to shift from art house strategies of reading to exploitation ones.[28] Raised to a trash aesthetic, these are qualities characteristic nowadays of prefabricated cult movies such as *Grindhouse* (U.S., Quentin Tarantino and Robert Rodriguez, 2007), in which art house consorts with exploitation with no hint of apology or detachment. It is an aesthetic pioneered and given uniquely troubling expression in *A Clockwork Orange*.

9

Visions of an English Dystopia
History, Technology and the Rural Landscape in The Tripods

LINCOLN GERAGHTY

The BBC adaptation of John Christopher's trilogy *The Tripods* (1984–1985) is seen as a relative failure in the corporation's long history of producing science fiction television for British audiences. Offered as replacement for *Doctor Who* (BBC, 1963–1989, 2005–), which underwent significant changes to its format in an attempt to bolster flagging audience ratings, *The Tripods* seemed set to fill the traditional Saturday tea-time slot. With a generous mix of location shooting, special effects, alien invasion, and boys-own adventure the series was promoted as children's science fiction television that would ensure audiences both young and old tuned in week after week to watch the narrative unfold as they had done with *Doctor Who*. However, originally intended for three seasons, *The Tripods* was axed after only two when it failed to gather a popular following. While reasons for *The Tripods*' early demise are linked to its production contexts — budgetary constraints at the BBC meant that expensive series were a gamble — this chapter maintains that the visual imagery of *The Tripods* may well have also played a part in the failure to attract a popular audience.

The look of science fiction and fantasy television — including visual tropes like spaceships and robots, location and landscapes such as outer space and the city, special effects, art and set design, and costume — contribute to the creation of fully imagined worlds. However, audience expectations of science fiction television tend to center on a futuristic aesthetic, one symbolic of the predictive nature of the genre. *The Tripods*, set on Earth in a post-apocalyptic future where humans live a pre-industrial, feudal, almost medieval existence, was a dystopian narrative whose landscape and Earth-bound physicality belied the high production values afforded to it. This meant that *The Tripods* looked more of a series set in the past than the future—even with gigantic alien machines stalking the land. The series' achievements in offering a realistic vision of a dystopian future and its failure to sustain a tea-time audience accustomed to high action space opera adventure are symptomatic of the dichotomy at the heart of the science fiction genre: it looks both forward and back, as Adam Roberts describes, it is a form of "prediction and nostalgia."[1] While *The Tripods* then can be seen as authentic science fiction because of this dual aesthetic, its mediocre reception during the Thatcher era (with economic recession and rioting in the inner cities) intimates that British science fiction television in the 1980s needed to look upon a future where life was going to be better than the present. Depictions of rural countryside and pastoral villages patrolled by giant, authoritarian machines were not what audiences wanted or needed.

British Science Fiction and Television Drama

One could look upon the 1980s as a relatively bleak time for the genre on U.K. television. The BBC had cut funding to its flagship series *Doctor Who* and the corporation was competing against the million dollar budgets of glossy and action-orientated American genre series such as *V* (U.S., NBC, 1984–1985). However, while British production of science fiction television series was on the wane, it was becoming cheaper for U.K. channels to import the big U.S. series and fill up the weekly schedules. The increase in American television alongside a decrease in British output meant that U.K. audiences were becoming familiar with the high production values imported from overseas. Early examples of this American dominance can be seen as far back as the 1960s when Irwin Allen's fantasy series such as *Voyage to the Bottom of the Sea* (U.S., ABC, 1964–1968) and Gene Roddenberry's *Star Trek* (U.S., NBC, 1966–1969) offered color, action and big budget thrills. Later series, such as *Battlestar Galactica* (U.S., ABC, 1978–1980) and *Buck Rogers in the 25th Century* (U.S., NBC, 1979–1981), relied heavily on the space opera format but again easily attracted a young audience in Britain. After *V* the rebirth of the *Star Trek* franchise with *Star Trek: The Next Generation* (U.S., Paramount, 1987–1994) signaled the beginning of a sustained period of investment in American science fiction series as part of the break-up in the television industry which saw cable and satellite channels challenge the dominance of the U.S. networks. In 1981, trying to match the influx of science fiction from the U.S., the BBC spent up its entire light entertainment special effects budget making *The Hitchhiker's Guide to the Galaxy* (1981), a sign that they were not only keen to produce series that looked like they were American but would also stand a chance of being exported back across the Atlantic to recoup some of the money. Indeed, the middle of the decade saw the BBC make children's drama series such as *The Box of Delights* (1984) and C.S. Lewis's *The Chronicles of Narnia* (1988–1990) directly for international sale, even part funded by American finance.[2] Mark Bould sees this financial bind as symptomatic of "an exhaustion of the genre — as if in the absence of the evolving production values of U.S. efforts, ideas, characters, and stories were no longer sufficient to hold an audience."[3] This assertion would seem to fit best with *The Tripods* as I shall go on to explore later in the chapter.

However, the genre still remained a fixture on the BBC and ITV, particularly in one-off drama or short serial adaptations. The critically acclaimed 1981 six half-hour-episode adaptation of John Wyndham's *The Day of the Triffids* exemplified the continued impact exerted by science fiction on television. The nature of the story, contemporaneous as it was with real-life events, meant little expenditure on large fantastic sets or props — other than the Triffids themselves — and the focus on the emotional and psychological trauma of central protagonists Bill and Jo, being two of only a few people who could still see, meant that the drama was relatively low key and confined to the studio rather than expensive outside shooting. Bould sees this short series as one of many "quality" dramas to be made in the 1980s, following in a tradition "developed out of the 1960s radical drama," many of which were, "often profoundly critical of Thatcherism — of policies that sold off nationalized industries and essential public services, increased the tax burden on the poorest, dismantled the welfare state and social security networks, tied defense and foreign policy to U.S. imperialism, and fashioned a reactionary, jingoistic, antiworker, 'dread of difference' culture."[4]

In *The Day of the Triffids* a critique of Thatcherism can be clearly read in the fact that little is learned or seen of the government or emergency services after the meteor shower makes the country's population blind and vulnerable to the Triffids' attacks. The blind are left to fend for themselves on the empty streets of London, small bands of looters and thugs terrorizing shopkeepers and stealing what supplies they can. Indeed, the government's greed and ignorance is shown to be one of the major causes of the Triffids' rise to dominance as Britain farmed the "alien" plants on an industrial scale, using them as an alternative to fossil fuels and traditional crops — which had been exhausted thanks to government mismanagement and poor planning.

British television drama in the 1980s, responding to commercially motivated shifts in audience viewing habits and interests, relied much more on the series and serial drama format to "maximise audiences in an increasingly competitive market-place."[5] While the science fiction genre was a reliable source of adaptable material for U.K. channels, the BBC's attitude towards supposed over-the-top and expensive cult series such as *Doctor Who* and *Blake's 7* (BBC, 1978–1981) meant that the original text had to be of a standard to warrant a large budgetary outlay, and be popular with a broad enough spectrum of people to guarantee a dedicated audience. Interestingly then, having had success with "quality" series adapted from classic science fiction texts, the BBC decided to commission a new Saturday afternoon series based on John Christopher's juvenile *The Tripods* trilogy. Choosing an adaptation that would necessitate high production values to fully realize a post-apocalyptic Britain ruled by an army of giant three-legged metal machines, the BBC clearly saw potential in the traditional post-apocalypse/invasion narrative.

With series one broadcast between September and December 1984 and series two between September and November 1985, one can see *The Tripods* fitting within a succession of children's literature adaptations for television including John Masefield's *The Box of Delights* and C.S. Lewis's *The Chronicles of Narnia* on the BBC and an adaptation of John Wyndham's *Chocky* (1984) on ITV. Alistair McGown's timeline of children's fantasy and science fiction television points to a growing trend in the late 1970s and early 1980s to produce serial drama specifically for a young audience: Arthurian legend and mother nature provided the inspiration for pre-industrial series such as *The Changes* (BBC, 1975) and *The Moon Stallion* (BBC, 1978); Englishness was explored in period fantasy tales such as *The Phoenix and the Carpet* (BBC, 1976–1977) and *The Enchanted Castle* (BBC, 1979); and with *Knights of God* (ITV, 1987), future Britain was again depicted as a feudal society this time under the rule of a fascist government.[6] Part of the BBC's drama provision for children, *The Tripods* can be seen as just one example of a number of programs that offered children a "service in miniature," defined by McGown as the BBC ambition to replicate "all of adult television's genres and formats for younger audiences"—a legacy left over from Mary Adams, producer of children's programming at the BBC in the 1940s, who wanted to make television from plays to encyclopedia programs specifically for children.[7]

Furthermore, where Dave Allen describes the BBC's fascination for adapting those children's books set in the English countryside combining magic and the ordinary, fantasy and the real, I would argue that this also characterizes elements of John Christopher's *Tripods* novels.[8] Following Allen's argument, these stories are "part of a far greater continuum of English creativity around the English landscape — often with metaphysical connotations." The rural, represented in literature, film and television as a garden idyll, "is perhaps most obviously a product of English romanticism in the early nineteenth century in poetry, literature, and art" with older roots stretching from William Blake to the British film director David Lean.[9] Considering links between BBC television drama and British art tradition is useful and provides further scope for visual analysis later in the chapter. For now, however, it is important to bear in mind how visions of the English landscape not only characterize the past but also stand in for Christopher's prediction of the future.

Screening the Novel

According to John Pfeiffer, the work of John Christopher (a pseudonym for Sam Youd, the popular adult and juvenile science fiction writer) explores the "fictional postcatastrophe behavior of people."[10] How they cope with the stresses and strains of life after environmental or nuclear disaster is the primary focus of almost all of his collected works for both adults and children. The conflict between civilization and savagery provides the backdrop for stories like *The Tripods* trilogy, "setting the stage upon which to analyze the behavior of humans in populations that will have to survive as small groups that become tribal."[11] Christopher was not the only British author using such a dystopian motif in their science fiction. As previously discussed in relation to *The Day of the Triffids*, John Wyndham's fiction often depicted a Britain right at the edge of extinction — its population under threat from alien plant invaders or sinister and powerful children. Catastrophe seemed entirely plausible and indeed imminent after the Second World War and the development of the H-Bomb, thus British science fiction in the 1950s and 1960s, when Christopher wrote *The Tripods* trilogy, merely reflected this fear of death, destruction and decay.

The overarching theme of this period was dystopia: the negative of utopia, a place or society depicted as worse or indeed a potential future of the contemporary world in which we live (see Hoffstadt and Schrey's chapter in this book). A common trope in the literary form of the genre, dystopias in the twentieth century are more often "critical dystopias" in that they neither celebrate the possibility of utopia nor entirely reduce the narrative to total despair. For Graham J. Murphy, the critical dystopia explores ways in which those marginalized by the corrupt or totalitarian regime can fight and change the system, perhaps even moving forward, thus offering a sense of hope as well as a vision of hopelessness.[12] What is more, dystopias offer social critique alongside pessimistic presentation: "the typical narrative structure of the dystopia (with its presentation of an alienated character's refusal) facilitates this politically and formally flexible stance."[13] This particular facet of the critical dystopia is most obvious in the decade's representation of the lone individual fighting the corrupt forces above him (as the protagonist is usually male) and offers an interesting twist on the American narrative of the self-made man who succeeds through individual endeavor and enterprise.

Adam Roberts summarizes the genre's developments in postwar Britain, suggesting that these authors were playing out fears of nuclear war and fallout in the U.K. in response to the deeply American concern for space opera and galactic exploration. However, he rejects the notion of the "cosy catastrophe," a term used by Brian Aldiss to describe British science fiction in this period, as it does not fully account for the unsettling visions of a future Britain that authors such as Christopher routinely recycled in his work. True, *The Tripods* trilogy "projected an increasingly insular aesthetic" common to the "cosy catastrophes" of Wyndham and Arthur C. Clarke,[14] however, the disposition of the juvenile protagonists in the novels dispels any sense of "cosiness" as they are determined to overturn the system imposed on them and the global population by the Tripods. They are not content with living comfortably or maintaining a simple lifestyle to avoid contact with their Tripod masters; they are set on rebellion, where a life free of authoritarian rule is preferable to a life where humanity no longer aspires to invention or creation.

For John Newsinger, *The Tripods* trilogy explores the "related notions of rebellion and power" while also expounding upon male friendship, teen angst and the hazards of adulthood. The child heroes of both the novels and the television adaptation do not fight "individual villains or dark conspiracies, against occupying armies or conquering empires" but instead they struggle "against the social order itself" and those who uphold it.[15] Little wonder that these books were popular with juvenile readers in their teens as they depict young people in the throes of revolution against adults who seek to quash any sense of individuality or autonomy. The children who decide to run away from their homes in rural England to join the rebellion against the Tripods do so in an attempt to overturn "the conformist, servile society that they have imposed on humankind":

> One important reason for the success of Christopher's juvenile science fiction is that he associates adolescent rebellion against adult authority, of the adventurous young against the conforming old, with rebellion against societies where authority seeks to control men's minds, reduce them to slavery and extinguish the very idea of freedom. The two rebellions are portrayed as one and the same.[16]

Perhaps this very point underscores why the BBC decided to take a gamble with adapting Christopher's work, they were trying to attract a young audience while also maintaining a sense of adult storytelling. Certainly, an anti-utopian tale of slaves and masters, rebellion and freedom fighting drew parallels with growing and youthful anti–Thatcher and Tory sentiment at the time and no doubt the BBC were less inclined to offer support for the Conservative government who were themselves attacking the television industry. When Margaret Thatcher established the Peacock Committee to investigate the funding of the BBC in 1985, science fiction programming on the channel would take a serious hit as it was seen by BBC1 Controller Michael Grade to be too expensive and too niche to continue production.[17] Yet, despite the important and timely themes that Christopher's *Tripods* adaptation brought to Britain's television screens, finance can be considered far more of a determinant for the series' content than its political contexts.

One could posit, however, that elements of Christopher's original novels — the postcatastrophe landscape, conflict between social conformity and individuality, the trials of adolescence — clearly emerge in the television adaptation and make up for the lack of money afforded to science fiction drama by the BBC in the middle of the decade. There is optimism in the original books that also comes through in the adaptations. For K.V. Bailey "harsh and even catastrophe-affected environments are certainly portrayed, but the lights of hope and idealism glimmer more brightly."[18] Indeed, those elements that emphasize the positive nature of Christopher's novels, such as the camaraderie and fondness felt between the original three boys that set out to seek the White Mountains, are transferred to the screen. The dystopian nature of the trilogy is plainly evident through the landscapes of wilderness and desolation depicted throughout the two series, yet it is perhaps what the children do and feel that makes the adaptation worthy science fiction. That *The Tripods* failed to maintain an audience for the second season points perhaps to a miscommunication of meaning between the production team and the audience, where the former sought to create drama and empathy over a span of thirteen episodes and the latter were expecting American production values, action, and peril week after week.

An English Nightmare

The pre-credit sequence of series one's first episode, "A Village in England, July, 2089AD," introduces us to the small village of Wherton (somewhere in the south but it is not made clear exactly where). Here people live a simple life: the mill grinds wheat for flour, horse-drawn carts provide transport, and the children have to fetch fresh water from the well. These kinds of activities and the rural, almost idyllic, setting belie the date given at the beginning of the episode, 2089. However, the quaintness of the scene is truly emphasized when the villagers' attention turns quickly to something approaching over the horizon; although not startling, the strange accompanying clarion call highlights the disconnect between the rural surroundings and the future in which this is supposed to be set. Newsinger describes the village in the novel as "semi-feudal," home to a "society that has turned its back on things technological."[19] Indeed, the most advanced piece of technology on screen appears to be the plate clock hanging on the wall of Will Parker's house (the fifteen-year-old main protagonist of the story). The pastoral scene is ruptured when we see what it was the villagers were watching on the horizon. Across the village lake a large metal foot descends, crashing into the water. As this happens the villagers stand back, revealing a man standing on the jetty looking ready to greet the coming metal monster. From the giant foot and leg the camera angle switches to focus on a large silver capsule sat atop; the metal monster, moving on three legs, comes closer to the lone man. As the Tripod reaches the water's edge it stops and a claw comes from within to reach down and grab the man, bringing him up to an open hatch. The final shot switches to reveal the sheer scale of the Tripod creature as it towers over the village and lake, the long armed claw dangling with its human cargo in a tight grip. From here the main credits begin and the audience is left wondering whether this was a scene from H.G. Wells's *The War of the Worlds* or a George Morland painting of a rural village brought to life.

It is revealed in the rest of the episode that the Tripod is in Wherton for "capping day," a day when all those who are of age (sixteen) are to be capped with a flat triangular piece of gold on the crown of their head. Will and his cousin Henry are wary of capping and what it means for those who have been capped. Everyone who has been capped seems to go through a personality change; they become subdued and appear to lose a sense of adventure and individuality that characterizes the nature of being a teenager. In fact, the cap is revealed to be a powerful alien device used by the Tripods to keep humans under control. It suppresses the more violent, yet still vital, tendencies of humanity so that the Tripods can rule unchallenged and maintain the feudal society which now characterizes England in 2089. Will encounters a vagrant called Ozymandias who tells him of how the Tripods came to be on Earth, arriving some one hundred years ago destroying the major cities and killing millions. After time later generations of survivors became reliant on the Tripods, their metal overseers remain stalking guardians of a backwards society devoid of technological know-how and scientific curiosity.

The mixture of past and future, the English countryside and alien invaders, serves to unsettle the audience as they learn of how England came to be mastered by the Tripods and all remnants of technology, civilization, and the present were wiped away. In the preface to the 2003 edition of *The White Mountains* (the first in the trilogy which was originally published in 1967) John Christopher reveals how he was inspired by the giant strides humanity was taking during the 1960s, with the Space Race dominating popular culture, and wanted to write a story of extra-terrestrial life and our progress toward the stars. Yet, when man did set foot on the Moon it seemed that reality did not live up to expectation; "I had seen the future, and found it disappointing," he points out. In a weird reversal Christopher turned his attention to the past: "the colour which had bleached out of our interplanetary speculations was still bright in human history and there was life there, and romance and action."[20] So, Christopher's future would be one set in the past, a feudal England that was not only under the control of powerful alien beings but had also returned to "a medieval hierarchical social structure."[21] Not concerned with envisioning a progressive future Christopher was keen to pick apart and investigate what a return to more basic times would do to contemporary society.

The results of the BBC's emphasis on the rural rather than the technological, like Christopher's own desire to depict a future that looks more like the past, fits neatly with how British television drama and indeed science fiction film looked during the 1980s. In this period heritage drama was a popular form of the genre, "not the industrial heritage of coal mines, factories or shipyards," the victims of Margaret Thatcher's social and economic reforms, "but the upper-class and aristocratic heritage of country houses and stately homes which features in the work of novelists from Jane Austen to Evelyn Waugh."[22] The tendency for heritage drama on British screens was often ascribed to "Thatcherism and its (highly selective) appeal to the values of the Victorians (self-sufficiency and family, but not public works),"[23] a philosophy, according to Lez Cooke, that Thatcher "felt had made Britain 'Great.'"[24] Indeed, the image of the pastoral on both British film and television in the 1980s provided an image of the national 'community' as 'one large family whose common concerns ride above any sectional interests.'"[25] Whether it was heritage, crime or soap opera drama during this period the effect Thatcherism had on the writers and producers of British television has been discussed by several critics.

In science fiction film, the past was used as backdrop for scenes of future Britain. The tone and design of the future in *Nineteen Eighty-Four* (Michael Radford, 1984) evoked "the grim postwar austerity of Orwell's" world. *Brazil* (Terry Gilliam, 1985), with its retro-fitted ducts and dark grey streets, represented more a Britain of the present than the future. For Linda Ruth Williams these depictions of dystopia were "future built from the past" and indicated the extent to which popular media were reacting to and challenging the nostalgic view of Britain promoted by the Conservative government at the time.[26] These films can be described as retrovisions, "a 'vision into or of the past' and [imply] an act of possessing the ability to read the past, in the way that one would possess a prophetic vision."[27] For Deborah Cartmell and I.Q. Hunter retrovisions are "makeovers of history" and as such these films imagine a future based on intertextual references to their generic predecessors and the visual look of the past.[28] Therefore, *The Tripods* can be described as a retrovision — not of the industrial Britain of the nineteenth and twentieth century but of the more pastoral eighteenth century when the English countryside was the living and breathing heart of the British economy.

Following a line of analysis prompted by John Caughie in his work on realist art and British television drama, I would suggest that comparing the details of the English landscape seen in *The Tripods* with works of art depicting the rural poor and countryside by artists such as George Morland gives further insight into how the aesthetics of that particular science fiction drama served to bring to life John Christopher's tale of rebellion against authority — a contributing factor in the alienation of the intended audience during the tea-time television slot as they would have been expecting a futuristic aesthetic familiar to *Doctor Who*. The rural settings created in *The Tripods* resemble the farmyard and village scenes painted by Morland in the late eighteenth century. He did not paint an idealized version of rural life, like most of his contemporaries, but instead pictured life as hard and unsentimental. Likewise, the village scenes and life on the open road depicted in the BBC's *The Tripods* is unforgiving, especially since the threat of capping or arrest for noncompliance looms large over those who inhabit Earth in the future. John Barrell describes Morland's art as illusory, in that he painted a picture of life in old England not romanticized or in praise of the social order but instead detailed the humble nature of England's poor; he focused on "tattered clothes, heavy boots and agricultural implements"[29]:

> Where his admirers wish to see the image of a unified society, he shows them a divided one; where they wish to see the poor as cheerful and industrious, he shows them as discontented, desperate, contemptuous, or defiantly idle; and there was no other painter of English rural life independent enough, or intimate enough with the lives of the people he portrayed, to achieve what Morland achieved.[30]

The notion of an egalitarian society at this time was painted out by Morland whose picturing of rural life illustrated "unity as artifice" rather than the *status quo*.[31] As Barrell further points out, English society in the eighteenth century was so divided and stratified that it was impossible to even distinguish between farmers and land-owners as in comparison the lowly laborers would see both "as the rich consumer of the fruits of their labour."[32] Ultimately, then, recognizing a homogenous and recognizable class in England during this period was impossible and Morland's painting highlighted this to great effect. Similarly, the hodge-podge of clothing styles, material and fabrics worn by farmers and village people in *The Tripods* flattens out a sense of hierarchy and supports the story's thematic concern for rebellion in the pursuit of freedom and social equality. The villagers in Wherton wear a strange mix of clothing, a result of the postcatastrophe scramble to survive and accumulate supplies, yet seeing women wearing dresses from the 1930s and men wearing britches and tri-corner hats from the regency period emphasizes the sense of social disorder that inspires Will and Henry to escape to the White Mountains and join the revolution, and will eventually result in the downfall of the Tripods. Nonetheless, at the same time, this visualization of a British pastoral past detracts from the futuristic aesthetic familiar to science fiction television drama imported from the U.S. in the 1980s and still popular among younger audiences.

Dans La Cité

On their journey to the White Mountains Will and Henry travel through postcatastrophe France, making friends with Jean Paul (Beanpole) who joins them to avoid his capping. There is a clear dichotomy drawn between rural England and superior France where technology and human ingenuity still exist in the form of steam powered trains and weapons such as machine guns and grenades. Upon the boys' entrance to Paris we are shown the remnants of the once beautiful city, buildings and monuments are left in ruins — only the Arc de Triomphe is recognizable in its decaying state. These scenes of destruction serve to further underline the backward nature of the English landscape where the boys started their journey. The divergent sense of space and place between the city (albeit destroyed) and countryside (albeit broken up by the irregular appearance of the Tripods) is a common trope in science fiction and has provided much scope for dystopic storytelling.

Cities not only provide a physical backdrop but also "the literal premises for the possibilities and trajectory of narrative action."[33] The urban science fiction experience as portrayed in film and television from *Metropolis* (Germany, Fritz Lang, 1927) in the 1920s to the present day, according to Vivian Sobchack, offers a "historical trajectory — one we can pick up at a generic moment that marks the failure of modernism's aspirations in images that speak of urban destruction and emptiness and that leads to more contemporary moments marked by urban exhaustion, postmodern exhilaration, and millennial vertigo."[34] Indeed, the ways we have imagined our fictional cities are clear indicators of how we continue to interact with the changing urban landscape. Images of the destroyed city are frequent in science fiction, whether the city is destroyed through war, alien invasion or simply the ravages of time. Science fiction, for Susan Sontag, is fundamentally about the visualization of disaster and its popularity as a genre stems from our fascination to witness our own destruction, and acknowledge our own part in it.[35] As such, Sobchack calls this visual decay "a response to the failure of the city's aspiration (and to the failure of 'modern' civilization)" and sees these characteristics employed in the nihilistic films of the 1970s such as *Soylent Green* (U.S., Richard Fleischer, 1973) where New York "no longer aspires but suffocates and expires."[36]

Series two, based on Christopher's *The City of Gold and Lead* (1967), saw the boys reach the White Mountains to join the resistance and set off on another journey, this time to carry out a secret mission to gain entry to the Tripods' City of Gold. Again, in stark contrast with the abundant scenes of pastoral life encountered throughout Europe, the Tripods' city is a vision of technological superiority and wonder. A giant dome over top hides and protects the alien inhabitants from the Earth's atmosphere which is poisonous to them. Will, acting as spy, witnesses the marvels of the Tripods' technical expertise. With him, the audience too is amazed as the BBC special and visual effects department seemingly went all out in envisaging a futuristic city complete with triangular skyscrapers and mid-air walkways. Whereas the first season emphasized both the physical and emotional journey of the three boys, often willingly sacrificing expensive special effects to add more character development, the six episodes set in the Tripod city emphasized the true nature of the Tripod threat. To bring this to the screen, producer Richard Bates brought in Bob Blagden as director, whose previous credits included creative designer for *Blake's 7*. The visual parallels between Blagden's city and the futuristic cities and sets of *Doctor Who* and *Blake's 7* are obvious, and warrant further exploration outside the scope of this chapter, but it is important to note here how far both narratively and visually *The Tripods* as a series had come from its humble beginnings in the fictional English village of Wherton, scenes so evocative of the Morland paintings as discussed earlier.

Conclusion

The Tripods and how their design was implemented (Christopher would reveal that he had inadvertently copied the visual nature of the three legged monsters with clawing tentacles from Wells' *The War of the Worlds*[37]) also contributed to the mixed reception the series received from viewers and critics. For example, the main criticism of the first season was that the Tripods were not seen enough and that too much time was spent filling out the story of how the three travelers survived on their journey south to the White Mountains, spending time holed away in French châteaux and vineyard farms instead of fighting the Tripods or building a resistance to their authority along the way. Four out of the thirteen episodes were devoted to this part of the story whereas it received barely five lines of space in the first book. For Alistair McGown, the audience "expected the post–*Star Wars* [U.S., George Lucas, 1977] hardware, but instead got something reminiscent of a wartime chase epic like *The Silver Sword* (BBC, 1957; 1971)."[38] With the first episode promising regular appearances of the three-legged machines yet the rest of the series failing to deliver, the primary threat posed to the boys on their journey to the White Mountains was the Black Guard — an enslaved human army of men who police the towns and villages, spying on potential dissidents and capturing vagrants to be returned to their Tripod masters. Clearly cheaper than using massive Tripod props and special effects, the Black Guard was the invention of screenwriter Alick Rowe who infused their function with the menace of Tolkein's Ringwraiths and the manner of Nazi soldiers.

Despite the lack of Tripods and the addition of the Black Guard, this fascination for the detail and building up of tension through the long chase served to underline John Christopher's original vision in the trilogy. The fact that the Tripods were not always in shot emphasized narratively that what posed the most threat to the survival of human civilization was not the technological superiority of the alien invaders but perhaps the idea that we were all too happy to accept the social order they imposed on us. Further to this, in response to readers' criticisms that the Tripods actually seemed inferior to human technology on their initial invasion (not having the ability to use infrared to track runways at night for example) Christopher maintains that the danger the aliens posed was rather more insidious: "the secret of success in battle lies often not so much in the use of one's own strength but in the exploitation of the other side's weaknesses."[39] In the prequel, *When the Tripods Came* (1988), Christopher reveals that humanity was taken in by Tripod propaganda broadcast through the television — our ignorance and gullibility, rather than superior technology, proving to be the real reason for our downfall.

Part of the genre's ability to depict different spaces is to make the familiar unfamiliar, what Vivian Sobchack sees as the "transformation of the absolutely familiar into the absolutely alien."[40] So while the first series of *The Tripods* ignored the extraterrestrial alien it did still visualize the alien through the estrangement of everyday objects and routines. Estrangement plays a vital role in the science fiction genre, as it juxtaposes what seems normal and everyday with the alien and otherworldly. As Sobchack further underlines, "it is the very plasticity of objects and settings in science fiction films which help define them as science fiction, and not their consistency."[41] Therefore, we might conclude *The Tripods* is by its very nature generically science fiction in that it depicts landscapes and people as familiar yet strange within a similar yet different time and place to that which we inhabit. The sense of wonder of the series does not lie in the fact that we may get a glimpse into the shell of the Tripod machines to see their alien pilots but exists in the very depiction of life to which we dearly hold on. This is where the difference perhaps lies between the British science fiction television of the time and the visually striking, yet narratively thin, American imports that were becoming popular in the 1980s: *The Tripods*' story, and indeed ominous threat, lay within the representation of an English future that was as primitive as its past. A vision all too recognizable in that for many it was a contemporary reality, with the social and cultural contexts of Thatcher's Britain impacting heavily on the series themes of cultural repression, totalitarianism and surveillance.

In addition, considering the nature of the series as children's television, we must recognize the industrial contexts within which *The Tripods* was developed and ultimately failed. Children's broadcasting has always come under great scrutiny from adults and regulators therefore the BBC is keen to monitor controversial stories and make programs within the strict guidelines laid down by themselves. Imported programs from America, so often "singled out as symptomatic of a perceived decline" in standards,[42] were in the case of *The Tripods* its inspiration and own worst enemy. Trying to keep up with genre programming across the Atlantic meant the BBC had to sacrifice quality for action yet in doing so it lost the very audience it was trying to attract. The visual look of the series did not match American output. Similarly, Alistair McGown states that if children's television is a "service in miniature" it is inevitably affected by the same forces that shape British broadcasting as a whole: a lack of funding, debates surrounding the death of drama, and an influx of imports.[43] Logically, then, *The Tripods* can be seen as a victim of circumstance. British television was going through a period of change during a time of cultural and economic uncertainty and to have a series, whose narrative and visual aesthetic depicted the tensions between the past and the future, the old and the new, meant that such problems seemed far too close to home to act as a form of Saturday afternoon entertainment.

10

The Future of History in Dennis Potter's *Cold Lazarus*

CHRISTINE SPRENGLER

Shortly after being diagnosed with terminal cancer in 1994, Dennis Potter scripted his last two serials, *Karaoke* and *Cold Lazarus*. First aired in 1996, they stand as a final testament to nearly thirty-five years in television drama and, as Potter himself described it, a life lived between two worlds, between a working-class mining community and the career path opened up to him as a "scholarship boy" at Oxford.[1] Potter was aware that he would never see *Karaoke* and *Cold Lazarus* completed and thus left explicit instructions for how each was to be realized, including the demand they be co-produced by the BBC and Channel Four (the first and last time this ever happened!). He knew full well the difficulties such an alliance would cause and likely relished the ensuing fracas as payback for the roadblocks he encountered at these institutions. But part of him had loftier and nobler ambitions in forcing this union between rivals. He did, after all, truly believe in what he thought was the "democratic potential" of television and its capacity to stimulate, educate and mobilize. With *Karaoke* and *Cold Lazarus*, Potter hoped to reach the widest possible audience to pay tribute to the heritage of British television, including, of course, his own contributions. However, he also used these works to issue a stern warning that the television he knew and practiced was on the verge of extinction and, along with it, British culture and access to history itself.

This is the manifest subject of *Cold Lazarus* and focus of this chapter. Following a few brief comments on authorship and reception, I want to consider the ways in which *Cold Lazarus* offers a stinging critique of postwar Americanization (as a process advanced by the Thatcherite policies that made possible the influence of media moguls like Rupert Murdoch) and how it led to the eradication of a collective history from the British national consciousness. I will argue that the effectiveness of this critique owes much to *Cold Lazarus*' status as science fiction, regardless of how haphazardly (or, as Glen Creeber implies, pastiche-like) it invokes certain tropes and conventions of the genre.[2] I want to suggest that the force and nuance of its engagement with the future of history depends in large part on its props, costumes and set design. In short, I want to attribute some of its merits — rather than its shortcomings — to its form and, specifically, its visual form as science fiction.

Potter's serials have been studied primarily through the lens of literary criticism with questions about narrative and autobiography dominating analysis. This is no doubt a logical approach to the work of someone who identified himself as a writer. But as valuable as this methodology has been in making sense of certain literary and narrative qualities, it tends to ignore one very important dimension: the visual. Reasons for this neglect are complicated and many, involving the cultural roots of British television and trends in television criticism. It can also be ascribed to the more specific tendency to revere Potter as an auteur and, as such, privilege manifestations of his authorial voice at the expense of what results from collaborative efforts among producers, directors, editors, and costume and set designers. The creative products of these collaborations are vital to the success and significance of many of his more remarkable dramas.[3] Thus, while some kind of acknowledgement of Potter's intentions or recourse to autobiography is unavoidable and indeed necessary, I want to supplement the insights already gained from an auteurist perspective with an enquiry into how *Cold Lazarus* produces meaning as a cultural text. That is, I am less concerned with whether or not Potter meant for certain props to appear in the world of *Cold Lazarus* than with how these props might operate in the context of the serial.

Shifting attention from Potter as the singular privileged author of his work to a consideration of style in the production of meaning need not require a significant conceptual leap, especially if we accept Rosalind Krauss's claim that the latter is actually a by-product of the former. She argues that efforts to identify intentions and define an author's signature opened up questions about the production of meaning in a text through visual, verbal and musical language.[4] For Krauss, this was a serendipitous consequence of the auteurist approach, one that precipitated a substantial methodological shift: years of auteur study eventually led to years of close textual analysis. I would like to enact a similar shift here on a much smaller scale, moving quickly on from questions about authorship to questions about the production of meaning through visual strategies. However, I am not arguing, as Krauss does, that a focus in the critical literature on Potter's authorship blocked recognition of "the truly radical aspects" of his work.[5] His intentions and narrative strategies matter. And, as the existing scholarship has shown, it also matters that Potter grew up in a mining community on the border with Wales, attended Oxford because of the 1944 Butler Education Act, wrote for the BBC during a specific period of its history, and lived through the social and political shifts of the postwar years and the turmoil of Thatcherism.[6] All this

10. The Future of History in Cold Lazarus (Sprengler)

constitutes a large part of what his entire *oeuvre* is ultimately about and, because of the reflective nature of *Karaoke* and *Cold Lazarus*, it constitutes the subject of these final serials too. But, in the case of *Cold Lazarus*, a focus on Potter's authorship has indeed blocked something. It has blocked consideration of how the series operates as science fiction.

Karaoke and *Cold Lazarus* concern the life and death of Daniel Feeld, an ornery, belligerent writer played by Albert Finney. *Karaoke* is set in 1994 and follows Feeld's attempt to finish his final two screenplays upon learning that he is terminally ill with cancer. He soon becomes convinced that strangers around him are speaking the lines of his script and, when he meets Sandra Sollars, he believes her to be the young woman for whom he has written a "nasty ending." Certain that his fiction is destined to materialize in her real life, he intervenes and shoots her would-be murderer. Interspersed throughout are comic exchanges between Feeld and a variety of characters representing the television industry that Potter had been part of for most of his life.

Cold Lazarus is set in 2368 and opens where *Karaoke* left off—with Feeld on his death bed. This is not part of the narrative's temporal reality. Instead it is a memory extracted from Feeld's cryogenically frozen head and visualized on a laboratory screen. The research team responsible for discovering this technology is led by British scientist Dr. Emma Porlock, yet owned and controlled by American pharmaceutical entrepreneur Martina Matilda Masdon. Their breakthrough in how to access memories of the deceased is accidentally witnessed by another American, David Siltz, media mogul and president of Universal Total Entertainment. He instantly sees the profit potential of this enterprise, especially in selling visual memories of real sex to a population accustomed to all things virtual. There is some resistance against such initiatives and the unbridled capitalism that defines this future dystopia, one in which England no longer exists as an independent political entity.[7] A group known as the RONs (Reality or Nothing) has initiated a terror campaign against the simulacral condition of their world. Dr. Fyodor Glasunov, a member of Porlock's team, belongs to this covert organization. And, though initially appalled by Siltz's plan to buy and sell Feeld's memories, he realizes that broadcasting images of the actual past—regardless of their distortion by the effects of trauma or workings of memory—could enable people to recognize their own oppressive conditions. He suspects that Feeld's memories might act as the necessary catalyst for revolution.

Karaoke certainly dabbles in Potter's signature non-naturalism through lip-synching and character doubling. But, whereas Potter's earlier uses of non-naturalistic devices in *Pennies From Heaven* (BBC, 1978) or *Blue Remembered Hills* (BBC, 1979) tend to be attributable to the psychological state of the protagonist and can be explained as the product of dreaming, psychosis or illness, in *Karaoke*, such devices extend beyond Feeld's imagination and into the world of others.[8] Hearing Sandra Sollars speak lines from his script may indeed stem from Feeld's delusions, but the danger she faces at the hands of Pig Mailion (Hywel Bennett), her pimp, is utterly real. And yet, however much Potter's brand of non-naturalism might seem to pave the way for a venture into science fiction, the kinds of innovative formal and narrative strategies pioneered by Potter and his production teams remain at a remove from the tropes and conventions of the genre. *Cold Lazarus* clearly revisits his usual themes of memory, class, childhood and popular culture in a way that is distinctly autobiographical. It even references key non-naturalistic devices through Daniel Feeld's lip-synching Bing Crosby's "Pennies From Heaven" and Albert Finney playing the ten year old Daniel in children's clothing. But these are references to earlier plays, memories extracted from a cryogenically frozen head, and not used as strategies in their own right in the diegetic reality of 2368. *Cold Lazarus* does not really offer a hybrid of, or bridge between, non-naturalism and science fiction. It abandons the former almost wholly in favor of the conventions of the latter. *Cold Lazarus* makes use of well-worn staples of science fiction: a dystopian future world, a laboratory setting, corporate villains, a scientist with humanist leanings, a scientific breakthrough that produces a moral dilemma, present day science in advanced manifestations from virtual reality to cryogenics and surveillance technology, and futuristically re-imagined everyday material objects like cars and chairs.

That Dennis Potter should select science fiction as the form to present what he knew to be his final work is surely significant. This was his one and only experiment with the genre and thus he was taking something of a chance speaking through a language with which he was not well-versed. According to Creeber, Potter chose science fiction because, as the most postmodern of all genres, it offered the perfect opportunity for him to critique postmodernism itself.[9] Though perhaps, like so many others, he also saw the potential for science fiction to clearly articulate and make fully explicit his desires and his anxieties about the future and, in particular, the future of Britain's past. Judging by the critical response, this was a risk that did not pay off. As science fiction, *Cold Lazarus* was deemed a failure.[10] For instance, Ken Trodd admitted the existence of a series of intractable problems, including a grossly inadequate budget. Although a reasonably elaborate set was constructed, they could not afford to shoot it on 35mm film.[11] The result was a lower production quality and a visual echo of earlier British television. Despite how appropriately nostalgic this may seem in theory, in practice, it had an adverse effect on its reception.[12]

Cold Lazarus may indeed look cheap. And its inability to offer a convincing future reality likely had an impact on audiences' willingness to believe in its fictional world. Reasons for its critical failure, though, are complex and go well beyond a simple visual inefficacy. If we want to ground its poor reception in its status as science fiction, we might look more closely at how *Cold Lazarus* was out of synch with contemporaneous examples of the genre. In fact, this is intricately tied to what Trodd sees as the main reason for *Karaoke* and *Cold Lazarus*' general rejection: they were profoundly out of step with the demands of a radically changed television industry in the 1990s. *Cold Lazarus* shares a greater affinity with the dystopian tenor of British science fiction television of the 1970s and even, to a point, with present-day cinematic productions like *V for Vendetta* (James McTeigue, U.K./U.S./Germany, 2006) or *Children of Men* (Alfonso Cuarón, U.K./U.S./Japan, 2006). Appearing in 1996, *Cold Lazarus* had little in common with the parodic, self-reflexive impulse that defined the decade's more successful offerings such as *Red Dwarf* (BBC, 1988–1999, 2009). It also had little in common with the cinematic quality of American imports like *The X-Files* (Fox, 1993–2002), a program that Catriona Miller credits for ushering in a new era for British science fiction television at the close of the millennium.[13]

As much as *Cold Lazarus* is a work of science fiction, it still bears many of the hallmarks of a Dennis Potter television serial. And, in the 1990s, this too was a liability. Murdoch-style programming of the era had precipitated a shift in audience tastes and expectations away from challenging drama. Moreover, negative reviews surfaced two weeks before the official air date. This initiated a flurry of negative press and articles proclaiming that Potter was an over-rated relic of the past. "Overindulged to the bitter end" read the title to A.A. Gill's review for *The Sunday Times*.[14] W. Stephen Gilbert called it "wandering" and "misshapen" while Garry Bushell proclaimed that Potter's "last works only confirm that this once-brilliant playwright degenerated into a hackneyed has-been."[15] Admittedly there are factors internal to the production of both *Karaoke* and *Cold Lazarus* that elicited derision, for criticisms were also levelled by devoted fans. These two serials were, after all, overtly sentimental and indulged in a kind of metonymic self-reflexivity through countless obscure references to friends and enemies alike. Trodd also attributes its shortcomings to strict conditions imposed on the script by Potter himself that left no room for creative interpretation. The inability to alter the script or contest directions resulted in the works feeling contrived and littered with moments that upset the syntax of episodes.[16]

In the end, *Cold Lazarus* deserves much of this criticism. As a television serial and as science fiction, it certainly does not rank among the best. Nevertheless, to dismiss it outright would be a mistake, and to ignore it as science fiction would be an even bigger one. For it is as science fiction that *Cold Lazarus* is a culturally significant work. It is in its creation of a futuristic dystopian landscape and the objects that inhabit it that *Cold Lazarus* issues an effective critique of the present's hand in adversely determining the fate of British culture and history. Thus, instead of pursuing reasons for its failures, I want to consider how we might find value and conceptual sophistication in its visual dimensions.

It goes without saying that science fiction film and television are dependant on production design and visual effects. Sets, props and costumes bear much of the burden of telling us about the nature of existence in alternate realms. In *Cold Lazarus*, they do this and more. Here, we find two types of props and aesthetic schemes that are juxtaposed to differentiate and evaluate distinctions between Britain and America as well as authentic and inauthentic nostalgia. They also reinforce narrative warnings about the demise of Britain and the loss of access to British history. They are comprised of, on the one hand, the commodity and material culture of 1950s America and, on the other, futuristic objects marked by "organic" traces that invoke the natural world.

Predictably, references to postwar American consumer culture are aligned with the American entrepreneurs Siltz and Masdon. One room in Siltz's London residence is decorated with turquoise sofas, atom-inspired furniture, a yellow Formica countertop and cabinetry with a speckled Formica veneer. Another contains a jukebox, pool table and movie memorabilia from early to mid twentieth century Hollywood. Siltz even owns a late 1950s tail-finned Cadillac modified to hover down the streets of 2368. In this future, these objects are antiques, museum-quality artifacts prized for their survival. But, they attest to more than a personal impulse to collect or to flex one's connoisseurial muscle. Siltz's collection includes objects firmly rooted in the material culture of the era that secured America's dominant position on the international political stage and in the arena of popular entertainment. They are icons of an age characterized by the proliferation of American material goods and culture and thus representative of the postwar export programs that precipitated what Richard Hoggart refers to as Britain's "Cultural Fall" — the beginning of the end of an autonomous British culture. As such, they reflect Siltz's own ambitions to perpetuate such expansionist practices.

For instance, despite its origins in the late nineteenth century, the jukebox functions as one such icon that testifies to the arrival of postwar American culture in Britain. Initially aligned with the 1950s through its contextualization by the visual media of this decade, the jukebox came to symbolize, for Hoggart and others, aggressive encroachment from across the Atlantic.[17] They perceived it as a threat to British music and youth and thus to the political consciousness of the next generation of the working-class. The jukebox is privileged in Hoggart's seminal 1957 *The Uses of Literacy* as the object that best symbolizes the Cultural Fall *and* it is privileged in Siltz's collection of objects that celebrate a key phase in the Americanization of Britain.

Yet, in spite of how well the jukebox signals a kind of cultural imperialism, it cannot celebrate the triumph of Americanization *at the expense* of Britain as effectively as the tail-finned Cadillac. Whereas jukeboxes did cross the Atlantic during the mid twentieth century, oversized automobiles only ever appeared on cinema screens. Thus, the existence of a tail-finned car in the London of 2368 speaks to the final stage and the ultimate triumph of Americanization. The cost of this process to British culture is most forcefully articulated by the image of tail-fins hovering amongst the rubble of an urban infrastructure that once failed to accommodate such a vehicle. As a privileged, canonical object in the visual culture of the American nostalgia economy, the tail-finned car communicates much about the mythic vision of the U.S. at mid century: adherence to the doctrine of conspicuous consumption, respect for the logic of planned obsolescence as well as an investment in futurity as embodied by the rocket-like tail fins. Fully loaded as a symbol of popular luxury, it was often associated through advertising with the cornerstones of the frontier myth: expansionism, mobility and rugged individualism.

It is hardly surprising that Siltz should own a tail-finned Cadillac and somehow wholly appropriate that he would summon it to chauffeur Dr. Porlock home after inviting her into a Faustian bargain. This particular bargain involves Siltz offering to fund Porlock's research on cryogenics in exchange for ownership of all memories extracted from Feeld's head. Though horrified by Siltz's failure to appreciate the scientific, moral and cultural implications of his scheme as well as his drive to commodify that which she thinks ought to be sanctified, Porlock's dire financial situation leaves her little choice but to accept his proposition. In this sequence, the car is fetishized through close-ups occupying thirty-eight continuous seconds of screen time as we come to appreciate the implications of Siltz's success in buying the only direct link to British history and his plans for discarding memories of historical significance in favor of those marketable as pornographic entertainment for his "Nostalgia Channels."

Siltz's 1950s relics may effectively remind him of the heavily mythologized era in American history when major economic shifts made his type of wealth and influence possible. Although clearly significant to him, they are not filmed or framed in ways to evoke a nostalgic response in the audience. As suggestive of a crass materialism, their status as commodities is foregrounded. They are symbols of American wealth in an otherwise impoverished Britain and thus objects to be reviled. In *Cold Lazarus*, these objects are not tasked with providing an emotional connection to the past, notwithstanding their dominant presence in the broader nostalgia economy of American popular culture. Instead, they contribute to a juxtaposition pitting objects representative of a contrived and manufactured nostalgia against Feeld's "real" and authentic memories and thus form part of a visual system differentiating between two types of national nostalgia.

Karaoke and *Cold Lazarus* are not only nostalgic, they are also ostensibly about nostalgia. *Karaoke* is defined by a kind of very personal, self-indulgent nostalgia. It is littered with references to Potter's works in a manner seemingly intended to elevate them from the status of television event to cultural event. *Cold Lazarus*, on the other hand, mourns not only the loss of a broader British working-class culture. It also mourns the loss of the memory of (and potential to feel nostalgia for) that culture. At first glance, it may seem odd to oppose an "authentic" British working-class nostalgia and an "inauthentic" nostalgia for American material and visual culture. One might assume the more logical opposition to be between working-class culture and the "heritage" imperative of British conservatives. However, consideration of who Potter holds responsible for his losses — especially the loss of authentic representations of the past in a futuristic world — reveals key political alliances between British and American conservatives. For Potter, the passing of the "golden age" of television and the disappearance of working-class culture are the result of Thatcherite policies that, through the adoption of free-market economics, further Americanized British life in a way that led to the destruction of working-class livelihoods and made possible the outrageous wealth and widespread influence of individuals like Rupert Murdoch.

Though Potter blamed Thatcher's domestic policies for irreparably damaging many aspects of British society, he held Murdoch responsible for not only lowering the standards of television, but also for luring what he saw as impressionable audiences with the gloss of American culture away from challenging and intelligent drama. Yet, as much as Potter hated Thatcher, he despised Rupert Murdoch even more (as is evident from his decision to name his malignant pancreatic tumor "Rupert" rather than "Maggie"). He held Murdoch responsible for destroying British television and the edifying programming that once defined it. And it is Murdoch that Potter reincarnates as Siltz, a fountain of free market rhetoric interested only in maintaining the passivity and loyalty of his vast audience. He is a purveyor of inauthentic emotions designed to prevent viewers from recognizing the conditions of their existence. Gone is all concern for the quality of programming and the potential for television to both entertain and educate. Siltz is only interested in keeping his audiences passive enough to stop them from questioning their participation as obedient consumers in a system designed to secure his power. Initially, he sees this contrived nostalgia for an artificial, commodified past as the most effective tool for suppressing class consciousness, for deterring his audience from joining protest groups like the RONs. Upon discovering the capabilities of the frozen head, however, he suspects his intentions might best be achieved by transforming Daniel Feeld's authentic sexual memories into virtual reality entertainment.

Juxtapositions designed to reinforce the distinction between authentic British nostalgia and inauthentic American nostalgia take many different forms and involve popular songs, narrative devices and character constructions. In what follows, I want to consider a few visual strategies that play a role in *Cold Lazarus'* warnings about the future of history.

Throughout the serial, Porlock and her team are continually shocked by the content of Feeld's memories, specifically by what they reveal about Britain's history. They are visibly moved by moments personal and collective, traumatic and mundane. On one occasion, a sequence of sentimental images from Feeld's personal and Britain's collective past are followed by a cut to Masdon and her lover, Nat (Jonathan Cake), who happen to be in the midst of their own revisitation of the twentieth century. Masdon has somehow managed to obtain an "authentic" cowboy outfit, an invaluable artifact that she instructs Nat to wear for their sexual role-playing exploits. She too is appropriately dressed for this Hollywood Western fantasy. With an elaborately adorned corset and feather boa, she looks the part of a prostitute who might well have inhabited the kind of brothel patronized by John Wayne. Thus, Masdon and Nat's return to the twentieth century is one informed by cinematic constructions, a set of mediated images that propagated its own myths about the past. Masdon's history is a cinematic one at a double remove from the "real" and thus lacking the authenticity that Dr. Porlock's team can claim for what they extract from Feeld's frozen head. In *Cold Lazarus*, Feeld's images are revered as the unmediated, raw material of memory and history, granting direct access to real embodied experiences.[18] And it is because they are so real, so "authentic," that they have the capacity to provoke intense emotional responses in even the most stolid, rational individuals. By contrast, Masdon and Nat's historical engagement is little more than absurdly perverse, at once comical and disturbing for what it suggests about the fate of the past.

This juxtaposition between the authentic and inauthentic depends for its force and nuance on visual tropes that bring one genre into collision with another. The distinction between the costumes that define the Western and the futuristic dystopian landscapes that define *Cold Lazarus*' brand of science fiction is visually striking and ostensible in a way that leads to a further set of *conceptually* striking distinctions: between real history and mediated history, between real emotions and manufactured ones. Here we are presented with a potent visual reference to a genre that has done much to entrench a particular vision of nineteenth century America in the historical consciousness — despite later revisionist efforts to undo this. And we are encouraged to think about this in the context and through the discursive lens of science fiction, the genre responsible for issuing some of the last century's most powerful cautionary tales.

Another subtle yet pervasive visual juxtaposition worth noting is achieved through the careful application of color schemes to costumes and sets. Throughout *Cold Lazarus*, American characters appear dressed in garish, brightly-colored costumes made from synthetic and often rigid materials. Their carnivalesque quality is distinct from the flowing, loose-fitting, textured and muted earth-tone costumes worn by the British. This is a visual opposition reinforced by the various interior spaces inhabited by these characters. Potter's request that Masdon occupy a house with a "David Hockney" feel to it was realized through a palette dominated by vibrant pinks, greens and blues.[19] Like Martina's sprawling estate, Siltz's properties also stand as testaments to conspicuous consumption. Siltz's London hotel seems to have been inspired by the look of postwar Technicolor Hollywood epics set in Roman gladiatorial times. As the camera tilts slowly upwards to scan the façade, an excerpt from a stereotypical epic film score underlines this cinematic reference. By contrast, nature, and not Hollywood, appears to have infiltrated otherwise highly futuristic British design and decor. Certain fixtures in Dr. Porlock's science lab — a space that lends itself to modernist, functionalist orthodoxy — are organic in shape. Mechanized chairs used by the scientists to dart across the laboratory look like curled leaves while support pillars resemble the trunks of trees in an old growth forest.

In a future devoid of vegetation, these allusions to nature are allusions to the past, to the pastoral idylls deeply entrenched in the British cultural consciousness. They also point to Potter's own personal idyll, the Forest of Dean, a place of trauma and joy, camaraderie and alienation, and one associated with his working-class childhood in most of his television serials. Perhaps these organic traces, these traces of nature, survive as persistent reminders of a "real" or, what is often described as an "organic," working-class culture. And perhaps these traces are reminder enough of what has been lost — even if only at an unconscious level — to facilitate the emergence of protest and the formation of the RONs. As their acronym suggests, RONs privilege reality over everything, regardless of how painful or challenging it might be. Once Dr. Glasunov realizes how Feeld might serve the RON agenda, he excitedly proclaims: "You should ... scrape out the poor creature's memories, and show billions of people out there that, yes, there were other ways to live. The past can stand in front of us for once, challengingly, and not be safely anaesthetized in the long, long ago. Let the past speak! Let it accuse!"

As a massive archive of historical information, the laboratory's central computer also plays a role in attempts to privilege the "real." Like Feeld, the computer can recall specific facts and events of twentieth century history. However, these are facts without emotional or even social context and can only be retrieved by precisely formulated questions. While virtual reality exists in a highly advanced form in the twenty-fourth century, artificial intelligence certainly does not. The computer is very un-human and little more than a repository of poorly organized facts. Its capacity to access history pales in comparison to Feeld's ability to show how life was lived and culture shared. He showed the scientists images from a working-class life that was unknown to them and not part of the supposedly comprehensive history contained in the computer. They were shocked to see images of working-class community, of places where people congregated in shared pursuits like a crowded football stadium. Feeld's memories may be triggered by a longing for that which has passed, they may even be distorted by trauma, but they remain much preferred to those offered up by the computer.

Although *Cold Lazarus* is set in the twenty-fourth century, its concern is with history, with how it is constructed, mediated and used, and with its capacity to effect change. And, the complexity with which *Cold Lazarus* probes history is, first and foremost, the province of its visual dimensions. Indeed, those aspects faulted for condemning the serial as bad or cheap-looking science fiction are ultimately the ones responsible for its sophisticated critiques. It is through props, costumes and set design that make use of culturally loaded objects and aesthetic schemes that *Cold Lazarus* evaluates and distinguishes between two types of nostalgia and two modes of engaging history.

It is in light of this that I would like to make a brief return to Creeber's alignment of Potter with Jameson in their mutual condemnation of postmodernism. Creeber is absolutely right to highlight their shared distaste for the harm postmodernism has apparently inflicted on our sense of history and our access to it. However, I think both Jameson and Potter are wrong about this, and *Cold Lazarus* shows why. The various constructions of visual pastness encountered throughout the serial play a central role in its judgement of postwar Americanization, Thatcherism and Murdoch-style entertainment. They do not obfuscate or sever our connection to the past as Jameson claims.[20] (Nor do they work against the critical aims of narrative as, Andrew Higson suggests, is the effect of visual spectacles at the heart of British heritage drama.[21]) Indeed, *Cold Lazarus* can be included amongst a growing number of films and television productions that mobilize various types of visual pastness in order to engage with history and the relationship between the past and the present.[22]

Accessing this particular aspect of the serial cannot be accomplished through an auteurist approach alone. It is certainly necessary to acknowledge how Potter's signature, biography, narrative strategies and intentions shape *Cold Lazarus* into what it is. But it is also crucial that we acknowledge how its visual devices — aspects that have received short shrift in Potter criticism — contribute immeasurably to the serial's critical nuance and complexity. As the product of countless and often undocumented collaborations, these fall outside the purview of the author-centered scholarship on Potter's work. Moreover, it is also crucial to consider how these visual devices — props, costume and set design — function in the context of the genre of the serial. For even though *Cold Lazarus* might disappoint as science fiction, in the end, it is its status as science fiction and its mobilization of a visually rich and richly layered future world to which we should attribute the depth and sophistication of its critique of the future of history and thus much of its value as a culturally significant television text.

11

Expatriate! Expatriate!
Doctor Who: The Movie *and Commercial Negotiation of a Multiple Text*

PETER WRIGHT

From 1963, the BBC's *Doctor Who* (1963–89, 2005–) was the quintessential manifestation of British television science fiction, even after its cancellation in 1989.[1] That changed on 14 May 1996, when *Doctor Who: The Movie*, an Anglo-American co-production financed by the BBC, its Worldwide division, Universal Television and Fox, aired on the Fox network.[2] To those familiar with the original serial, it was obvious that *Doctor Who* had undergone substantial reinvention for U.S. television. Charges of "commercialization" and "Americanization" inevitably followed. These assessments were never substantiated, however, and the nature of *Doctor Who*'s revision has remained largely unexplored. Given *Doctor Who*'s importance as a British popular cultural phenomenon, this chapter examines its adaptation for a wider viewing public. It discusses how the telefilm employs intertextuality and shifts in genre to transform the ideology of *Doctor Who* in an attempt to secure an ill-defined mass audience. It also demonstrates how the producer, director and writer tried to reconcile old and new viewers while "clawing back" the Doctor to a point of socio-centrality.[3] Finally, it argues that rather than being subject to some vague process of "Americanization," *Doctor Who: The Movie* reflects a specific form of cultural imperialism.

Essentially, Universal aimed to use the film to gain sufficiently high North American ratings to make a future series viable.[4] Of course, the film also had to appeal to existing fans, since they formed an important market for the product and attendant merchandising. The film's hybrid crew reflected this desire to satisfy both American and British audiences. Philip Segal, the producer and motivating power behind the telefilm, epitomized "two cultures colliding on set."[5] Segal was born in Essex, England, but spent most of his professional life in Hollywood. In

1991 he joined Steven Spielberg's Amblin Television as Head of Production, where he created the disappointing *Seaquest DSV* (1993–1996). He also secured a production deal for *Doctor Who* having pursued the option for almost six years.[6] His motivation derived wholly from being a fan who was "not interested in tearing the fabric of the show apart."[7] Nevertheless, Segal felt that the program relied "too much on its own history instead of broadening its outlook."[8] He believed the show's consistent intratextuality opposed wider popularity by alienating new viewers.

Despite Segal's presence, American involvement in *Doctor Who* caused consternation amongst fans who feared the program might be "Americanized."[9] Suppressing his own reservations about the "cultish" nature of the BBC production, Segal reassured fans that this would not occur. Speaking as Head of Production at Amblin in 1995, he admitted: "I do not think 'Americanising' the show is healthy for *Doctor Who* ... Fans should know that one of the guarantees I have made to the BBC is that I am not going to do anything to damage the 'Britishness' of the show."[10]

The notion of "Britishness" to which Segal refers requires some explanation, since without an understanding of the characteristics of the 1963–1989 series it is difficult to comprehend fully its later transformation. In *Doctor Who: The Unfolding Text* (1983), John Tulloch and Manuel Alvarado identify the fundamental qualities underlying the program's lauded "Britishness." Primarily, they see *Doctor Who* as "an institution in British cultural life" wherein the Doctor is "very much the English gentleman."[11] Unlike many American television protagonists, the Doctor is neither superhuman nor invulnerable. He is fallible and often idiosyncratic. Throughout his various incarnations he remains "an alien, an outsider, with an egocentric and often solipsistic aestheticism," dedicated to overthrowing despotism.[12] He "consistently adopted that liberal populist role in criticising 'sectionalist' forces of 'Left' and 'Right,' and in rebuking the 'official' and the powerful in big business, the military, government or militant unions."[13] As a liberal, the BBC Doctor occupied neutral political ground from where he criticized socially, morally, and aesthetically, the mores of his contemporary audience. His neutrality and critical role reflected the BBC's self-professed political and social agenda, which made him an extension of programming policy. Hence, he was not merely an English gentleman, but an English gentleman grounded in the British socio-political context, acting as a spokesman for or, at least, a symbol of the BBC. It is this cultural embedding that engendered the program with much of its inimitable and contemporaneous "Britishness."

This "Britishness" was developed further through the program's creative remit. Originally conceived to assist the teaching of science and history to children, *Doctor Who* was informed intermittently by explicit and implicit pedagogic discourses. As Tulloch and Alvarado argue, it drew on the soft science of its Wellsian model to investigate alternate cultures and advocate "a responsible cultural perspectivism."[14] Accordingly, it promotes "a liberal discourse of 'tolerance' and 'balance' against the militaristic tendencies of the Bug Eyed Monster (BEM) syndrome."[15]

When Segal stated that he wished to preserve the serial's "Britishness," it seems likely he intended to translate the Doctor's eccentricity, his liberalism, and his critical role to an American context. He explained that unless the financiers were "willing to embrace the mythology and everything that makes the show what it is, we're not going to do it. We're not going to turn the Doctor into something he is not."[16] Read in the light of the film, these assurances seem naïve, possibly because Segal did not appreciate how important the BBC's public service broadcasting (PSB) role was to its British ambience. Indeed, it is likely that Segal found his idealism impossible to sustain due to the commercial criteria to which he was forced to adhere. By 1996, Segal's drive for fidelity had been diluted by commercial necessity: "It was very important for me to tell a story that American audiences could enjoy, without having to understand all the mythology," he admitted. "I think that's the responsibility of doing what I call an international *Doctor Who*."[17]

In sacrificing his commitment to *Doctor Who*'s "mythology," Segal adopted the attitude of British director Geoffrey Sax. A realist, Sax understood the film had "to be accessible and understandable to a whole new audience. But at the same time, we do need to keep happy the people who have stuck with *Doctor Who* over the years, so we've included certain references which, even if they are lost on a new audience, won't make any difference to their understanding."[18]

Sax's perspective — and strategy of balancing new audience enjoyment and comprehension with fannish references — was shared by British screenwriter Matthew Jacobs. As Steve Eramo notes, "not only did he [Jacobs] have to make the new *Doctor Who* film recognisable and entertaining to die hard *Who* fans but also interesting enough to the uninitiated viewer looking to watch a fantastical adventure and love story."[19] Jacob's brief, and his perceptions of how an American audience might react to the film, made him concentrate on certain fundamentals.[20] "What I really wanted to do," he explained:

> was write a story where the audience's main task is understanding the Doctor.... This meant you need to have the show's most accessible villain in the movie, which in many ways is the Doctor's rival Time Lord, the Master. Through their battle with each other the audience finds out who the Doctor is, why he's here as well as the fact that the Master does not care the least about saving Earth. The Doctor does though because of who the Doctor is.[21]

Collectively, Segal, Sax and Jacobs generated an adventure intended to "internationalize" the Doctor. As Sylvester McCoy (the Seventh Doctor) observed, "I think it's [the film's] now becoming a worldwide thing rather than an American thing."[22] This observation suggests that any attempt to categorize the telefilm as an Americanization because it is made within an American production system for a largely American audience simplifies the form of the adaptation and denies the global origins of some of the images, intertexts and allusions informing the text.[23]

Ironically, despite all the discussion of new and international audiences, Segal and his co-workers had little awareness of their target audiences. One might expect, then, that the involvement of the Fox Network would shape the production towards its audience demographic. This was not the case. In 1995, Fox's demographic base was largely African-American and Latin American men aged eighteen to twenty-five. This was a less-than-ideal market for *Doctor Who: The Movie*, a white drama whose only ethnic character is Chang Lee (Yee Jee Tso), a Chinese hoodlum who robs, opposes, and sacrifices himself for the Doctor.[24] Even allowing for the kind of negotiated interaction found by Elihu Katz and Tamar Liebes in their 1984 study of the subcultural reception of *Dallas* (U.S., CBS, 1978–1991), it seemed unlikely that ethnic audiences would find the telefilm engaging — a supposition borne out by its poor U.S. viewing figures.[25]

Hence, the co-production developed with only the vaguest attention paid to potential audiences. With no-one actively identifying viewers, or considering how the film might be tailored for certain audiences, the film's producers seemed to settle on strategies they believed capable of attracting as many viewers as possible. From textual evidence, the methods applied were the deployment of a utilitarian intertextuality, intended to reconcile existing and new audiences, and revisions to the show's generic character. As Ien Ang has argued, the formulation of institutional strategies unrelated to actual audiences is not unusual since

> in the considerations of the institutions that possess the official power to define, exploit and regulate the space in which television is inserted in the fabric of culture and society [the] subjective, complex and dynamic forms of audiencehood [...] disappear in favour of a mute and abstract construction of "television audience" onto which large-scale economic and cultural aspirations and expectations, policies and planning schemes are projected.[26]

Segal and his collaborators were, as Ang remarks of PSB and commercial television producers, adopting

> an instrumental view of the audience as an object to be conquered. Whether the primary intention is to transfer meaningful messages or to gain and attract attention, in both cases the audience is structurally placed at the reception end of a linear one-way process.[27]

To "transfer meaningful messages," to guide interpretation and direct comprehension, *Doctor Who: The Movie* uses intertextuality for four interrelated purposes, although the forms are not as discrete in their narrative positioning as the following critically convenient categories suggest. Firstly, "familiarizing intertexts" reassure new audiences that *Doctor Who* is not an exotic artifact but is situated within familiar generic territory. Secondly, "commercial intertexts" attempt to secure the loyalty of *Who*'s commercially important fandom by maintaining continuity between BBC-produced *Doctor Who* and the telefilm. Thirdly, "explicative intertexts" clarify the more idiosyncratic elements of *Doctor Who*— regeneration particularly — to unfamiliar audiences. Finally, "revisionist intertexts" transform the Doctor's character and establish a foundation for the generic alterations occurring simultaneously. In each case, the term "intertext" refers to "one or more texts the reader [or viewer] must know in order to understand a [text] [...] in terms of its overall significance."[28] While a partial understanding of the process of adaptation can be obtained from apprehending one or two of these forms of intertextuality, a complete comprehension of the "overall significance" of the film can only be gained by perceiving all four forms and their various interrelationships.

The process of familiarizing new audiences using intertextuality begins with the telefilm's opening graphics sequence. Amalgamating the vortex-tunnel from original *Doctor Who* with *Star Trek*-like sound effects, the film heralds, not a velocity-distorted U.S.S. *Enterprise* but American-style credits that list the "Special Guest Star" and those "Guest Starring" in the production. Although the presence of the vortex may reassure *Who* fans, the derivative aural and visual intertexts to *Trek* seem intended to seduce *Star Trek's* enormous North American audience. The new arrangement of the *Doctor Who* theme is more strident and upbeat, recalling the score of the 1966–69 *Star Trek* (U.S., NBC). This transition, through which *Doctor Who* recalls *Star Trek*, however temporarily or superficially, facilitates the new viewer's understanding of the telefilm as television genre science fiction, as something familiar. Paradoxically, and intelligently, the title sequence attempts to reassure and inform a new audience with its allusions to *Star Trek* just as it reassures existing audiences with its celebrated imagery and theme music. Indeed, the presence of aural references to *Star Trek* establishes the criteria of familiarization utilized throughout the film.[29] As the narrative develops, such "familiarizing intertexts" become increasingly interwoven with "commercial intertexts."

Commercial intertexts were seen as vital to the success of the movie. As many *Doctor Who* fans consume related merchandise maintaining continuity with the series, it was necessary for the telefilm to exhibit a similar continuity if it was to exploit comparable markets.[30] Although "the fans' total membership will amount to about half a percent of the audience at the absolute maximum,"[31] they are financially significant. Hence, Segal's treatment was intertextually linked to the original series. The film opens by showing the last minutes of the Doctor's seventh incarnation, thereby linking *Doctor Who: The Movie* to the last televised BBC adventure, Rona Munro's ironically titled "Survival" (1989). This continuity qualifies the telefilm as canonical *Doctor Who* and seeks to exploit fan loyalty. In turn, for completists, the video release, script and novelization all become potential acquisitions with varying degrees of importance. The profitability of maintaining continuity was demonstrated later by the film's merchandizing sales, which included 150,000 copies of the video release (worth £2.25 million in retail sales), 55,000 copies of Gary Russell's novelization (£330,000) and 15,000 copies of Jacob's script (£105,000).[32] (The profitability of the DVD edition of the film, released in August 2001, is unknown.)

In terms of its narrative, the film falls into two distinct sections. The first twenty-two minutes leading to the Doctor's seventh regeneration are designed for followers of the original series. Beginning with a methodical and reflective introductory voiceover by the (as yet unknown) Eighth Doctor, the film establishes economically the major elements of its slender plot. The viewer learns that the Master, now awaiting execution on "the planet Skaro," is the "old enemy" of the narrator who introduces himself as "the Doctor, a rival Time Lord." Like the Master, he hails from Gallifrey. The croaking, electronic voices of (the unnamed and unseen — presumably for copyright reasons) Daleks intrude, rasping "Exterminate! Exterminate!" and reduce the Master to cinders.

Anyone familiar with *Doctor Who* will recognize, and is likely to be reassured by, the presence of the Doctor and the Master. The mention of Skaro (the Dalek homeworld) and the inclusion of the strangely remodulated Dalek voices are keyed to appeal to initiated viewers by remaining obscure. Such individuals will recognize the intertexts and "conspire" with the film's producers behind the backs of those unfamiliar with the series to appreciate more than the newcomer. In short, the opening narration invites existing *Who* audiences to congratulate themselves on observing how these intertextual references are embedded and how their full referential potential is available only to a (privileged?) minority. However, while viewers may compliment themselves for apprehending such references, they may overlook the essentialism of the introduction and its redundancy for followers of the program.

For those new to *Doctor Who*, the introduction is vital for establishing the characters of, and the antagonism between, the Doctor and the Master, and for emphasizing their alien origins. They are Time Lords, an allusive phrase that suggests their power over the temporal flow. To new audiences, "Skaro" and the Dalek voices possess no resonance; they transmit little information that is critical or relevant. They are simply a curious neologism and a babble of peculiar sound effects. The reduction of the Daleks from cultural icon and powerful metaphor for totalitarian authority to a gaggle of off-screen, apolitical voices is emblematic of the irrelevance of most "concessions" to continuity.

Such intertextual ornamentation, which implies continuity without sustaining it, is explicit as the Seventh Doctor settles himself in the marvellously redesigned TARDIS console room. A cavernous area of non-time, the console room is a complex synthesis of Edwardian furnishing, Gothic architecture, and "Steampunk" retrograde technology littered with relics from the Doctor's past, including his famous sonic screwdriver. Such relics, which connote the program's history, remind the initiated audience of the Doctor's colorful past and that his character is subject to transformation. Though they might continue to reassure the informed viewer that, despite stylistic differences, elements of canonical *Doctor Who* are being preserved, they are as redundant as the Daleks.[33] Segal emphasizes the superficiality of the presence of such icons when he observes, "Over the years, fans got to enjoy different things — jelly-babies, sonic screwdrivers, sticks of celery, yo-yos, umbrellas — all of those things that became symbols of each character. And I think we've taken a lot of these things and put them into the show."[34] Not only does this observation imply Segal's simplistic view of what appeals to fans, but also the "taking and putting in" approach reflects how he mistakes presence for resonance, how he believes the mere appearance of these objects will, in some ambiguous manner, evoke the sensibility of the original program.

Situated amongst the commercial intertexts of the opening console scene, yet anticipating later revisionist intertexts, is a copy of H.G. Wells's *The Time Machine* (1895). The novel has two functions. Firstly, it reminds existing viewers of the Doctor's literary origins and, secondly, it provides a vital intertextual reference point for unfamiliar audiences. *Doctor Who*'s connection with *The Time Machine*, which is perfectly justifiable providing it is located within the show's larger context and rich narrative history, appears intended to provoke existing audiences into acknowledging that the program was already a retelling of an older story. Of course, once *Doctor Who* has been identified as a version of Wells's novel, what uniqueness it acquired throughout its preceding twenty-six seasons is undermined. With its claims to originality challenged, it is vulnerable to adaptation, to transformation, since it has been revealed as a variation of an earlier conceit itself. By exposing *Doctor Who* as an adaptation in the first place, Segal apparently attempts to forestall any objections raised against his contemporary reworking.

For new viewers, *The Time Machine* has a vital explicative function, signposting the nature of the Doctor and his TARDIS. By providing the Doctor with a book that is both the source of, and an analogy with, *Doctor Who* itself, the filmmakers supply the disorientated viewer with a cultural artifact from which they can obtain orientation, providing they are familiar with Wells's novel. Importantly, though, unlike later explicative intertexts, *The Time Machine* is not a revisionist intertext since it does not change fundamentally the nature of *Doctor Who* itself.

When the Master escapes as slime from his casket — a clear allusion to Pandora's Box — he forces the TARDIS to land in San Francisco on 30 December 1999. At this point, the film abandons much of its derivative commercial intertextuality in favor of intertexts from alternative cultural sources seemingly designed to familiarize new audiences further and revise *Doctor Who* for a new, global reception.

Although this familiarization began with the insertion of *The Time Machine*, the retention of *Doctor Who*'s existing audience left Segal with a problem: how to explain the Doctor's regeneration into a younger man hypothetically more suited to a mass audience. His solution was to introduce what can be termed "revisionist intertexts." A revisionist intertext is one which, when introduced into an episodic serial (in this case BBC-produced *Doctor Who*), causes fundamental changes in the defining features of that textuality, whether in terms of characterization, narrative structure, or socio-political perspective. This notion is illustrated best by considering the regeneration sequence, the appearance of the Eighth Doctor, and their effects on narrative development.

After crash-landing on Earth, the Doctor is shot by street gangs in a sequence wholly at odds with the visibly contrived action of the original and strongly reminiscent of American police dramas. The Doctor's shooting marks the point of departure from the conventions of "traditional" *Doctor Who*. As he falls victim to random crime, it is obvious that the Seventh Doctor, wry, mysterious, and Machiavellian, is not a fit candidate for an "international" Doctor Who; framed as powerless, he has ceased to be at the center of events. His vulnerability is emphasized after Chang Lee takes him to Walker General Hospital. In the emergency room — a location which acts, like the allusions to *Star Trek*, as a point of reference for any new viewer accustomed to *ER* (U.S., NBC, 1994–2009) or *Chicago Hope* (U.S., Fox, 1994–2000) — the surgeons detect his irregular heartbeat.[35] Believing the x-ray of the Doctor's bi-cardial cardiovascular system to be a double exposure, the resonantly named Doctor Grace Holloway (Daphne Ashbrook) attempts to correct the fibrillation, despite the Doctor's protests that he is "not human." He "dies" during the procedure.[36]

With the Seventh Doctor dead, the telefilm's intertextuality seems intended to satisfy two requirements: firstly, to communicate the nature of the Doctor's regeneration through explicative intertexts and, secondly, to transform the characters of the Doctor and his archenemy, the Master, using revisionist intertexts. In contrived parallel sequences, the Doctor and the Master undergo rebirths figured through such explicative and revisionist material. Having escaped the TARDIS, the Master insinuates himself in the home of paramedic Bruce (Eric Roberts). As Bruce sleeps, the Master reappears as a translucent cobra (an image the BBC thought clichéd[37]). He rears over Bruce's open mouth and plunges down his throat. At this point two intertexts inform the narrative. Firstly, the act of oral rape recalls those occurring in the *Alien* films and connotes the invasive power of the Master. Secondly, and more significantly, his appearance as a snake equates him with the Edenic serpent and Satan, a character rescripting exploited throughout the remainder of the film.

In the hospital morgue, the camera crosscuts between the Doctor on his slab and Pete the attendant (William Sasso) watching *Frankenstein* (U.S., James Whale, 1931) on television. "It's alive! It's alive!" proclaims Henry Frankenstein (Colin Clive) as a further crosscut links the Monster's (Boris Karloff's) twitching hand with the spasmodic movements of the Doctor's fingers. As the Monster lurches so the Eighth Doctor jerks upright. A blade of light slashes across his eyes, recalling a similar — and now iconic — shot of Bela Lugosi in *Dracula* (U.S., Tod Browning, 1931).

Whilst these visual parallels are a homage to Universal's most famous productions, the visual references to *Frankenstein* and, less obviously, to *Dracula* facilitate the new viewer's understanding of Time Lord regeneration. In this way, the film reflects its understanding of a phenomenon first observed by Michael Riffaterre, who argues that:

> The urge to understand compels the reader [or viewer] to look to the intertext to fill out the text's gaps, spell out its implications and find out what rules of ideolectic grammar account for the text's departures from logic, from accepted usage (that is, from

the sociolect), from the cause-and-effect sequence of the narrative, and from verisimilitude in the descriptive [...].[38]

In the context of the telefilm, the gap the unfamiliar viewer has to "fill out" is an understanding of the Doctor's regeneration. The intertext, present on the screen, provides a popular culture parallel (approximately equivalent to the "accepted usage" Riffaterre refers to and deriving from the "sociolect" of classic horror film) to explain the roles of the "ideolectic grammar" or the peculiar conventions of *Doctor Who*'s transformations of its main character. The ease with which unfamiliar viewers can make such a connection is also emphasized by Riffaterre: "[...] obviously, when the culture which the text reflects is still within reach, the readers' task is facilitated by the frequency of references to well-known signposts, or just by chance encounters with them [...]."[39] Clearly, classic Hollywood movies are still very much "within reach" of contemporary television audiences and provide a multinational currency of intertexts in which to trade.

The intertextual presence of *Frankenstein* indicates that the Doctor is undergoing a process of rebirth, or resurrection, analogous to that experienced by the Monster. Of course, such a comparison risks provoking an aberrant decoding in the audience by associating the Doctor with a "monster" rather than anticipating the hero he will become. To counter this potential aberrant decoding, the references to *Frankenstein* and *Dracula* are augmented by revisionist intertexts identifying the Doctor explicitly with Christ. As the Doctor regenerates, galvanic flashes illuminate his covering sheet. This Frankensteinian imagery is hybridized by the sight of his form radiating though the cover and recalling the Shroud of Turin. When the Doctor bursts from his vault, his emergence recasts the events at Gethsemane. Again, the Doctor's rebirth is mediated through familiar iconic imagery. That is, "ideolectic" peculiarities are explained through "sociolectic" allusions.

The association between Christ and the Doctor is developed further when he lurches into an abandoned ward. Here he hums a melody from Puccini's *Madame Butterfly* (1898) (identified for the audience earlier in the film), an explicative high culture aural cue to his miraculous transformation that affirms the popular cultural reference to *Frankenstein*. In the empty ward, Sax bombards the viewer with visual clues to the Doctor's confused mental state. Wandering dazedly, he sees eight images of himself in a fractured mirror, each symbolizing his eight incarnations. The separation of these images implies that his composite persona is detached from its own past. A broken baby doll with its head turned backwards symbolically suggests the Eighth Doctor's innocence, his recent rebirth, and his need to look back memoriously in dense visual shorthand that can only be appreciated on re-watching. When the Doctor falls to his knees and cries, "WHO AM I?" from the depths, according to Jacobs's screenplay, of his "very soul,"[40] the desperate, agonized question sees the Doctor, arms widespread, crucified by incomprehension. He looks up (to God?) and folds himself in the sheet he has worn from the morgue. With his wild hair and robe-like costume, the Doctor is framed authoritatively and unequivocally as Christ.

If this sequence was not sufficiently explicit, Pete later remarks how the Doctor "was wearing a shroud and a JD tag on his toe." Grace regards him sceptically and replies, "Somehow, I don't think the Second Coming happens here." Grace's line provides an important disclaimer: the Doctor's recovery is a secular parousia. To avoid offending Christian viewers with its potential blasphemy, the film attempts to deny the religious parallels it establishes. Later, as the Doctor explains his rivalry with the Master, Grace asks: "This Master — is he like the Devil?" "No! The Master is a rival Time Lord. Pure evil," he reassures her (and the audience). This denial only serves to emphasize that the Satanic and Christ-like imagery deployed around the two Time Lords is present to facilitate understanding. To frame a conflict between two incompletely understood aliens as antagonism between the more familiar Western cultural figures of Christ and the Devil is to assist comprehension in an audience unfamiliar with the lengthy war of personalities, egos and morals fought between the Doctor and his archenemy.

The visual, explicative shorthand that associates the Doctor and the Master with Christ and Satan is so conspicuous that primary school children were able to make the connections. The observations of the children at Ibstock School, South London,[41] indicate how closely — and successfully — the film controls its audiences' decoding of the text. Although this perspective denies the ability of audiences to read texts variously, Morley understands that "the power of viewers to reinterpret meanings is hardly equivalent to the discursive power of centralized media institutions to construct the texts which the viewer then interprets; to imagine otherwise is simply foolish."[42]

Hence, to talk about an institutionally-shaped adaptation of *Doctor Who* with an intended interpretation and associated effects does not seem inappropriate, particularly when the text "activates or mobilises" intertexts to leave "little leeway to" viewers and thereby "closely controls their response."[43] As John Fiske remarks, "No text is simply a pattern of signifiers: a text is a bearer of meanings and relating signifiers to meaning is not just a matter of applying them to appropriate signifieds. Rather they limit the area within which the meanings may be found."[44] By defining the locations where meaning may be found, the producers of *Doctor Who: The Movie* seek to ensure comprehension of the characters before developing the plot.

The recasting of the Doctor and his archenemy as Christ and Satan is more important than this, however. Such rescripting of characters marks the point where the conventions and qualities of the BBC's *Doctor Who* begin to be revised by the telefilm's intertexts. Having visually and explicitly circumscribed the seemingly mythic natures of its antagonists, the film deploys an apocalyptic plot, punctuated with further familiarizing and explicative intertexts.

With Bruce's body decaying around him like Brundlefly (Jeff Goldblum) in *The Fly* (U.S., David Cronenberg, 1986), the Master, now dressed like the Terminator (as played by Arnold Schwarzenegger in *The Terminator* [U.S./U.K., James Cameron, 1984]) plans to invade the Doctor's more suitable Gallifreyan form. To achieve this, he uses a hypnotized Chang Lee to open the Eye of Harmony, the TARDIS's power source.[45] This initiates a battle for the Doctor's body and soul. As the Doctor explains to Grace: "if I look into the Eye of Harmony my soul will be destroyed and he [the Master] will take my body." For the first time, *Doctor Who* obtains a spiritual dimension which weakens the rationalism underpinning the BBC's conception and moves the film away from the specificity of the Christ-Satan conflict into a more generalized spiritual battle. The loss of his soul is not the only danger the Doctor must face, however. With the Eye now open, the Earth is likely to be pulled through the TARDIS's power source at the turn of the millennium.

Against this apocalyptic background, the Doctor searches for an atomic clock with which he can "close the Eye." He eventually gains access to the Institute of Technological Advancement and Research where (somewhat fortuitously) a beryllium clock is about to be started. As the Doctor steals the beryllium chip, the camera focuses on the gold cross embossed on its surface. Nowhere are the religious parallels conveyed more directly than here. What was once a secular struggle between two Time Lords is now a spiritual conflict for souls, futures and (somewhat punningly) states of Grace.

Back at the TARDIS, the Doctor and Grace realize the Eye has been open too long to save the world; the Doctor must move the TARDIS back in time to before the Eye opened. As he attempts this, the Master neutralizes Grace and captures the Doctor. Using an apparatus reminiscent of the device employed for conditioning Alex (Malcolm McDowell) in *A Clockwork Orange* (Stanley Kubrick, 1971) and the Crown of Thorns, Lee helps the Master chain the Doctor above the Eye. The final conflict sees Lee rebel against the Master, who kills him, and Grace liberated from the Master's power. In the console room, Grace invokes God and, according to Jacobs's screenplay, "connects two wires — the right wires. The finger of God! A massive spark [...]."[46] erupts as the TARDIS dematerializes. In the finale, the Master is sucked into the Eye and Grace is killed. Grief-stricken, the Doctor moves the TARDIS back to 29 December 1999 when Lee and Grace are miraculously resurrected by golden radiance pouring from the Eye. Grace assures the Doctor that "There is nothing to be scared of," thereby completing the film's underlying spiritual message. Her resurrection also overturns an unwritten but fundamental rule of the *Doctor Who* universe, which states that once the TARDIS has landed in a specific time and place, the events precipitated by its arrival cannot be revised through any convenient jaunts back in time to "set things right."[47]

The inclusion of Christian-derived intertexts, the battle for the Doctor's body and soul, and the miraculous restoration of Earth, Grace and Lee, effects a substantial shift in *Doctor Who*'s usual political foci. In associating the Doctor with Christ, the producers no longer characterize him as a social reformer. Rather than continuing in his critical "liberal populist role," the Doctor is rescripted as a conservative. Although his association with Christ appears to raise him "above" worldly politics, he is a savior disinterested in resolving the power relationships and injustices of the contemporary status quo. Capitalists, dictators, terrorists, reformers, liberals, conservatives, and socialists are all restored, in their current political positions, when the Doctor saves Earth. He is, in effect, a spent force for social justice and reformation.

Unlike the BBC Doctor, the "helper of the underdog, the underprivileged, and all those who [...] are discriminated against [...] in a word not the 'fantastic' man of the all–American dream but the general human good guy,"[48] the Eighth Doctor is a "fantastic" man. He derives not from the American dream but from a politically sanitized vision of the Christian savior whose love for humanity is boundless. Unfortunately, that love, which remains understated and mysterious throughout the BBC serial, is inextricably associated in the telefilm with his need to save himself. Consequently, the salvation of Earth is moved into the background while the antagonism between the Doctor and the Master takes center stage. The narrative's emphasis on the personal battle between rival Time Lords conceals the Doctor's (and the film's) conservative position since the Doctor and the Master are depicted as generalized representatives of good and evil, rather than Left or Right, oppressor and oppressed. Accordingly, the film becomes a shadow play of abstract notions rather than the political parable an audience familiar with *Doctor Who* might expect. It seems probable that this abstract quality was designed to avoid alienating any potential viewer who might find *Doctor Who*'s traditional political stance oppositional.

The revisionist intertexts re-presenting the Doctor and his nemesis as mythic figures begin the process by which they, and *Doctor Who* as a cultural document, are clawed back to a socio-central political position through an emergent and uncritical conservatism and an uncharacteristic faith in technology. This process is extended by the generic shifts occurring as the narrative unfolds.

Central to the Doctor's social repositioning is the introduction of a romantic subplot which moves *Doctor Who* towards the romance-adventure genre. The main consequence of this is the heterosexualization of the Doctor. Between 1963 and 1989, the Doctor was never coded as a sexual figure. Historically, his lack of romantic interest in his companions lent him an aesthetic asexuality that contributed to his mysteriousness and allowed speculation regarding his sexual orientation. This speculation is rendered obsolete when the Doctor kisses Grace. This one incident, which provoked more controversy amongst fans than any other aspect of the telefilm, marks a shift in character and in genre. The Doctor, once a celibate intellectual, is recast as a romantic hero. Unwilling to tolerate even the possibility of the Doctor being read as gay, the film heterosexualizes him for what are probably pragmatic and commercial reasons.

The Doctor's heterosexualization does not exist in a vacuum. Opposite his relationship with Grace is the Master's recruitment of the impressionable Chang Lee. Since these are the only close relationships the Time Lords form with humans, the narrative parallels are explicit. Where the Doctor enlists Grace with his eccentric charm and good looks, the Master's "seduction" of Chang Lee is based on lies and promises of wealth and power. Having already witnessed the Master's phallic-form orally penetrating and, in a gross visual pun, "getting inside" Bruce, the viewer recognizes that the Master is framed, subtextually and homophobically, as a predatory queer. His corruption of naïve youth Lee plays on this monstrous notion. Indeed, his acknowledgement of Lee as "the son I always yearned for" has a distinct paedophilic resonance, given the ambiguity of "yearn."

Although the Master's possible homosexuality is never stated openly, the campness he expresses at the end certainly provides him with a queer resonance. His scarlet Time Lord robes associate him visually with Q (John DeLancie) from *Star Trek: The Next Generation* (U.S., Paramount, 1987–1994), a character who almost demands a queer reading through his "evocation of subcultural codes of camp performance."[49] "I always dress for the occasion," intones the Master as he sweeps down the stairs of the TARDIS's cloister room with more than a nod to Tim Curry's performance as Frank 'n' Furter in *The Rocky Horror Picture Show* (U.K./U.S., Jim Sharman, 1975). Added to the Master's subsequent pawing of Lee, these connotations identify him as a monstrous queer with a pseudo-incestuous desire for his "son."[50]

By "reassuring" the audience that the Doctor is straight and his archenemy a dangerous queer, the telefilm reflects and sustains conservative and homophobic attitudes by associating heterosexuality with "goodness" and homosexuality with rape and paedophilia. By pandering to a hypothetically homophobic audience, the film valorizes heterosexual relationships. Again, the Doctor's potential to question the status quo — here through his traditionally ambiguous sexual orientation — is undermined by the fixing of his sexuality.

The movement towards adventure-romance raised a problem: how to ensure that those who enjoy romances are not discomfited by the idea of an alien hero initiating sexual contact with a nice American thirty-something — a source of horror in Fox's main science fiction show, *The X-Files* (U.S., Fox, 1993–2002). Accordingly, the Doctor was clawed back further. In the scene following the Doctor's first kiss, the Master is studying the Doctor's eye in the TARDIS's cloister room. With surprise, the Master exclaims: "The Doctor is half-human!" Later, the Doctor admits to Grace he is "half-human. On my mother's side." This disclosure, which reaffirms other New Testament parallels, serves no narrative purpose. It is a commercial decision in which mainstream ideology — to be heterosexual and human is "normal" and, therefore, acceptable — further alters conventional *Doctor Who*. Unfortunately, the Eighth Doctor's acknowledgement of his parentage contradicts the Seventh Doctor's earlier insistence that "I am not human." Although this allows for the possibility of him being *half-human*, somewhere between the two avowals the film has broken down under the weight of trying to unify old and new audiences and turn a profit. Somewhat perversely, a television series intended to promote tolerance and equality is reinvented as a vehicle prohibiting interracial (through the metaphor of interplanetary) relations.

Segal's "international" *Who* is, then, the adventure that Christianized, depoliticized, sexualized, and humanized the previously rational, alien, aesthetic and politically liberal Doctor. Working from a position of almost complete ignorance regarding possible audiences, Segal pursued a hypothetical mainstream viewing public that subscribed to, or at least sympathized with, typical Western values: Christian morality, heterosexuality and conservative politics. This is not an unusual stance for a producer to adopt, as Scott Siegler, former CBS vice-president for drama development explains, because television's "audience is a mass audience [...] the audience tastes are so diffused and so general that you've got to be guessing [...] you can never really know."[51]

Here lies the explanation for Segal's strategies. His intertextual signposts to cinema and television are attempts to exploit the popularity of ideas and images that have worked before. Segal's sociological assumptions depended, apparently, on statistical suppositions: there are more Christians — whether practising or not — in the West than any other religious group, there are more straight people than gay or lesbian individuals, and there are more political conservatives than there are radicals. By embracing these notions, Segal sought to attract his desired international audience.

He failed. Gaining 5.5 million viewers in North America, less than 9 percent of the available audience, the *Doctor Who* franchise was insufficiently commercial for further investment. In the U.K., the film's 9.08 million viewers constituted a much more significant 36 percent audience share,[52] possibly because it attracted followers and fans starved of *Doctor Who* for seven years who were prepared to accept any *Who* as better than no *Who* at all. Despite its success in Britain, however, the BBC declined the immediate opportunity of producing further *Doctor Who* on financial grounds, although it did see the film as an affirmation of the abiding popularity of the program. In response, it reclaimed the rights to produce its own *Doctor Who* novels from Virgin Publishing, whose license was due for renegotiation.[53]

To deny the telefilm's significance because of its international failure or its inability to secure an immediate future for the Doctor on British television is to overlook its relevance as a particular form of cultural imperialism. In seeking to popularize *Doctor Who*, Segal effected its colonization by ideas and ideologies wholly at odds with its original socio-political mandate. In seeking as large an audience as possible, Segal produced something, as John Fiske observes of much satellite-broadcast television, with a "non-controversial content, a bland homogeneity that will offend no one and appeal in some, relatively superficial, way to everyone."[54]

Revisionist intertexts, character transformations and the generic shift described above brought *Doctor Who: The Movie* into line with the homogenized products of the international television age. It *is* bland, non-controversial (from a conservative perspective) and superficial. Such homogenization is important since it forms a significant element of cultural imperialism. As Chris Barker observes, "in the context of discussions about power, the idea of cultural imperialism does have strength, especially in relation to television, where people are *denied* a cultural experience as a result of the homogenization of production."[55]

In this case, it is followers and fans of BBC-produced *Doctor Who* who were denied their cultural experience. Where "cultural imperialism is [usually] understood in terms of the imposition of one *national* culture upon another"[56] what *Doctor Who: The Movie* indicates is the imposition of the conventions and values of much Western popular culture on an identifiable subculture, which had previously followed a drama program often at odds with those values. For dedicated fans, the film represented a double blow. On the one hand, it undermined all that the Doctor once stood for and, on the other, its commercial failure in America jeopardized future televized adventures.

Whilst the temporary loss of *Doctor Who* (it eventually returned to British television in 2005 influenced substantially by the telefilm) may not have been a significant blight on popular cultural heritage, it was symptomatic of how commercialism continually disenfranchises the consumer of choice, the follower of favored entertainment, and the fan of new inspiration for the activities of fandom. The imperatives acting upon popular sub-cultural documents are entirely conservative and leave the fan with little to resort to but nostalgia.

The disappointed or disillusioned fan may have found some minor compensation in Terrance Dicks's *The Eight Doctors* (1997), the first BBC novel in their range of new adventures focusing on the Eighth Doctor. The Prologue addresses and corrects many of the liberties taken with *Doctor Who* mythology in the film, correcting errors and bringing *Doctor Who* mythology back into context. Significantly, the Doctor's experiences during the telefilm are dismissed as "a weird, fantastic adventure, full of improbable, illogical events."[57] The condemnation of the telefilm is clear and the fact remains that Segal's efforts to both reassure and educate new viewers through intertextuality and to move the Doctor to a point of an assumed universally appealing centrality, resulted in the removal of any trace of originality or idiosyncrasy possessed by the original series.

Ultimately, *Doctor Who: The Movie* epitomizes the worst quality of much popular cultural production: an intellectually numbing, politically complicit, and culturally stagnant sameness. It failed to challenge the status quo (as *Quantum Leap* [U.S., NBC, 1989–1994] once did) or to encourage its audience to question the continued validity of that status quo (as *Babylon 5* [U.S., PTEN/TNT, 1993–1998] did). Lacking the sophistication and skepticism of other science fiction shows of the period (like *The X-Files*), *Doctor Who: The Movie* put commerce before content, safety before story, and style before substance. In attempting to expatriate the Doctor, Segal exterminated him and his laudable crusade against political and social injustice more effectively than the Daleks ever could.

12

Invasion of the Brit-Snatchers
National Identity in Contemporary Science Fiction Cinema

AIDAN POWER

This chapter deals with the increasingly eclectic and transnational nature of contemporary British-based science fiction cinema. Taking into account an array of factors, amongst them the influence of foreign directors, multi-national casts and funding, it seeks to examine the state of the genre and question the continued relevance of the prefix "British." Focusing specifically on two international co-productions, the James McTeigue directed *V for Vendetta* (U.S./U.K./Germany, 2006) and Alfonso Cuarón's *Children of Men* (U.K./Japan/U.S., 2006), this chapter will scrutinize the influence of the aforementioned factors, using Danny Boyle's *28 Days Later* (U.K., 2002) as a counterpoint. Ultimately, should the nationalities of creative personnel impede upon the reception of the film they help create, or indeed in the current climate of cultural homogenization, is it merely tribalism that leads to filmgoers laying claim to productions as their own? Furthermore, are such claims merely an extension of marketing ploys deliberated to make films appeal to the widest common audience, while striving simultaneously to appear "authentically" regionalized?

As a genre, dystopian science fiction has long raged against the death of the individual. An array of dystopian productions have featured meditations on the nature of personal freedoms, and are centered on the plight of individuals who seek to assert their individuality in the face of societal or governmental oppression. Salient examples of this theme range from Fritz Lang's seminal *Metropolis* (Germany, 1927), through Francois Truffaut's *Fahrenheit 451* (France, 1966) to Terry Gilliam's *Brazil* (1985). A common thread that links such productions (and these films as representative examples) is the need to address the balance between the creation of an alternate reality, one that inspires suitable awe amongst audiences and the necessity of anchoring such depictions in the familiar and thus engendering a sense of uncanny familiarity. As Thomas B. Byers notes, "visions of the future that extrapolate contemporary trends to envision their possible consequences have long been part of cultural discourse and debate."[1] Whilst this study is limited to an investigation of three high profile productions, it is interesting to note the similarities between them — most significantly, mutual concerns over the power of the military, the severance of roots through death and the eventual rebirth of society. In this particular instance, I will argue that the discrepancies between national and transnational productions are not as pronounced as one may presume, and whilst interpretations of British life may vary, thematic, political and representational similarities are in evidence throughout.

In a recent letter to *The Guardian* newspaper, the prominent Spanish director Pedro Almodóvar strongly contested what he perceived to be critical comments made in an article by the critic Paul Julian Smith. Smith had questioned the director's apparent pre-eminence in Spanish cinema, wondering aloud if the Spanish film industry was in danger of being held back by the exploits of its most famous exponent.[2] Almodóvar, Smith claimed, had become something of a national icon, a touchstone for critics when debating the merits of Spanish cinema, so much so that his output dwarfed that of any would be contemporaries. Taking umbrage at alleged insinuations of national dominance, Almodóvar pointed out that he had been nothing if not an ambassador for Spanish cinema, one who frequently encouraged and publicized the work of other Spanish directors. *The Guardian* responded by way of editorial that it was never their intention to denigrate Almódovar's motives, but merely to highlight his success as an internationally recognized filmmaker. The point of relaying this episode here is not to debate the pros and cons of the specific argument, but instead to highlight a prevalent mode (one of many) of coding national cinemas. Without wishing to delve too deeply into the field of auteur studies, it is worth relaying this continuing trend to relate national entities to key individuals. Naturally, in an age of large-scale migration, such categorization must be aware of transnational paradigms and multicultural realities. The experiences of diasporic communities and ethnically diverse populaces have been depicted in new emerging genres such as French *beur* cinema and Black British Cinema, where key personnel can lay claim to more than one nationality. Stretching this theme, this chapter will focus on the spectre of internationally cofunded productions, set in Britain, but directed by foreign directors and featuring multinational casts, in an effort to decode endemic aesthetic and political representations. Both *Children of Men* and *28 Days Later* directly interact with questions of transnationalism, featuring racially diverse characters, some with more than one fixed national identity. Conspicuous amongst those portrayed in the former film is the pregnant refugee Kee, whose plight is worsened by the refusal of the British government to recognize the rights of non-nationals, while the latter production concerns the flight of a subtly postcolonial group into the wilderness and their subsequent struggle against a British army unit. *V for Vendetta*, meanwhile, is set in a dystopian future where minorities have been stripped of their civil rights and the concept of "Britishness" is delineated along racial lines that leave little room for cultural diversity.

In seeking to present a trans-border argument for these films, one must first take into account the spectre of national cinema itself. Much of the thinking behind modern concepts of national cinemas still harks back to Benedict Anderson's concept of an "imagined community,"[3] one that is continually relevant in relation to prominent diasporic directors such as the German/Turkish director Fatih Akin or the French/Moroccan Ismaël Ferroukhi, for example, filmmakers whose work often seeks to reconcile chasms arising from cultural duality. Building upon Anderson's treatise, Andrew Higson argues that in light of continuous migration, all nations are "in some sense diasporic" and calls for a greater awareness of the "diversity of reception" amongst audiences.[4] Higson's argument is pertinent, in particular when one considers not just the ethnic diversity of British (and in particular English) cities, but also the drive toward devolution in contemporary Britain. However, in spite of these trends, one need only gauge the vociferous nature of any argument surrounding the perceived diminution of British sovereignty, an example being the rejection of the Euro currency, to appreciate that for all its diversity, Britain as a region is still a binding communal entity for many millions of inhabitants. If a central trope of transnational existence is an identity that is in a state of flux and/or in constant negotiation with itself, then this is a state of being that surely correlates with the idea of nationhood. As Higson goes on to suggest, nations are "thus forged in the tension between unity and disunity, between home and homelessness."[5] In order to analyze the transnational nature of contemporary British science fiction cinema, one must first make allowances for this interstitial relationship between the national and the transnational, a relationship described by Hamid Nacify in his exposition of "accented" cinema as being "simultaneously local and global."[6] For Nacify, such accented films remark upon diaspora and transnationalism by "expressing, allegorizing, commenting upon, and critiquing the home and host societies and cultures and the deterritorialized conditions of the filmmakers."[7] In critiquing host territories in such a fashion, filmmakers such as Alfonso Cuarón with *Children of Men* for example, are subsequently complicit (whether consciously or not) in marketing nations in a certain manner. It is specifically this correlation between cinematic representations of community and belonging, and the resultant marketing of identities, both subconscious and explicit, that invites interrogation, calling upon Thomas Elsaesser's contention that in response to outside interest, European cinema has not been beyond developing a "retroactive national vernacular,"[8] one that posits itself as being a simulacrum of reality, one in keeping with perceived "outside" expectations.

V for Vendetta

Film studies' concern with the role of cinema in the nation is inherently internalist. Its central concern is with how — if at all — the production, circulation and consumption

> of the moving image is constitutive of the national collectivity. However, this internalism is necessarily tempered by the awareness of exteriority as a shaping force.[9]

Philip Schlesinger's above argument is striking insofar as it highlights the paradoxical relationship between the conceit elicited by the existence of a national cinema and the realization that quite often such cinemas are laced with multinational intonations. This uneasy balance between the local and the international seems to be brought into sharp relief whenever a Hollywood film studio turns its attention to the graphic novels of Alan Moore. The Northampton-born author has been vociferous in his opposition to filmic interpretations of his work and has publicly distanced himself from a number of productions, culminating in his refusal of both a screen credit and monetary royalties from the recent *Watchmen* (U.S., Jack Synder, 2009). Unlike *Watchmen*, which is set in an alternate 1980s New York, but in a similar vein to other Moore works such as *The League of Extraordinary Gentlemen* (U.S./U.K./Germany/Czech Republic, Stephen Norrington, 2003) and *From Hell* (U.S., Albert and Allen Hughes, 2001), *V for Vendetta* is set in England and informed by specifically British nuances. A 1990s set meditation on the potential ramifications of Thatcherism, Moore's novel is transported to the near future by screenwriters Larry and Andy Wachowski, and tinged instead with allusions to the Bush administration.

Centered around the exploits of a masked freedom fighter, the eponymous V, *V for Vendetta* concerns itself with a Britain that has turned to fascism in a desperate attempt to address rampant crime, widespread disease and rising anxieties about increased levels of immigration, stoked in part, by a histrionic media. Under the autocratic rule of Chancellor Adam Sutler, whose Norsefire party espouses a somewhat incoherent yet familiar mix of nationalism and selective Christianity, Britain is in a veritable state of lockdown. Those whose lifestyles do not adhere to the conventions set out by the government (Muslims and homosexuals are mentioned explicitly in this regard) have their civil liberties infringed upon, are deported and in many instances "disappear." Interestingly, the film makes several references to the supposed threat posed by the Muslim world, as well as the role of the government and media in exploiting resultant fears for their own gain. A diegetic television program, for example, crassly depicts a white woman being tortured by an Islamic terrorist replete with thawb and headscarf whilst a sensationalist newscaster describes the systematic reduction of civil rights amongst minorities as a necessary patriotic act. Furthermore, the filmic adaptation of Moore's graphic novel sanitizes V's extremist political views. In place of Moore's stated anarchist agenda for V, the screenplay has the hero fighting for the familiar, if vaguely circumspect concept of "freedom." The democratic (and somewhat idealized) nature of this freedom is revealed when V states his intention to give power back to the people, a further departure from the source text where the collapse of governance creates a chasm filled by violence and uncertainty.

This seeming disenfranchisement of British sensibilities at the heart of the film's plot is mirrored by the presence of the American Wachowskis, the Australian James McTeigue as director, as well the studio backing of Warner Bros. as financiers. However, owing largely to the geographical specificity of the source text, the film is set in London and makes liberal use of prominent landmarks, such as the Old Bailey, Trafalgar Square and the Houses of Parliament in Westminster. As with *Children of Men*, *V for Vendetta* is foregrounded by repeated glimpses of internationally renowned landmarks, ensuring that even the most inattentive of viewers can be left in no doubt as to the setting. This deliberate foregrounding mirrors strategies endemic in a host of recent successful European releases, amongst them *Goodbye Lenin!* (Germany, Wolfgang Becker, 2003), *Le Fabuleux Destin d'Amélie Poulain / Amelie* (France/Germany, Jean-Pierre Jeunet, 2001) and *Nuovo Cinema Paradiso / Cinema Paradiso* (Italy/France, Giuseppe Tornatore, 1988), recording the familiar, albeit through the aperture of a distinctly ordered aesthetic. Writing about this marketing device, Thomas Elsaesser notes that "references to the nation, the region and the local have also become second-order realities, whenever they function as self advertisement for (the memorializable parts of) the past, for lifestyle choices or for (tourist) locations."[10] When viewed through this prism, depictions of the local, Elsaesser argues, provide "access points for the international and global cinema markets."[11] *V for Vendetta* seeks to assert its credentials by using the tale of Guy Fawkes as a framing device, thus tying the production to a noted historical event and lending the resultant narrative a veneer of authenticity. Like Fawkes, who sought to eradicate Protestant rule by blowing up the Houses of Parliament, V too attempts to overthrow a reigning government by means of force, a plan he unveils to Evey Hammond, a young personal assistant, after saving her from an attempted rape by corrupt policemen.

An unfortunate side-effect of such "access points" as articulated by Elsaesser, is that they can extend to people too, and arguably, the Wachowskis' view of the English is a somewhat lazily conceived one. Where V speaks with the considered eloquence of a vaudevillian actor, as encapsulated by his lengthy opening monologue, wherein he displays his linguistic dexterity by referencing almost exclusively adjectives beginning with the letter V, many of those he seeks to "liberate" are little more than poorly drawn stereotypes. Responding to her rescuer's monologue, Evey, seemingly channeling the crasser depictions of the working-classes prevalent in nineteenth century publications such as *Punch* magazine, blurts out: "are you some kind of crazy person?"[12] Natalie Portman's uneven accent, surreptitiously dropping "h's" and elongating her "r's" in an attempt to emulate a cockney English accent, is part of the problem here, but also one could argue that Evey (a character considerably re-imagined from the graphic novel) embodies traits that are prevalent amongst the film's depictions of the lower classes, characteristics that do not require the viewer to stray far from the imaginative confines of stereotype. A succession of crooked policemen, security guards and bar dwellers do little but intone unconvincingly in quasi-mellifluous cockney accents — stock characters certainly, but moreover, ones imagined by, and arguably for, "foreigners." That they are in need of deliverance from peril by the suave and hyper-literate V, merely serves to highlight their passivity. They learn of his deeds via state-controlled television, yet do little to contribute to their own restitution but continue to sit, smoke, drink and watch. Cheered by V's rhetoric, they nonetheless remain idle and it would appear clear that despite their misgivings over the state of their nation, they would sooner while away their time in taverns than actively pursue a change in regime. Such indolence is merely accentuated when set alongside V's mobility and it is telling that the more daring of his actions are cross-cut with images of a pub-dwelling few, an all too convenient microcosm of the working-classes at large. This theme of foregrounding the foreign in the familiar serves to put the international viewer at ease and to locate the film visually as well as culturally, albeit in a manner that can appear contrived. One does not need great finance, nor imagination, to depict a specific locale in this manner — for instance if it is London, it must be black taxi cabs and sporadic shots of Big Ben (for New York one need but substitute the building and change the hue of the taxi). In a similar vein and in this particular instance, large sections of whole populations are represented by cardboard characterizations, a "select" few standing in for the masses. Such methods can appear highly derivative and at this remove it is tempting to equate such aesthetic rendering of time and place with the specter of foreign (in this instance American and Australian) influence, one keen to pigeon-hole the local into a neatly packaged caricature, in order to maximize core demographics.

However, while locations and people may do little to challenge stereotypical views of the local, the politics that inform such localities are all too frequently international. Where Alan Moore's target was the Conservative government of the 1980s, here the critique is reserved for the American Republican Party. Illustrating the rise of a right-wing Christian leadership that seeks to eradicate at all costs the perceived threats posed by Muslim extremists, Moore's view that the film is merely "a Bush-era parable by people too timid to set a political satire in their own country"[13] is difficult to dismiss. In the film's climactic scene, V's corpse is laid to rest in a train carriage residing in an abandoned underground station. Prepared by V, the train is rigged with explosives and bound for Westminster, where in an extravagant set-piece, the Houses of Parliament shall be blown asunder. The potential for metaphorical readings of these events is manifold, but the image of a national parliament being destroyed is surely symbolic in light of any criticism of the film's regard for the local. Britain, it would then appear logical to argue, is being stripped of its identity by Hollywood productions such as *V for Vendetta*, where an insistence on making all politics global (and by extension, as leader of the "free world," American) is depriving the local of its own distinctive voice. Several factors militate against this exclusive reading however, as shall be shown in the following discussion of *Children of Men* and finally of the British made and directed *28 Days Later*, where several "international" trends continue to manifest themselves.

Children of Men

Like *V for Vendetta*, *Children of Men* benefits from American studio backing (in the guise of Universal Pictures), and although its cast is comprised of mainly British actors (with the notable exception of Julianne Moore), it is directed by the Mexican Alfonso Cuarón, who had earned the trust of Hollywood producers after helming a film in the *Harry Potter* series (2004's *Harry Potter and the Prisoner of Azkaban* [U.K./U.S.]). Also, like *V for Vendetta*, it has its source in another medium, the novel *The Children of Men* (1992) by the English author P.D. James. Cuarón departs from several plot devices of James's text however, most notably in his switching of the cause for humankind's inability to reproduce from male sterility to female infertility. The central plot remains the same: Theo, a cynical former political activist finds himself responsible for the safety of a young refugee Kee, who against all odds is pregnant. Cuarón gradually weaves a road narrative, as Theo and his companions flee the attention of both the authorities and resistance fighters who are desperate to exploit the political potential of presenting a pregnant woman to a sterile world bereft of children. As in *28 Days Later*, a racially diverse group of individuals are forced to band together and navigate through a hostile countryside, one presided over by a domineering military. Reaching the southern coast of England, now used as a large make-shift detention center for refugees, Theo and Kee take to the water in anticipation of the arrival by trawler of the Human Project, a near-mythical group of humanitarians. As their small rowboat rocks amongst the waves, Kee gives birth to a boy while Theo succumbs to the effects of a bullet wound and dies, thus encapsulating neatly the circle of life. In his analysis of the film, Slavoj Žižek notes that the presence of the boat serves as a metaphor for the rootlessness of contemporary identity, saying that "the condition of the renewal means you cut your roots."[14] This lack of roots, I would argue, can similarly be read into the motif of the car, itself the site of much of the journey, and a vessel for the melding and shaping of identities as disparate as the production team that brought *Children of Men* to the screen. As Kristin Ross asserts, "the car can compensate for the destruction it has created — it can protect the driver and offer solace." Like the people it transports, the car has a fixed shelf-life. Not unlike human beings, it causes environmental destruction and is subject to the limitations of the environs that surround it. Nonetheless it remains a source of comfort for its passengers and provides a comparatively secure platform for human interaction to take place, a "protected interior space that takes on value" and in the process becomes a "home from home."[15] Like *V for Vendetta*'s Evey Hammond, who is forced to flee her home and job after coming to the aid of V, the once bitter Theo is reawakened to the possibilities of existence after forgoing the comforts of anonymity. The perspective provided by his journey to the coast and the harrowing experiences of characters he encounters along the way, force Theo to re-evaluate his priorities. Where once he was apathetic to the plight of the marginalized in society, he is now prepared to sacrifice himself for what he perceives to be the greater good. While Hugo Weaving's V is prepared to raze London to the ground in order to lay the groundwork for a rebirth of society, Theo's actions are more modest in scale, even if his intentions are similar — by protecting the mother of a child, he seeks to provide hope for the future, in an increasingly nihilistic world.

As with *V for Vendetta's* thinly disguised attacks on the Bush administration, *Children of Men*, in the hands of Cuarón, engages in notable acts of ideological disenfranchizement, underscoring British settings and scenarios with wide-ranging and internationally relevant critiques. Whilst one can no doubt accuse the Tony Blair-led Labour government of, at the least, being unwittingly compliant in the more unsavory acts perpetuated by the Bush administration, such as the torture of prisoners in Abu Ghraib, or the prolonged detention of terror suspects in Guantanamo Bay, James's source novel was published in 1992, three years before George W. Bush became Governor of Texas and some nine years before he was sworn in as President of the U.S. The film nonetheless directly references the maltreatment of Iraqi prisoners in Abu Ghraib, in a scene where Theo and Kee pass through a prison camp in a refugee-filled bus. As Theo attempts to allay Kee's considerable pre-natal anxiety, visible outside the bus is a direct recreation of the infamous Abu Ghraib torture photos, replete with a hooded detainee being physically and verbally assaulted. The film abounds with direct and indirect references to the "War on Terror," but here the critique manifests itself most tangibly, via a direct visual indicator that has its genesis in iconography so striking and omnipresent, that it has segued into the very zeitgeist of popular culture. Again, a British-set dystopian future has, under the direction of a foreign director and foreign financiers, been coded with strong references to the perceived wrongdoings of the American government, references that are without precedent in the text that informs it. Amongst the sights that Theo and Kee encounter after leaving the detention center is a group of armed Islamic radicals who parade through the streets in open opposition to the authorities imposed upon them, in a scene not unlike those witnessed in Iraq or the Gaza Strip on a near daily basis at the time of the film's release. Again, one could argue that such imagery serves as an allegorical meditation on the ramifications of continued British interference in the Middle East, yet it is hard to escape the notion that the central target for criticism is not Britain at all, but the aggressive foreign policies of the Bush administration. That such a critique should be heavily coded in Christian symbolism merely sharpens the view that the ideologies of the neo-conservative American right are under scrutiny. Released in America on Christmas Day 2006, and concerning a story about a marginalized pregnant woman who flees into the wilds to give birth to an iconic child, *Children of Men* takes its cue from religious texts as much as it comments upon political uncertainty. Taking the wide-ranging scale of the film's political and religious commentary into account then, would it not be reasonable to ask if Cuarón's use of a British setting is thus somewhat incidental, if

P.D. James's novel could just as easily have been transported elsewhere? After all, if the politics are global, are the intricacies of the local not subsumed in the maelstrom of wider contextual concerns? In a bid to place these concerns within a suitable contextual sphere, it is instructive to look to Danny Boyle's *28 Days Later* as a contrapuntal and British-made example of the post-apocalyptic subgenre.

28 Days Later

Writing about the phenomenon of heritage cinema in 2005, Tim Bergfelder argued that foreign involvement in British national cinema need not be construed as a "them and us" scenario; instead, he called for a broader and more flexible construction of identity itself. Instead, the process of collaboration with outside parties, Bergfelder stated, "ought to be understood as adding new discursive and aesthetic layers, which irrevocably change but also contribute to the continuing evolution of, national cultures."[16] Pointing to the collaborative nature of cinematic production, Bergfelder could just as easily be referring to contemporary science fiction when he suggests that the erection of rigid (and all too frequently arbitrary) cultural boundaries can lead to a myopic level of interiority, one hampered by a lack of perspective. Furthermore, he points to the history of European cinema when he states that it is "more than just the sum total of separate and divergent national film styles. In terms of production, cinemas in Europe have, since the late nineteenth century emerged out of cultural hybridization processes, and processes of economic diversification."[17] We have already seen how the transnational productions *V for Vendetta* and *Children of Men* juxtapose distinctly British concerns with thinly veiled critiques of American foreign policy, but how do they compare to (and contrast with) *28 Days Later*, a distinctly more localized affair? Written by the London native Alex Garland and under the direction of Manchester-born Danny Boyle, *28 Days Later* depicts an England that has been struck by a "rage" virus epidemic, a malady passed on through blood that reduces its victims to a state of murderous dementia. Although regarded in many quarters as a horror, or indeed "zombie" film, *28 Days Later* has strong thematic links to the science fiction genre, taking its cue from amongst other sources, Richard Matheson's 1954 dystopian novel *I Am Legend*. Incorporating characteristic tropes of both science fiction and horror, the film is something of a hybrid, reimagining zombies as fast-moving predators who hunt in packs amidst a dystopian environment that has been shaped in part by the consequences of animal testing at a scientific clinic. Waking from a coma in an abandoned London hospital, Boyle's central protagonist Jim wanders disbelievingly through a seemingly deserted cityscape before banding with a group of three other survivors in a bid to escape to the presumed sanctuary of the countryside. Funded in part by the British government lottery franchise scheme (a Labour backed initiative to try to stimulate the local film industry), *28 Days Later* features an almost exclusively British and

Irish cast as well as a Scottish producer and an English cinematographer and composer. Regional differences acknowledged, it is thus, by most rational criteria a British film. Free from foreign infringement then and released some four years before both *V for Vendetta* and *Children of Men*, it would be reasonable to assume that Boyle's film would differ considerably in content and context from either production and yet, closer inspection suggests that conversely, the similarities between them are manifold.

While Alfonso Cuarón and James McTeigue adapted their films directly from pre-existing texts (albeit somewhat loosely, as we have seen), Garland's, though influenced by an array of sources, was an original screenplay. Ostensibly, the film's concerns are British; landmarks of the Empire pockmark the opening scenes of the film as Jim passes Westminster Abbey, Trafalgar Square and London Bridge, whilst a brief shot of a billowing Union Jack flag further provides a two-pronged nationalistic device, one that serves the dual purpose of locating the spatial construct of the nation state while simultaneously signaling its collapse. Fittingly, in a motif that encapsulates the collapse of society and heritage, Jim and the survivors he encounters — Selena, a chemist, Frank, a taxi driver and his teenaged daughter Hannah — are not assigned surnames, while Jim's parents are referred to in both the film and closing credit sequence as "Jim's father and mother." In this historically frozen Britain, one's genealogy is of little consequence; as with *Children of Men* and *V for Vendetta*, we are transported to the site of the death and subsequent rebirth of society. Jim, like *Children of Men's* Theo, is coerced into travelling across Britain with a racially diverse group. That the group is subtly postcolonial, is hinted at by Boyle and made clearer when later set in opposition to the arrival of a British army unit in the second half of the film. Jim's Irishness is casually relayed, his accent and that of his father are subtly intonated, but indubitably Irish all the same, while Selena is not coded as "other" until she comes into contact with an army garrison, when she is referred to disparagingly as "the black one" by a resident soldier. Although the identity of Selena's ethnic origin is not revealed, the presence of her and Jim present a colonized counterpoint to the colonizers as represented by the British army, while their ultimate survival signifies further the collapse of Empire. The old order, as represented by shots of unattended London war memorials and by the crumbling edifice of a country manor (now requisitioned and refigured into a military barracks), is seen to be fading, and Selena and Jim are not alone in questioning its continued relevance. The status of the nation, it would appear, is of secondary importance when set against wider concerns and indeed, a broader and more universal understanding of belonging is being called for. Interestingly, it is another colonial subject, the Scottish Sergeant Farrell, who openly questions the future of a Britain that has seemingly been cut off from the rest of the world. Arrested for insubordination, Farrell remarks that the world at large is indifferent to Britain's plight, and that far from being a glorious empire, Britain is merely "a diseased little island." History, it is implied, will not save Britain, and the inflexibility of the military ultimately leads to its downfall and annihilation. As with *V for Vendetta*, British rule is seen to collapse into its own self-interest, while the arrival of aid comes in the shape of a Finnish fighter jet in much the same way as the Human Project's trawler arrives from abroad to intervene in *Children of Men*.

Like Theo, and Natalie Portman's Evey Hammond in *V for Vendetta*, Jim's flight into the unknown is made possible by the untimely death of his family — a forceful severing of roots, and Zizek's stated "condition for renewal." Tellingly, the vehicle for this renewal is a black taxi cab, a famed and instantly recognized staple of London life and a literal site for the act of tourism itself. Coupled with Boyle's predilection for filming touristic landmarks in *28 Days Later* (one considerably removed for example, from his depiction of Edinburgh in *Trainspotting* [1996], wherein "Boyle tries to obliterate the differences between Edinburgh and other British, or indeed, European cities"[18]), this motif of the taxi locates the action in the realm of the familiar, making Boyle's Britain palatable to a universal audience, in much the same way that Cuarón and McTeigue play upon the familiar to create alternate realities. Through the binding communal space of the cab, Boyle's survivors become a temporary embodiment of a surrogate family and in the process, regain their humanity. Selena states as much when she reneges on her earlier assertion that "staying alive is as good as it gets," and goes on to quietly extol the virtues of companionship and family. Indeed the theme of family occurs on several occasions throughout the film as Boyle searches for ways to reconcile his characters' immense personal losses with their relentless fervor for continued existence. Most notable in this regard is the film's conclusion, a rare scene of calm domesticity that restores the specter of the family unit. In a lakeside cottage, Selena sews in the kitchen and Jim sleeps upstairs while Hannah, playing outdoors, hails the imminent arrival of a reconnaissance plane. Jarring with the overall aesthetic of the film, which is shot largely with hand-held digital video cameras, this concluding sequence is filmed in 35mm widescreen, adding to an incongruous warmth that is at odds with what precedes it, dovetailing with conventional Hollywood denouements as well as conservative political ideologies. Such a representation of family echoes the aforementioned closing scene in *Children of Men*, where Theo's death in the rowboat is the thematic signifier for the rebirth of society as coded by the birth of Kee's son and the subsequent arrival of the Human Project's trawler. In *28 Days Later*, it is Hannah's father Frank who sacrifices himself for the greater good. Having successfully driven the group to their Manchester destination, Frank contracts the rage virus and dies; in the process lending the surrogate family a more orthodox appearance and forcing Jim to fill the role of proactive patriarch. Like *V for Vendetta*'s V, he becomes a further martyr for the greater good, his body laid out alongside the vehicle that expedited his journey of self-discovery. It is here that the survivors encounter the military unit that are keen to uphold the values of a crumbling Empire, one that readily employs aggressive and brutal tactics to achieve its goal — the attempted rape of Hannah and

Selena — in a bid to regenerate society. The conviction of the all-male unit that they are acting in the best interest of society is tempered somewhat by a wish to satiate their latent sexual desires whilst also calling to question the nature of the society which they wish to preserve. This linkage in all three films between death and vehicles and martyrdom and rebirth, lend themselves neatly to readings of the transience of the journey, and, by extension, universal themes of life and of the restorative nature of sacrifice.

Conclusion

A priori, interpretations of sacrifice as listed above could quite easily be applied to current conflicts in Iraq or Afghanistan for example, should one wish to seek justification for U.S.–led incursions into both nations. In turn, this reading leads to vexing questions as to whose ideological framework and subsequent image new societies (both onscreen and off) are being modeled upon. Is Boyle's new Britain more authentic than those of McTeigue and Cuarón because it is ostensibly "more" British? At this remove, it is worth noting Higson's contention that "the debates about national cinema need to take greater account of the diversity of reception, the recognition that the meanings an audience reads into a film are heavily dependent on the cultural context in which they watch it."[19] Such a consideration is pertinent when seeking to dissect the ambiguity of British science fiction cinema, although while taking on board Higson's argument, it is necessary to invert his theory in this particular instance. Released in the U.S. after the events of 9/11 and in the midst of a feared SARS epidemic, it is difficult to imagine how American viewers could view *28 Days Later* as being divorced from wider political machinations. Reviewing the film for *Entertainment Weekly*, Owen Gleiberman noted that "*28 Days Later* was completed before the arrival of SARS (though after 9/11), yet it overlaps with that recent news event in a way that's timely enough to make the coincidence feel vaguely sinister, as if the movie knew something,"[20] while the resident critic for *The Atlanta Journal-Constitution*, Eleanor Ringel Gillespie, commented that "in a series of surreal scenes, Jim wanders past a stilled Big Ben, through an eerily empty Trafalgar Square. He also comes across a poignant message board covered with pictures and names of the missing that's all too reminiscent of 9/11."[21] Such shots of Piccadilly Circus noticeboards laden with posters seeking missing persons and photos of deceased loved ones are particularly resonant, amongst images of iconic buildings providing a backdrop to streets strewn with debris. In a similar vein, the aggression and hidden motives of the film's military unit play upon popular concerns relating to the power of the American army (a point elucidated upon in the film's sequel *28 Weeks Later* [U.K./Spain, Juan Carlos Fresnadillo, 2007][22]).

It would be somewhat disingenuous to ignore the duality of audience reception at play here, for although "the movement of films across borders" may introduce exotic elements to the "indigenous" culture,"[23] the opposite as evinced in *Children of Men* and *V for Vendetta* can also be true: namely that the introduction of exotic elements in the shape of foreign production crews can reinvigorate representations of the local. Fresh perspectives on local issues can certainly provide what Bergfelder describes as "new aesthetic and discursive layers,"[24] but what is striking also, are the similarities between seemingly disparate depictions of dystopian Britain. Ultimately, commercial concerns (not to mention the prominence of the U.S. in global affairs), ensure that local issues will often be funnelled through the interpretations of international filmic personnel, yet the juxtaposition of local and global concerns need not be mutually exclusive. It is undeniable that *Children of Men* and *V for Vendetta*, in particular, utilize British texts as a prism through which international concerns can be subjected to interrogation, yet as we have seen, a distinctly British production such as *28 Days Later* is not beyond scrutiny in this regard, often looking outward for its political critique. On another level still, it is surely misleading to claim that national audiences (complex as their composition may be), are concerned only with national and by association local affairs. Here it is important to note that the relevancy of local issues need not be dwarfed by wider concerns, but to state instead that in cinema, as in culture at large, there is ample room for both. Whilst critics are within their rights to question the pervasiveness and influence of Hollywood productions, surely the application of such arguments to the science fiction genre are merely an extension of oft-restrictive debates about the nature of national communities themselves? In other words, while Hollywood undoubtedly continues to enjoy considerable influence in the British market, it does not render British films redundant as a consequence. Nor are its depictions of British life (while undoubtedly grating at times) necessarily an affront to the "realities" evinced in more localized productions, as we have seen here. In terms of quality, production, budget and originality, the three films surveyed here differ markedly, yet distinct thematic and political similarities are in evidence throughout, lending credence to the idea that intrinsic "Britishness," itself a somewhat overstated concept, is in no immediate danger.

13

A Cosy Catastrophe
Genre, National Cinema, and Fan Responses to 28 Days Later

BRIGID CHERRY

The theme of this collection is British science fiction, but what of the British science fiction audience? Genre films have long been a staple of British cinema, but although the histories of British genres have been largely reclaimed, the audiences for British science fiction and related genres have not always been as well explored. Certainly, as evidenced by box-office takings and television viewing figures, British audiences have a voracious appetite for science fiction and, as demonstrated by the accompanying fan discourse and productivity, the fan audience segments are particularly active. In recent decades, though, British science fiction audiences have been limited in the range of British films which they can see and their choice of viewing is often restricted — at least as far as new releases — to predominantly American products supplemented with the occasional British or foreign film.[1] In the areas of fantasy, science fiction and horror cinema, British films have always tended (with the exception perhaps of the work of the Hammer studio) to be overshadowed by their American counterparts. In an increasingly multi-media environment defined by convergence of both industry and technology, as well as the marginalization of national culture, film consumption has taken on new dimensions. This forces us to examine not just the high and low dichotomy of the cultural economy of fandom[2], but the global marketplace of American-dominated free trade and cultural imperialism. Of concern here is that American cultural forms elide the national culture, particularly within genre cinema in general and specifically within the "fantastique" genres of science fiction and horror.[3] In theorizing taste in relation to nationality and identity, accounts of film in Europe and elsewhere have repeatedly sought to address issues arising from cultural imperialism.[4] In this context, questions of whether the tastes of domestic audiences are affected by an American-dominated monoculture must be addressed. And if tastes are influenced, do British genre audiences respond to British genre films in ways that might either acknowledge a national cinema or be attributed to aspects of national and cultural identity? Do they, accordingly, make specific meanings from British texts?

In focusing on genre here, I want to make clear that the analysis that follows is not limited solely to discussion of science fiction film fans alone. The audience for a single, specific genre is not easy to isolate. Fans — as Jenkins has shown[5] — are nomadic and individual viewing choices are often eclectic. Any genre is, in any case, a site of contested meaning. The preferences and viewing patterns of the audience for fantastic genres tend to be broad (taking in television and literature, as well as film) and their conceptions of the boundaries of these genres are fluid (with horror fans often classing science fiction films as amongst their favorite horror films[6]) and often contested.[7] There are clearly many overlaps between science fiction and horror, particularly in the history of British cinema and literature. In being described by its filmmaker as an "apocalyptic horror-thriller"[8] and with many reviews equating it to the zombie subgenre, *28 Days Later* (Danny Boyle, 2002) — the central focus of this chapter — is a typically hybrid film. It is both horror and science fiction, and is thus positioned within a history that encompasses Mary Shelley, Robert Louis Stevenson, H.G. Wells, John Wyndham, John Christopher and J.G. Ballard, as well as British telefantasy such as *Survivors* (BBC, 1975–1977), *Doctor Who* (BBC, 1963–1989, 2005–) and the *Quatermass* serials. Many of these epitomize the popular perception of the British science fiction subgenre, the "cosy catastrophe" — a term coined by Brian Aldiss to describe post-apocalyptic narratives following the lives of a small group or community of survivors.[9] Although science fiction and associated fandom groups do seem on the surface to have a very narrow focus, often single texts, fan discourse is frequently positioned across genres or moves freely from one genre to another with little recognition of the boundaries. It is not at all unusual to find *The Lord of the Rings* films discussed by *Star Wars* fans and *Doctor Who* regarded as a reverential text by horror fans: these examples typify the broad tastes of many fans who migrate across a wide range of fan cultures.

We might therefore expect the majority of fan audience members to have heterogeneous tastes and viewing preferences — but the question of how important the national culture is to these viewers remains. Since fans make up an active and vocal (and thus identifiable) segment of the audience, studies of fans should help us to model the importance of national cinema texts in a wider context. Research into fan audiences in order to ascertain the patterns of consumption and range of responses remains important particularly in respect of understanding the place of national cinema. To this end, the research presented here focuses on the reception of the British science fiction/horror/thriller *28 Days Later* by British fans. The need to ascertain whether nationality and other aspects of identity are factors either in patterns of taste amongst genre audiences or in the reception of particular films is especially relevant in the context of media convergence (and I include the international nature of the Internet here), the impact of American texts on British culture and the wider questions of cultural imperialism.

In addressing the issues this raises, qualitative data obtained from a study of British genre fans in the science fiction and horror communities is analyzed in order to determine whether fan responses or activities might be related, if at all, to national or cultural identity. The fans participating in this research (and from whom the quotes below are drawn) were recruited from fan groups dedicated to *Doctor Who*, *Spaced* (Channel Four, 1999–2001), *Stargate SG-1* (U.S., Showtime/SCI FI, 1997–2007), British science fiction and telefantasy in general, and science fiction and horror cinema in a wider context.[10] Research was carried out between October 2002 (in the run up to the release of *28 Days Later* in the U.K. on 1 November) and August 2003 (three months after the DVD release on 19th May), this period being designed to take in the peaks of discussion around the film's exhibition and initial availability on DVD. It should be noted that the participants quoted throughout were predominantly white and middle-class, and a majority were male, although they ranged in age from their twenties to their fifties. This research is not then a study of *28 Days Later* fans, nor an analysis of fan culture and behavior in general. Rather it is a study of the reception of a film — the responses and readings — by fans of fantastic genres in a national context. In this way it is a study of an audience segment (one composed of fans of related texts) for a particular film which might be expected to hold particular significance in a national and cultural context (a British film made by a highly regarded British filmmaker in a subgenre which has a specifically British history) and which focuses solely on aspects of the text of interest to this audience. A number of factors have emerged with respect to genre fans and their behavior both as audience members and as participants in fan cultures. Where these are related to nationality — including aspects of taste and identity — they prove to be crucial in respect of the formation of discourses circulating amongst genre audiences. Of particular note here are the fans' privileging of the "Britishness" of the film, particularly in terms of aesthetic and narrative breaks with the dominant forms of Hollywood genre, their identification with its characters and locations as obviously British, and their fondness for British filmmakers.

Unsurprisingly, given the hybrid nature of *28 Days Later*, one of the main concerns of many fans was the generic classification of the film. Boyle's "apocalyptic horror-thriller" was claimed as both science fiction and horror, or more specifically a zombie film, highlighting the problems of classification of any film which exhibits generic hybridity. As Ross and Nightingale suggest,[11] genre is a key factor in interpretive practice, particularly amongst fan audiences, and according to Fiske,[12] the meta-polysemic nature of fantastic genres marks such texts out as particularly producerly.[13] The following discussion illustrates the hesitation of some fans. G (M, 30s, Horror)[14] claims that: "Any reviews I read before hand [sic] compared it to Romero's *Dawn* or *Day of the Dead* and to be honest that about sums it up," whilst J (M, 40s, Horror) states "NO it's not a zombie film, but it's supposed to be about something a bit different which gives its victims slightly ... okay VERY zombie like behaviour." It may well be that fans wish to lay claim to the film for the primary genre of their fan affiliations. Whilst these members of a horror fan group debate its status as a horror film, science fiction fans are more likely to defend it as science fiction. Z (F, 20s, *Spaced*), for example, states that:

> *28 Days Later* is a work of science fiction, in fact it is so blatantly fixed in this genre it amazes me that it ever gets called a horror film. The first thing to note is that "the infected" are far from zombies, not only do they not look like zombies they also don't behave like zombies. The second is that the film is not about the infected's attempts to kill the protagonists, but rather the protagonists attempts to survive. This film is about character development and human relationships, it is not a series of increasingly inventive attacks by monsters.

These classifications are based on the same elements of the texts, given appropriately different (and meta-polysemic) readings that suit a particular generic claim. However, for the majority of fans the question of whether the film belongs in any particular category of genre or subgenre is not one in the end that impeded their enjoyment of the film. A small number of fans, however, seem to have been offended by what they regard as generic mislabelling. RF (M, 30s, Horror), for example, who thought it was "a terrible film [which] looked nice, but that was about it!," stated that he was:

> under the misapprehension that it was going to be a zombie film, that is a film about humans fighting zombies. Imagine my disappointment when it became an almost offensive storyline about soldiers who can't go for a month without needing a shag, so they set up an elaborate plan to lure women to up north in order to rape them!

Regardless of the feminist stance implied in RF's initial response to the film, the exchange which followed illustrates the way fans tend to develop expectations for a new film depending on their own past preferences and opinions of older films and this can work both with and counter to marketing campaigns for a film. O (M, 20s, Horror) replied with a remark suggesting that RF had misread the marketing: "Quite how you came to that conclusion is beyond me. Every single advertising campaign for the film stated 'It's not a zombie film'!" RF responded by making light of his assumptions, but again asserting that the film was misrepresented, even going on to attack the film further: "Guess I must be thick," he says, "or overwhelmed by subliminal advertising that told me it was! Certainly tried to rip enough zombie movies off for a non-zombie film!" What is important here is that established genre conventions or canonical texts are used as a yardstick against which new texts are measured, marking genre out as a key factor in interpretive practice and responses.

In this respect, many fans (especially, but not solely, the fans active in the horror groups) do make specific comparisons to zombie films, locating *28 Days Later* in the category horror, as much as in science fiction. Primary references are to the George Romero *Dead* series and the more recent *Resident Evil* (U.K./Germany/France, Paul W. S. Anderson, 2002)—films that have tended to define the zombie subgenre in recent American horror cinema. *28 Days Later* is seen as superior to *Resident Evil*—a film widely derided as an example of the decline of Hollywood cinema in terms of being derivative, hackneyed and narratively underdeveloped. "Okay," said J, for example, "there wasn't a lot of gore or big jumps etc. [in *28 Days Later*], but if you want that, go and watch *Resident Evil*." There are similarities here with the responses to British texts such as *Judge Dredd* and *Lord of the Rings*, specifically in respect of the "Hollywoodization" that fans so often fear and despise.[15] Like them, fans such as KK (M, 20s, SF) express scorn towards Hollywood texts: "I loved it [*28 Days Later*]. It was a breath of fresh air (along with *Dog Soldiers* [U.K./Luxembourg/U.S.A., Neil Marshall, 2002]) and a great relief from the Hollywood mainstream horror we are forced to suffer." There is a clear suggestion here of resistance to the imposition of an American cultural norm (what might be deemed imperialism) — or at the very least a dislike of the Hollywood narrative styles on offer (that "we are forced to suffer"). In this respect some fans are much more interested in complex or novel films which play with (or indeed subvert) the generic conventions — and this includes the mix of science fiction, horror and thriller conventions in *28 Days Later*, rather than what are regarded as clichéd and/or simplistic special effects-driven Hollywood-style films. In relation to a fan canon, the Romero films are used to define and epitomize the zombie subgenre. For many fans, *28 Days Later* is not, however, seen as inferior but as different. VoD (F, 30s, Vampire) says:

> I loved it but [it's] getting a lot of flack. [I] Think people were expecting a Romeroesque creation. I was pleasantly surprised. I love Romero (who can't?) but *28* ... was very artistically done ... i.e. [the] blood and crow's beak, empty London, burning civilization flashing by through a car window....

In many respects, the dislike for Hollywood is related to narrative and character development and, as suggested by the above quote, aesthetics and modes of emotional affect are also extremely important for many fans who are looking for something other than the straightforward jumps and gore of Hollywood films. A typical comment is made by LR (M, 40s, Who) who states that he is "a sucker for atmosphere." Significantly in a British context (and what leads to the film being read as a cosy catastrophe), he cites *The Village of the Damned* (Wolf Rilla, 1960) as a prime example of atmosphere (a film adaptation of John Wyndham's *The Midwich Cuckoos* (1957) — a key text in the cosy catastrophe form of British literary science fiction). Another common complaint is that Hollywood does not provide films that make a lasting impression on the viewer, something that *28 Days Later* does. T (M, 30s, Horror), for example, states: "I really enjoyed [*28 Days Later*], but I wouldn't class it as a very 'jumpy' film, especially in the latter stages. It's definitely disturbing, though." Again, affect is mentioned as a key factor in relation to nationality by some fans; S (M, 30s, DVD) states that: "*28 Days Later* is so far removed from [the Romero] films for quality. Maybe it's the Britishness of the style or something that makes it more psychologically disturbing that it really should be." It must be noted here that these opinions are shared by some American fans with broad tastes and knowledge of and love for European and other national genre cinemas — in this way, we might regard such fans as connoisseurs of the genre and this indicates that nationality is not the only factor at play here.

In terms of genre comparisons (and thus definitions), the British fans (and also the American connoisseurs to some extent) tend to make cultural comparisons to a wide range of texts, though these — as with *Village of the Damned*— were predominantly other examples of British science fiction-horror and cosy catastrophe, for example, *The Day of the Triffids* (BBC, 1981), *Doomwatch* (BBC, 1970–1972), *Survivors* (BBC, 1975–1977) and *Dog Soldiers*; American connoisseurs made cultural comparisons to titles such as *The Last Man on Earth* (Italy/U.S.A., Ubaldo Ragona, 1964) and *The Omega Man* (U.S., Boris Sagal, 1971). It is clear from these selections that these fans do not limit themselves to film, and they freely migrate back and forth between film and television in their viewing choices. With very few British science fiction films being produced, the fans seem more than content with telefantasy, but when a British film does appear some do seek to embrace and find whatever enjoyment in it they can. This raises their expectations in a particular way. The following comment (from G) suggests that fans have been cultivated not to have very high expectations of British cinema:

> *28 Days Later* is a pretty good film which is a bit surprising because not only is it British, it's also [...] a very British looking film as well which is quite refreshing considering the subject matter.

It is the history of British science fiction that provides a backdrop to the fans' reception of the film as "refreshing." Thus the film is seen in a positive light when compared to the majority of American films, but it may also work against the film when compared to other British texts or become the subject of debate. The cultural competencies of the fans are important here and these work as a benchmark against which the film is held up. CF (M, 30s, Who) maintains that: "As a depiction of a wasted London it ain't a patch on 'The Dalek Invasion Of Earth.'" *Doctor Who*— this reference is to an early story from the series — is a common point of comparison for these telefantasy fans, along with other defining texts of British science fiction literature, television and film. As we might expect though, fans do not always agree: CoD (M, 20s, Who) thought that "The deserted London scenes blow 'Dalek Invasion' away, much more creepy, quiet and disturbing." For yet other fans, the return of an older type of story — one for which they had fond memories — was a welcome one and a comparison was not necessary. TG (M, 50s, Who), for example, said "It was the glossy bastard child of *Survivors*, *Day of the Triffids* and 'Dalek Invasion of Earth'. You could sense Terry Nation dancing in heaven — it's been thirty years but someone understands again!"[16] Literary sources are also important, particularly John Wyndham. AM (M, 25, Who) states "I thought it was closer to Wyndham's post-apocalyptic England than to Nation's, I must say. As such, I thought it was wonderful," and PHJ (M, 40s, Who) agrees: "I found it to be a thoroughly enjoyable film, but then I am a massive fan of John Wyndham."

Again, the establishment of a fan canon is at work here, but the fan's personal history is also a key factor and fans have frequently invested in the texts they watched when young and which were formative in the establishment of their fan identity. With respect to national identity, the formative texts in this context are commonly British cosy catastrophes. This is strongly related to the processes of projection and introjection described by Jackie Stacey,[17] in which perceptions of and relationships to cultural objects can be part of the construction of self. Matt Hills's proposition regarding the "biographical continuity between the transitional object and cultural experience" is also important; the responses reported here are associated very strongly with childhood objects and thus have direct relevance to Hills's theory.[18] Some fans hold these formative texts as extremely important on a personal level and it is this — as much as any fan canon — which influences their responses. FLF's (M, 30s, SF) responses are a case in point:

> The first 15 minutes or so were great, but it was all downhill from there. It echoed Wyndham in places (one of my favourite authors) but lacked the power of his work. [...] I'm a big fan of 'after the fall of humanity' style stories, but *28 Days Later* scores pretty low on my list of favourites. I loved *Survivors* and the BBC version of *Day of the Triffids*, as well as movies such as *The Quiet Earth* [New Zealand, Geoff Murphy, 1985], *Le Dernier Combat* [France, Luc Besson, 1983], *Threads* [BBC, 1984] and *Virus* [/*Fukkatsu no hi* (Japan, Kinji Fukasaku, 1980)].

Such is this fan's love for and knowledge of the genre that a more recent text appears to have almost too much to live up to. It is also worth noting that for the *Doctor Who* fans, Christopher Ecclestone's role in the film has taken on increased significance since his casting as the Doctor in the new series. "Eccles," as TG (typical of the fans) refers to him, "was excellent. He's fluidly real, really, isn't he?" whilst JP (M, 20s, Who) thought: "He's fantastic. He really is. And it's interesting how he's doing it in his posh accent that just makes it seem even creepier...."

28 Days Later is thus equated with British apocalyptic science fiction and horror. It is the shared narrative conventions which allow fans, in the manner of Hills's biographical continuity, to recall their early viewing experiences, likes and dislikes, and are often what originally attracted them to the genre. These features include the post-apocalyptic storyline, the isolated survivor and the reliance on everyday resources or inner strengths. More recent developments in the genre, particularly within Hollywood cinema (conventions such as technology, weapons and action-style heroism), are accordingly not as well liked — though not necessarily because the conventions themselves are not appreciated. Rather it is the way in which they are used — and overused — within the genre. Through overuse, the American generic conventions are seen by the fans as clichés and unrealistic. Alongside this, many British fans as well as some Americans found the play on the typical zombie movie conventions in *28 Days Later* a refreshing change from the typical Hollywood style. One significant factor in the difference between *28 Days Later* and Hollywood films is suggested by B (M, 30s, SF):

> I'm fond of *28 Days Later* because it has the utter gall, in this day and age, of being a film with an actual, honest-to-goodness happy ending! Yes, that's right, instead of phoney modern-day nihilism, we actually have a happy ending! You could actually leave the film with a feeling of hope and a smile on your face ... after the hour-and-a-half of claustrophobic fear the release of tension with the happy ending is wonderful. I wish more filmmakers had the courage these days to have happy endings. It's not always cool or hip to end with a nihilistic shocker ... sometimes it's just the sign of a paucity of imagination and a dead soul.

This is certainly suggestive of nostalgic feelings for a tradition not often seen in contemporary mainstream examples of the genre. Again, there do seem to be strong indications of resistance to Hollywood culture. M (M, 30s, Spaced) typifies this:

> This film does what all the American films in its genre want to do, lashings of projectile gore, characters being killed off, left right and center. [...] But what we have here is not only cliché questions but questions of how certain persons would be treated in these situations and how they would react, morals and ethics are both questioned here, rape, procreation, materialism, murder, death, survival of the fittest and not necessarily because you've got an SA80 in yer mits.

For many fans, as here, the subtext and the philosophical or political questions raised by the film are extremely important. Issues mentioned include road rage, the outbreak of foot and mouth disease in 2001, and the behavior of British soldiers. CoD, for example, is concerned about the latter: "Squaddies have a testosterone-filled, overly macho culture about them ... we still hear about soldiers, sex and discipline (or lack thereof)." Thus, both genre and theme are key issues and these can be related to national identity in respect of contemporary news stories or the history and forms of the national cinema, both of which have a strong influence on taste. As the comparisons with British television suggest, the fans (whether their primary allegiance is to horror, science fiction or a single television text) appear to have a similar set of transitional objects. Furthermore, it was the ability to scare that gave the film much of its standing amongst the fans. The Channel Four website states that: "Boyle turned the zombie movie on its head with his DV-shot horror. Set against the backdrop of a post-apocalyptic Britain, 'the infected' in his film are rampaging monsters that chase down the living to quench their thirst for blood."[19] It was this very "turning on its head" in a British setting (and the address to relevant national concerns) that appealed to many British fans. Most fans agree that the film is classifiable as horror because they find it scary (emotional affect is a major factor in fan definitions of horror[20]), but it is a horror very firmly rooted in a recognizable Britain that reflects earlier science fiction/horror texts in general, and the cosy catastrophe in particular.

This goes a long way towards explaining the film's acceptance by many fans and this is echoed in the responses of the wider audience. In Channel Four's poll of the "hundred scariest moments" in film and television, *28 Days Later* was voted eighteenth. Significantly, the film's "most chilling moment" (to quote from the Channel Four website): "comes right at the beginning, when Cillian Murphy wakes from a coma and wanders out to find London completely deserted." It is this setting — a deserted capital and country — that is a key dimension of the horror for the British fans, as this quote from BBF (M, 20s, SF) illustrates: "Being set in England and opening with some pretty effective shots of a dead London the film's first half manages to get a grip on you simply through recognition of locations." Certainly, familiarity in terms of a national context was important to some British fans. Significantly this is linked with strong character identification driven by nationality (here an anonymous fan):

> The atmosphere generated within the first half of the film is fantastic and due to the opening London locations it does start to leave you in a "what if I ..." frame of mind and making every step Jim makes after his initial encounter with the infected fraught with implied danger.

In the same vein, realistic actions and reactions by characters in a national context also provide further pleasures. J, defending the film against negative reactions making what he saw as unfair comparisons with Hollywood films, said:

> I really did enjoy this film — it's more about "what would you do" which is exactly the point a lot of people miss, not everyone can hotwire a car/fly a helicopter/etc. etc. etc. — most people would get shit scared, run like hell and try and find more people to team up with.

In this way questions of quality and — as with the comparisons with generic conventions outlined above — *28 Days Later* is often seen as being good because it rejects the typical modes of American horror cinema which are themselves seen as unrealistic. As with identification with realistic characters, a realistic plot is also seen as important, as this quote from C (M, 20s, SF) typifies:

> [It has a] better sense of reality than other examples of the genre: *28 Days Later* eschews the macho gun posturing in the main for a well told story and effective set pieces.... It manages to get a better sense of realism to the situation, which may be a bit of an odd thing to say (after all have any of us been in a zombie invasion ... no thought not) but still it's a lot more real because the heroes can't suddenly fly planes, have access to vast quantities of ammo etc.

Such notions of quality are linked by the fans to the presence of a British director and British production context, demonstrating not just an awareness of nationality as represented within the text, but of the careers of filmmakers in the U.K. and with British film production in general. As GTL (M, 20s, Spaced) illustrates, fans can have detailed knowledge of national cinema:

> I love the director ... his stuff is always completely contemporary with a hint of visual retrospect at the same time. *Trainspotting* [Boyle, 1996] was very much of the time that it was brought out and so was *28 Days Later*. It's refreshing to see that instead of all the harking back to old times [...] that we seem to get a lot of. A good British movie over all.

Here, there is a sense in which genre fans crave home-grown films, yet at the same time feel that they are not catered for by the national cinema — which is more widely known and respected for its costume dramas to which this fan is referring (indicative of his own set of tastes and preferences, he describes these as "wanks"). There is also a sense for G in which Danny Boyle breaks the usual pattern of a British director turning his back on British film for Hollywood: "Hats off to Danny Boyle, after some of his latter big bucks films this is the last thing I expected him to do next." As many of these responses suggest, the reasons why British fans liked the film were attributed not simply to nationality but to issues of quality that are bound together with "Britishness." As outlined here by G again, quality is linked to production values (*28 Days Later* is considered to be a well-made film) and emotional effect:

> Danny Boyle [...] paints a brilliantly grim picture, the scenes of a deserted London are chilling and the new way of life survivors have to adapt to keeps the film flowing. There's plenty of action along the way too which means the film never becomes tiresome or boring.

Of course, not all British fans liked the film. Plot holes and two-dimensional characters were the main concerns. Similarly, the subverting of the generic conventions did not appeal to all British fans. It was pejoratively linked with Dogme films, for example, as if art and avant garde and other forms of specialist cinema all had negative appeal (evidence of the cultural economy at work, perhaps). This also illustrates the fact that some British fans have more in common with the American mainstream fans (just as the American connoisseurs have much in common with some British fans). Certainly, it suggests that these fans have "bought in" to the cultural colonization of British cinema and television by American texts. Another example of the impact of cultural imperialism on audiences is suggested in the remark by JO (M, teens, SF) that *28 Days Later* is "another overhyped Hollywood movie"—though the error was quickly pointed out by other fans. Some fans might, then, seem to be unaware of the production contexts of the film or are dismissive of British cinema, though I do not want to stress this too heavily—it may well be that these are younger or novice fans and/or fans with less generic knowledge or competence. In general, fan audiences can be amongst the most knowledgeable and informed of viewers, yet it may take some time to acquire such cultural competence.[21] Indeed, some British fans did take up considered positions in their dislike of the film. Some, such as Q (M, 30s, SF), felt that it did not merge British realism with Hollywood-style effects very successfully:

> The question is whether to go for realism (making some kind of comment about society today) or to go for an out and out fantasy gorefest (showing off your creative make-up skills). Well, in my opinion, *28 Days Later* still didn't know which option it wanted to adopt at the end of the movie.

Similarly, P (M, 20s, SF) found it to be "a dumb, clichéd movie that mixes Zombies and a large portion of [...] BBC SF and ends up being less than the sum of its parts...," suggesting that the attempt to adopt American styles or values is a flaw. However, many British fans regarded any flaws as unimportant, acknowledging them but preferring to forgive them or not let them impede their enjoyment of the film. G had:

> only two minor quibbles, the story behind the virus [...] could have been explained a bit more. I suppose we are seeing things through the main characters perspective, but I felt it lacked a bit here. Secondly, the second half of the film (at the army base) seems to become a bit detached from the original idea in the first half. But these are only quibbles.

In this way, some British fans establish a kind of "ownership" of British films such as *28 Days Later*, loving them whilst accepting their faults, defending their own preferences as they excuse the flaws in individual films that they love or even in the genre as a whole. A particular liking for a text should not therefore be taken as a rose-tinted view of the quality or artistic merits of that text.

British science fiction fans are not an homogenous group, but as the evidence here suggests, British cinema can exert a strong influence on tastes and preferences. Nationality is not necessarily a key factor in establishing identity within fan communities, particularly online, but it is often relevant to the formative experiences of the fans. National identity appears to exert a strong influence not only on personal taste, but in relation to the development of a science fiction canon centered around film, television and literary texts associated with cosy catastrophe. And whilst U.K.–based fan groups tend to fragment around very specific primary tastes (*Doctor Who*, *Spaced*), this does not restrict discussion of other texts and even seems to encourage discussion of key British canonical films, television programs and literature. Individual fans do move between groups, but more importantly particular interpretations tend to be repeated in different groups, providing a clear indication of a distinct interpretive community. It must not be forgotten, however, that factors relating to national difference are not always clear-cut; whilst nationality is a key factor in predicting responses to a text, other aspects of identity — including gender — invariably complicate any such patterns. In this context, however, nationality is foregrounded — particularly in relation to a popular culture dominated by American texts and where patterns of taste are determined by cultural background. British films may (and do) hold special significance for British audiences either through strong identification with British characters and locations, or in terms of aesthetic and narrative breaks with the dominant forms of the genre (usually Hollywood), or even fondness for British filmmakers. In this respect, discourses circulating around national cinema are important — particularly in respect of divergent narrative styles, sets of generic conventions and production values, within which notions of comparative quality highlight the differences between British and American texts.

14

Desiring the Doctor
Identity, Gender and Genre in Online Fandom

REBECCA WILLIAMS

There is little doubt that the British science fiction series *Doctor Who* (BBC, 1963–1989, 2005–) has achieved outstanding success, both critical and popular, since its re-launch in 2005. Furthermore, scholarly work has enthusiastically examined the show from a range of perspectives, leading to the emergence of "*Doctor Who* studies."[1] Admittedly, analysis of *Doctor Who* is not exclusive to the post–2005 incarnation (hereafter referred to as "new *Who*") and work such as Tulloch and Jenkins's *Science Fiction Audiences*,[2] Tulloch and Alvarado's *The Unfolding Text*,[3] and Alan McKee's writing on "classic *Who*"[4] have much to say about the text, production and reception of the series in its classic forms. However, this chapter seeks to contribute to an understanding of "new *Who*" and to address some of the gaps in analysis of the show and in studies of science fiction fans more widely.

One of the primary omissions has been the responses of female fans of the show which have tended to be sidelined even though "new *Who*" actively sought to attract a female science fiction audience through the centrality of strong companions such as Rose, Martha, Donna and Amy.[5] Related to this is the fact that, despite the productive ways in which female fans can use science fiction texts to form supportive communities or resist dominant ideologies,[6] there remains an ongoing cultural assumption that science fiction is a genre which primarily attracts male audiences. This chapter explores this by examining the responses of female fans of "new *Who*" with particular emphasis on how they read the program through the figure of The Doctor, as played by David Tennant (2005–2010).[7] Much prior work on fandom both within and beyond the science fiction genre has examined how female fans are often dismissed as silly or trivial and those who express overly sexualized desire for celebrities or characters are frequently devalued. When such expressions *are* permitted they can often only be articulated in "safe" female spaces such as women-only message boards or online list-servs.[8] Related to such notions of female fans as silly, hysterical or immature is the figure of the "fangirl" who is assumed to embody these traits and who is often devalued for her irrational attraction to characters or celebrities.[9] This chapter seeks to argue that, *contra* the devaluation of these feminized responses, desire and attraction might be displayed as a positive aspect of the fan practices of certain female fans of "new *Who*" and, more specifically, David Tennant. Thus, although Christopher Ecclestone (the ninth Doctor) and Tennant's star personae have been analyzed,[10] my emphasis is on how a specific actor's embodiment of the role contributes to how certain fans read the show. In particular, given that "*Doctor Who's* connection with British public service ideals, its eccentric lead character and its sometimes less-than-glossy production values have all caused it to be thought of as a very British program,"[11] I consider whether it is David Tennant's performance as a specific type of Doctor and a particular form of masculinity (commonly referred to as "geek chic"[12]) which contributes to these fans' discussions of the program. Thus, approaching fandom as performative, I will examine how status as "fangirls" might be embraced, reclaimed, and displayed.[13] In considering female fans of "new *Who*" and David Tennant, the chapter draws upon this case study to more generally engage in debates within British science fiction fandom. Indeed, as the chapter will illustrate, whilst fandom which focuses upon attraction to Tennant might be valued by certain viewers, such readings remain contentious and are not welcomed by all fans of *Doctor Who*. Thus, the chapter also examines how male and female fans differ in their interpretations of the show and relates these issues to how the boundaries of the fandom are policed in various ways.

Having set up the aims of the chapter, I now briefly outline how this research into fans of "new *Who*" was undertaken and how the fan comments used were gathered. Given that television fandom is often performed online, the focus of analysis for this chapter is one Internet forum devoted to discussion of *Doctor Who*. Cyberethnography is a common method in fan and cultural studies, allowing consideration of "critical and exegetical discussions of [...] program[s]."[14] Thus, although this chapter draws on "snapshots" from a range of online posts, rather than engaging in sustained participant observation over a long period of time, it remains indebted to the methodological and theoretical principles of cyberethnography. Data was drawn from the *Doctor Who Forum* (formerly *Outpost Gallifrey*) which was the largest online *Doctor Who* fansite with over 39,000 members at the time of writing.[15] Although the site requires a username and password to log in and read and post, there is academic precedent for using quotes from the site.[16] Whilst online spaces are subject to competing issues of ethics and access, brevity prevents more comprehensive discussion of these here.[17] However, use of online quotes from the forum adheres to basic principles of anonymity as all names of posters have been omitted to protect their identity and quotes used are identified by thread name and post number. Such moves protect an individual's identity (even if they can only be identified by online pseudonyms) but they also offer a level of academic accountability in that quotes can be traced and verified by others. Having briefly outlined the approach undertaken when examining online fans of *Doctor Who*, the chapter now considers how discourses of gender and appropriate fan behavior were performed and policed in this online space.

OMG! Squeeing Fangirls!!!: Fandom, Gender and Identity

Despite its alleged mainstreaming and the fact that an increase in online fandom has allowed "fan expression and fan identity to leak out into, and potentially permeate, the fan's everyday life,"[18] certain forms of fan practice remain devalued. This dismissal can be undertaken by wider society, as in Matt Hills's example of Michael Jackson fans that were attracted to the star,[19] or within popular media coverage of the *Twilight* saga (a series of books and films about vampire romance) which has described its fans "using Victorian era gendered words like 'fever,' 'madness,' 'hysteria,' and 'obsession.'"[20] However, such devaluation can also occur *within* specific fan cultures. For example, Andrea MacDonald notes how female fans of the U.S. science fiction series *Quantum Leap* (U.S., NBC, 1989–1994) who wished to discuss the lead actor Scott Bakula were dismissed by male viewers,[21] whilst male fans of *The X-Files* (U.S., Fox, 1993–2002) disliked it when "women begin sharing lustful thoughts about the actors,"[22] and attempted to close down such expressions of attraction whilst simultaneously discussing their own desires for female characters/actresses.[23] However, sometimes female fans themselves make distinctions between "appropriate" and "inappropriate" fan behavior. For example, Nash and Lahti examined fans of Leonardo DiCaprio and found that many emphasized their interest in his acting abilities in order to distance themselves from "(other) girl fans' more common (and less appropriate) focus on his looks or his place in romantic fantasies."[24] Similarly, Hills and Williams analyzed how predominantly female fans of *Buffy the Vampire Slayer* (U.S., The WB/UPN, 1997–2003) actor James Marsters were keen to disassociate themselves from fans who appeared "too hysterical or 'immature'" and from those who went to see the star's rock band, not for the music, but for the chance to see the desired character he played in the flesh.[25]

This insistence on not being immature or hysterical highlights how female fans' responses are often constructed through the constructed figure of the "fangirl." Whilst "fanboys" are depicted as nerdy and overly obsessed with trivia and collecting merchandise,[26] fangirls are characterized as hysterical, excessively emotional, and obsessive. It is telling that whilst the fanboy is largely associated with traits which suggest repression, order, and being socially inept (quite often with women), fangirls embody the antithesis of this. The threat of the fangirl lies in their hysteria, their frenzy, their emotionality and desire; all traits which imply an unruly body which cannot be contained. For example, images such as frantic girls screaming at Beatles' concerts have reinforced the cultural stereotype that "fangirls together [...] are supposed to whip each other up into a hysterical frenzy, their expression of desire reduced to fits of crying and screaming."[27] As Rhiannon Bury argues, however, the figure of the fangirl is a discursive construct and labeling someone as a fangirl performs a clear role in positioning and disciplining both female desire and appropriate fan behavior: "The fangirl quickly became a powerful heteronormative minus-male subject position offered to those of us with female bodies who express admiration for a male celebrity."[28] Thus, there is always a "balancing act undertaken by female fans that admire male celebrities and yet are concerned about being dismissed as fangirls."[29] As Bury's work makes clear, for some the label of the fangirl is to be avoided at all costs for its association with immaturity, hysteria, and a sense of uncontained and unregulated sexuality and femininity. Indeed, oppositions abound between restraint and intellect and the unruly body and desires of the fangirl.

Despite such negative associations, not all female fans reject the fangirl label and its associations with desire and emotionality. Instead, some fans actively seek to reclaim and perform the identity of the fangirl and, having outlined how female fandom and fangirls have been previously approached, I turn now to more specific discussion of the fandom displayed at the *Doctor Who Forum*. Fandom has been approached as a site of performance and as "an identity which is (dis-)claimed, and which performs cultural work,"[30] and this chapter examines how status as "fangirls" might be embraced, reclaimed, and performed. For many female fans of "new *Who*" their first contact with the show has been in its post–2005 incarnation and many are unconcerned with the show's history, nor with revisiting old episodes. For these fans the new version of the show forms the primary text which they are interested and invested in. For a smaller subset of these fans, their reading of the show functions through the "filter" of David Tennant, highlighting that: "we absorb media messages through a range of filters. We mediate through reference groups, we actively and selectively sift through media content."[31] Moreover, discussions surrounding Tennant often make explicitly clear that these fans perceive him as an object of desire and, whilst they might discuss his acting abilities, other roles, or other aspects of *Doctor Who*, their attraction to him is paramount. As one fan comments: "Its the Talent. The Voice. The Big Brown Eyes. The Smile. The Freckles. The Dimples. The Lean Sexy Body. The Sweetness. The Tee Shirts. DT has it ALL."[32] Such interpretations clearly oppose more masculinized fan readings since "derision of those [fans] who 'fancy' cast members suggests that sexual attraction should not be the primary terms of evaluation."[33] However, for some female *Doctor Who* fans, attraction does indeed form the "primary term of evaluation" and one key way in which female fans of "new *Who*" express their fandom is through the notion of "squee squads," allowing them to form groups of fellow fans who share the same interests. For example, Busse and Hellekson note that squeeing is "a squeal of uncontained appreciation or excitement."[34] The enactment of squeeing allows online fans to articulate their excitement and enthusiasm for characters, actors, or narrative events from *Doctor Who* (and its sister show *Torchwood* [BBC, 2006–]). However, although originating within fandom, fan concepts such as "squeeing" have begun to be commented on within the mainstream media since Tennant's status as a "sexy" Doctor was articulated in wider press coverage and because the show had enormous cultural impact. For example, in a comparison of the three "new *Who*" Doctors (Christopher Ecclestone, Tennant, and Matt Smith), one article comments that: "Tennant turned the show from 'Doctor Who' to 'Doctor phwoargh.' Hardcore fansites were horrified by the sudden influx of newly minted girl-fans screaming 'skweeee!'"[35] This suggests that female fans who read "new *Who*" via their attraction to David Tennant might not be entirely oppositional since their readings have, to some extent, been sanctioned by the media's positioning of Tennant as the "sexy Doctor." However this comment also makes clear that such responses are not welcomed by all fans of "new *Who*." Online fans seem to back this up through comments such as "Tiresome shippers [those who support on-screen romantic relationships] and squeers defy all rational explanation,"[36] or descriptions of squeeing as "a sound of unjustified excitement which normally precedes being punched very hard in the face."[37] Although the latter comment cannot be taken as a genuine threat of violence, these posts demonstrate some posters' frustration with fans that are irrationally excited by certain aspects of fandom. It is also perhaps telling that the latter comment was posted in a thread devoted to classic series toys and merchandise, indicating that this poster is both a fan of the older *Doctor Who* episodes (which some Tennant fans express no interest in) and is also a potential collector of *Doctor Who* items. As discussed above, the practices of stereotypical fanboys often include the collection of such objects which tends to oppose the practices of fangirls. It may be, then, that the overexcitement of the fangirls and "Squee squads" is too different from this fans' own practices and behaviors and, thus, must be discursively controlled and dismissed.

David Tennant, Geek Chic, and Masculinity

Although the male fans quoted above appear to dismiss female viewers who support on-screen relationships or display unacceptable excitement towards the show, the fact remains that David Tennant has attracted a significant female fanbase. Given the hostility of many male fans, why do fangirls continue to overtly display their attraction to him and to perform this identity so consciously on the *Doctor Who Forum*? One answer might be to view their fan practices as overt performances of femaleness, as exaggerated displays of appropriate hegemonic femininity. There have been clear links made between the figure of the fan and the "nerd" or the "geek," which suggests that fangirls may also be aligned with these archetypes. Furthermore, nerd identity (and, we can also argue, fan identity) is closely linked to issues of gender and sexuality as: "nerdism in both men and women is held to decrease sexual attractiveness. [...] In women, lack of sexual attractiveness is a far greater sin."[38] Indeed, "nerds are presumed male [...]. This connection between nerdism and masculinity may be what makes a nerd identity so damaging to women's potential and perceived sexual desirability."[39] Fanboys similarly need to negotiate threats to their gender identity as "the fan-boy clearly shares some of the (albeit stereotypical) characteristics of the [...] failed masculinity of the nerd."[40] Given the close links between fans and the figures of the nerd and the geek might we not be able to view the performance of a fangirl identity as a way to counter both this apparent desexualization but also to ward off any defeminization which occurs via the correlation of the geek/fan/nerd figure with masculinity? If, as argued, fan identity is performative and not natural, then assuming the mantle of the fangirl might actually offer a space for enactment of culturally feminized and devalued traits such as displaying attraction to desirable male figures.

In addition to the common focus on David Tennant as a figure of desire is a tendency towards discussion of the type of masculinity which he and his Doctor embody. There is a sense that his portrayal of The Doctor through costuming and styling, which connotes a "geek chic," contributes to his appeal for many female fans. The masculinity and desirability of Tennant's Doctor appears to resonate with cultural constructions and stereotypes of the nerd or the geek but also relates to *Doctor Who*'s status as a specifically British science fiction program.

To deal with the first of these issues we need to consider popular cultural constructions of "the fan," a figure who, despite the alleged mainstreaming of fandom, is still often prone to negative stereotyping, stigma, and ridicule. As noted above, fans who express libidinal attraction for celebrities/characters often form one of these groups, but the wider stereotype of the fan as "sad and pathetic, lacking a grasp of reality and obsessed with the unimportant" also endures.[41] Indeed, "Fans, geeks and nerds — overlapping but not identical social and cultural categories — have long been vilified in the mass media with 'get-a-life' stereotypes and marginalized by images of social, sexual and economic incompetence."[42] Given this ongoing cultural denigration it is perhaps unsurprising that fans often gravitate towards fan objects which seem to reflect traits associated with fandom or which appear sympathetic to them. For example, in discussion of *Buffy the Vampire Slayer* actor James Marsters, Hills and Williams note that the actor often situates himself as an outsider or a "freak," positioning himself as similar to fans in order to engender their support.[43] Whilst it can surely be argued, given Tennant's self-identification as a long-time fan of *Doctor Who*,[44] that he is positioned as "close to" fans of the show, I am more interested here in how his characterization of the Tenth Doctor as "geeky" and intelligent might work to encourage fan identification and, in the case of female fans, attraction and desire.

Despite cultural stereotyping, representations of the geek or nerd are not always associated with technology and computing, nor are they always linked to notions of failed masculinity.[45] For example, within the rock and indie music scenes there has been a reappropriation of "geek cool" which displays and valorizes being "introspective, insecure and self-deprecating."[46] Thus, indie and geek chic can offer "an alternative articulation of masculinity" which opposes the more aggressive males of rock and punk music.[47] Here, the label of the geek is actively claimed and performed and used to construct a softer and more welcoming masculinity. Similarly, one way in which geeks can address potential stigma surrounding their identities is to "embrace their outsider status and assert 'geek pride' as an exercise of power and resistance,"[48] and this is often achieved by wearing clothing which emphasizes one's geek status, by dressing stylistically in "geek chic." Thus, the notion that the geek chic which Tennant's Doctor embodies might actually engender attraction and desire from certain female viewers no longer seems so implausible. In fact, given the strong cultural linkage between the figures of the fan, the geek, and the nerd, the fact that female fans might be attracted to male characters or actors who appear to embody similarities with them makes sense. If fangirls are positioned as largely devalued and as "sad," much like the discursively constructed geek, then their reading of *Doctor Who* via Tennant's portrayal of The Doctor suggests a level of identification, as well as emotional investment and libidinal attraction. In "The Record Long David Tennant Appreciation Thread," for example, fans debate their attraction to the actor. One states, "I dont think DT has conventional Good Looks either. I like that [actor John] Barrowman said DT is not what you would call Classically Good Looking, but that he is a sexy Guy. That's soooo true,"[49] whilst another attests "SEXY is definitely the right adjective for DT."[50] Such comments suggest that part of Tennant's appeal is that he is not typically good-looking or unattainably handsome. His lack of stereotypical "good looks" are valued by these fans who remain attracted to him even though he does not typify cultural norms of attractiveness and is not, as these fans note, "classically good looking." However, Tennant's own star persona may play a further part here, given his high cultural links to the Royal Shakespeare Company and his playing of Hamlet in 2008–2009[51] which might further feed into his construction as an intelligent, non-traditional figure of masculinity that female fans could identify with. Finally, given that "the character [of The Doctor] has become wedded to imagined notions of British cultural identity,"[52] it may be that part of Tennant's appeal for some female fans is his embodiment of a very British masculinity which is softer, more feminized, and more accessible. Furthermore, fan attraction to the actor can also be linked to current trends in contemporary science fiction television more broadly as, whilst early science fiction depicted "handsome American heroes [fighting] against evil, the genre's current representations of masculinity are rather less stable."[53]

Policing the Genre: British Science Fiction and "Appropriate" Readings

Having outlined some of the ways in which female fans of "new *Who*" read the show through David Tennant, I now consider the distinctions which operate within this online fan space, paying particular attention to how debates over appropriate readings of the show are gendered. Drawing on the case study of *Doctor Who* as a British science fiction show, this section considers how the issues examined in this chapter might relate more broadly to fan debates about science fiction as a genre and to wider discussions over *what* can be discussed and *who* can be permitted to speak.

As noted above, male and female fans often diverge in their discussions of fan objects since online male fans tend to dislike "frivolous" chat[54] and, in MacDonald's study of *Quantum Leap* fans, objected to "long discussions of the characters' relationships" and off-topic chat about posters' real lives.[55] However, such attempts to restrict "female" conversations or to drive women to their own separate message boards clearly demonstrate fans' attempts to police the boundaries of acceptable conversation. Indeed, one of the most common ways in which fandom has been theorized is through analysis of how subcultures form their own distinctions, appropriate behavior, and discourses which tend to replicate the cultural hierarchies of mainstream culture.[56] This is often achieved by determining who is part of a fan culture, and fans make "constant attempt[s] to project internal purity by identifying inauthentic outsiders who must be rejected and shunned."[57] Indeed, a common way in which some fans of *Doctor Who* attempt to police the boundaries of the fandom is through devaluing those who display attraction to David Tennant, dismissing them as not being "true" lovers of *Doctor Who* and being unfamiliar with the show's prior history. It is here that the label of the fangirl is often deployed as a derogatory term which aims to feminize and infantilize those who perform their fandom in this way. Indeed, whilst the gendered element of the term is clear, invoking the notion of the "girl" suggests childishness and immaturity; traits which are often disavowed within other fan cultures.[58]

For example, in a thread entitled "New school fans — too much self-loving?," one poster suggests that many of these fans "just say 'ugh classic is boring, new is best, David Tennant OMGLOLBESTDRSEXGODLOL,'"[59] whilst another comments, "I agree that there's a hugely irritating trend amongst some New fans to equate 'talented actor playing a compelling character' and 'omg so haaaawt!!!!1one' [...]. There's a certain giggling schoolgirl mindset to a particular kind of New Who fan."[60] Comments such as these demonstrate fans' irritation with female fans' attraction to David Tennant which is here stereotyped as "giggling schoolgirls" and a tendency to substitute coherent language for text-speak and enthusiastic declarations of attraction. This indicates the infantilization of such fans and their responses, characterizing them as childish and somewhat ridiculous. By rendering those who deviate from apparently masculinized "proper" readings of *Doctor Who* (that is, respecting the history of the program, offering rational argument, suppressing emotional responses) as both feminized and immature, certain groups of fans work to enforce "an officially constituted reading formation which supervises reading of the show."[61] This dismissal of Tennant fans continues in a debate over whether certain fans would keep watching after the actor departed the show. Notions of fangirls as obsessive and concerned with the attractiveness of the lead character are clearly displayed in the following posts:

> I don't think he was referring to actual fans more the kinda people that're like: "David Tennant is the best Doctor ever ^_^! Matt Smith will be rubbish because he isn't sexy! He's so damn ugly, am I right Middle-aged Housewife Number 7?" They'll all be gone come next year, those people aren't fans. I can't understand the mentality of somebody who watches a show just 'cus the main character is hot.[62]

> I'd be surprised if the fangirls creeping him out and his reputation as a pin-up didn't factor into his leaving. Wasn't there one report of them having to stop filming cus the squeers took their obsession with him too far? I find people discussing the paint on the TARDIS more endearing than people slagging off his girlfriends and digging and obsessing over his life to feel closer to him.[63]

Clearly here certain readings and behaviors are deemed appropriate within the science fiction genre whilst others are not. However, many fans of David Tennant do not retreat from the battlefield over meaning and interpretation. One female poster angrily responds by devaluing the discussions of older fans and those who watched pre–2005 *Doctor Who*:

> im sorry you dont get to choose who are fans of this show and personaly its a good thing you dont, the so called squee squad bring a different aspect to fandom that i for one love hearing about the reading about and its good for fandom to not just be 40 year olds talking about tardis paint and how its different now than it was in the key to time![64]

For this fan, and others like her, it is the reading of *Doctor Who* through the figure of Tennant that is "appropriate," and it is the more masculinized responses of discussing minutiae such as the color of the TARDIS which are deemed to be deviating from the norm. Furthermore, instead of treating the term fangirl as an insult or an attempt to belittle them, many seek to reclaim the identity and use it as a badge of defiance against those fans whose readings differ from their own. One female fan responds with "There is nothing wrong with being a 'middle-aged squeeing fangirl,' it's not a 'men only' fanclub after all. Mind you, some men do seem to be a bit intimidated and fed up with all the squeeing (which will only make us SQUEEE even louder!)."[65] Another replies to the suggestion that fangirls and "squee squads" occupy a "dank corner of fandom"[66] by rejecting the male poster's attempt to belittle and devalue female fan practices through sidelining them. She posts, "The Squee section of fandom is not dank, neither is it in a corner. It's here, full bloodied and to stay. Welcome to your worst nightmare!"[67]

However, practices such as squeeing and lusting over David Tennant are not always unproblematically embraced by female fans. Indeed, the term fangirl has always been open to contestation and ambiguity with many fans operating a dual usage of the label as a fan might "post a diatribe about a 'stupid fangirl' on her/his Livejournal one day, but may write a very excited and only semi-coherent entry another day and clearly label it as being 'fangirl-mode.'"[68] For example, some fans worked on a project to present to David Tennant, with one commenting "perhaps I should put something about how I objected because he is so much more handsome with all his face showing, and his hair too. I don't want to get too 'obsessed stalker fangirl' ish though!"[69] Even though this fan is posting in the "David Tennant appreciation thread" and is obviously enough of a fan of the actor to contribute a lengthy letter to the project, she still works to maintain a line between herself and the constructed "Other" of the fangirl. Here, fangirls are characterized as obsessive and as potential stalkers and the threat of association with this clearly comes from the fan's discussion of how handsome Tennant is. Here the link is clear — too much attention paid to the attractiveness of a celebrity is characteristic of the fangirl, a figure which this fan still seeks to maintain a distance from. Another thread, which although titled "Could *Torchwood* survive without Jack?" discusses *Doctor Who*, debates the definition of the term fangirl and the assumptions associated with it. One male fan states,

> In general terms I don't like people equating being a "fangirl," "fanboy," "fanperson," whatever, with having a crush on the actor/actress/being. Certainly not the case with myself considering I'm readily identified as a "Freema fanboy" and can assure myself that I don't have anything in the realm of a crush on her.[70]

For this poster, it is not the label itself which is problematic (he quite happily identifies as a Freema Agyeman fanboy) but, rather, the implication that such an identity is based solely on attraction and desire. What this poster imagines other aspects of fanboy identity to be remains unclear but this comment clearly illustrates that fans themselves negotiate the terms of "fangirl" and "fanboy." Furthermore, other (female) fans comment:

> Another reason I took exception to [the] generalization about fangirls is the immediate, negative connotation of "fangirl" [...]. I've liked John Barrowman since I saw "The Empty Child." I've enjoyed sci-fi and fantasy for decades. So saying only "JB fangirls" think [*Torchwood*] wouldn't work without him? No.[71]

> Well DT is my first Doctor so speaking as a "middle-aged squeeing fangirl" I have to say that while I think he's fabulous (and fanciable) and I am sorry he's leaving, what I'm most appreciative of is the fact that he led me to this wonderful show. [...] I'm most definitely going to stick with DW no matter what. I enjoyed Eccleston too and I look forward to Matt Smith.[72]

For these female posters being a "fangirl" and being attracted to certain celebrity figures stands in clear opposition to their longer standing fandom of the science fiction genre more generally. For the first fan, her opinion that *Torchwood* would not work without the presence of actor John Barrowman is apparently based on her knowledge of the genre, rather than on any personal interest in the star. Of course, we cannot necessarily take this declaration at face value and it must be viewed, as with all online postings, as a performative display of fan identity. In this case, then, it might be that, well aware of the negative connotations of "fangirl," these fans seek to remove their interest in *Torchwood* and *Doctor Who* from the devalued realm of female fandom by aligning themselves with the more culturally masculinized genres of science fiction and fantasy, or by describing how initial interest in the figure of David Tennant has led to a wider appreciation of the "wonderful show" of *Doctor Who* more generally.

Conclusion

As this chapter has illustrated, John Tulloch's suggestion of a homogenous and stable interpretation of *Doctor Who* which "establish[es] an officially constituted reading formation" can no longer be sustained.[73] The advent of the Internet and the relaunch of "new *Who*" in 2005 has led to wider fragmentation of the audience and the formation of often disparate groups who read the show through different "filters" such as the long-standing history of the show, the auteur figure of Russell T. Davies, or various characters or actors. What this chapter has sought to contribute is an analysis of responses of certain female fans of *Doctor Who*, a component of the audience whose interpretations have been largely sidelined. More broadly, however, the chapter has related this case study of female David Tennant fans to wider issues within British science fiction through examining how fans with opposing views operated mechanisms of distinction to police the boundaries of what was appropriate for fans of *Doctor Who* and for the science fiction genre more broadly. Whilst gender divisions within fandom are not new, this chapter has brought these issues together with an exploration of how some female fans might recuperate and reclaim the often devalued term of the "fangirl" in order to perform their fan identities. Furthermore, whilst "women within fandom are often either attacked or dismissed,"[74] this case study of fans of a specific British science fiction television show has sought to offer some nuanced understandings of how fan identities are performed and are always subject to issues of distinction regarding who, and what, is appropriate and permitted within the realm of science fiction fandom. Indeed, even academic work which discusses the figure of the fangirl often goes to great lengths to argue that these fans are "more than" this — that their relationships with one another may have originated from mutual desire for specific celebrities but that they have grown and developed into friendships which transcend "drooling" or emotional responses.[75] What this chapter therefore proposes is that female fans' desires and responses (whether we call these fans fangirls or not) need to be addressed on their own terms and should be situated within wider debates over gender and genre in science fiction fandom. Indeed, if this chapter poses a question, let it be this: why can we not address female fans without feeling the need to rationalize or justify their desires or their emotional responses? Ultimately, it seeks to ask, within the fandom of a British science fiction television show, what is so wrong about desiring The Doctor?

15

Invaders from Space, Time Travel and Omnisexuality
The Multi-Layered Narrative of Torchwood

LEE BARRON

The twenty-first century has seen something of a renaissance occur for British science fiction television, most notably with the triumphant return of *Doctor Who* (BBC, 1963–1989, 2005–), which (aside from a one-off feature film made in 1996) had been off-air since 1989. The revamped *Doctor Who* was headed by television writer Russell T. Davies, whose previous credits had included early work in children's television and a series of acclaimed dramas such as *Bob and Rose* (ITV, 2001), *The Second Coming* (ITV, 2003), *Casanova* (BBC, 2005) and most notably, *Queer as Folk* (Channel Four, 1999–2000). But in addition to establishing a new incarnation of the Doctor character, a new female companion, and a pantheon of new alien enemies in addition to resurrected old favorites, Davies's *Doctor Who* also featured a male "co-hero" character: Captain Jack Harkness played by the Scottish/American actor John Barrowman. Although the Doctor had periodically had male companions during the program's 1963–1989 run (such as Ian Chesterton, Ben Jackson, Jamie McCrimmon, Harry Sullivan and Adric), Jack Harkness was different. Undertaking a series of adventures with the Doctor (as played by Christopher Eccleston and then David Tennant), the Captain Jack character instilled an unmistakable and unprecedented sense of sexuality into *Doctor Who*. And while the Captain Jack character would ultimately be an on-off companion, he would prove to have such a level of popularity that the character would be granted a spin-off series, *Torchwood* (BBC, 2006–), its title an anagrammatic homage to *Doctor Who* and featuring Captain Jack as the main character.

As with its progenitor series, *Torchwood* would also exemplify classic tropes and iconography of science fiction such as spacecraft, robots and extraterrestrials but with the added centrality of time travel and inter-dimensional invasion. However, *Torchwood* would feature an extra set of "boundary erosions," those of sexuality, profanity, graphic violence and post-watershed transmission slot. Because, unlike the family-oriented *Doctor Who*,[1] *Torchwood* would rapidly prove itself to be a radical alternative. And it is the issue of boundaries, in terms of worlds, dimensions, temporal zones, and sexuality within *Torchwood* that will be explored within the chapter. The onus on boundary erosion is a factor that illustrates both the continuities and discontinuities that marks *Torchwood*, in terms of long-established science fiction tropes and traditions, but especially so in contrast to *Doctor Who*. Nonetheless, *Torchwood* is also a very different expression of science fiction than that of *Doctor Who* in spatial terms. *Torchwood's mise-en-scène* is set predominantly within a single location: contemporary Cardiff. And yet, the series is centrally concerned with the idea of flux; it is a multilayered text that is centrally concerned, via its central plot-device, the Rift: a temporal-spatial anomaly that allows slippage to occur between time and space and which enables alien creatures to gain access to Earth. This plot conceit, central to the action of the majority of episodes, typifies the entire narrative. *Torchwood* is a text that is characterized by slippage, rifts and collisions; from the literal and visually-rendered movements that occur between space and time, to the tonal shifts that are endemic throughout the series. Furthermore, with a level of sexuality not present within *Doctor Who*, *Torchwood* possesses a cast of characters, primarily the central protagonist Captain Jack, but also many of the supporting characters, who express flexibility with regard to sexual boundaries. Therefore, *Torchwood*, a narrative about boundary slippage, is intrinsically characterized by this process in multiple ways, some which enhance the serial, marking it off as a progressive and groundbreaking example of modern British science fiction television, and a text that has pushed the boundaries of what can be explored within the television genre of science fiction.

Weevils, Timeslips and Stopwatches

Although there are a number of "proto-science fiction" literary works, from Johannes Kepler's *Somnium* (1634), Bishop Godwin's *The Man in the Moone* (1638), Voltaire's *Micromegas* (1752) to Mary Shelley's *Frankenstein* (1818) and C.I. Defantenay's *Star au Psi de Cassiopée* (1854), it was with the works of Jules Verne and H.G. Wells that science fiction became a recognisable genre or subgenre, even though the term "science fiction" would not come into existence until 1926, the year Hugo Gernsback launched the pulp magazine *Amazing Stories*.[2] *Amazing Stories* was the first self-described science fiction magazine, or, using Gernsback's self-coined term, "Scientifiction" to describe the work of Verne and Wells, writing that, in the view of Gernsback, were "romances ... intermingled with scientific fact and prophetic vision."[3] With a descriptive (and marketable) tag established, the literary genre/subgenre[4] developed through works by writers such as: Poul Anderson, Isaac Asimov, Arthur C. Clarke, Robert A. Heinlein, A.E. van Vogt,

Ray Bradbury and John Wyndham, in addition to the 1950s science fiction "explosion" that saw the production of numerous examples in science fiction magazines, anthologies, novels, cinema, and towards the end of the 1950s and into the 1960s, television.[5] Although a varied field, Brian McHale would argue that science fiction is a genre predominantly predicated upon the staging of "close encounters between different worlds, a genre that places discrete worlds in direct confrontation."[6] Hence, science fiction is the genre typified by what Robert Scholes calls "fabulation." It is a form of fiction "that offers us a world clearly and radically discontinuous from the one that we know, yet returns to confront that known world in some cognitive way."[7] Classically, fabulation, as McHale notes, conventionally takes two distinct but frequently complementary strategies: the transportation (through space, time or "other dimensions") of representatives of Earth to a different world, and (utilizing Thomas Pynchon's phrase) another world's intrusion into "ours." To illustrate, McHale cites various examples which include the invasion from space tales such as H.G. Wells's *The War of the Worlds* (1898), or tales of manned space travel, as in Wells's *The First Men in the Moon* (1901), Ray Bradbury's *The Martian Chronicles* (1950), and Edgar Rice Burroughs's John Carter Martian adventures (1912–1940). What typifies such narratives is the sense of confrontation that occurs "between our world and some other world or worlds somehow adjacent or parallel to our own, accessible across some kind of boundary or barrier."[8] Although identifiable in numerous literary works, such characteristics would also be discernible in the development of science fiction television, and in Britain, perfectly illustrated by the serial *Doctor Who*.

Although predated by programs such as the *Quatermass* serials (BBC, 1953–1957) and *A for Andromeda* (BBC, 1961), *Doctor Who* was first broadcast in 1963 during a period that witnessed the medium of television become the dominant domestic entertainment technology and (inspired by the threat of ITV) a subsequent drive by the BBC to embrace new television genres, among them, science fiction.[9] Heavily influenced by the works of H.G. Wells, primarily *The Time Machine* (1895) and *The War of the Worlds*,[10] *Doctor Who* consisted of a narrative predicated upon the principle of time, space, and inter-dimensional travel, coupled with extraterrestrial invasion tales. The series would run from the 1960s until the end of the 1980s, a longevity based upon quality writing, but also a distinctive ability to move with the times. This included its embracing of different generic modes and the series' unique characteristic, the Time Lord Doctor's ability to regenerate into a new body at the point of death (solving the problem of actors leaving the role), with each successive Doctor exhibiting a particular style and identity brand.[11] However, within the second generation of *Doctor Who* in 2005, not only would the series continue to explore and exhibit the "worlds in confrontation" motif that McHale argues is the hallmark of science fiction, it would do so with the added value of a much higher budgets and more impressive CGI-created special effects. Furthermore, its success on the BBC would result in Russell T. Davies's creation of a spin-off series, *Torchwood*. But while *Torchwood* would contain obvious narrative and thematic continuities with *Doctor Who*, it would also exhibit a highly distinctive sense of identity of its own that wholly set it apart from its "meta-series."

As a direct offshoot operating within the same narrative universe as *Doctor Who*, *Torchwood* inevitably would inherit and express the motifs of spatial and temporal effacement and slippage. But from the outset, *Torchwood* would be very different in its approach and representation of such themes. Unlike the narrative of *Doctor Who*, which is predicated upon the constant traveling through time and space, *Torchwood*'s narrative is rooted to a singular location, Earth, or more precisely, contemporary Cardiff. Indeed, if *Torchwood* demonstrates any direct continuity, barring periodic crossover episodes featuring Captain Jack and *Doctor Who* companions, then it is with the era of the Third Doctor (Jon Pertwee) from 1970 to 1974, the period that saw the Doctor act as an adjunct to UNIT (United Nations Intelligence Taskforce). Moreover, Captain Jack is not the *deus ex machina*–like Doctor, appearing almost magically at moments of peril, but is rather an employee, a professional heading the Torchwood Institute, the organization initiated in 1899 by Queen Victoria as a defense force against extraterrestrial incursions. Furthermore, *Torchwood* is an ensemble series. Captain Jack does not have "companions," but a professional team that is organized along strict principles of division-of-labor. The team consists (in series one) of former WPC Gwen Cooper, technology expert Toshiko "Tosh" Sato, medical officer Owen Harper, and "teaboy" Ianto Jones, and it is a group that is subject to a high mortality rate (by the climax of series three, only Gwen and Captain Jack remain alive). The tone and pace of *Torchwood* is quickly established in the opening episode, "Everything Changes." The episode opens, not ostensibly in any science fiction setting, but rather with a crime scene, the site of a murder. Present at the scene, in addition to Forensics officers, is PC Gwen Cooper, who is confused by the arrival of "Special Ops"— the Torchwood team, whose authority outranks all other officers. Torchwood's arrival signifies not only the introduction of the team, but also immediately denotes the stark difference that exists between *Torchwood* and *Doctor Who*. This difference expressed by a Forensic officer's reaction to the sweeping executive powers of the Torchwood group —"it's a fucking disgrace"— signalling the narrative differences the series has in comparison to *Doctor Who* and the freedom granted to explore and express adult themes through its 9:00 P.M. broadcast slot on BBC2.

Opening in a manner akin to a crime series, *Torchwood*'s science fiction credentials are only confirmed with Jack's statement, "I love this planet," immediately followed by the use of the "Resurrection Glove," an alien technology that can bring the recently dead back to life for two minutes. This is the incident that is witnessed by Gwen, who then undertakes her own investigative mission to uncover the identities of both Torchwood and Captain Jack Harkness, on behalf of herself, and to provide the necessary exposition for the audience. Although the plot of "Everything Changes" begins with a murder, the result of Torchwood member

Suzie Costello's attempt to master the Resurrection Glove, the episode centrally establishes the main themes and characteristics of the series: Gwen's entrance into the clandestine and subterranean Torchwood III with its laboratory of alien technology and state-of-the art surveillance equipment, her discovery that Jack was an American RAF volunteer who mysteriously vanished in 1941, and her subsequent joining of the Torchwood team.

The principal vein of elucidation within "Everything Changes" concerns why Torchwood III is located in the unlikely location of Cardiff (a running joke throughout the series), and why the Torchwood Institute exists. As Jack reveals to Gwen, Torchwood is an entity that is separate from the government, outside the police and beyond the United Nations. He is also an "alien-catcher," who, with his team, is centrally concerned with scavenging alien technology for use in a coming twenty-first century threat to humanity. Furthermore *Torchwood* is located in Cardiff because it is at the center of a space/time anomaly. As Jack explains: "There's a rift in space and time running right through the city. The Weevils didn't come in a spaceship. They just slip through. All sorts of things get washed up here. Creatures, timeshifts, space junk, debris, flotsam and jetsam." But the Rift is more than this—the Rift is the central narrative driving force of *Torchwood*, and it is what grants the program its distinctive characteristic.

The Oxford English Dictionary defines the word "rift" as: "a crack or split in an object; an opening in a cloud etc; a cleft or fissure in earth or rock" or "to tear or burst apart."[12] All of these descriptions communicate the form and function of the Rift within *Torchwood*. With parallels to *Doctor Who* and with hints of the legacy of H.G. Wells, *Torchwood* is filled with extraterrestrial invasions. These range from episodes such as "Day One," that features an alien life-form landing on Earth and wreaking havoc via possessing human bodies, and most notably, the 2009 mini-series, "Children of Earth." But the main thrust of *Torchwood* is related to the Rift and the state of spatial and temporal flux that it creates. As such, the Rift acts as the main narrative crux of the series. It is the dramatic axis on which the events of episodes typically revolve, the source of threat or anomalous phenomena.

The central *mise-en-scène* of series one and two (it is destroyed in series three), the Torchwood base (dubbed "The Hub" and complete with pet pterodactyl) is located at the epicenter of the Rift, and "Rift activity" is the staple of these series. It would, in terms of production, also show a different and modern face of Britain in terms of its Welsh production locations, and move away from the strict London/Home Counties/English focus of the original *Doctor Who*.[13] Although there are numerous incursive forces that make use of it, the consistent "face" of the Rift is the feral alien species dubbed "Weevils," who slip through the Rift from their world to take up residence in the Cardiff sewer system, but which periodically ascend to the surface and attack humans. Although some episodes have featured threats that were not Rift-related at all, for example, the ghost motif of "Random Shoes," the fairies of "Small Worlds," or the human cannibalistic clan of "Countrycide," the Rift and its effacement of time/space boundaries *is* the major focus of *Torchwood*. Moreover, as the series progresses, the Rift acquires a complexity and multilayered nature, effectively becoming a character in its own right within the narrative. This facet is especially emphasized in the episode "Adrift" which reveals and explores the unpredictability of the Rift, establishing, as it does, that it not only allows non-human life-forms to cross into Cardiff, but that it can also draw people into it, dispersing them across the universe. The core of the episode rests upon the discovery that the Rift frequently returns its "abductees" to Earth, albeit frequently in a state of unnaturally advanced age and bearing physical and mental damage. Thus, the Rift is a "portal" between worlds. Furthermore, the Rift also acts as a means to introduce classic tropes of the science fiction genre into *Torchwood*, principally that of time travel, a theme that dominates the episode "Out of Time." In this instance, the Torchwood team do not react to any threat that has emerged from the Rift, but rather, they must act as counselors to three passengers of an airplane that has crossed from 1953 to 2006, an occurrence that allows for further exposition concerning the exact nature of the Rift. As Jack states to the bemused pilot of the lost aircraft, Diane Holmes: the Rift is a transcendental portal, "a door in time and space." "Out of Time" represents something of a change of pace from other episodes, concentrating on the effects and trauma of the Rift and the ways in which the people from the past must reconcile themselves with the present and forget their previous era, or, like Diane, attempt to re-enter the Rift and return to the past.

Continuing with a time travel theme, the most complex and multilayered exploration of Rift-related boundary effacement is exemplified in the two-part finale of series one, "Captain Jack Harkness" and "End of Days," both centrally based upon time travel and the movement between discrete worlds. "Captain Jack Harkness" is an episode that is thematically driven by the depiction of parallel worlds, with a narrative based upon the idea of time-slip. This episode sees Jack and Tosh drawn to the apparently "haunted" and long-derelict Ritz Dancehall to investigate reports of the sounds of 1940s-style music coming from within it. However, on entry, they are transported back in time to 1941, becoming trapped there. As the episode progresses, the narrative subsequently continually shifts back and forth between 1941 and 2006, with an increasing level of slippage amid the worlds becoming evident, initially through communications and equations written by Tosh in the past which are discovered in the present, followed by the more dramatic collision of the two temporal zones as the "walls" separating the epochs steadily wear down. This begins with Gwen hearing the period music in the present and intensifies as Owen opens the Rift, visualized in the scene that has Jack and Tosh step over the temporal threshold to return to the twenty-first century. "Captain Jack Harkness" also introduces a mysterious villain character, Bilis Manger, a time traveler who, as he states to Gwen, "can step across eras," and whose ultimate scheme is revealed in the series one finale, "End of Days," set amidst a Cardiff that is undergoing spatial and dimensional trauma due to the partial opening of the Rift that enabled Jack and Tosh's escape from the past.

"End of Days" is centrally predicated upon the issue of boundary collapse, in which the plot sees Cardiff experiencing the effects of time splintering, with "cracks" appearing in the barriers between temporal spaces that mean that historical eras begin to co-mingle. This ranges from the appearance of an aggressive Latin-speaking Roman soldier to the hospital admitting a woman from the middle-ages who has the Black Death. Consequently, past, present and future threaten to collide to the extent that the Earth will be destroyed. The episode culminates in a Bilis-inspired mutiny by the team against Jack and the opening of the Rift to "let it suck back what it has let through." But what the opening of the Rift achieves is the realization of Bilis's scheme, the release of Abaddon, the Great Devourer — Son of the Great Beast — who has been imprisoned beneath the Rift. Thus, in addendum to the episode's Biblical/Satanic/apocalyptic overtones (and at one stage Ianto reads from the Book of *Revelation*), this further element of worldly invasion also suggests the influence of the American "weird fiction" writer, H.P. Lovecraft, whose tales of the return of the "Old Ones" or "Elder Gods" were invariably set "in the fear-haunted towns of an imaginary area of Massachusetts or in the cosmic vistas that exist in dimensions beyond space and time."[14] Lovecraft's tales would be filled with details of these extraterrestrial Gods which existed on Earth before humanity and who seek to return through various portals. And, with a distinctly Lovecraftian touch, the newly released and gigantic Abaddon stalks across Cardiff, his shadow causing the deaths of everyone it falls upon, his reign only (rather rapidly, it must be noted) curtailed by Captain Jack who absorbs his shadow and whose immortality proves fatal to the creature, exhibiting yet another further level of boundary erosion manifest in the series, and central to Captain Jack — that of life and death.

With an influential nod to the recuperative powers of Gerry Anderson's 1960s iconic science fiction hero Captain Scarlet, who was "made indestructible after surviving a Mysteron attack,"[15] Captain Jack cannot die, nor does he appear to age. Captain Jack, born in the fifty-first century, is therefore a man out of time, and his central uniqueness is his immortality (he describes himself as being "a fixed point in time") and indestructibility, a result of exposure to the time vortex in the *Doctor Who* episode "Parting of the Ways." And it is as the *Torchwood* narrative unfolds across (to date) three series that Jack's identity is steadily revealed, in an elliptical fashion. For example, his role as an off-world "Time Agent" is hinted at within "Kiss Kiss, Bang Bang," he appears within an early twentieth century film reel within "From Out of the Rain" engaged in an early Torchwood mission and utilizing his immortality as a circus act, "Exit Wounds" reveals the loss of his family and the existence of a brother, and the flashback-themed "Fragments" reveals his actual recruitment to the Torchwood Institute in 1899. But, the narrative progressively casts Captain Jack's existence in a permanent "in-between-state" as an ultimately melancholic state. For instance, within "Children of Earth," it is revealed that Jack has a daughter, Alice and a grandson, Steven. Yet, his contact is minimized by Alice because she is doomed to age and die while he will not. Furthermore, and again illustrating his Captain Scarlet-like status, Captain Jack is utterly impervious to attempts to kill him. Thus, although subject to numerous gunshots throughout the narrative which apparently kill him (in addition to being buried alive), this proves to be only a temporary condition from which he awakens. This ability is particularly explored and tested within "Children of Earth," five episodes that see Jack shot on numerous occasions, poisoned, entombed in concrete and, most spectacularly and graphically, blown into pieces by a bomb, only to slowly regenerate back to his former state. However, it is also significant that Gwen also reflects a distinct sense of "alienation," not due to being immortal, but related to the pressure of living simultaneously in two very different spaces, and maintaining a relationship with a fiancée, Rhys. As she states of her life in the episode "Out of Time": "it's like there's two separate worlds — there's Torchwood, and then there's real life." But even then, they eventually come together with Rhys discovering the existence of both Torchwood and the Rift.

Therefore, from the temporal/spatial nature of the Rift, to Captain Jack's immortal fixed-point ontological status, *Torchwood* is a text that extensively articulates the idea of boundary erosions. It is a series about a world that is on the fault-line of parallel worlds and an unstable temporal/spatial/dimensional doorway that is unpredictable. In this regard, it has clear parallels with previous modes of science fiction texts that feature "portals," from Wells's *The Time Machine* to *Doctor Who*, the latter having a particular focus upon this theme in Davies's writing. However, there is yet another level to the way in which *Torchwood* plays with the issue of boundaries and boundary effacement, and one that decisively sets it apart from its older *Doctor Who* heritage, and this is the issue of sexuality and fluid sexual identities.

With reference to his previous work as a television writer, most notably in writing the groundbreaking Channel 4 drama, *Queer as Folk* (complete with its *Doctor Who*-loving character, Vince), the U.K. tabloid, *The Sun*, greeted the announcement that Davies was heading the revamp of the long-defunct *Doctor Who* with the headline, "Doctor Queer."[16] And in some senses, they were not too far off the mark because the *Doctor Who* of the twenty-first century would, under Davies's vision, contain a sexual edge that the original run utterly lacked. Though the 1963–1989 series would see periodic reference to a range of political issues such as fascism, ethnic persecution, feminism and class conflict,[17] sexuality was not paramount, nor was there any real indication that there could be any romantic liaisons between the Doctor and his companions.[18] So while the character of the mysterious and otherwordly Doctor would range from the avuncular, impish, and eccentric, he was most assuredly chaste. Even with the companionship of numerous female (and some male) companions, from (to name but a few) the resourceful Sarah Jane, the warrior Leela, the Time Lord Romana, and the "streetwise" Ace, while representations of femininity would vary, the issue of sexuality was notably absent.[19] On the other hand, within Davies's 2005 *Doctor Who* version, a romantic narrative link between the Doctor and companions *would* become more manifest, particularly involving the Tenth Doctor and his companion, Rose Tyler. Moreover, in addition to romance, the new *Doctor Who* also introduced within the episode "The Empty Child" the "roguish" Captain Jack Harkness, then a time traveling bisexual conman.[20] Captain Jack's introduction came in the role of the rescuer of Rose, who was perilously hanging from a rope attached to a barrage balloon drifting over Blitz-era London in the midst of a German air raid. Saving Rose with an alien tractor beam, and in possession of a Chula alien spacecraft, Jack, like the Doctor, was represented as an otherworldly figure. Ostensibly an American volunteer with the RAF, Jack's immediate attraction to Rose was obvious, yet, as suggested by Jack's earlier banter with his fellow officer, Algernon, who is euphemistically described by Jack as being "not Rose's type," Jack would be sexually complex. Indeed, he would be *sexual*. Hence, the revamped *Doctor Who* would not also boast impressive CGI effects and introduce a cavalcade of new villains/monsters that differentiated it from its previous incarnation, but it would, under Davies's authorial guidance, also introduce sexual jealousy and desire, homosexuality, and a dashing character who actively seeks out sexual pleasure in a variety of forms. As the Doctor explains to Rose about Jack's self-defined "omnisexual" nature:

> THE DOCTOR: Relax. He's a fifty-first century guy. He's just more flexible when it comes to dancing.
> ROSE: How flexible?
> THE DOCTOR: So many species. So little time.

Hence, Davies's version of *Doctor Who* was conspicuous with regard to its distinctive and unprecedented politically progressive modern sexual dynamic. As the actor John Barrowman states of his character and his sexual orientations: "Russell had made it clear to me that Jack's character would be unlike any other in the classic *Doctor Who* series. As a result, the subtle sexual chemistry among all three characters — the Doctor, Rose and Jack — was always in play."[21] However, with the character of Captain Jack further established and fleshed out in *Torchwood*, with the added advantage of a broadcast slot after the BBC watershed (9 P.M.) the sexuality of the character would be more explicitly and unambiguously represented as the series was starkly differentiated from the family-oriented *Doctor Who*, as evidenced by this dialogue interchange within the episode "Meat":

> GWEN: Have you ever eaten alien meat?
> JACK: Yeah.
> GWEN: What was it like?
> JACK: He seemed to enjoy it.

So, in addition to the worldly boundaries disrupted by the Rift, sexual boundaries within *Torchwood* would also be routinely effaced. Subsequently, as with the idea of boundary slippage being central to the narrative, this process would also be mirrored in its representational strategy concerning sexuality. As a result, within *Torchwood* the boundaries of sexual preference are routinely unstable and unpredictable, so much so that the characters Gwen, Owen, Ianto and Toshiko, although formally "straight," have all periodically engaged in bisexuality. But it is of course Captain Jack who is the locus of such fluctuation, a principle that is most potently articulated within the pivotal episode, "Captain Jack Harkness," as discussed earlier, which not only interweaves the science fiction subjects of time travel and differing worlds overlapping, but combines this with a boundary-crossing approach to sexual worlds and "heteronormative cultures." Whereas the *Doctor Who* episodes "The Empty Child" and "The Doctor Dances" subtly indicated a sexual relationship between Jack and Algernon, "Captain Jack Harkness" would go further to suggest that *Torchwood* could display a degree of sexual/gender politics not typically present within science fiction television, or indeed, many wider forms of drama.

Even though "Captain Jack Harkness" is concerned with the team combating the apocalyptic plans of Bilis in 1941, the episode contains a subplot involving Jack and the real Jack Harkness, an American volunteer fighter pilot with the 133rd Squadron from whom it is revealed Jack has taken his "Captain Jack" identity. Against the background of two temporally and spatially-distinct narratives, Jack's history and sexuality is subsequently explored and revealed. The relationship the two Jacks forge is initially framed upon a clichéd eve-of-battle "buddy" routine, with "Jack" urging Jack to go to his English sweetheart, Nancy, to "make tonight the best night of your life" as he will be killed in action the following day. But, the consequence of this advice confirms the real Jack's hitherto repressed homosexual desires, and, in the course of a single night, the two Jacks recognize a mutual sexual attraction, which is acted upon and publicly demonstrated. In terms of Gary Needham's analysis of this moment, the episode confronts a further "impossibility" in the midst of the fantastical dimensions of the narrative, that of expressing openly homosexual desire in 1940s Britain. Within the episode, it is, as Needham states, the Rift that enables such expression, and the relationship culminates in the two Jacks taking to the dance floor and, moments before the Rift reopens to allow Jack and Tosh to return back to the future, the two men engage in "one of the longest gay kisses on television."[22]

Therefore, *Torchwood* represents not only a contemporary example of British science fiction television, but also a counter to a British television broadcasting history that until comparatively recently has been dominated by heteronormativity,[23] the cultural reinforcement of heterosexual relationships as the social norm and the general invisibility of homosexual representation. And *Torchwood* has continually represented homosexual relationships, most notably and poignantly in relation to the Ianto/Jack sexual relationship, a liaison that progresses from recreational and playful sex (involving naked hide-and-seek, and an enigmatic "stopwatch" game) into a stable relationship in "Children of Earth." Accordingly, against the backdrop of Rift-activity and fantastic events, if not always subtle, *Torchwood* would establish an adult discussion and representation of sexuality as a persistent subtextual seam running throughout the series and consequently forming a continuum with earlier progressive British television drama representations of homosexuality that politically pushed the boundaries of heteronormativity, from *The Naked Civil Servant* (BBC, 1975) and *Oranges Are Not the Only Fruit* (BBC, 1989) to, most notably, Davies's own *Queer as Folk* . However, it must be noted that from an authorial perspective, Davies has consistently denied that there is any overt "gay agenda" within his scripts for *Doctor Who* or in relation to the character of Captain Jack, arguing that "Jack's sexuality should be read progressively as a non-issue,"[24] which is the point of the character within *Doctor Who* and *Torchwood*, that he hails from a future in which sexual difference is non-existent, the point so poignantly underscored within the episode "Captain Jack Harkness."

Nonetheless, deliberate introduction of an adult-oriented tone does mean that, particularly in the first series but also evident in subsequent episodes, the tone of *Torchwood* is at times unstable. Of course, as John Tulloch and Henry Jenkins argue of the original *Doctor Who*, its adaptability and adoption of features from alternative genres (the historical romance and Gothic horror, for example) was a key factor to explain the series' longevity.[25] *Torchwood*, although displaying its own distinctive identity also engages in generic cultural borrowings, but more explicitly than *Doctor Who*. For instance, the episode "Everything Changes" contains cultural references and genre influences that range from to *CSI: Crime Scene Investigation* (U.S., CBS, 2000–) and *Men in Black* (U.S., Barry Sonnenfeld, 1997) to outright horror motifs, most notably expressed in the first screen appearance of a Weevil, which attacks a hospital orderly and tears out his throat in a scene of gushing blood. Such an incident is more common to the horror film rather than science fiction but was clearly deliberate as *Doctor Who*, tailored for an early Saturday evening broadcast slot, had been governed by a rule that kept it distinct from horror. Thus, while it was meant to be "scary," it would feature "no blood and no human doing violence to another human."[26] *Torchwood*, alternatively, could and would feature violence, horror and references to horror texts. For instance, within "Everything Changes," Gwen Cooper later encounters a Weevil imprisoned within the Torchwood Institute in a manner that is clearly a visual homage to Agent Starling's first meeting with Hannibal Lecter in *The Silence of the Lambs* (U.S., Jonathan Demme, 1991) in his plastic-fronted dungeon-like cell, while the series two episode "Sleeper" simultaneously fuses cinematic references to the violent science fiction movies *Terminator 2: Judgment Day* (U.S./France, James Cameron, 1991) and *Predator* (U.S., John McTiernan, 1987) with not-so-subtle hints of government-sanctioned torture and hidden urban terrorist cells then staples in current affairs and news media. Alternatively, the episode "Something Borrowed" plays as broad farce with a hint of Sam Raimi's low-budget horror film *The Evil Dead* (U.S., 1981) thrown in for good measure, while "Countrycide" is pure horror with its theme of cannibalistic-motivated murder and focus upon humans doing violence to humans (as there are no aliens, nor any Rift phenomenon).

Nevertheless, aside from such vaguely "postmodern" stylistic homage, the narrative mix of science fiction staples (time travel, alien invasion, cyborgs) with sexuality, violence and particularly liberal profanity (with words such as "shit," "fuck," "bollocks," "piss" and "twat" routinely employed throughout the series), is abrupt, jarring and even a little uncomfortable within the science fiction setting. For example, within "Everything Changes," Owen uses alien pheromone spray in a bar to stimulate instant and irresistible sexual attraction in a woman, using it again on the woman's enraged boyfriend, an action that results in a passionate on-screen male-on-male kiss and which acts as the prelude to a torrid (off-screen) threesome. But while the scene is intentionally amusing and further serves to emphasize the fluidity of sexual boundaries that underscores *Torchwood*, nevertheless, Owen's strategy is effectively that of "date rape." Subsequently, the attempt to distance *Torchwood* from *Doctor Who* is sometimes excessive and blunt, and the adult themes and transmission time serve to close off the series from younger viewers who are fans of Captain Jack from his *Doctor Who* appearances. This aspect of the series would be the source of negative reactions. For instance, as one reviewer stated of series one, and "Everything Changes" in particular: "the sex and violence added to justify the post-watershed slot feel tacked on, as most of the characters display an adolescent naivety and gormlessness that make it hard to engage with them on a truly 'adult' level."[27] However, although series one was arguably erratic in terms of tone and consistency, the series established a firm sense of identity in series two and a level of dramatic edge and depth seldom seen in science fiction in series three ("Children of Earth"). With the Torchwood team reduced to Jack, Gwen and Ianto in the wake of the deaths of Owen and Tosh, and with a plot vaguely reminiscent of *Quatermass* (ITV, 1979), with its emphasis on alien designs on children and young people, "Children of Earth" was less of a series and more a television "event." Graduating from BBC2 to BBC1 and transmitted consecutively over five nights, "Children of Earth" demonstrated the popular status *Torchwood* had achieved, and presented a plot that combined the classic science fiction motif of extraterrestrial threat with a narrative that was simultaneously grim and tragic, but which also acted as a sharp political allegory and critique of Britain's New Labour government's culture of media "spin," a PR strategy argued to constitute "manipulative or deceptive communication."[28] Furthermore, "Children of Earth" would continue with the progressive unpeeling of the multilayered character of Captain Jack, principally with the revelation of his family and the revelation that he was complicit in the delivery of twelve children to the alien race known as the "456" (from the radio frequency they broadcast messages to Earth) in 1965 — a factor made all the more poignant when their fate as a source of "chemical high" to the 456 is ultimately revealed. Therefore, "Children of Earth" would add to the generic influences that characterize the series, adding political conspiracy overtones and the action/paranoia of iconic

American dramas such as *24* (U.S., Fox, 2001–2010), whereby Jack and the Torchwood team must not only fight an alien menace but also face more pressing and immediate danger from their own government's state-sanctioned assassins. Hence, "Children of Earth" was, with its emphasis on alien invasion, in keeping with themes present within *Doctor Who*, but simultaneously discontinuous, exploring themes and ideas that the Time Lord's adventures could not address. And to illustrate the differences between the series, Russell T. Davies, within his book *The Writer's Tale* (2010), articulates the intrinsic nature of the *Doctor Who* narrative: "The Doctor's life never stops, no matter how sad things get. Dry your tears, move on. New Adventures to come. Otherwise, you might remember *Doctor Who* as a sad and bleak thing, which is maybe not so good if you're eight years old."[29] But, pitched at an adult audience, and capitalizing on the thematic scope the post-watershed slot brought, Davies had the creative freedom to end "Children of Earth" on a thoroughly bleak note, and in the process emphasizing the key source of differentiation that separates *Doctor Who* from *Torchwood*.

Torchwood and Russell T. Davies's Science Fiction Universe

In Patrick Parrinder's view, "science fiction, in many obvious and not-so-obvious ways, reflects the nature of modern society."[30] *Torchwood* is no exception. Though sometimes prone to tonal inconsistency, particularly in series one in which plots would jump from aliens, fairies, ghosts to human cannibals, it has nevertheless established its own narrative identity, a sense of individuality that, in amongst its alien creatures and Rift-created threats, also has come to represent a populist challenge to cultural heteronormativity within a science fiction context. As Davies has confessed of the Captain Jack character, he "loves the thought that somewhere a young boy might watch Captain Jack with his family and say, 'actually, I've got something to tell you.'"[31] Consequently, the product of one of the most famous and influential science fiction series in television history, *Torchwood* has established for itself a distinctive identity of its own bearing the unmistakable narrative "stamp" of Russell T. Davies.

While *not* demonstrably a filmmaker or director, Davies has established himself as a science fiction television auteur. A scriptwriter of repute prior to *Doctor Who*, Davies has become synonymous with British science fiction television within *Doctor Who* and its offshoots. As Sarris notes, in relation to the French New Wave origins of the term, auteur technically means "author," and represented an application of a literary mode to the process of film direction "as a form of creation."[32] Furthermore, while it was patently the case that not all film directors could be auteurs, "nor are all auteurs necessarily directors."[33] This conception of auteur aligns with Davies's role within *Doctor Who* perfectly, because the auteur tradition concerned the stamping of personality on studio products in the face of the "uniformity of the classical Hollywood system."[34] Such perceptions of the auteur are apposite to the status of Davies and his creative influence in relation to *Doctor Who*, having written over half of its episodes (between 2005 and 2009) and being indelibly and visibly connected with its productive process and marketing. Indeed, this is the point made by Matt Hills, that the 2005 version of *Doctor Who* represents a striking example of "authored TV."[35] And *Torchwood* is all the more striking in that it too displays Davies's inimitable influence and stylistic touches even though of the thirty-one episodes of *Torchwood* Davies has written/co-written only four of them. Yet, the series still displays that quintessential auteur aspect, the intrinsic "personal factor"[36] of its creator, especially the traces of the ribald and sexually frank *Queer as Folk*.

Furthermore, in the wake of *Torchwood*, Davies would create *The Sarah Jane Adventures* (2007–). But whereas *Torchwood* was pitched at an adult audience, *The Sarah Jane Adventures* returned to the spirit of the original *Doctor Who*, as it is primarily targeted at a child/ "tween" audience and broadcast at 4:30/4:45 P.M. on the satellite/cable BBC channel CBBC. While filled with incidents of peril and danger, it would obviously lack the violent and sexual edge of *Torchwood*. Nonetheless, while *Torchwood* and *The Sarah Jane Adventures* represent two very distinct threads that stand apart from *Doctor Who*, the narratives and characters from all of Davies's serials would come together within the *Doctor Who* adventure "Journey's End" to defeat Davros and the Daleks, with Jack toning down his sexual confidence to the level of mild flirtatious remarks in relation to Sarah Jane's alien-created adopted son, Luke (Thomas Knight).

At the climax of "Children of Earth," in the wake of the deaths of Ianto and Jack's own grandson (who Jack sacrificed to save millions of children from the 456), for all of its emphasis on sexuality and political commentary, *Torchwood* concludes with a staple science fiction moment — that of Captain Jack Harkness beaming aboard a waiting spacecraft to explore the universe in self-imposed exile from Earth. Consequently, *Torchwood* comes full circle back to the Doctor, with Captain Jack's last onscreen appearance occurring within the *Doctor Who* adventure, "The End of Time," in which the Doctor, in the face of impending regeneration, bids all of his companions farewell. Thus, whether Captain Jack returns from the stars is, at the time of writing, still uncertain, but if "Children of Earth" is the final *Torchwood* adventure, it is one that demonstrates the myriad boundaries that can be explored and effaced within contemporary science fiction, especially when that series is centrally predicated upon boundary erosion and unpredictability in the form of the Rift. But, while the machinations of the Rift invariably provide the plot motifs and the source of the action, the series exhibits other potent examples of multilayers and slippage, most significantly and most controversially, in its progressive explorations of sexuality and its representation of fluid sexual identities and sexual pleasure.

So, while *Torchwood* is erratic in tone at times and may not fit together aliens and profanity always harmoniously, nevertheless, as "Children of Earth" ably illustrated, contemporary British science fiction television can deliver edge, drama, character development, and harrowing tragedy in amongst alien creatures and extraterrestrial threats. All of which illustrates just how far science fiction has come since *Doctor Who* first materialized onto British television screens at 5:15 P.M. on Saturday 23 November 1963.

Chapter Notes

Introduction

1. A note on the use of references to films and television programs throughout the book: unless otherwise stated, all titles have been produced in the United Kingdom. The abbreviation "BBC" refers to the British Broadcasting Corporation. All references to the national production status of films have been taken from the Internet Movie Database.

2. For example, writing in *The Guardian* newspaper, Mark Lawson noted parallels between the storyline of the episode "Cold Blood" (broadcast on 29 May 2010) and contemporary events in British politics. The episode involved the brokering of power-sharing between two hostile tribes, thus mirroring the recent negotiation and formation of a Coalition government by the Conservative and Liberal Democrat parties. See Mark Lawson, "TV Matters: Doctor Who," *The Guardian*, 3 June 2010, available at http://www.guardian.co.uk/tv-and-radio/2010/jun/03/doctor-who-coalition (accessed 30 June 2010).

3. Gordon Brown, "PM's Question Time," *Radio Times*, 17–23 April 2010, p. 25.

4. Figures according to the Broadcasters' Audience Research Board (BARB), "Weekly Top 30 Programmes," available at http://www.barb.co.uk/report/weeklyTopProgramsOverview (accessed 1 July 2010).

5. Laura Roberts, "Writer Defends *Doctor Who* from Stephen Fry's Charges of 'Infantilism,'" *The Telegraph*, 17 June 2010, available at http://www.telegraph.co.uk/culture/tvandradio/doctor-who/7834280/Writer-defends-Doctor-Who-from-Stephen-Frys-charges-of-infantilism.html (accessed 30 June 2010).

6. See http://www.sfx.co.uk/2010/05/03/guest-blog-terry-pratchett-on-doctor-who/ (accessed 30 June 2010).

7. *Doctor Who* and its spin-off shows have generated numerous journal articles and chapters in academic collections, and also a number of monographs and edited collections. These include: Kim Newman, *Doctor Who* (London: British Film Institute, 2005); James Chapman, *Inside the TARDIS: The Worlds of Doctor Who* (London and New York: I.B. Tauris, 2006); *Time and Relative Dissertations in Space: Critical Perspectives on Doctor Who*, ed. by David Butler (Manchester: Manchester University Press, 2007); John Kenneth Muir, *A Critical History of Doctor Who on Television* (Jefferson, NC: McFarland, 2008); Jim Leach, *Doctor Who* (Detroit: Wayne State University Press, 2009); Matt Hills, *Triumph of a Time Lord: Regenerating Doctor Who in the Twenty-First Century* (London and New York: I.B. Tauris, 2010); *Illuminating Torchwood: Essays on Narrative, Character and Sexuality in the BBC Series*, ed. by Andrew Ireland (Jefferson, NC: McFarland, 2010).

8. I.Q. Hunter, "Introduction: The Strange World of the British Science Film," in *British Science Fiction Cinema*, ed. by I.Q. Hunter (London and New York: Routledge, 1999), pp. 1–15 (p. 7).

9. Ibid., p. 14, and John Oliver, "Science Fiction: Britain's Distinctive Take on the Future," *Screenonline*, available at http://www.screenonline.org.uk/film/id/446205/index.html (accessed 5 July 2010).

10. Ibid., Oliver.

11. See, for example, Henry Jenkins and John Tulloch, *Science Fiction Audiences: Watching Star Trek and Doctor Who* (London and New York: Routledge, 1995).

12. See John R. Cook and Peter Wright, "'Futures Past': An Introduction to and Brief Survey of British Science Fiction Television," in *British Science Fiction Television: A Hitchhiker's Guide*, ed. by John R. Cook and Peter Wright (London and New York: I.B. Tauris, 2006), pp. 1–20.

13. Ibid., p. 19.

14. James Chapman, "Onward Christian Spacemen: *Dan Dare*—*Pilot of the Future* as British Cultural History," *Visual Culture in Britain*, 9.1 (2008), 55–79.

15. David Quantick, "Sci-fi Britannica," *SFX*, December 2008, pp. 9–11.

16. See, for example: M. Keith Booker, *Science Fiction Television* (Westport, CT: Praeger, 2004); Catherine Johnson, *Telefantasy* (London: British

Film Institute, 2005); *The Essential Science Fiction Television Reader*, ed. by J.P. Telotte (Lexington: University Press of Kentucky, 2008); Rebecca Feasey, *Masculinity and Popular Television* (Edinburgh: Edinburgh University Press, 2008); *The Routledge Companion to Science Fiction*, ed. by Mark Bould, Andrew M. Butler, Adam Roberts and Sherryl Vint (Oxon and New York: Routledge, 2009); *Channeling the Future: Essays on Science Fiction and Fantasy Television*, ed. by Lincoln Geraghty (Lanham, MD: Scarecrow, 2009), M. Keith Booker and Anne-Marie Thomas, *The Science Fiction Handbook* (Chichester: Wiley-Blackwell, 2009); *The Essential Cult TV Reader*, ed. by David Lavery (Lexington: University Press of Kentucky, 2010).

Chapter 1

1. Richard Hodgens, "A Brief, Tragical History of the Science Fiction Film," *Film Quarterly*, 13.2 (1959), 30–9 (p. 30).
2. Barry K. Grant, "Looking Upward: H.G. Wells, Science Fiction and the Cinema," *Literature/Film Quarterly* 14.3 (1986), 154–63 (p. 154).
3. H.G. Wells, *Things to Come: A Film by H.G. Wells* (New York: Macmillan, 1935), p. viii.
4. Don G. Smith, *H.G. Wells on Film: The Utopian Nightmare* (Jefferson, NC: McFarland, 2002), *passim*. See also Paul Jensen, "H.G. Wells on the Screen," *Films in Review* 18.9 (1967), 521–7. Jensen's filmography includes two films not cited by Smith: a production of *The First Men in the Moon* (Bruce Gordon and J.L.V. Leigh) by the Gaumont Company in 1919 and an experimental short film of *The Door in the Wall* (Glenn H. Alvey Jr.) by the British Film Institute in 1959.
5. Smith identifies the Filipino horror films *Terror Is a Man* (Gerado de Leon, 1959) and *The Twilight People* (Eddie Romero, 1972) as unacknowledged adaptations of *The Island of Doctor Moreau*.
6. *The Invisible Man* (1958–1959) was a British-made series produced by Ralph Smart for ATV in which the protagonist is a scientist who turns invisible in a failed laboratory experiment and thereafter becomes an undercover crimefighter. This was also the premise of NBC's *The Invisible Man* (1975) and the U.S. Network's *The Invisible Man* (2000–2002). None of these series takes anything from Wells's *The Invisible Man* other than the title. *War of the Worlds* (1988–1989) was a sequel to the 1953 film of *The War of the Worlds*, in which the remains of the alien invaders are revived when terrorists attack the military base where they are stored.
7. H.G. Wells, *Experiment in Autobiography: Discoveries and Conclusions of a Very Ordinary Brain (Since 1866)* (London: Victor Gollancz, 1934), p. 563.

8. Robert Silverberg, "Introduction," in *The War of the Worlds: Fresh Perspectives on the H.G. Wells Classic*, ed. by Glenn Yeffeth (Dallas, TX: Benbella, 2005), pp. 1–13 (p. 1). The Paramount "Special Collector's Edition" DVD of the 1953 *The War of the Worlds* includes a supporting documentary entitled *H.G. Wells: The Father of Science Fiction*.
9. There is an extensive critical literature: see, for example, John Huntingdon, *The Logic of Fantasy: H.G. Wells and Science Fiction* (New York: Columbia University Press, 1982); Peter Kemp, *H.G. Wells and the Culminating Ape* (London: Macmillan, 1982); Frank McConnell, *The Science Fiction of H.G. Wells* (Oxford: Oxford University Press, 1981); and Patrick Parrinder, *Shadows of the Future: H.G. Wells, Science Fiction and Prophecy* (Liverpool: Liverpool University Press, 1995).
10. Quoted in *The Definitive Time Machine: A Critical Edition of H.G. Wells's Scientific Romance with Introduction and Notes*, ed. by Harry M. Geduld (Bloomington: Indiana University Press, 1987), p. 198.
11. Quoted in Rachael Low, *The History of the British Film 1906–1914* (London: George Allen and Unwin, 1949), p. 180.
12. Smith, p. 155.
13. H.G. Wells, *H.G. Wells in Love: Postscript to An Experiment in Autobiography*, ed. by P.G. Wells (London: Faber and Faber, 1984), p. 207.
14. See Jamie Sexton, "The Film Society and the Creation of an Alternative Film Culture in Britain in the 1920s," in *Young and Innocent? The Cinema in Britain 1896–1930*, ed. by Andrew Higson (Exeter: University of Exeter Press, 2002), pp. 291–305.
15. H.G. Wells, *The King Who Was a King: The Book of a Film* (London: Ernest Bell, 1929).
16. On Wells's involvement with the British film industry in the 1920s, see Sylvia Hardy, "H.G. Wells and British Silent Cinema: The War of the Worlds," in *Young and Innocent? The Cinema in Britain 1896–1930*, ed. by Andrew Higson (Exeter: University of Exeter Press, 2002), pp. 242–55.
17. *Kinematograph Weekly*, 9 January 1936, p. 80A.
18. The production history of *Things to Come* is documented in Christopher Frayling, *Things to Come* (London: British Film Institute, 1995); Rachael Low, *The History of the British Film 1929–1939: Film Making in 1930s Britain* (London: Allen and Unwin, 1985), pp. 172–3; and Karol Kulik, *Alexander Korda: The Man Who Could Work Miracles* (London: W.H. Allen, 1975), pp. 146–53.
19. J. Danvers Williams, "'I Wrote This Film for Your Enjoyment,' says H.G. Wells," *Film Weekly*, 29 February 1936, pp. 8–9.
20. Wells, *H.G. Wells in Love: Postscript to an Experiment in Autobiography*, pp. 211–2.

21. British Film Institute Unpublished Scripts Collection S6235: *Whither Mankind? A Film of the Future* by H.G. Wells. Based on his two books, *The Shape of Things to Come* and *The Work, Wealth and Happiness of Mankind* (no date).
22. British Film Institute microfiche on *Things to Come*: *Kinematograph Weekly*, 27 February 1936, p. 31; *Monthly Film Bulletin* 3.26 (February 1936), p. 25; "Magnificence of 'Things to Come,'" *Morning Post*, 22 February 1936; "The Film That Is a Film," *Observer*, 23 February 1936; *Inquirer*, 29 February 1936; "Mr. Wells Sees Us Through," *Listener*, 18 March 1936, p. 545.
23. Michael Korda, *Charmed Lives: A Family Romance* (London: Allen Lane, 1980), p. 123.
24. For commentary see Timothy Travers, "*The Shape of Things to Come*: H.G. Wells and Radical Culture in the 1930s," *Film and History*, 6.2 (1976), 31–41; Leon Stover, *The Prophetic Soul: A Reading of H.G. Wells's 'Things to Come'* (Jefferson NC: McFarland, 1987); Frayling, *Things to Come*; and Jeffrey Richards, "*Things to Come* and Science Fiction in the 1930s," in *British Science Fiction Cinema*, ed. by I.Q. Hunter (London: Routledge, 1999), pp. 16–32.
25. See, for example, John Brosnan, *Future Tense: The Cinema of Science Fiction* (London: Macdonald and Jane's, 1978).
26. Wells, *H.G. Wells in Love*, pp. 212–3.
27. Richards, p. 28.
28. James C. Robertson, *The Hidden Cinema: British Film Censorship in Action, 1913–1975* (London: Routledge, 1992), pp. 55–7.
29. R.C. Sheriff, *No Leading Lady: An Autobiography* (London: Gollancz, 1968), p. 291. On the making of *The Invisible Man*, see James Curtis, *James Whale: A New World of Gods and Monsters* (Minneapolis: University of Minnesota Press, 2003), pp. 196–201.
30. Keith Williams, *H.G. Wells, Modernity and the Movies* (Liverpool: Liverpool University Press, 2007), pp. 64–5.
31. Quoted in Thomas Doherty, *Pre–Code Hollywood: Sex, Immorality, and Insurrection in American Cinema 1930–1934* (New York: Columbia University Press, 1999), p. 312.
32. For a comparison of the book and the film, see Joseph D. Andriano, *Immortal Monster: The Mythological Evolution of the Fantastic Beast in Modern Fiction and Film* (Wesport, CT: Greenwood, 1999), pp. 136–42.
33. John Ellis, "The Quality Film Adventure: British Critics and the Cinema 1942–1948," in *Dissolving Views: Key Writings on British Cinema*, ed., by Andrew Higson (London: Cassell, 1996), pp. 66–93.
34. Victoria O'Donnell, "Science Fiction Films and Cold War Anxiety," in Peter Lev, *History of the American Cinema Volume 7: Transforming the Screen 1950–1959* (Berkeley: University of California Press, 2003), pp. 169–96.
35. Crystal Downing, "Deconstructing Herbert: *The War of the Worlds* on Film," *Literature/Film Quarterly*, 35.4 (2007), 274–81 (p. 277).
36. Benjamin Shapiro, "Universal Truths: Cultural Myths and Generic Adaptation in 1950s Science Fiction Films," *Journal of Popular Film and Television*, 18.3 (1990), 103–11 (p. 107).
37. Williams, p. 131.
38. For commentary see Jonathan Bignell, "Another Time, Another Space: Modernity, Subjectivity, and *The Time Machine*," in *Alien Identities: Exploring Differences in Film and Fiction*, ed. by Deborah Cartmell, I.Q. Hunter, Heidi Kaye and Imelda Whelehan (London: Pluto, 1999), pp. 87–103.
39. Other Scheer/Harryhausen films, all produced for Columbia, included *Earth vs. the Flying Saucers* (U.S., Fred F. Sears, 1956), *Twenty Million Miles to Earth* (U.S., Nathan Juran, 1957), *The 7th Voyage of Sinbad* (U.S., Nathan Juran, 1958), *The Three Worlds of Gulliver* (U.S., Jack Sher, 1960) and *Jason and the Argonauts* (U.S., Don Chaffey, 1963).
40. See James Chapman, "*Quatermass* and the Orgins of British Television SF," in *British Science Fiction Television: A Hitchhiker's Guide*, ed. by John R. Cook and Peter Wright (London: I.B. Tauris, 2005), pp. 21–51.
41. Christopher Dunkley, *Financial Times*, 10 October 1984, p. 23.
42. Geoff King, *Spectacular Narratives: Hollywood in the Age of the Blockbuster* (London: I.B. Tauris, 2000), pp. 28–39.
43. Wells also appears as a character in the *Doctor Who* serial "Timelash" (1985) and in the "Tempus Fugitive" (1994) episode of *Lois & Clark: The New Adventures of Superman* (U.S., ABC, 1993–1997).
44. Williams, p. 135.
45. Kim Newman, "War of the Worlds," *Sight and Sound*, 15.9 (September 2009), p. 84.
46. Remarkably, Spielberg's epic was one of three versions of *The War of the Worlds* released in 2005. *H.G. Wells' War of the Worlds* (U.S.), directed by David Michael Latt for Asylum Home Entertainment, was another updated version set in Washington, D.C., released straight to DVD. *H.G. Wells' The War of the Worlds*, directed by Tim Haines for Pendragon Pictures, maintained the setting in Victorian England and was shot in sepia tones to approximate the "look" of early cinema. This also went straight to DVD and is now somewhat elusive.
47. Smith, p. 184.
48. The influence of *The Time Machine* can be seen in *Time Flies* (Walter Forde, 1944), *Planet of the Apes*, *Time After Time*, *Time Bandits* (Terry Gilliam, 1981) and *Back to the Future* (U.S., Robert Zemeckis, 1985), and in the television se-

ries *Doctor Who*, *The Time Tunnel* (U.S., Fox, 1966–1967) and *Timeslip* (ATV, 1970–1971). There have been myriad alien-invasion films, but the one that most closely resembles *The War of the Worlds* is Roland Emmerich's *Independence Day* (U.S., 1996), in which the seemingly all-powerful aliens are finally defeated by introducing a computer virus into their mothership—a technological equivalent of Wells's bacteria.

Chapter 2

1. Bill McGuire, *Global Catastrophes: A Very Short Introduction* (Oxford: Oxford University Press, 2002), p. xi.
2. Isaac Asimov, "Social Science Fiction," in *Modern Science Fiction: Its Meaning and Its Future*, ed. by Reginald Bretnor (Chicago: Advent, 1979), p. 160.
3. Susan Sontag, "The Imagination of Disaster," in *Liquid Metal: The Science Fiction Film Reader*, ed. by Sean Redmond (London: Wallflower, 2004), pp. 40–7 (p. 45).
4. Dunja M. Mohr, "Transgressive Utopian Dystopias: The Postmodern Reappearance of Utopia in the Disguise of Dystopia," *Zeitschrift für Anglistik und Amerikanistik*, 57.1 (2007), pp. 5–25 (p. 9).
5. Ibid., p. 7.
6. H.G. Wells, *The Time Machine* (New York: Signet Classic, 2002), p. 97.
7. However, the credit for the first depiction of the consequences of a world war fought with nuclear weapons goes to another novel by Wells. *The World Set Free*, published in 1914, not only anticipated the use of "atomic bombs" by more than thirty years, but also coined that term and reportedly even influenced the actual invention.
8. Mick Broderick, "Surviving Armageddon: Beyond the Imagination of Disaster," *Science Fiction Studies*, 20.3 (no. 63, 1993), pp. 362–82.
9. Martha Bartter, "Nuclear Holocaust as Urban Renewal," *Science Fiction Studies* 13.2 (no. 39, 1986), pp. 148–58 (p. 158).
10. Sontag, p. 42.
11. Ibid., p. 42.
12. Ibid., p. 41.
13. Broderick, p. 362.
14. David Dowling, *Fictions of Nuclear Disaster* (London: Macmillan 1987), p. 86.
15. Most notable is Nicholas Ruddick, *Ultimate Island: On the Nature of British Science Fiction* (Westport, CT: Greenwood, 1993).
16. Jeffrey Richards, "Things to Come and Science Fiction in the 1930s," in *British Science Fiction Cinema*, ed. by I.Q. Hunter (London: Routledge, 2001), pp. 16–32.
17. Sontag, p. 47.
18. Richmond Crinkley, "Endgame: Looking at Nuclear Aesthetics," *National Review*, 24 August 1984, pp. 28–33 (p. 29).
19. See Tony Shaw, "The BBC, the State and Cold War Culture: The Case of Television's *The War Game* (1965)," in *English Historical Review*, 494 (2006), pp. 1351–1384.
20. David Seed, "TV Docudrama and the Nuclear Subject: *The War Game*, *The Day After* and *Threads*," in *British Science Fiction Television: A Hitchhiker's Guide*, ed. by John R. Cook and Peter Wright (London: I.B. Tauris 2006), pp. 155–72 (p. 161).
21. Brian W. Aldiss, *Billion Year Spree: The True History of Science Fiction* (New York: Doubleday, 1973), p. 294.
22. Christopher Priest, "British Science Fiction," in *Science Fiction: A Critical Guide*, ed. by Patrick Parrinder (London: Longman, 1979), pp. 187–202 (p. 194).
23. Aldiss, p. 294.
24. For a more detailed analysis of *Survivors* and the motif of self-sufficiency, see Andy Sawyer, "Everyday Life in the Post-Catastrophe Future: Terry Nation's *Survivors*," in *British Science Fiction Television: A Hitchhiker's Guide*, ed. by John R. Cook and Peter Wright (London: I.B. Tauris, 2006), pp. 131–53.
25. Mark Bould, "Science Fiction Television in the United Kingdom," in *The Essential Science Fiction Television Reader*, ed. by J.P. Telotte (Lexington: University Press of Kentucky, 2008), pp. 209–30 (p. 220).
26. Neil Wilkes, "Julie Graham talks Survivors," *Digital Spy*, 1 August 2008, available at http://www.digitalspy.co.uk/tv/a117932/julie-graham-talks-survivors.html (accessed 27 March 2008).
27. Hans Krah, *Weltuntergangsszenarien und Zukunftsentwürfe. Narrationen vom "Ende" in Literatur und Film 1945–1990* (Kiel: Verlag Ludwig, 2004), p. 354.
28. See Sue Short, "'No Flesh Shall Be Spared.' Richard Stanley's *Hardware*," in *British Science Fiction Cinema*, ed. by I.Q. Hunter (London: Routledge, 2001), pp. 169–80.
29. Rüdiger Heinze and Jochen Petzold, "No More Room in Hell: Utopian Moments in the Dystopia of *28 Days Later*," *Zeitschrift für Anglistik und Amerikanistik*, 57.1 (2007), pp. 53–68 (p. 60).

Chapter 3

1. Jason Mittell, *Genre and Television: From Cop Shows to Cartoons in American Culture* (London: Routledge, 2004) p. 4.
2. "*Spaceways*" program listing, *Radio Times*, 25 January 1952, p. 31.
3. "*Journey Into Space*" program listing, *Radio Times*, 18 September 1953, p. 19.

4. See Leon Stover, *Science Fiction from Wells to Heinlein* (Jefferson, NC: McFarland, 2002).
5. April 1926 issue of *Amazing Stories*. Quoted in Brian Stableford, John Clute and Peter Nicholls, "Definitions of SF," in John Clute and Peter Nicholls, *Encyclopedia of Science Fiction* (London: Orbit/Little, Brown, 1993), pp. 311–14.
6. Brian Stableford, "Scientific Romance," *The A to Z of Science Fiction Literature* (Oxford: Scarecrow, 2005), p. 306.
7. Brian Attebury, "The Magazine Era: 1926–1960," in *The Cambridge Companion to Science Fiction*, ed. by Edward James and Farah Mendlesohn (Cambridge: Cambridge University Press, 2003), p. 34.
8. Arthur Koestler, "The Boredom of Fantasy," *The Listener*, 28 May 1953, p. 893.
9. Ibid.
10. David Pringle, *Science Fiction: The 100 Best Novels* (London: Xanadu, 1985), p. 14.
11. George Orwell, "Boys' Weeklies," *Essays* (London: Penguin, 1984), p. 92.
12. Christopher Priest, "British Science Fiction," in *Science Fiction: A Critical Guide*, ed. by Patrick Parrinder (London: Longman, 1979), p. 194.
13. Kingsley Amis, *New Maps of Hell* (London: Four Square, 1963), p. 7. Brian Aldiss also remembers "The discovery of *Marvel, Amazing*, and *Astounding* on Woolworth's counter." See *Hell's Cartographers: Some Personal Histories of Science Fiction Writers*, ed. by Brian W. Aldiss and Harry Harrison (London: Weidenfeld and Nicholson, 1975), p. 184.
14. Richard Hoggart, *The Uses of Literacy* (London: Penguin, 1992), p. 217.
15. Ibid., p. 248.
16. Ibid.
17. Koestler, p. 891.
18. Nigel Kneale quoted in Julian Petley and Kim Newman, "The Manxman," *Monthly Film Bulletin*, 56.662 (March 1989), p. 91.
19. Rudolph Cartier to C. Moodie, Air Ministry, 12 June 1953, BBC Written Archives Centre (hereafter BBC WAC) T5/418.
20. Ibid.
21. Michael Lewis, "Did You Hear That? Children's Comics," *The Listener*, 13 December 1951, p. 1007.
22. Horace King, *Hansard, Commons*, 30 November 1954, column 76.
23. Ibid., column 77.
24. Martin Barker, *A Haunt of Fears: The Strange History of the British Horror Comics Campaign* (London: Pluto, 1984), p. 82.
25. N.J. Shaw, Letter, "Viewers Write to the 'Radio Times,'" *Radio Times*, 29 August 1952, p. 38.
26. Lionel Hale, "Mystery Story," *Radio Times* (U.K.), 15 August 1952, p. 38.
27. "Mystery Story" listing, *Radio Times* (U.K.), 15 August 1952, p. 38.
28. "The Scanners," "Twenty-One Years Non-Stop," *Radio Times* (U.K.), 30 January 1953, p. 15.
29. Ibid.
30. Kenneth A. Hurren, "Number Three" listing, *Radio Times* (U.K.), 30 January 1953, p. 14.
31. Rick Altman, *Film/Genre* (London: British Film Institute, 1999), p. 57.
32. Peter Hayes, "A Threat from Outer Space," *Radio Times* (U.K.), 25 November 1955, p. 8.
33. Dorothy Berry, "When Hugh Went to School," *Radio Times* (U.K.), 25 March 1955, p. 27.
34. George Orwell, "Riding Down From Bangor," *Essays* (London: Penguin, 1994), p. 400.
35. Alan Dixon, "Redskins and Palefaces," *Radio Times* (U.K.), 1 April 1955, p. 21.
36. Altman, p. 36.

Chapter 4

1. Only recently has there started to emerge some nascent critical attention on this subject. See, for example, Robert Shail, "Terence Fisher and British Science Fiction Cinema," *Science Fiction Film and Television*, 2.1 (Spring 2009), 77–90.
2. David Pirie, *A New Heritage of Horror: The English Gothic Cinema* (London: I.B Tauris, 2008), p. 150.
3. Ibid., p. 91.
4. *British Science Fiction Cinema*, ed. by I.Q. Hunter (London: Routledge, 1999).
5. Pirie, p. 153
6. See also: Peter Hutchings, *Terence Fisher* (Manchester: Manchester University Press, 2002) and Paul Leggett, *Terence Fisher: Horror, Myth and Religion* (Jefferson, NC: McFarland, 2002).
7. Pirie, p. 15.
8. Hutchings, p. 119
9. Jonathan Rigby, *English Gothic: A Century of Horror Cinema* (London: Reynolds and Hearn, 2006), p. 50.
10. Marcus Hearn and Jonathan Rigby, *X The Unknown Viewing Notes* (London: DD Video, 2003), p. 15.
11. Rigby, pp. 51–52.
12. Ibid., p. 52.
13. Ibid., p. 49.
14. Julian Petley and Kim Newman, "*The Manxman*," *Monthly Film Bulletin*, 56.662 (March 1989), p. 26.
15. Rigby, pp. 54–55.
16. Ibid., pp. 55–56
17. Roslynn D. Haynes, *From Faust to Strangelove: Representations of the Scientist in Western Literature* (Baltimore: John Hopkins University Press, 1994), p. 4.
18. Pirie, p. 83
19. Ibid., p. 92.

20. Marcus Hearn and Alan Barnes, *The Hammer Story* (London: Titan, 1997), p. 41.
21. John Oliver, "*The Damned*," in *Screenonline*, available at http://www.screenonline.org.uk/film/id/556215/ (accessed 2 April 2009).
22. Hearn and Barnes, p. 80.
23. Rigby, p. 124.
24. Pirie, p. 89.
25. Rigby, p. 168.
26. Peter Hutchings, *Hammer and Beyond: The British Horror Film* (Manchester: Manchester University Press, 1993), p. 49.
27. Hearn and Barnes, p. 129.
28. Ibid., p. 129.
29. Pirie, p. 93.

Chapter 5

1. My reference is to Walter Benjamin's very well-known essay, "The Work of Art in the Age of Its Technological Reproducibility" (second version), transl. by Annie Bourneuf, in Walter Benjamin, *The Work of Art in the Age of Its Technological Reproducibility and Other Writings on Media* (Cambridge, MA: Harvard University Press, 2008), pp. 19–55.
2. The entry for Fuest on the *Internet Movie Database* begins: "Well regarded for his stylish genre work of the 1970's, Robert Fuest may not [sic] a very extensive list of feature film credits, but the quality of his output is what matters, not the quantity." See "Robert Fuest," *Internet Movie Database*, available at http://www.imdb.com/name/nm0297523/bio (accessed 30 May 2010).
3. Susan Sontag, "Notes on Camp," in Susan Sontag, *Against Interpretation* (New York: Delta/Dell, 1966) p. 288.
4. "Robert Fuest," "Talent Bios" by Jonathan Sothcott, bonus material, *And Soon the Darkness*, DVD, Anchor Bay, 2002. Sothcott's source is an interview that Fuest gave for a magazine called *Bizarre*. Fuest does not say which publication anointed him as "High Priest of Pop Art." We should note that Pop had itself become mass marketed. In his incisive contemporary analysis of Pop, critic and jazz musician George Melly observes that by 1966 the word "Pop" was "applied indiscriminately": some of the many examples of such indiscriminate application that he gives include Union Jacks, petrol pumps, the films of Jean-Luc Godard, and James Bond. See George Melly, *Revolt into Style: The Pop Arts in Britain* (London: Allen Lane/Penguin, 1970) p. 172.
5. See, among many others, Toby Miller, *The Avengers* (London: British Film Institute, 1997), *The Avengers Companion*, ed. by Alain Carrazé and Jean-Luc Putheaud, with Alex J. Geairns, trans. by Paul Buck (San Francisco: Bay, 1998), and Piers D. Britton and Simon J. Barker, *Reading Between Designs: Visual Imagery and the Generation of Meaning in The Avengers, The Prisoner, and Doctor Who* (Austin: University of Texas Press, 2003) for a variety of discussions of the centrality of "style" in *The Avengers*.
6. Julian Critchley, "*Avengers* Still Good with Miss Thorson," *The Times*, 10 October 1968, no page reference.
7. Gary A. Smith, *Uneasy Dreams: The Golden Age of British Horror Films, 1956–1976* (Jefferson, NC: McFarland, 2000), p. 315.
8. Sothcott reproduces the poster in color. It is reproduced in black and white in Smith, p. 315. For more about the history of the film's production and release, see also Gary A. Smith, *The American International Pictures Video Guide* (Jefferson, NC: McFarland, 2009), pp. 171–172.
9. James Robert Parish and Steven Whitney, *Vincent Price Unmasked* (New York: Drake, 1974), p. 131.
10. See Parish and Whitney, *Vincent Price Unmasked* (New York: Drake, 1974) p. 130, 239, 131, and 239, respectively.
11. Michael Moorcock, "Introduction," in *New Worlds: An Anthology*, ed. by Michael Moorcock (New York: Thunder's Mouth, 2004), p. xiii.
12. I am relying here on Colin Greenland's primary research and chronology of events. See Colin Greenland, *The Entropy Exhibition: Michael Moorcock and the British 'New Wave' in Science Fiction* (London: Routledge and Kegan Paul, 1983), pp. 16–21, and p. 229.
13. Melly observes, astutely, that the directions of high and mass became confused at the end of the Pop phenomenon (for Melly, the late 1960s), with high culture emulation of or homage to mass culture and mass culture's marketing versions of that high cultural emulation back as mass culture. See Melly, p. 127.
14. For the most comprehensive history and analysis of the Independent Group currently available, see the catalogue of the IG retrospective from 1990: *The Independent Group: Postwar Britain and the Aesthetics of Plenty*, ed. by David Robbins (Cambridge, MA: The MIT Press, 1990). In his autobiography, *Miracles of Life: Shanghai to Shepperton: An Autobiography* (London: Fourth Estate, 2008), Ballard recalls at length the effect the IG's exhibition, *This Is Tomorrow*, which opened in August 1956 in Whitechapel, had on him (p. 188). In the same autobiography, Ballard writes of later getting a stripper, the wonderfully named Euphoria Bliss, to perform a striptease at the ICA to the reading of a scientific paper (p. 210). Ballard's notorious installation of three crashed cars went on display at the New Arts Laboratory in London in 1970 (pp. 238–9).
15. Christopher Finch, "Language Mechanisms: A Review of the Work of Eduardo Paolozzi," reprinted in *New Worlds*, pp. 375–9.

For a discussion of the institutional positioning of the avant-garde in general, see Peter Bürger, *Theory of the Avant-Garde*, trans. by Michael Shaw (Minneapolis: University of Minnesota Press, 1984) pp. 35–54.
  16. Greenland, p. 65.
  17. Ibid., p. 65–6.
  18. Ibid., p. 3.
  19. Greenland is quoting Leslie A. Fielder, "The New Mutants," in *Collected Essays Volume II*, ed. by Leslie A. Fielder (New York: Stein and Day, 1971), pp. 379–400.
  20. Brain Aldiss, *Billion Year Spree: The True History of Science Fiction* (New York: Schocken, 1973), p. 308.
  21. Ronald Firbank (1886–1926) was the very incarnation of camp dandyism in life as well as in a small body of novels that utilize indirection, obliquity, and nonsequitur to generate structure and multiple meanings—or no meaning at all, depending on the reader's perspective. See Ronald Firbank, *The Complete Firbank* (London: Picador, 1988). Sontag lists Firbank with Wilde in her "pocket history of camp." See Sontag, p. 281.
  22. "*All art constantly aspires towards the condition of music*" (italicized in the original). See Walter Pater, "The School of Giorgione," in *The Renaissance: Studies in Art and Poetry*, ed. by Donald L. Hill (Berkeley: University of California Press, 1980), pp. 120–22 (p. 106).
  23. Michael Moorcock, *A Cure for Cancer*, p. 144. My dates for the first publications of the four novels, first published in the U.K. by Allison and Busby, come from Michael Moorcock, *The Cornelius Quartet* (New York: Thunder's Mouth, 2001). All subsequent page references are to this edition. Parts of *The Final Programme* were first published in *New Worlds* in 1965 and 1968.
  24. Ibid., p. 855.
  25. John Clute, "The Repossession of Jerry Cornelius," in Michael Moorcock, *The Cornelius Chronicles* (New York, Avon, 1977), pp. vii–viii.
  26. Moorcock, p. viii.
  27. Michael Moorcock, "Introduction: My Times, My Lives," in Michael Moorcock, *The Lives and Times of Jerry Cornelius: Stories of the Comic Apocalypse* (New York: Four Walls Eight Windows, 2003), p. vi.
  28. Ibid., p.vii.
  29. *The Final Programme* in Michael Moorcock, *The Cornelius Quartet* (New York: Thunder's Mouth, 2001), pp. 6, 13, 20, and 96. All subsequent page references will be to this edition.
  30. Ibid., p. 22.
  31. Ibid., p. 18.
  32. Ibid.
  33. Ibid., p. 47.
  34. Ibid., pp. 136–37.
  35. Ibid., p. 137.
  36. Ibid.
  37. Ibid., p. 138.
  38. Ibid., p. 139.
  39. Ibid., p. 142.
  40. Ibid., pp. 90–91. Greenland asserts that the Mad Astronaut becomes a stock figure of the British New Wave, from Moorcock's Newman to David Bowie's Major Tom. See Greenland, p. 49.
  41. Ibid., p, 8.
  42. Ibid., p. 57.
  43. Ibid., p. 144.
  44. Ibid., p. 855.
  45. Eco writes that in Fleming's work "nineteenth century tradition and science fiction, [...] adventurous excitement and hypnosis [...] [are] fused together to produce an unstable *bricolage*, which often hides its ready-made nature by presenting itself as literary invention." See Umberto Eco, "Narrative Structures in Fleming," in *The Role of the Reader: Explorations in the Semiotics of Texts*, ed. by Umberto Eco (London: Hutchinson, 1981), pp. 144–74 (p. 172). Eco's text first appeared in Italian in 1965 and was translated into English in 1966.
  46. Smith is typical: "An unsuccessful attempt to bring the oblique visions of author Michael Moorcock to the screen. [...] This incoherent film tries hard to be clever and camp but really doesn't succeed with either." See Smith, 2000, p. 109.
  47. "Perhaps this conflation [of sexual and commodity] fetishes is historically new to this moment: [...] it is only foregrounded in Pop, which acts out this super–fetishism in ways that are excessive but demonstrative," writes Foster. See "On the First Pop Age," *New Left Review*, 19 (January/February 2003), p. 101.
  48. In the novel, we may note, Miss Dazzle is "equipped with the daintiest masculine genitals." See Moorcock, p. 25.
  49. Guy Debord's trenchant analysis of how spectacle itself becomes a kind of super–commodity remains relevant. See Guy Debord, *The Society of the Spectacle*, trans. by Donald Nicholson-Smith (New York: Zone, 1995).
  50. Andrew Ross analyzes the relationship between modes of production and the emergence of camp in the 1960s as an issue for intellectuals as well as for Pop artists like Andy Warhol. He defines camp as the "re-creation of surplus value from forgotten forms of labour." See Andrew Ross, *No Respect: Intellectuals and Popular Culture* (London: Routledge, 1989), p. 151.
  51. Paolozzi's *As Is When* series can be seen on the Tate website at http://www.tate.org.uk/servlet/ViewWork?cgroupid=999999961&workid=11190&searchid=17542 (accessed 30 June 2010).
  52. Jerry kills both, too, Catherine by accident and Frank during a fight that precedes the finding of the microfilm.
  53. For a classic analysis of Romantic and decadent motifs, see Mario Praz, *The Romantic Agony*, trans. by Angus Davidson (New York: Meridian, 1956).

54. See the entries for "lotus" and "hermaphrodite" in J.E. Cirlot, *A Dictionary of Symbols*, trans. by Jack Sage (New York: Barnes and Noble, 1971).
55. Moorcock, p. 47.
56. The poster is reproduced in color in Sothcott. It is also reproduced as a black and white advertisement for the film on the inner cover of *Films and Filming*, 20.2 (November 1973), no page reference. In the latter, the tagline is below the needle gun and not divided by it as in the color poster.
57. Victor Arwas, like many other critics, comments on the centrality of imagery of the hermaphrodite in Jones's work from the early 1960s on. Victor Arwas, *Allen Jones* (London: Academy Editions/Ernst and Sohn, 1993) p. 35.
58. Greenland glosses the "multiverse" as "an infinite set of possible worlds, all the possible results of all the possible outcomes of all decisions and chances. These equivalent universes coexist." See Greenland, p. 128. Greenland also remarks that the multiverse "has some standing as a convention in sf [sic], having facilitated plots for many writers from the thirties to the present" (p. 127).
59. *The Last Days of Man on Earth* was the U.S. title of *The Final Programme*. The phrase, "the comic apocalypse" occurs in the subtitle of Moorcock's anthology of his own shorter work, *The Lives and Times of Jerry Cornelius: Stories of the Comic Apocalypse*.

Chapter 6

1. This chapter refers to Gerry Anderson as the creator of the programs discussed, but the situation was actually more complex, with Gerry mainly responsible for company management and planning special effects filming, his wife, Sylvia, for character origination, and directing of actors, and numerous collaborators contributing to the program realization.
2. Jonathan Bignell, "And the Rest Is History: Lew Grade, Creation Narratives and Television Historiography," in *ITV Cultures: Independent Television Over Fifty Years*, ed. by Catherine Johnson and Rob Turnock (Maidenhead, England: Open University Press, 2005), pp. 57–70.
3. Robert Sellers, *Cult TV: The Golden Age of ITC* (London: Plexus), p. 92.
4. Simon Archer and Stan Nicholls, *Gerry Anderson: The Authorised Biography* (London: Legend, 1996), p. 55.
5. Sellers, pp. 86–7.
6. Nicholas J. Cull, "The Man Who Made Thunderbirds: An Interview with Gerry Anderson," in *British Science Fiction Television: A Hitchhiker's Guide*, ed. by John Cook and Peter Wright (London and New York: I.B. Tauris, 2006), pp. 116–30 (p. 126).
7. Sellers, p. 112.
8. Sylvia Anderson, *My FAB Years* (Neshannock, PA: Hermes), p. 21.
9. Sellers, pp. 89–90.
10. Archer and Nicholls, p. 86.
11. Sellers, p. 83.
12. Cull, p. 120.
13. Anderson, p. 35.
14. Sellers, p. 82.
15. Ibid., p. 80.
16. Anderson, p. 39.
17. Ibid., pp. 84–9.
18. Archer and Nicholls, pp. 82–3.
19. Sellers, p. 113.
20. Jonathan Bignell, "Writing the Child in Media Theory," *Yearbook of English Studies*, 32 (2002), pp. 127–39.
21. John R. Cook, "The Age of Aquarius: Utopia and Anti-Utopia in Late 1960s' and Early 1970s' British Science Fiction Television," in *British Science Fiction Television: A Hitchhiker's Guide*, ed. by John R. Cook and Peter Wright (London and New York: I.B. Tauris, 2006), pp. 93–115 (p. 110).
22. James Chapman, *Saints and Avengers: British Adventure Series of the 1960s* (London and New York: I.B. Tauris, 2002).
23. Sellers, p. 95.
24. Anderson, p. 26, and p. 30.
25. Steve Neale, "Transatlantic Ventures and Robin Hood," in *ITV Cultures: Independent Television Over Fifty Years*, ed. by Catherine Johnson and Rob Turnock (Maidenhead, England: Open University Press, 2005), pp. 73–87.
26. Bernard Sendall, *Independent Television in Britain, vol. 1: Origin and Foundation, 1946–62* (Basingstoke and New York: Macmillan, 1982), p. 371.
27. Cull, p. 121.
28. Joyce Kolko and Gabriel Kolko, *The Limits of Power: The World and United States Foreign Policy, 1945–1954* (New York: Harper and Row, 1972).

Chapter 7

1. Other Anderson acronyms included, from *Stingray* (ATV/ITC, 1964–1965), WASP (World Aquanaut Security Patrol); from *The Secret Service* (Century 21/ITC, 1969), BISHOP (British Intelligence Service Headquarters — Operation Priest); from *Joe 90*, WIN (World Intelligence Network) and BIGRAT (Brain Impulse Galvanascope Record and Transfer); and from *Captain Scarlet and the Mysterons*, SIG (Spectrum Is Green). FAB was the standard call response in *Thunderbirds* but although the term sounded like an acronym, it actually stood for nothing.

2. Bill Osgerby, "'Stand By for Action!' Gerry Anderson, Supermarionation and the 'White Heat' of Sixties Modernity," in *Unruly Pleasures: The Cult Film and Its Critics*, ed. by Xavier Mendik and Graeme Harper (Guildford: FAB, 2000), pp. 123–35 (p. 126).

3. Ibid., p. 135.

4. John R. Cook, "The Age of Aquarius: Utopia and Anti-Utopia in Late 1960s' and Early 1970s' British Science Fiction Television," in *British Science Fiction Television: A Hitchhiker's Guide*, ed. by John R. Cook and Peter Wright (London and New York: I.B. Tauris), pp. 93–115 (p. 104).

5. For a relevant discussion of science fiction cinema, see: H.B. Franklin, "Visions of the Future in Science Fiction Films from 1970 to 1982," in *Alien Zone: Cultural Theory and Contemporary Science Fiction Cinema*, ed. by Annette Kuhn (London: Verso, 1990), pp. 19–31.

6. Christine Cornea, *Science Fiction Cinema: Between Fantasy and Reality* (Edinburgh: Edinburgh University Press, 2007), p. 79.

7. For a discussion of the latter, see: David Garland, "Pulling the Strings: Gerry Anderson's Walk from 'Supermarionation' to 'Hypermarionation,'" in *Channeling the Future: Essays on Science Fiction and Fantasy Television*, ed. by Lincoln Geraghty (Lanham, MD: Scarecrow, 2009), pp. 61–74.

8. The first landing on the Moon took place during *UFO*'s production.

9. Cornea, p. 80.

10. See for instance the interview with him in: Nicholas J. Cull, "The Man Who Made *Thunderbirds*: An Interview with Gerry Anderson," in *British Science Fiction Television: A Hitchhiker's Guide*, ed. by John R. Cook and Peter Wright (London and New York: I.B. Tauris), pp. 116–130.

11. *The Secret Service*, Anderson's final "Supermarionation" television show before beginning work on *UFO*, also incorporated some live-action inserts.

12. Anderson has indicated that he fashioned his puppet shows with an adult audience in mind alongside the main children's audience. The intended departure from children's programming with *UFO* appears to have been more problematic.

13. Anderson on "Confetti Check A-OK": "Oddly enough, I was heavily criticised for that, particularly by ITC in New York. They reacted by saying 'Now come on, you're dealing with married life, for God's sake, and this is supposed to be a science fiction series.'" See Chris Bentley, *The Complete Book of Gerry Anderson's UFO* (London: Reynolds and Hearn, 2003), p.50.

14. Apparently the shot of the alien eyeball was so discomforting to potential merchandisers of the show, who presumably were looking for the next *Thunderbirds*, that some of them walked out of preview screenings of the first episode. Reported in Bentley, p. 172.

15. Cook, p. 106.

16. It is interesting in this respect that the woman who Alec attempts to pick up in the first episode, Virginia Lake (played by Wanda Ventham), would replace him as SHADO second in command in the last nine episodes. For the second time in *UFO*'s production history, a female character received an unplanned promotion "in the field," so to speak.

17. The fact that these two operatives are a white woman and a black man but that the episode never refers to this is a clear indication, also evident in other episodes, of the series' desire to include progressive representations of race. That, from a present day perspective at least, it does this so awkwardly arguably reflects the tenor of the times more than it does any shortcomings on the part of the program makers.

18. For a relevant discussion of *The Prisoner*, see: Sue Short, "Countering the Counterculture: *The Prisoner* and the 1960s," in *British Science Fiction Television: A Hitchhiker's Guide*, ed. by John R. Cook and Peter Wright (London and New York: I.B. Tauris), pp. 71–92.

19. Some sample transmission schedules are collected in Bentley, pp. 169–70.

Chapter 8

1. This is a revised version of an article first published in *Recycling Cultures*, ed. by Sara Martin, Felicity Hand and Isabel Clúa (Newcastle upon Tyne: Cambridge Scholars Publishing, 2008), pp. 11–20. Published with the permission of Cambridge Scholars Publishing.

2. On Kubrick's place within British science fiction, see James Chapman, "'A Bit of the Old Ultra-Violence': *A Clockwork Orange*," in *British Science Fiction Cinema*, ed. by I.Q. Hunter (London: Routledge, 1999), pp. 128–37.

3. Janet Staiger, "The Cultural Productions of *A Clockwork Orange*," in *Stanley Kubrick's A Clockwork Orange*, ed. by Stuart Y. McDougal (Cambridge: Cambridge University Press, 2003), pp. 37–60 (p. 44); Matthew Sweet, *Shepperton Babylon: The Lost Worlds of British Cinema* (London: Faber and Faber, 2005), p. 272.

4. Eric Schaefer, *"Bold! Daring! Shocking! True!" A History of Exploitation Films, 1919–1959* (Durham, NC: Duke University Press, 1999), p. 77.

5. On British sexploitation, see I.Q. Hunter, "Take an Easy Ride: Sexploitation in the 1970s," in *Seventies British Cinema*, ed. by Robert Shail (London: British Film Institute, 2008), pp. 3–13. On exploitation generally, and especially its parasitism on the mainstream, see I.Q. Hunter, "Exploitation as Adaptation," *Scope: An Online Journal*

of *Film and TV Studies* 15 (November 2009), and *Cultural Borrowings: Appropriation, Reworking, Transformation*, ed. by Iain Robert Smith (eBook), pp. 8–33, available at http://www.scope.nottingham.ac.uk/cultborr/chapter.php?id=5 (accessed 22 June 2010).

6. Justin Smith, *Withnail and Us: Cult Films and Film Cults in British Cinema* (London and New York: I.B. Tauris, 2010), p. 68.

7. Sweet, p. 272. On generational conflict in British science fiction in the 1960s, see I.Q. Hunter, "*The Day the Earth Caught Fire*," in *British Science Fiction Cinema*, ed. by I.Q. Hunter (London: Routledge, 1999), pp. 99–112.

8. The best account of class and generation in British horror is Leon Hunt, *British Low Culture: From Safari Suits to Sexploitation* (London: Routledge, 1998), pp. 142–59. See also I.Q. Hunter, "Deadly Manors: The Country House in British Exploitation Films," in *Locating Identity: Essays on Nation, Community and the Self*, ed. by Paul Cooke, David Sadler and Nicholas Zurbrugg (Leicester: De Montfort University, 1996), pp. 45–55; and Steve Chibnall, *Making Mischief: The Cult Films of Pete Walker* (Guildford: FAB, 1998).

9. John Fraser, *Violence in the Arts* (London and New York: Cambridge University Press, 1974), p. 17.

10. Fraser, pp. 24–5.

11. Robin Wood, "Introduction," in *The American Nightmare: Essays on the Horror Film*, ed. by Robin Wood and Richard Lippe (Toronto: Festival of Festivals, 1979), pp. 7–28.

12. See Joan Hawkins, *Cutting Edge: Art-Horror and the Horrific Avant-Garde* (Minneapolis: University of Minnesota Press, 2000), pp. 5–32; and Janet Staiger, *Interpreting Films: Studies in the Historical Reception of American Cinema* (Princeton: Princeton University Press, 1992), p. 185.

13. Hawkins, p. 23.

14. On *A Clockwork Orange* as a cult film, see Ali Catterall and Simon Wells, *Your Face Here: British Cult Movies Since the Sixties* (London: Fourth Estate, 2002), pp. 114–35; and Smith, pp. 63–86. On Kubrick as a cult auteur, see David Church, "The 'Cult' of Kubrick," *Offscreen*, 10.5 (31 May 2006), available at http://www.offscreen.com/index.php/phile/essays/cult_kubrick (accessed 22 June 2010).

15. Margaret DeRosia, "An Erotics of Violence: Maculinity and (Homo)sexuality in Stanley Kubrick's *A Clockwork Orange*," in *Stanley Kubrick's A Clockwork Orange*, ed. by Stuart Y. McDougal (Cambridge: Cambridge University Press, 2003), pp. 61–84.

16. Krin Gabbard and Shailja Sharma, "Stanley Kubrick and Art Cinema," in *Stanley Kubrick's A Clockwork Orange*, ed. by Stuart Y. McDougal (Cambridge: Cambridge University Press, 2003), pp. 85–108 (p. 88).

17. Jon Lewis, *Hollywood v. Hard Core: How the Struggle over Censorship Saved the Modern Film Industry* (New York and London: New York University Press, 2002), p. 226.

18. Staiger, pp. 37–60.

19. See Thomas Elsaesser, "Screen Violence: Emotional Structure and Ideological Violence in *A Clockwork Orange*," in *Approaches to Popular Culture*, ed. by C. W. E. Bigsby (London: Edward Arnold, 1976), pp. 171–200.

20. Letter from Stephen Murphy to N.C. Haslegrave, 20 January 1972, BBFC file on *A Clockwork Orange*.

21 Pauline Kael, "Stanley Strangelove," *New Yorker*, 1 January 1972, pp. 50–3; Andrew Sarris, "Films in Focus," *Village Voice*, 30 December 1971, pp. 49–50.

22. Kael, p. 50.

23. Smith, pp. 77–8.

24. Fredric Jameson, *Signatures of the Visible* (New York: Routledge, 1990), p. 1.

25. Linda Ruth Williams, *The Erotic Thriller in Contemporary Cinema* (Edinburgh: Edinburgh University Press, 2005), p. 397.

26. I.Q. Hunter, "*A Clockwork Orgy*: A User's Guide," in *Realities and Remediations: Film and the Limits of Representation*, ed. by Elizabeth Wells and Tamar Jeffers McDonald (Newcastle Upon Tyne: Cambridge Scholars Publishing, 2007), pp. 101–11 (pp. 104–5). Reprinted in *Peep Shows: Cult Film and the Cine-Erotic*, ed. by Xavier Mendik (London and New York: Wallflower, 2011).

27. Vivian C. Sobchack, "Décor as Theme: *A Clockwork Orange*," *Literature/Film Quarterly*, 9.2 (1981), pp. 92–102 (p. 98).

28. Robert B. Ray, *A Certain Tendency of the Hollywood Cinema, 1930–1980* (Princeton, NJ: Princeton University Press, 1985), pp. 140–3.

Chapter 9

1. Adam Roberts, *Science Fiction* (London: Routledge, 2000), p. 30.

2. Alistair McGown, "Children's TV Drama," *Screenonline*, available at http://www.screenonline.org.uk/tv/id/682920/index.html (accessed 2 March 2010).

3. Mark Bould, "Science Fiction Television in the United Kingdom," in *The Essential Science Fiction Television Reader*, ed. by J.P. Telotte (Lexington: University Press of Kentucky, 2008), pp. 209–30 (p. 222).

4. Ibid.

5. Lez Cooke, *British Television Drama: A History* (London: British Film Institute, 2003), p. 142.

6. Alistair McGown, "Children's Fantasy and SF," *Screenonline*, available at http://www.screenonline.org.uk/tv/id/1383217/index.html (accessed 2 March 2010).

7. Ibid.
8. Dave Allen, "Secret Gardens and Magical Realities: Tales of Mystery, the English Landscape, and English Children," in *Channeling the Future: Essays on Science Fiction and Fantasy Television*, ed. by Lincoln Geraghty (Lanham, MD: Scarecrow, 2009), pp. 93–109 (p. 94).
9. Ibid., p. 106.
10. John R. Pfeiffer, "John Christopher (Sam Youd)," in *British Fantasy and Science Fiction Writers, 1918–1960*, ed. by Darren Harris-Fain (Detroit: Gale, 2002), pp. 14–29 (p. 16).
11. Ibid., p. 17.
12. See Graham J. Murphy, "Dystopia," in *The Routledge Companion to Science Fiction*, ed. by Mark Bould, Andrew M. Butler, Adam Roberts, and Sherryl Vint (London: Routledge, 2009), pp. 473–77.
13. Raffaella Baccolini and Tom Moylan, "Introduction: Dystopias and Histories," in *Dark Horizons: Science Fiction and the Dystopian Imagination*, ed. by Raffaella Baccolini and Tom Moylan (New York: Routledge, 2003), pp. 1–12 (p. 6).
14. Adam Roberts, *The History of Science Fiction* (London: Palgrave, 2005), p. 210.
15. John Newsinger, "Rebellion and Power in the Juvenile Science Fiction of John Christopher," *Foundation: The Review of Science Fiction*, 47 (1990), 46–54 (p. 46).
16. Ibid., p. 47.
17. James Chapman, *Inside the TARDIS: The Worlds of Doctor Who* (London and New York: I.B. Tauris, 2006), p. 154.
18. K.V. Bailey, "Masters, Slaves, and Rebels: Dystopia as Defined and Defied by John Christopher," in *Science Fiction for Young Readers*, ed. by C. W. Sullivan III (Westport, CT: Greenwood, 1993), pp. 97–112 (p. 97).
19. Newsinger, p. 50.
20. John Christopher, *The White Mountains* (1967; repr. New York: Simon Pulse, 2003), p. ix.
21. Pfeiffer, p. 23.
22. Cooke, p. 157.
23. John Caughie, *Television Drama: Realism, Modernism, and British Culture* (Oxford: Oxford University Press, 2000), p. 212.
24. Cooke, p. 128.
25. Andrew Higson cited in Paul Dave, *Visions of England: Class and Culture in Contemporary Cinema* (Oxford: Berg, 2006), p. 6.
26. Linda Ruth Williams, "Dream Girls and Mechanic Panic: Dystopia and its Others in *Brazil* and *Nineteen Eighty-Four*," in *British Science Fiction Cinema*, ed. by I.Q. Hunter (London: Routledge, 1999), pp. 153–68 (p. 159).
27. Sarah Neely, "Cool Intentions: The Literary Classic, the Teenpic and the 'Chick Flick,'" in *Retrovisions: Reinventing the Past in Film and Fiction*, ed. by Deborah Cartmell, I.Q. Hunter and Imelda Whelehan (London: Pluto, 2001), pp. 74–86 (p. 74).

28. Deborah Cartmell and I.Q. Hunter, "Introduction: Retrovisions: Historical Makeovers in Film and Literature," in *Retrovisions: Reinventing the Past in Film and Fiction*, ed. by Deborah Cartmell, I.Q. Hunter and Imelda Whelehan (London: Pluto, 2001), pp. 1–7 (p. 7).
29. John Barrell, *The Dark Side of the Landscape: The Rural Poor in English Painting, 1730–1840* (Cambridge: Cambridge University Press, 1980), p. 6.
30. Ibid., pp. 128–9.
31. Ibid., p. 5.
32. Ibid., p. 2.
33. Vivian Sobchack, "Cities on the Edge of Time: The Urban Science fiction Film," in *Alien Zone II: The Spaces of Science Fiction Cinema*, ed. by Annette Kuhn (London: Verso, 1999), pp. 123–43 (p. 123).
34. Ibid., p. 124.
35. See Susan Sontag, "The Imagination of Disaster," in *Liquid Metal: The Science Fiction Film Reader*, ed. by Sean Redmond (London: Wallflower, 2004), pp. 40–7.
36. Sobchack, 1999, pp. 132–3.
37. John Christopher, *The City of Gold and Lead* (1967; New York: Simon Pulse, 2003), p. viii.
38. Alistair McGown, "Tripods," available at http://www.screenonline.org.uk/tv/id/1386667/index.html (accessed 2 March 2010).
39. John Christopher, *When the Tripods Came* (1988; New York: Simon Pulse, 2003), p. vi.
40. Vivian Sobchack, *Screening Space: The American Science Fiction Film* (New Brunswick, NJ: Rutgers University Press, 1998), p. 133.
41. Ibid., p. 87.
42. Alistair McGown, "Children's Television," *Screenonline*, available at http://www.screenonline.org.uk/tv/id/445547/index.html (accessed 2 March 2010).
43. Ibid.

Chapter 10

1. *Karaoke* first aired between 29 April and 20 May 1996 and *Cold Lazarus* between 26 May and 17 June 1996.
2. Glen Creeber, *Serial Television: Big Drama on the Small Screen* (London: British Film Institute, 2004), p. 68.
3. In fact, the depression-era music so central to *Pennies from Heaven* (BBC, 1978) was not Potter's passion, but Ken Trodd's, the serial and Potter's long-term producer. In 1971, Trodd published *Lew Stone—A Career in Music*, on the notable 1930s musician.
4. Rosalind Krauss, "Dennis Potter and the Question of the Television Author," in *Film and Theory: An Anthology*, ed. by Robert Stam and

Toby Miller (Oxford: Blackwell, 2000), pp. 7–15 (p. 12–13).

5. Krauss, p. 12.

6. See, for example, the following significant and thorough publications on Potter's television serials: Peter Stead, *Dennis Potter* (Bridgend, Mid Glamorgan: Poetry Wales, 1993), John R. Cook, *Dennis Potter: A Life on Screen* (Manchester: Manchester University Press, 1998), Glen Creeber, *Dennis Potter: Between Two Worlds — A Critical Reassessment* (London: Macmillan, 1998) and *The Passion of Dennis Potter: International Collected Essays*, ed. by Vernon Gras and John R. Cook (London: Macmillan, 2000).

7. Potter feared England's assimilation into Europe almost as much as he did its control by the United States. In fact, Potter was rather conservative and isolationist in his views. In *Cold Lazarus*, the British Isles are now part of the larger territory known as "Western Europe."

8. The line between fiction and reality is blurred even more in *Karaoke* than it is in *The Singing Detective* (BBC1, 1986), a serial renowned for its erasure of the boundaries between these two realms.

9. Creeber, p. 72. I will return to this point in the conclusion where I will briefly address Potter's (Fredric) Jamesonian critique of postmodernism.

10. Consider the following biting review: "Potter dips into science fiction completely ignorant of the genre, an arrogance from which *Cold Lazarus* never quite recovers. [...] The design struggles bravely with a television budget and can't help but recall the old, pre–Hollywood *Doctor Who*; the acting is uneven at best, often embarrassing to all concerned, and the tonal swings between satire, comic book futurism and woolly intellectual discussion are not managed confidently." Ray Cathode, "The Box," *Sight and Sound*, 6.6 (June 1996), pp. 32–3 (p. 32).

11. Ken Trodd, Personal Interview, 16 March 2000.

12. Of course high production quality does not necessarily translate into successful science fiction. Knowing the high cost of the genre, Absolutely Television invested a great deal of money in *The Strangerers* (Sky, 2000), but it flopped anyway.

13. Catriona Miller, "British Apocalypse Now — or Then?: *The Uninvited, Invasion: Earth* and *The Last Train*," in *British Science Fiction Television: A Hitchhiker's Guide*, ed. by John R. Cook and Peter Wright (London and New York: I.B. Tauris, 2006), pp. 263–82 (p. 266).

14. A. A. Gill, "Overindulged to the Bitter End: Profile — Dennis Potter," *The Sunday Times*, 28 April 1996, available at <http://global.factiva.com.proxy2.lib.uwo.ca:2048/ha/default.aspx> (accessed: 15 January 2009).

15. See W. Stephen Gilbert, "Cold Comforts," *The Independent*, 24 May 1996, available at http://www.independent.co.uk/arts-entertainment/cold-comforts-1348922.html (accessed 15 January 2009) and Garry Bushnell, "On the Box: Television," *The Sun*, 1 May 1996.

16. Ken Trodd, Personal Interview, 18 February 2000. It is difficult to determine what translates well from script to screen and others often provided criticism that, in the end, improved upon what Potter had envisioned.

17. See Richard Hoggart, *The Uses of Literacy* (New Brunswick, NJ: Transaction, 1998), pp. 188–91.

18. The problem of whether any experience escapes mediation is not addressed in *Cold Lazarus*.

19. Dennis Potter, *Karaoke and Cold Lazarus* (London: Faber and Faber, 1996), p. 207.

20. See Fredric Jameson, *Postmodernism, or The Cultural Logic of Late Capitalism* (1991; Durham, NC: Duke University Press, 1999), pp. 16–19.

21. See Andrew Higson, "Re-Presenting the National Past: Nostalgia and Pastiche in the Heritage Film," in *British Cinema and Thatcherism*, ed. by Lester Friedman. (London: UCL, 1993), pp. 109–29.

22. I offer an extended discussion of several examples of this in *Screening Nostalgia: Populuxe Props and Technicolor Aesthetics in Contemporary American Film* (Oxford: Berghahn, 2009).

Chapter 11

1. This is a revised version of an article first published as Peter Wright, "Intertextuality, Generic Shift and Ideological Transformation in the Internationalising of *Doctor Who*," *Foundation: The International Review of Science Fiction*, 33.92 (Autumn 2004), 64–90.

2. The $5 million finance for *Doctor Who: The Movie* was divided between Fox ($2.5 million), the BBC (£300,000), BBC Worldwide and Universal Television (who collectively contributed $2.2 million). See Philip Segal and Gary Russell, *Doctor Who: Regeneration: The Story Behind the Revival of a Television Legend* (London: HarperCollins Entertainment, 2000), p. 97.

3. In *Reading Television*, John Fiske and John Hartley use the term "claw back" to describe how bardic television draws "into its own central position both the audience with which it communicates and the reality to which it refers [...] The bardic mediator constantly strives to claw back into a central focus the subject of its messages. This inevitably means that some features of the subject are emphasized rather than others" (pp. 86–7). Throughout this article the term is used

somewhat differently to indicate how the figure of the Doctor is brought back from his eccentric position as an aesthetic, asexual alien outsider to a more central location in Western culture. See John Fiske and John Hartley, *Reading Television* (London: Routledge, 1978).

4. See *Bidding Adieu: A Video Diary* (Bill Baggs, 1996).

5. Garry Jenkins, "New Doctor Who," in *TV Zone: The Monthly Magazine of Cult Television*, 77 (April 1996), p. 43.

6. See Tom Beck, "The Man Who Owns Doctor Who," in *Doctor Who Magazine*, 226 (June 1995), pp. 36–7.

7. Philip Segal cited in "*Doctor Who*: Return of the Time Lord," *Radio Times*, 25–31 May 1996, p. 2.

8. Segal and Russell, p. 13.

9. See *Doctor Who Magazine* for the 1993–1996 period.

10. Segal, cited in Beck, p. 37.

11. John Tulloch and Manuel Alvarado, *The Unfolding Text* (London: Macmillan, 1984), p. 1 and p. 35.

12. Ibid., p. 47.

13. Ibid., p. 54.

14. Ibid., p. 41.

15. Ibid., pp. 41–2.

16. Segal, cited in Beck, p. 37.

17. Segal, cited in "*Doctor Who*: Return of the Time Lord," p. 2.

18. Geoffrey Sax, cited in "*Doctor Who*: Return of the Time Lord," p. 2.

19. Steve Eramo, "Matthew Jacobs: Writing for Who," *TV Zone* 80 (July 1996), p. 27.

20. For a detailed account of Jacobs's brief and the various drafts Jacobs undertook, see Segal and Russell, pp. 98–111.

21. Matthew Jacobs, cited in Eramo, p. 28.

22. Sylvester McCoy, *Bidding Adieu*.

23. Notably, *Doctor Who: The Movie* does not have the sense of Americanism that characterizes *Star Trek*, the original *Battlestar Galactica* (U.S., ABC, 1978–1979), or *Buck Rogers in the 25th Century* (U.S., NBC, 1979–1981). For a discussion of the American qualities of these programs see John Tulloch and Henry Jenkins, *Science Fiction Audiences: Watching Doctor Who and Star Trek* (London: Routledge, 1995), pp. 114–5.

24. I am indebted to Gary Russell for alerting me to these facts in conversation.

25. For a brief description of Katz and Liebes findings, see John Fiske, *Television Culture* (London: Routledge, 1987; repr. 1999), pp. 71–2.

26. Ien Ang, *Desperately Seeking the Audience* (London: Routledge, 1991), p. 2.

27. Ibid., pp. 31–2.

28. Michael Riffaterre, "Compulsory Reader Response: The Intertextual Drive," in *Intertextuality: Theories and Practices*, ed. by Michael Worton and Judith Still (Manchester: Manchester University Press, 1990), pp. 56–78 (p. 56).

29. A later and more explicit reference to *Star Trek* occurs when the TARDIS's chameleon circuit is renamed a "cloaking device," a technological conceit appearing in several *Star Trek* films and episodes.

30. For a discussion of the importance of continuity in fan loyalty, see Tulloch and Alvarado, pp. 65–9 and p. 83.

31. Tony Howe, cited in John Tulloch and Henry Jenkins, *Science Fiction Audiences: Watching Doctor Who and Star Trek* (London: Routledge, 1995), p. 160.

32. These figures are taken from David J. Howe and Stephen James Walker, *Doctor Who: The Seventh Doctor Handbook—The McCoy Years 1987–1996* (London: Virgin, 1998).

33. Another example of this strategy occurs when the Doctor is taken to Walker General Hospital by Chang Lee. When questioned by the paramedic attending the Doctor, Lee gives the Doctor's name as "John Smith," the pseudonym employed by the Third Doctor during his exile on Earth.

34. Segal, cited in *TV Zone* 77 (April 1996), p. 43.

35. During a meeting between the BBC's executive producer Jo Wright and Philip Segal, the BBC voiced its concerns that Matthew Jacobs's script had resulted in something like "a script for *ER*." See Segal and Russell, p. 108.

36. The Doctor, a redoubtable hero for twenty-six years, is "killed" by human interference, but his death is freighted with sly humor that emphasizes the underlying project of the film — to transform the provincial British world of *Doctor Who* into a viable commercial product. Hence, it is entirely fitting, and not a little symbolic, that an American kills the last truly "British" Doctor. He is doubly alien (he is a British figure abroad and a Gallifreyan on Earth) and wholly vulnerable in the context of commercialized and commercializing late twentieth century America. It hardly seems coincidental that (the possibly facetiously named) Doctor Roger Swift is discussing fund-raising while Grace operates on the Doctor. Swift's presence underpins the importance of raising money, of turning a profit, and thereby self-consciously textualizes the purpose of the telefilm.

37. Segal and Russell, p. 108.

38. Riffaterre, p. 57.

39. Ibid., p. 58.

40. Matthew Jacobs, *Doctor Who: The Script of the Film* (London: BBC, 1996), p. 34.

41. See Gary Gillat's limited audience study "Second Sight," *Doctor Who Magazine*, 242 (August 1996), p. 9.

42. David Morley, *Television Audiences and Cultural Studies* (London: Routledge, 1992), p. 31.

43. Riffaterre, p. 57.
44. Fiske, *Television Culture*, p. 84
45. According to the BBC mythology, the Eye of Harmony is the artificial black hole engineered by the Time Lord Omega and tamed by his co-worker Rassilon. Located beneath the Panopticon, the centerpiece of the Capitol on Gallifrey, the black hole provides the Time Lords with the enormous power they require to travel at will through the space-time vortex. By redefining the Eye of Harmony as the TARDIS's engine, screenwriter Jacobs unnecessarily simplifies a significant amount of Time Lord history, a fact which angered fans of the series.
46. Jacobs, p. 118.
47. In Season Nineteen's "Timeflight" (by Peter Grimwade), the Doctor refuses to go back in time to save the life of his companion Adric (Matthew Waterhouse), killed in the preceding adventure, Eric Saward's "Earthshock."
48. Tulloch and Jenkins, p. 98.
49. Ibid., p. 261.
50. Interestingly, the decision to cast Eric Roberts as the Master may have contributed to a reading of the character as a predatory queer. In 1996, Roberts was known for delivering a sympathetic performance of a man dying of AIDS in gay director Randal Kleiser's autobiographical *It's My Party* (U.S.), which premiered at Sundance on 11 January before receiving a general U.S. release on 22 March. Therefore, at the time of the casting, shooting and airing of *Doctor Who: The Movie* Roberts was familiar to American audiences for having recently played a gay man. Although *It's My Party* is certainly not a homophobic text, Roberts' involvement in the film added an additional, extratextual resonance to the telefilm's insinuations regarding the Master's sexuality.
51. Seigler cited in Ang, p. 40.
52. See Gary Gillatt, "An Englishman Abroad," *Doctor Who Magazine*, 264 (May 1998), p. 14. Viewing figures are from Segal and Russell, p. 143,
53. The notion that any televised *Doctor Who* was welcome is an attitude shared amongst the many fans who aired their opinions in various issues of *Doctor Who Magazine* in the months following the airing of the telefilm. In terms of the BBC's reappropriation of its publishing rights, a cynic might suggest that the Corporation used Segal's film as an extended advertisement for its own products, taking the opportunity to use outside investment to rejuvenate the brand and, hence, capitalize on the resurgence of interest in *Doctor Who* to market its own comparatively low-cost merchandise.
54. Fiske, p. 319.
55. Chris Barker, *Television, Globalisation and Cultural Identities* (Oxford: Oxford University Press, 1999), p. 43.
56. Ibid., p. 37.
57. Ibid., p. 1.

Chapter 12

1. Thomas B. Byers, "Commodity Futures," in *Alien Zone: Cultural Theory and Contemporary Science Fiction Cinema*, ed. by Annette Kuhn (London: Verso, 2000), pp. 39–50 (p. 39).
2. Paul Julian Smith, "The Curse of Almodovar," *The Guardian*, 17 June 2008, available at http://www.guardian.co.uk/film/2008/jun/17/worldmusic.pedroalmodovar (accessed 28 June 2010).
3. Benedict Anderson, *Imagined Communities: Reflections on the Origin and Spread of Nationalism* (London: Verso, 1991).
4. Andrew Higson, "The Limiting Imagination of National Cinema," in *Cinema and Nation*, ed. by Mette Hjort and Scott McKenzie (London: Routledge, 2000), pp. 63–74 (p. 16).
5. Ibid.
6. Hamid Nacify, *An Accented Cinema: Exilic and Diasporic Filmmaking* (Princeton, NJ: Princeton University Press, 2001), p. 4.
7. Ibid. p. 5.
8. Thomas Elsaesser, *European Cinema: Face to Face with Hollywood* (Amsterdam: Amsterdam University Press, 2005), p. 115.
9. Philip Schlesinger, "The Sociological Scope of National Cinema," in *Cinema and Nation*, ed. by Mette Hjort and Scott McKenzie (London: Routledge, 2000), pp. 19–31 (p. 24).
10. Elsaesser, p. 82.
11. Ibid., p. 82.
12. Published in Britain from 1841 to 1992, and later revived in the mid 1990s, *Punch* was especially popular in the latter parts of the nineteenth century. Nominally a satirical magazine, *Punch* often depicted the working-classes, as well as minorities such as the Irish, in an unflattering light. As Jamie W. Johnson notes: "The working-classes only appear in Punch in relationship to the dominant classes. Servants rarely appear as subjects in their own right, except to demonstrate the ridiculousness of their natures." Jamie W. Johnson, "The Changing Representation of the Art Public in 'Punch,' 1841–1896," *Victorian Periodicals Review*, 35.3 (2002), pp. 272–94 (p. 274).
13. Vineyard, Jennifer, "Alan Moore: The Last Angry Man," in *Movies on MTV.com*, available at http://www.mtv.com/shared/movies/interviews/m/moore alan 060315/ (accessed 30 May 2009).
14. Slavoj Žižek, *Children of Men*, DVD commentary (Universal, 2006).
15. Kristin Ross, *Fast Cars, Clean Bodies: Decolonization and the Reordering of French Culture* (Cambridge, MA: MIT Press, 1995), p. 55.
16. Tim Bergfelder, "National, Trans-National or Supranational Cinema? Rethinking European Film Studies," *Media, Culture and Society*, 27.3 (2005), pp. 315–31 (p. 321).
17. Ibid., p. 329.

18. Ewa Mazierska and Laura Rascaroli, *From Moscow to Madrid: Postmodern Cities, European Cinema* (London and New York: I.B. Tauris, 2003), p. 197.
19. Higson, p. 19.
20. Owen Gleiberman, "28 Days Later," *Entertainment Weekly*, 27 June 2003, available at http://www.ew.com/ew/article/0,,458308,00.html (accessed 25 June 2010).
21. Eleanor Ringel Gillespie, "*28 Days Later*," *Atlanta Journal Constitution*, 26 June 2003, available at http://www.accessatlanta.com/movies/content/shared/movies/reviews/numbers/28dayslater.html (accessed 26 June 2010).
22. Released in 2007 under the direction of the Spanish filmmaker Juan Carlos Fresnadillo, *28 Weeks Later* portrays the aftermath of U.S. intervention against the "rage" virus. Now quarantined and under strict military supervision, London is re-imagined as an occupied territory wherein personal freedoms are limited, in an ultimately futile attempt to re-establish social order. The re-emergence of the virus leads to chaos on the streets and amidst military efforts to quell the disturbances, a considerable level of "collateral damage" is accrued, as dozens of non-infected civilians are shot and killed.
23. Higson, p. 19.
24. Bergfelder, p. 321.

Chapter 13

1. It is also worth noting that since *28 Days Later* British science fiction television has seen a successful resurgence with series such as the rebooted *Doctor Who*, its spin-off *Torchwood* (BBC, 2006-), *Primeval* (ITV, 2007-), *Life on Mars* (BBC, 2006-2007) and the remake of *Survivors* (BBC, 2008-2010).
2. John Fiske, "The Cultural Economy of Fandom," in *The Adoring Audience: Fan Culture and Popular Media*, ed. by Lisa Lewis (London: Routledge, 1992), pp. 30-49 (p. 30).
3. In part, the reason for these genres being particularly marginalized has to do with Hollywood blockbuster budgets and the high costs of special effects cinema which British cinema cannot often match.
4. Tino Balio, "Adjusting to the New Global Economy: Hollywood in the 1990s," in *Film Policy: International, National and Regional Perspectives*, ed. by Albert Moran (London: Routledge, 1996), pp. 23-38.
5. Henry Jenkins, *Textual Poachers: Television Fans and Participatory Culture* (London: Routledge, 1992), pp. 24-7.
6. Brigid Cherry, "Refusing to Refuse to Look: Female Viewers of the Horror Film," in *Identifying Hollywood Audiences: Cultural Identity and the Movies*, ed. by Melvin Stokes and Richard Maltby, eds., (London: British Film Institute, 1999), pp. 187-203 (p. 194).
7. Mark Jancovich, "Genre and the Audience: Genre Classifications and Cultural Distinctions in the Mediation of *The Silence of the Lambs*," in *Hollywood Spectatorship: Changing Perceptions of Cinema Audiences*, Melvin Stokes and Richard Maltby, eds. (London: British Film Institute, 2001), pp. 33-45.
8. As described by Boyle on the official website (site no longer active), http://www.28dayslaterthemovie.co.uk/main.html (accessed 27 March 2004).
9. Brian Aldiss and David Wingrove, *Trillion Year Spree: The History of Science Fiction* (London: House of Stratus, 1986), pp. 278-79.
10. Discourses and data are taken from the British Science Fiction Association Forum at http://www.bsfa.co.uk, Outpost Gallifrey at http://www.gallifreyone.com/, Spaced Out at http://www.spaced-out.org/, The Yahoo! Groups UK-SG1 at http://tv.groups.yahoo.com/group/UK-SG1/ and the Vampire Exchange and Information Network at http://groups.yahoo.com/group/vein/, and the Google Groups uk.media.dvd, rec.arts.sf.movies and alt.horror.
11. Karen Ross and Virginia Nightingale, *Media and Audiences: New Perspectives* (Maidenhead: Open University Press, 2003), pp. 120-45.
12. John Fiske, "The Cultural Economy of Fandom," in *The Adoring Audience: Fan Culture and Popular Media*, ed. by Lisa Lewis (London: Routledge, 1992), pp. 30-49.
13. A text can be deemed meta-polysemic if it offers diverse reading positions which provide something for everyone and encourage different forms of identification, both contextually and at the level of character. A viewer (or reviewer) of *28 Days Later* might thus take up a reading position in the context of several different generic templates.
14. Background information is given on each participant as sex (male or female), age (by ten-year range), and membership of forum or discussion group ("Horror" indicates the alt.horror Google group, "Spaced" the Spaced Out forum, "Vampire" the VEIN Yahoo! group, "Who" the Outpost Gallifrey forum for Doctor Who fans, and so on).
15. Martin Barker and Kate Brooks, *Knowing Audiences: Judge Dredd, Its Friends, Fans and Foes* (Luton: University of Luton Press, 1997).
16. Terry Nation is a significant figure in British science fiction. He was a writer for *Doctor Who*, creating the Daleks, as well as the originator of *Survivors* (BBC, 1975-1977) and *Blake's 7* (BBC, 1978-1981)
17. Stacey, Jackie, *Star Gazing: Hollywood Cinema and Female Spectatorship* (London: Routledge, 1994), pp. 228-34.

18. Matt Hills, *Fan Cultures* (London: Routledge, 2002), p. 108.
19. See http://www.channel4.com/film/news features/microsites/S/scary/results_20-11_1.html (accessed 30 June 2010).
20. Brigid Cherry, "Subcultural Tastes, Genre Boundaries and Fan Canons," in Lincoln Geraghty and Mark Jancovich, eds., *The Shifting Definitions of Genre: Essays on Labeling Films, Television Shows and Media* (Jefferson, NC: McFarland, 2008), pp. 201–15 (pp. 205–7).
21. Mark Kermode, "I Was a Teenage Horror Fan," in *Ill Effects: The Media Violence Debate*, ed. by Martin Barker (London: Routledge, 2001), pp. 126–34 (p. 127).

Chapter 14

1. Matt Hills, *Triumph of a Time Lord: Regenerating Doctor Who in the Twenty-First Century* (London and New York: I. B. Tauris, 2010), p. 2.
2. John Tulloch and Henry Jenkins, *Science Fiction Audiences: Watching Doctor Who and Star Trek* (London: Routledge, 1995).
3. John Tulloch and Manuel Alvarado, *The Unfolding Text* (London: Macmillan, 1984).
4. Alan McKee, "How to Tell the Difference Between Production and Consumption: A Case Study in *Doctor Who* Fandom," in *Cult Television*, ed. by Sara Gwenllian-Jones and Roberta E. Pearson (Minneapolis: University of Minnesota Press, 2004), pp. 167–85; Alan McKee, "Why is 'City of Death' the Best *Doctor Who* Story?," in *Time and Relative Dissertations in Space: Critical Perspectives on Doctor Who*, ed. by David Butler (Manchester: Manchester University Press, 2007), pp. 233–45.
5. Nicholas J. Cull, "Tardis at the OK Corral: *Doctor Who* and the U.S.," in *British Science Fiction Television: A Hitchhiker's Guide*, ed. by John R. Cook and Peter Wright (London and New York: I.B. Tauris, 2005), pp. 52–70. (p. 67).
6. See Camille Bacon-Smith, *Enterprising Women: Television Fandom and the Creation of Popular Myth* (Philadelphia: University of Pennsylvania Press, 1992) and Constance Penley, *NasaTrek* (London: Verso, 1997).
7. Actor Matt Smith took over the role as the Eleventh Doctor, first appearing after Tennant's Doctor regenerated at the end of the episode "The End of Time" and featuring in his first full-length story "The Eleventh Hour" in April 2010.
8. Sarah Elizabeth Bird, *The Audience in Everyday Life: Living in a Media World* (London: Routledge, 2003), p. 77.
9. See Rhiannon Bury, *Cyberspaces of Their Own: Female Fandoms Online* (New York: Peter Lang, 2005); Christine Scodari, "You're Sixteen, You're Dutiful, You're Online: 'Fangirls' and the Negotiation of Age and/or Gender Subjectivities in TV Newsgroups," in *Girl Wide Web: Girls, the Internet, and the Negotiation of Identity*, ed. by Sharon R. Mazzarella (New York: Peter Lang, 2005), pp. 105–20.
10. Hills, pp. 151–65.
11. Matt Hills, "*Doctor Who*," in *Fifty Key Television Programs*, ed. by Glen Creeber (London: Arnold, 2004), pp. 75–9 (p. 76).
12. Jackie Storey and Megan Lane, "Doctor Who, Fashion Icon," *BBC News U.K.* (2005), available at http://news.bbc.co.uk/2/hi/uk_news/magazine/4717755.stm (accessed 21 February 2009).
13. Matt Hills, *Fan Cultures* (London: Routledge, 2002), p. xi.
14. Steve Bailey, *Media Audiences and Identity: Self-Construction in the Fan Experience* (London: Palgrave Macmillan, 2005), p. 185.
15. Shaun Lyons, *The Doctor Who Forum*, Home page, 2000–2009, http://www.doctorwhoforum.com/ (accessed 10 March 2009). Since the writing of this chapter, the website has morphed into *Gallifrey Base*, available at http://gallifreybase.com/forum (accessed 4 April 2010).
16. Matt Hills, "*Doctor Who* Discovers... Cardiff: Investigating Trans-Generational Audiences and Trans-National fans of the (2005) BBC Wales production," *Cyfrwng: Media Wales Journal*, 3 (2006), pp. 56–74
17. Amy Bruckman, "Ethical guidelines for research online" (2002), available at http://www.cc.gatech.edu/~asb/ethics/ (accessed 4 April 2010).
18. Hills, *Fan Cultures*, p. 129.
19. Matt Hills, "Michael Jackson Fans on Trial? 'Documenting' Emotivism and Fandom in Wacko About Jacko," *Social Semiotics*, 17 (2007), 459–77.
20. Melissa Click, "'Rabid,' 'Obsessed,' and 'Frenzied': Understanding *Twilight* Fangirls and the Gendered Politics of Fandom," *Flow TV*, 11: 4 (2010), available at http://flowtv.org/?p=4638 (accessed 3 April 2010).
21. Andrea Macdonald, "Uncertain Utopia: Science Fiction Media Fandom and Computer Mediated Communication," in *Theorizing Fandom: Fans, Subculture and Identity*, ed. by Cheryl Harris and Alison Alexander (Cresskill, N.J.: Hampton Press, 1998), pp. 131–52.
22. Susan Clerc, "Estrogen Brigades and 'Big Tits' Threads: Media Fandom Online and Off," in *Wired Women: Gender and New Realities in Cyberspace*, ed. by Lynn Cherny and Elizabeth Reba Weise (Seattle: Seal, 1996), pp. 73–97 (p. 86).
23. Rhiannon Bury, "Waiting to X-Hale: A Study of Gender and Community on an All-Female *X-Files* Mailing List," *Convergence: The Journal of Research into New Media Technologies*, 4 (1998), pp. 59–83 (p. 62–63).
24. Melanie Nash and Martti Lahti, "'Almost Ashamed to Say I Am One of Those Girls': *Titanic*, Leonardo DiCaprio and the Paradoxes of Girls' Fandom," in *Titanic: Anatomy of a Blockbuster*, ed. by Kevin S. Sandler and Gaylyn

Studlar (New Brunswick, NJ: Rutgers University Press, 1999), pp. 67–88 (p.75).

25. Matt Hills and Rebecca Williams, "It's all My Interpretation: Reading Spike Through the 'Subcultural Celebrity' of James Marsters," *European Journal of Cultural Studies*, 8 (2005), pp. 345–65 (p. 353).

26. Matthew Pustz, *Comic Book Culture: Fanboys and True Believers* (Jackson: University Press of Mississippi, 1999), pp. 71–9.

27. Bury, p. 205.

28. Ibid., p. 37.

29. Ibid., p. 41.

30. Hills, *Fan Cultures*, p. xi.

31. Gwyn Symonds, "Bollocks! Spike Fans and Reception of *Buffy the Vampire Slayer*," *Refractory: A Journal of Entertainment Media*, 2 (2003), available at http://www.sfca.unimelb.edu.au/refractory/journalissues/index.htm (accessed 1 March 2009).

32. "The Record Long David Tennant Appreciation Thread [Part 130]," Post #610, http://www.doctorwhoforum.com/showthread.php?t=214303&highlight=record+david+tennant&page=16 (accessed 5 March 2009).

33. Mark Jancovich and Nathan Hunt, "The Mainstream, Distinction and Cult TV," in *Cult Television*, ed. by Sara Gwenllian-Jones and Roberta E. Pearson (Minneapolis and London: University of Minnesota Press, 2004), pp. 27–45 (p. 33).

34. Kristina Busse and Karen Hellekson, "Introduction: Work in Progress," in *Fan Fiction and Fan Communities in the Age of the Internet*, ed. by Karen Hellekson and Kristina Busse (Jefferson, NC: McFarland, 2006), pp. 5–32 (p.11).

35. Caitlin Moran, "Will Doctor 11 Have the Phwoargh Factor of Doctors 9 and 10?," *The Times Online*, 18 March 2010, available at http://entertainment.timesonline.co.uk/tol/arts_and_entertainment/tv_and_radio/article7068066.ece (accessed 4 April 2010).

36. "Anyone Looking Forward to a Future of Doctor Who Not Involving David Tennant?," Post #10, http://www.doctorwhoforum.com/showthread.php?t=221598&highlight=school (accessed 5 March 2009).

37. "Classic Series Toys and Merchandise [Part 19])," Post #646, http://www.doctorwhoforum.com/showthread.php?t=211072&highlight=Classic+series+merchandise+%5BPart&page=17 (accessed 5 March 2009).

38. Lori Kendall, "'Oh No! I'm a Nerd!' Hegemonic Masculinity on an Online Forum," *Gender & Society* 14 (2000), 256–74 (p. 265).

39. Ibid., p. 266.

40. Jacinda Read, "The Cult of Masculinity: From Fan-Boys to Academic Bad-Boys," in *Defining Cult Movies: The Cultural Politics of Oppositional Taste*, ed. by Mark Jancovich, Antonio Lazaro Reboll, Julian Stringer, and Andrew Willis (Manchester: Manchester University Press, 2003), pp. 54–70 (p. 64).

41. Nathan Hunt, "The Importance of Trivia: Ownership, Exclusion and Authority in Science Fiction Fandom," in *Defining Cult Movies: The Cultural Politics of Oppositional Taste*, ed. by Mark Jancovich, Antonio Lazaro Reboll, Julian Stringer, and Andrew Willis (Manchester: Manchester University Press, 2003), pp. 185–201 (p. 185).

42. Ed Wiltse, "Fans, Geeks and Nerds, and the Politics of Online Communities," *Proceedings of the Media Ecology Association*, 5 (2004), available at http://www.media-ecology.org/publications/MEA_proceedings/v5/Wiltse05.pdf (accessed 20 March 2009).

43. Hills and Williams, p. 350.

44. BBC, "Tennant to Take Over the Tardis," *BBC NewsUK* (2005), available at http://news.bbc.co.uk/2/hi/entertainment/4450285.stm (accessed 13 April 2009).

45. Lori Kendall, "Nerd Nation: Images of Nerds in U.S. Popular Culture," *International Journal of Cultural Studies*, 2 (1999), pp. 260–83 (p. 262).

46. Marion Leonard, *Gender in the Music Industry* (Aldershot: Ashgate, 2007), p. 48.

47. Ibid.

48. Jason Tocci, "The Well-Dressed Geek," *Media in Transition*, 5 (2007), 6, available at http://web.mit.edu/comm-forum/mit5/papers/Tocci.pdf (accessed 14 February 2009).

49. "The Record Long David Tennant Appreciation Thread [part 132]," Post #221, available at http://www.doctorwhoforum.com/showthread.php?t=217628&highlight=Record+David+Tennant+Appreciation+Thread+%5BPart&page=6 (accessed 5 March 2009).

50. Ibid., Post #174

51. Hills, *Triumph of a Time Lord*, p. 159.

52. Hills, "*Doctor Who*," p. 76.

53. Rebecca Feasey, *Masculinity and Popular Television* (Edinburgh: Edinburgh University Press, 2008), p. 56.

54. Susan Clerc, "DDEB, GATB and Ratboy: The X-Files Media Fandom, Online and Off," in *Deny All Knowledge: Reading the X-Files*, ed. by David Lavery, Angela Hague and Marla Cartwright (London: Faber and Faber, 1996), pp. 36–51 (p. 41).

55. MacDonald, p. 148.

56. Cornel Sandvoss, *Fans: The Mirror of Consumption* (London: Polity, 2005), pp. 32–42.

57. Jancovich and Hunt, p. 28.

58. See Will Brooker, *Using the Force: Creativity, Community and Star Wars Fans* (New York and London: Continuum, 2002); Matt Hills, "Putting Away Childish Things: Jar Jar Binks as an Object of Fan Loathing," in *Contemporary Hollywood Stardom*, ed. by Thomas Austin and Martin Barker (London: Arnold, 2003), pp. 74–89.

59. "New School Fans — Too Much Self-Lov-

ing?," Post #21, available at http://www.doctorwhoforum.com/showthread.php?t=157933&highlight=giggling+schoolgirl (accessed 6 March 2009).
    60. Ibid., Post #34.
    61. Tulloch and Jenkins, p. 145.
    62. "Anyone Looking Forward to a Future of Doctor Who Not Involving David Tennant?," Post #17.
    63. Ibid., Post #80.
    64. Ibid., Post #76.
    65. Ibid., Post #99.
    66. Ibid., Post #88.
    67. Ibid., Post #99.
    68. Sandra Youssef, "Girls Who Like Boys Who Like Boys: Ethnography of Online Slash/Yaoi Fans" (unpublished thesis, Mount Holyoke College, Department of Anthropology, 2003), p. 51, available at http://yuuyami.com/luce/thesis.pdf. (accessed 8 March 2009).
    69. "The Record Long David Tennant Appreciation Thread [Part 130]," Post #510.
    70. "Could Torchwood Survive without Jack?," Post #36, available at http://www.doctorwhoforum.com/showthread.php?t=218265&highlight=fangirl (accessed 5 March 2009).
    71. "Could Torchwood Survive without Jack?," Post # 37.
    72. "Anyone Looking Forward to a Future of Doctor Who Not Involving David Tennant?," Post #62.
    73. Tulloch and Jenkins, p. 145.
    74. Jancovich and Hunt, p. 32.
    75. Clerc, p. 87.

Chapter 15

    1. Alan McKee, "Is Doctor Who Political?," *European Journal of Cultural Studies*, 7.2 (2004), pp. 201–17.
    2. See Darko Suvin, *Positions and Presuppositions in Science Fiction* (Basingstoke: Macmillan, 1988); Fredric Jameson, "Progress Versus Utopia; or, Can We Imagine the Future?," *Science Fiction Studies*, 27.9 (1982), pp. 147–58.
    3. Eric. S. Rabkin, "Defining Science Fiction," in *Reading Science Fiction*, ed. by James Gunn, Marleen S. Barr and Matthew Candelaria (Basingstoke: Palgrave, 2008), pp. 15–23 (p. 17).
    4. See Jameson.
    5. Rick Worland, "Sign-Posts Up Ahead: The Twilight Zone, The Outer Limits, and TV Political Fantasy 1959–1965," *Science Fiction Studies*, 8.23, Part 1 (1996), pp. 103–22.
    6. Brian McHale, *Postmodernist Fiction* (New York and London: Methuen, 1987), p. 60.
    7. Robert Scholes, *Structural Fabulation: An Essay on Fiction of the Future* (Notre Dame and London: University of Notre Dame Press, 1975), p. 29.

    8. McHale, p. 61.
    9. John R. Cook, "Adapting Telefantasy: The Doctor Who and the Dalek Films," in *British Science Fiction Cinema*, ed. by I.Q. Hunter (London and New York: Routledge, 1999), pp. 113–28.
    10. James Chapman, *Inside The TARDIS: The Worlds Of Doctor Who* (London and New York: I. B. Tauris, 2006).
    11. See Nicholas Cull, "'Bigger on the Inside ...': Doctor Who as British Cultural History," in *The Historian, Television and Television History*, ed. by Graham Roberts and Philip M. Taylor (Luton: University of Luton Press, 2001), pp. 95–111; John Tulloch and Henry Jenkins, *Science Fiction Audiences: Watching Doctor Who and Star Trek* (London and New York: Routledge, 1995); and John Tulloch and Manuel Alvarado, *Doctor Who: The Unfolding Text* (Basingstoke: Palgrave Macmillan, 1983).
    12. Della Thompson, ed., *The Oxford Compact English Dictionary*, (Oxford: Oxford University Press, 1996), p. 874.
    13. See Chapman and Matt Hills, *Triumph of a Time Lord: Regenerating Doctor Who in the Twenty-First Century* (London and New York: I.B. Tauris, 2010).
    14. Clive Barker and Stephen Jones, *Clive Barker's A to Z of Horror* (London: BBC, 1997), p. 52.
    15. Simon Archer and Stan Nicholls, *Gerry Anderson: The Authorised Biography* (London: Orbit, 1998), p. 121.
    16. Esther Walker, "After the Tardis: Russell T. Davies," *The Independent*, 4 October 2008, available at http://www.independent.co.uk/arts-entertainment/tv/features/after-the-tardis-russell-t-davies-950816.html (accessed 30 June 2010).
    17. See Tulloch and Jenkins.
    18. See Kim Newman, *Doctor Who* (London: British Film Institute, 2005), p. 49.
    19. See Katherine Stannard, "Technology and the Female in the Doctor Who Series: Companions or Competitors?," in *Politics, Gender, and the Arts: Women, the Arts, and Society*, ed. by Ronald Dottere and Susan Bowers (Selinsgrove, PA: Susquehanna University Press, 1992), pp. 64–71.
    20. See Chapman.
    21. John Barrowman and Carole E. Barrowman, *Anything Goes: The Autobiography* (London: Michael O'Mara Books, 2008), p. 242.
    22. Gary Needham, "Scheduling Normativity: Television, the Family, and Queer Temporality" in *Queer TV: Theories, Histories, Politics*, ed. by Glyn Davis and Gary Needham (London and New York: Routledge, 2009), pp. 143–158 (p. 54).
    23. See, for instance, Alexander Doty and Ben Gove, "Queer Representation in the Mass Media," in *Lesbian and Gay Studies: A Critical Introduction*, ed. by Andy Medhurst and Sally R. Munt (London and Washington: Cassell, 1997),

pp. 84–99; and Sue Thornham and Tony Purvis, *Television Drama* (Basingstoke: Palgrave, 2005).
  24. Hills, p. 36.
  25. See Tulloch and Jenkins.
  26. Hills, p. 117.
  27. Sergio Angellini, "Torchwood — Series 1, Part 1," *Sight & Sound*, 17.3 (March 2007), p. 84.
  28. David Miller and William Dinan, *A Century of Spin* (London: Pluto, 2008), p. 2.
  29. Russell T. Davies and Benjamin Cook, *Doctor Who: The Writer's Tale* (London: BBC, 2010), p. 323.
  30. Patrick Parrinder, *Science Fiction: Its Criticism and Teaching* (London and New York: Methuen, 1980), p. 29.
  31. Cole Moreton, "Russell T. Davies: Return of the (Tea) Time Lord," *The Independent*, 6 April 2008, p. 2.
  32. Andrew Sarris, "Towards a Theory of Film History," in *Movies and Methods: An Anthology*, ed. by Bill Nichols (Berkeley: University of California Press, 1976), p. 244.
  33. Ibid., p.250.
  34. David Bordwell and Kristin Thompson, *Film Art: An Introduction* (New York: McGraw-Hill, 2008), p. 461.
  35. Ibid., p. 17.
  36. James Monaco, *The New Wave* (New York: Oxford University Press, 1976), p. 7.

Select Bibliography

Aldiss, Brian W. *Billion Year Spree: The True History of Science Fiction*. New York: Doubleday, 1973.

_____ and Harry Harrison, eds. *Hell's Cartographers: Some Personal Histories of Science Fiction Writers*. London: Weidenfeld and Nicolson, 1975.

Andriano, Joseph D. *Immortal Monster: The Mythological Evolution of the Fantastic Beast in Modern Fiction and Film*. Wesport, CT: Greenwood, 1999.

Baccolini, Raffaella, and Tom Moylan, eds. *Dark Horizons: Science Fiction and the Dystopian Imagination*. New York: Routledge, 2003.

Barker, Martin, and Kate Brooks. *Knowing Audiences: Judge Dredd, Its Friends, Fans and Foes*. Luton: University of Luton Press, 1997.

Bartter, Martha. "Nuclear Holocaust as Urban Renewal." *Science Fiction Studies*, 13.2 (no. 39, 1986), pp. 148-58.

Booker, M. Keith. *Science Fiction Television*. Westport, CT: Praeger, 2004.

_____ and Anne-Marie Thomas. *The Science Fiction Handbook*. Chichester: Wiley-Blackwell, 2009.

Bould, Mark, Andrew M. Butler, Adam Roberts and Sherryl Vint, eds. *The Routledge Companion to Science Fiction*. Oxford and New York: Routledge, 2009.

Bretnor, Reginald, ed. *Modern Science Fiction: Its Meaning and Its Future*. Chicago: Advent, 1979.

Britton, Piers D., and Simon J. Barker. *Reading Between Designs: Visual Imagery and the Generation of Meaning in The Avengers, The Prisoner, and Doctor Who*. Austin: University of Texas Press, 2003.

Brooker, Will. *Using the Force: Creativity, Community and Star Wars Fans*. New York and London: Continuum, 2002.

Brosnan, John. *Future Tense: The Cinema of Science Fiction*. London: Macdonald and Jane's, 1978.

Butler, David, ed. *Time and Relative Dissertations in Space: Critical Perspectives on Doctor Who*. Manchester: Manchester University Press, 2007.

Cartmell, Deborah, I.Q. Hunter, Heidi Kaye and Imelda Whelehan, eds. *Alien Identities: Exploring Differences in Film and Fiction*. London: Pluto, 1999.

Chapman, James. *Inside The TARDIS: The Worlds of Doctor Who*. London and New York: I.B. Tauris, 2006.

_____. "Onward Christian Spacemen: *Dan Dare — Pilot of the Future* as British Cultural History." *Visual Culture in Britain*, 9.1 (2008), 55–79.

Clute, John, and Peter Nicholls. *Encyclopedia of Science Fiction*. London: Orbit/Little, Brown, 1993.

Cook, John R. *Dennis Potter: A Life on Screen*. Manchester: Manchester University Press, 1998.

_____ and Peter Wright, eds. *British Science Fiction Television: A Hitchhiker's Guide*. London and New York: I.B. Tauris, 2006.

Cornea, Christine. *Science Fiction Cinema: Between Fantasy and Reality*. Edinburgh: Edinburgh University Press, 2007.

Creeber, Glen. *Dennis Potter: Between Two Worlds—A Critical Reassessment*. London: Macmillan, 1998.

Crinkley, Richmond. "Endgame: Looking at Nuclear Aesthetics." *National Review*, 24 August 1984, pp. 28–33.

Downing, Crystal. "Deconstructing Herbert: *The War of the Worlds* on Film." *Literature/Film Quarterly*, 35.4 (2007), 274–81.

Dowling, David. *Fictions of Nuclear Disaster*. London: Macmillan 1987.

Frayling, Christopher. *Things to Come*. London: British Film Institute, 1995.

Geduld, Harry M., ed. *The Definitive Time Machine: A Critical Edition of H.G. Wells's Scientific Romance with Introduction and Notes*. Bloomington: Indiana University Press, 1987.

Geraghty, Lincoln, ed. *Channeling the Future: Essays on Science Fiction and Fantasy Television*. Lanham, MD: Scarecrow, 2009.

Grant, Barry K. "Looking Upward: H.G. Wells, Science Fiction and the Cinema." *Literature/Film Quarterly*, 14.3 (1986), 154–63.

Gras, Vernon, and John R. Cook, eds. *The Passion of Dennis Potter: International Collected Essays*. London: Macmillan, 2000.

Greenland, Colin. *The Entropy Exhibition: Michael Moorcock and the British "New Wave" in Science Fiction*. London: Routledge and Kegan Paul, 1983.

Gunn, James, Marleen S. Barr and Matthew Candelaria, eds. *Reading Science Fiction*. Basingstoke: Palgrave, 2008.

Haynes, Roslynn D. *From Faust to Strangelove: Representations of the Scientist in Western Literature*. Baltimore: Johns Hopkins University Press, 1994.

Heinze, Rüdiger, and Jochen Petzold. "No More Room in Hell: Utopian Moments in the Dystopia of *28 Days Later*." *Zeitschrift für Anglistik und Amerikanistik* 57.1 (2007), pp. 53–68.

Hills, Matt. "*Doctor Who* Discovers ... Cardiff: Investigating Trans-Generational Audiences and Trans-national Fans of the (2005) BBC Wales Production." *Cyfrwng: Media Wales Journal*, 3 (2006), 56–74.

_____ *Triumph of a Time Lord: Regenerating Doctor Who in the Twenty-First Century*. London and New York: I.B. Tauris, 2010.

Hodgens, Richard. "A Brief, Tragical History of the Science Fiction Film." *Film Quarterly*, 13.2 (1959), 30–9.

Hunter, I. Q., ed. *British Science Fiction Cinema*. London and New York: Routledge, 1999.

Huntingdon, John. *The Logic of Fantasy: H.G. Wells and Science Fiction*. New York: Columbia University Press, 1982.

Hutchings, Peter. *Terence Fisher*. Manchester: Manchester University Press, 2001.

Ireland, Andrew, ed. *Illuminating Torchwood: Essays on Narrative, Character and Sexuality in the BBC Series*. Jefferson, NC: McFarland, 2010.

James, Edward, and Farah Mendlesohn, eds. *The Cambridge Companion to Science Fiction*. Cambridge: Cambridge University Press, 2003.

Jancovich, Mark, Antonio Lazaro Reboll, Julian Stringer and Andrew Willis, eds. *Defining Cult Movies: The Cultural Politics of Oppositional Taste*. Manchester: Manchester University Press, 2003.

Jenkins, Henry, and John Tulloch. *Science Fiction Audiences: Watching Star Trek and Doctor Who*. London: Routledge, 1995.

Jensen, Paul. "H.G. Wells on the Screen.," *Films in Review*, 18.9 (1967), 521–7

Johnson, Catherine. *Telefantasy*. London: British Film Institute, 2005.

Kemp, Peter. *H.G. Wells and the Culminating Ape*. London: Macmillan, 1982.

King, Geoff. *Spectacular Narratives: Hollywood in the Age of the Blockbuster*. London: I.B. Tauris, 2000.

Krah, Hans. *Weltuntergangsszenarien und Zukunftsentwürfe: Narrationen vom "Ende" in Literatur und Film 1945–1990*. Kiel: Verlag Ludwig, 2004.

Kuhn, Annette, ed. *Alien Zone: Cultural Theory and Contemporary Science Fiction Cinema*. London: Verso, 1990.

Leach, Jim. *Doctor Who*. Detroit: Wayne State University Press, 2009.

McConnell, Frank. *The Science Fiction of H.G. Wells*. Oxford: Oxford University Press, 1981.

McDougal, Stuart Y., ed. *Stanley Kubrick's A Clockwork Orange*. Cambridge: Cambridge University Press, 2003.

McKee, Alan. "Is Doctor Who Political?"

European Journal of Cultural Studies, 7.2 (2004), 201–17.

Mohr, Dunja M. "Transgressive Utopian Dystopias: The Postmodern Reappearance of Utopia in the Disguise of Dystopia." *Zeitschrift für Anglistik und Amerikanistik*, 57.1 (2007), pp. 5–25.

Muir, John Kenneth. *A Critical History of Doctor Who on Television*. Jefferson, NC: McFarland, 2008.

Newman, Kim. *Doctor Who*. London: British Film Institute, 2005.

Newsinger, John. "Rebellion and Power in the Juvenile Science Fiction of John Christopher." *Foundation: The Review of Science Fiction*, 47 (1990), 46–54.

Parrinder, Patrick. *Shadows of the Future: H.G. Wells, Science Fiction and Prophecy*. Liverpool: Liverpool University Press, 1995.

_____, ed. *Science Fiction: A Critical Guide*. London: Longman, 1979.

Redmond, Sean, ed. *Liquid Metal: The Science Fiction Film Reader*. London: Wallflower, 2004.

Roberts, Adam. *Science Fiction*. London: Routledge, 2000.

Ruddick, Nicholas. *Ultimate Island: On the Nature of British Science Fiction*. Westport, CT: Greenwood, 1993.

Scholes, Robert. *Structural Fabulation: An Essay on Fiction of the Future*. Notre Dame, IN: University of Notre Dame Press, 1975.

Shail, Robert. "Terence Fisher and British Science Fiction Cinema." *Science Fiction Film and Television*, 2.1 (Spring 2009), 77–90.

Shapiro, Benjamin. "Universal Truths: Cultural Myths and Generic Adaptation in 1950s Science Fiction Films." *Journal of Popular Film and Television*, 18.3 (1990), 103–11.

Shaw, Tony. "The BBC, the State and Cold War Culture: The Case of Television's *The War Game* (1965)." *English Historical Review*, 494 (2006), 1351–1384.

Smith, Don G. *H.G. Wells on Film: The Utopian Nightmare*. Jefferson, NC: McFarland, 2002.

Sobchack, Vivian C. "Décor as Theme: *A Clockwork Orange*." *Literature/Film Quarterly*, 9.2 (1981), pp. 92–102.

_____. *Screening Space: The American Science Fiction Film*. New Brunswick, NJ: Rutgers University Press, 1998.

Stead, Peter. *Dennis Potter*. Bridgend, Mid Glamorgan: Poetry Wales, 1993.

Stover, Leon. *The Prophetic Soul: A Reading of H.G. Wells's "Things to Come."* Jefferson NC: McFarland, 1987.

Suvin, Darko. *Positions and Presuppositions in Science Fiction*. Basingstoke: Macmillan, 1988.

Telotte, J.P., ed. *The Essential Science Fiction Television Reader*. Lexington: University Press of Kentucky, 2008.

Travers, Timothy. "*The Shape of Things to Come*: H.G. Wells and Radical Culture in the 1930s." *Film and History*, 6.2 (1976), 31–41.

Tulloch, John, and Henry Jenkins. *Science Fiction Audiences: Watching Doctor Who and Star Trek*. London: Routledge, 1995.

Williams, Keith. *H.G. Wells, Modernity and the Movies*. Liverpool: Liverpool University Press, 2007.

Worland, Rick. "Sign-Posts Up Ahead: The Twilight Zone, The Outer Limits, and TV Political Fantasy 1959–1965." *Science Fiction Studies*, 8.23, Part 1 (1996), 103–22.

Wright, Peter. "Intertextuality, Generic Shift and Ideological Transformation in the Internationalising of *Doctor Who*." *Foundation: The International Review of Science Fiction*, 33.92 (Autumn 2004), 64–90.

Yeffeth, Glenn, ed. *The War of the Worlds: Fresh Perspectives on the H.G. Wells Classic*. Dallas: Benbella, 2005.

About the Contributors

Lee Barron teaches in the Department of Media at Northumbria University (U.K.). His main research and teaching interests are in the areas of popular culture and media, including music, film, television, and celebrity. His writings have appeared in journals such as *Postcolonial Studies, The Journal of Popular Culture, Nebula, Fashion Theory, Chapter and Verse, International Review of the Aesthetics and Sociology of Music,* and *Disability and Society*. He has also published in a number of books, including *Illuminating Torchwood* (2010).

Jonathan Bignell is a professor of television and film at the University of Reading (U.K.). His recent books include *Beckett on Screen* (2010), *A European Television History* (2008) (edited with Andreas Fickers), *Big Brother: Reality TV in the Twenty-First Century* (2006), and *Postmodern Media Culture* (2000). His publications about science fiction include the book *Terry Nation* (2005) (with Andrew O'Day) and articles on *Doctor Who, The Time Machine* and *The Handmaid's Tale*. He serves on the editorial boards of the journals *New Review of Film and Television Studies, Symbolism: An International Annual of Critical Aesthetics* and the *Journal of Science Fiction Film and Television*.

James Chapman is a professor of film studies at the University of Leicester (U.K.). He has wide-ranging research interests in British cinema, television and popular culture. His books include *Past and Present: National Identity and the British Historical Film* (2005), *Licence to Thrill: A Cultural History of the James Bond Films* (2007), *War and Film* (2008) and, co–authored with Nicholas J. Cull, *Projecting Empire: Imperialism and Popular Cinema* (2009).

Brigid Cherry is a senior lecturer in film and popular culture at St. Mary's University College (U.K.), where she teaches courses on horror cinema, cult film and television, youth culture and music video. She is the author of *Horror* in the Routledge Film Guidebooks series, and is the co–editor of *21st Century Gothic*. She is working on a monograph on the *Doctor Who* online audience and has written widely on science fiction and horror audiences and fan cultures. She has also published work on the contemporary Gothic and vampire cinema.

Michael du Plessis is an associate professor (teaching) of comparative literature and English at the University of Southern California in Los Angeles and has published on topics ranging from Goth subculture to nineteenth century French fiction and in journals such as *Oxford Literary Review* and *Film and Philosophy*. He is working on a book about science fiction and style in the 1960s and 1970s.

Lincoln Geraghty is a principal lecturer in film studies and subject leader for media and film studies at the University of Portsmouth (U.K.). He serves as editorial advisor for *The Journal of Popular Culture, Reconstruction,* and *Atlantis*, with interests in science fiction film and television, fandom, and collecting in popular culture. He is author of *Living with Star Trek: American Culture and the Star Trek Universe* (2007) and *American Science Fiction Film and Television* (2009), and the editor of *The Influence of Star Trek on Television, Film and Culture* (2008) (with Mark Jancovich), *The Shifting Definitions of Genre: Essays on Labeling Film, Television Shows and Media* (2008), and *Channeling the Future: Essays on Science Fiction and Fantasy Television* (2009).

Tobias Hochscherf is a professor of audiovisual media at the University of Applied Sciences Kiel in Germany and visting lecturer at Northumbria University (U.K.). He has published widely on European cinema and television history and is co-editor of *Divided, but Not Disconnected: German Experiences of the Cold War* (2010), and author of *Continental Connection: German-speaking Émigrés and British Cinema, 1927–45* (2011). His research interests include British cinema, early television history, contemporary reality television, and transnational film cultures.

Christian Hoffstadt was awarded his doctoral degree at the University of Karlsruhe, Germany. He is an academic coordinator at the Karlsruhe House of Young Scientists, Karlsruhe Institute of Technology, Germany. His research areas include game and film studies, the philosophy of popular culture and the philosophy of medicine.

I.Q. Hunter is a principal lecturer in film studies at De Montfort University, Leicester (U.K.). He edited *British Science Fiction Cinema* (1999), and is writing *British Trash Cinema*.

Peter Hutchings is a professor of film studies at Northumbria University (U.K.). He has a particular interest in horror cinema and his recent books include *Terence Fisher* (2002), the British Film Guide on *Dracula* (2003), *The Horror Film* (2004) and *The Historical Dictionary of Horror Cinema* (2009). He has also published on science fiction film and television, realism in British cinema, and the British psychological thriller.

Derek Johnston was awarded his Ph.D. from the University of East Anglia (U.K.) in 2010 for his thesis "Genre, Taste and the BBC: The Origins of British Television Science Fiction." He has published on the history of science fiction film and television in the *Science Fiction Film and Television* journal, *When Worlds Collide: The Critical Companion to Science Fiction Film Adaptations* (forthcoming), *The Routledge Companion to Science Fiction* (2009) and *It Came from the 1950s* (forthcoming), the latter two pieces in collaboration with Mark Jancovich.

James Leggott lectures on film and television at Northumbria University (U.K.). He is the author of *Contemporary British Cinema: From Heritage to Horror* (2008), and has published on various aspects of British film and television culture, including reality television, television comedy, traditions of social realism, and the work of the Amber collective.

Aidan Power is a Ph.D. candidate in film studies at University College Cork (Ireland). His thesis deals with motifs of mobility and identity in European cinema. His research focuses on science fiction, road movies and the cinema of Michael Haneke and his areas of interest include westerns, classical Hollywood and national cinemas.

Dominik Schrey is a university teacher at the Faculty of Humanities of the Karlsruhe Institute of Technology in Germany. He has published articles on various aspects of media culture and is working on his doctoral dissertation on media change and nostalgia. His research interests include media and cultural theory, film history and animation studies.

David Simmons is a lecturer in American literature, film and television studies. He has published material on a wide range of subjects related to twentieth century popular culture, including a number of books on the 1960s countercultural movement, work on H.P. Lovecraft, the American horror film, and contemporary genre television. He is editing a collection on the television series *Heroes*.

Christine Sprengler is an associate professor in the Visual Arts Department at the University of Western Ontario (Canada). She is the author of *Screening Nostalgia: Populuxe Props and Technicolor Aesthetics in Contemporary American Film* (2009) as well as articles on British and American film and television. Her research interests include experimental film, video installation, and representations of the 1950s in contemporary visual culture.

Rebecca Williams is lecturer in communication, cultural and media studies in the School of Creative and Cultural Industries at the University of Glamorgan (U.K.). She has written about fandom for *Continuum: Journal of Media and Cultural Studies* and co-authored articles in *European Journal of Cultural Studies* and *Television And New Media*.

Peter Wright is a reader in speculative fictions at Edge Hill University (U.K.). He is author of *Attending Daedalus: Gene Wolfe Artifice and the Reader* (2003). He has written numerous articles and has contributed to Blackwell's *A Companion to Science Fiction* (2005), *The Routledge Companion to Science Fiction* (2009) and *Fifty Key Figures in Science Fiction* (2009). In 2005, he co-edited *British Science Fiction Television: A Hitchhiker's Guide* with John Cook. His *Shadows of the New Sun: Wolfe on Writing/Writers on Wolfe* (2007) was a finalist for the Locus Award for nonfiction in 2008. He is working on *When Worlds Collide: The Critical Companion to Science Fiction Film Adaptations*.

Index

A for Andromeda 3, 180
A la conquête du pole/The Conquest of the Pole 14
The Abominable Dr. Phibes 60–2
Adams, Douglas 3
Adams, Mary 107
The Adventures of Robin Hood 74
The Adventures of Twizzle 74, 79
After London 30
The Airship Destroyer 14
Akin, Fatih 145
Aldiss, Brian 35, 63–4, 108,157
Alien 135
All Quiet on the Western Front 19
Allen, Dave 107
Allen, Irwin 105
Almodóvar, Pedro 144
Alphaville, une étrange aventure de Lemmy Caution 4
Altman, Rick 46
Alvarado, Manuel 129, 167
Amazing Stories 13, 178
Amblin Television 129
American Mutoscope and Biograph Company 14
Amis, Kingsley 43
And Soon the Darkness 61
Anderson, Benedict 145
Anderson, Gerry 7–9, 58, 73–95, 184
Anderson, Poul 179
Anderson, Sylvia *see* Thamm, Sylvia
Andress, Ursula 77
Andrews, Harry 71
Andy Warhol 100
Andy Warhol's Dracula 99
Ang, Ien 131
Ann Veronica 13
Armstrong, Louis 43
Ashes to Ashes 3
Asimov, Isaac 29, 179
Askwith, Robin 97
Asquith, Anthony 15
Associated Television (ATV) 74, 82
Attebury, Brian 42
Austen, Jane 111
The Avengers 60–1, 74, 81

Babylon 5 142
BAFTA (British Academy of Film and Television Arts) 2
Bailey, K.V. 109
Bainbridge, Beryl 98
Baker, Roy Ward 51, 57–8
Bakula, Scott 169
Ballard, J.G. 4, 62–3, 100, 157, 198*n*14
Barbarella 72
Barker, Chris 141
Barker, Martin 45
Barrell, John 112
Barrowman, John 173, 176, 178, 186
Barry, Gene 26
Barry, Iris 15
Bartter, Martha 31
Bates, Richard 114
Battlestar Galactica 105
Bava, Mario 72
BBC *see* British Broadcasting Corporation
The Bed Sitting Room 36
Beethoven, Ludwig van 102–3
Being Human 3
Bergfelder, Tim 151, 155
Berry, Dorothy 47
The Bible 48, 102
Billington, Michael 90
Biró, Lajos 15
Bishop, Ed 90
Blagden, Bob 114
Blair, Tony 150
Blake, William 107
Blake's 7 3, 106, 114
Bliss, Arthur 15
The Blob 52
Blood on Satan's Claw 98
Blue Remembered Hills 119
Bob and Rose 178
Bond, James 77, 81, 83
Bonnie and Clyde 99
Bould, Mark 105–6
The Box of Delights 105, 107
Boyle, Danny 3, 4, 37, 143, 151–4, 158, 163–5
Bradbury, Ray 46, 180
Brando, Marlon 24

Brave New World 29, 42
Brazil 72, 112, 143
Bride of Frankenstein 20
Briggs, Raymond 33
Brimstone and Treacle 98
British Broadcasting Corporation (BBC) 1–2, 5, 7, 13, 22, 24, 33, 35, 40–49, 52, 57, 78, 104–7, 109, 111–2, 114, 116–8, 128–135, 137–8, 141–2, 162, 165, 180–1, 186, 189, 191, 204n2, 205n35, 206n45, 206n53
British Science Fiction Cinema 3
British Science Fiction Television: A Hitchhiker's Guide 5
Broderick, Mick 32
The Brothers 92
Brown, Gordon 2
Brunel, Adrian 15
Buck Rogers in the 25th Century 105
Buffy the Vampire Slayer 169, 172
Buñuel, Luis 102
Burgess, Anthony 97, 101
Burroughs, Edgar Rice 180
Burroughs, William 63
Bush, George W. 26, 146, 148, 150
Bushell, Garry 121
Busse, Kristina 170
Bussell, Jan 40
Byers, Thomas B. 144

The Cabinet of Dr Caligari 56
Calder-Marshall, Anna 61
Campbell, Joseph W. 42
Cape Fear 98
Čapek, Karel 40
Captain Scarlet 75, 77, 79, 83, 87, 184–5
Captain Scarlet and the Mysterons 85, 93
Carreras, Michael 59
Cartier, Rudolph 2–3
Cartmell, Deborah 112
Casanova 178
Catherine the Great 15
Caughie, John 112
CBS 74, 141
Century 21 Productions 75, 76, 80, 87
The Changes 36, 107
Channel Four 117, 173
Chicago Hope 135
The Children 98
The Children of Light 56
Children of Men 4, 7, 37–9, 121, 143–55
Chocky 107
Christopher, John 8, 104, 106–7, 111, 112, 115, 157
The Chronicles of Narnia 105, 107
Churchill, Winston 1, 95
Citizen Kane 21
The City of Gold and Lead 114
Clarke, Arthur C. 42, 108, 179
Clemens, Brian 61
A Clockwork Orange 4, 9, 56, 96–103
Close Encounters of the Third Kind 25
Clute, John 64

Cold Lazarus 7, 9, 117–127
The Condition of Muzak 64, 67
Confessions of a Window Cleaner 97
Connery, Sean 36
Cook, John R. 5, 81, 87, 91
Cooke, Alistair 18
Cooke, Lez 111
Cool It Carol! 97
Corbusier, Le 65
Cornea, Christine 88, 93
Creeber, Glen 118, 120, 126
Critchley, Julian 61
CSI: Crime Scene Investigation 188
Cuarón, Alfonso 4, 143, 145, 149
A Cure for Cancer 64, 67
The Curse of Frankenstein 52, 54
Cushing, Peter 53, 56

Daleks 1–2, 9, 80, 133, 142, 191
Dallas 131
The Damned 55–6, 97
Danger: Diabolik 72
Dare, Dan 6
Darwin, Charles 12
Davies, Russell T. 177–8, 180, 190
The Day After 34
Day of the Dead 158
The Day of the Triffids (book) 3, 35,37–8, 43 161
The Day of the Triffids (1962 film) 3, 34
The Day of the Triffids (1981 TV series) 3, 36, 106–8, 161–2
The Day of the Triffids (2009 TV series) 3
Defantenay, C.I. 179
Le Dernier Combat 162
The Desperate Hours 98
Destination Moon 21
The Devils 100
The Devil's Rain 62
diCaprio, Leonardo 169
Dick Barton Strikes Back 52
Dicks, Terrance 142
Dr. No 77, 81
Dr. Phibes Rises Again 60–1
Doctor Who 1–3, 7–9, 24, 35, 76, 80, 104–6, 112, 114, 128–142, 157–8, 161–2, 166–92
Doctor Who: The Movie 128–42
Dog Soldiers 160–1
Donleavy, Brian 52
Doomsday 35–8
Doomwatch 161
Doppelganger 89
Dowling, David 32
Dracula 19, 55–6, 135–6
Drake, Gabrielle 90

Ecclestone, Christopher 162, 168, 171
Eco, Umberto 67
Eden Lake 98
The Eight Doctors 142
El Topo 99
Eleventh Hour 3

Elsaesser, Thomas 12, 23
Empire of the Ants 12
The Enchanted Castle 107
The English Assassin 64, 66
English Gothic: A Century of Horror Cinema 51, 53–4
U.S.S. *Enterprise* 132
ER 135
Eramo, Steve 130
The Evil Dead 188
The Evil of Frankenstein 56
The Exorcist 99
Eyes Wide Shut 102

Le Fabuleux Destin d'Amélie Poulain 147
Fahrenheit 451 4, 143
Fantastic Voyage 23
Fawkes, Guy 147
Feely, Terence 90
Fennell, Albert 61
Ferroukhi, Ismaël 145
The Final Programme (book) 60–72
The Final Programme (film) 8–9, 60–72
Finch, Christopher 63
Firbank, Ronald 64
Fireball XL5 74–5, 77, 81
The First Men in the Moon (book) 12
The First Men in the Moon (film versions) 12
Fisher, Terence 51–2
Fiske, John 137, 141, 158
Fleming, Ian 64, 199n45
The Fly (1957) 51
The Fly (1986) 137
The Food of the Gods (book) 12
The Food of the Gods (film) 12
Foster, Hal 68
Four Feather Falls 74, 79
The Four Sided Triangle 51
Fox Network 128, 131
Francis, Freddie 56
Frankenheimer, John 24
Frankenstein films 19–20, 45, 50–9, 135–6, 179
Frankenstein (novel) 54
Frankenstein and the Monster from Hell 59
Frankenstein Created Woman 56–7
Frankenstein Must Be Destroyed 58
Fraser, John 98
Die Frau im Mond 4
Frightmare 98
From Faust to Strangelove: Representations of the Scientist in Western Literature 54–5
From Hell 59, 146
From the Earth to the Moon 14
Fry, Stephen 2
Fuest, Robert 60–72
Fulton, John P. 20

Gabbard, Krin 99
Garland, Alex 151
Garner, James 77
Gernsback, Hugo 13, 41–3, 179

Get Smart 80
The Ghost Goes West 15
Gilbert, W. Stephen 121
Gill, A.A. 121
Gillespie, Eleanor Ringel 154
Gilliam, Terry 72, 143
Girl in the Moon see *Die Frau im Mond*
Gleiberman, Owen 154
Godal, Edward 15
Godard, Jean-Luc 4, 100
The Godfather 99
Godwin, Bishop 179
The Gold Bug 62
Goodbye Lenin 147
Gordeno, Peter 90
Gould, Graydon 77
Grade, Lew 74–5, 89
Grade, Michael 109
Grant, Barry Keith 11
Grant, Cary 77
Gray, Barry 79, 86
The Great Ecstasy of Robert Carmichael 98
Greenland, Colin 63
Greenstreet, Sydney 77
Grindhouse 103
Guest, Val 52
Gulliver's Travels 42

Hall, Andrew 24
Hamilton, Richard 68
Hammer films 50–59, 97, 156
Hammer House of Horror 59
Hammer House of Mystery and Suspense 59
Hardware 36
Harold and Maude 99
Harris, John Beynon 42
Harry Potter and the Prisoner of Azkaban 149
Harryhausen, Ray 23
Haskin, Byron 12, 22
Hawkins, Joan 99
Haynes, Rosylnn D. 54
Heinlein, Robert A. 179
Hellekson, Karen 170
Hell's Angels on Wheels 97
A Heritage of Horror 51
High Treason 14
Higson, Andrew 127, 145, 154
Hill, Reg 74
Hills, Matt 162, 169, 191
Hinds, Anthony 54
The History of Mr Polly 11
The Hitchhiker's Guide to the Galaxy (BBC, 1981) 105
The Hitchhiker's Guide to the Galaxy (book and radio series) 3
Hodgens, Richard 11
Hoggart, Richard 44, 122
Horror Hospital 98
The Horror of Frankenstein 58–9
House of Whipcord 98
House on the Edge of the Park 98

The Human League 6
Hunter, I.Q. 51
Huxley, Aldous 29
Huxley, Julian 15
Huxley, Thomas 12
Hyperdrive 3

I Am Legend 151
I, Claudius 15
ICA *see* Institute for Contemporary Art
IG *see* Independent Group
Independent Group (IG) 63, 198n14
Independent Television (ITV) 73–5, 78, 82, 106–7, 178, 180
Independent Television Corporation/Incorporated Television Company (ITC) 74, 94
Injury Time 98
Institute for Contemporary Art (ICA) 63
Invaders from Mars 22
Invasion of the Body Snatchers 22
The Invisible Fluid 14
The Invisible Man (book) 12, 14
The Invisible Man (film) 12, 14, 19–21, 26
The Invisible Man (TV, 1984) 24
The Invisible Man (TV versions) 12, 194n6
L'Invisible Voleur/The Invisible Thief 14
Irving, Charles 46, 49
The Island of Doctor Moreau (book) 12–3
The Island of Doctor Moreau (film versions) 12
The Island of Dr. Moreau (1996 film) 24
The Island of Lost Souls (film) 12
ITC *see* Independent Television Corporation
ITV *see* Independent Television

Jackson, Michael 169
Jacobs, Matthew 130
Jagger, Mick 97
James, P.D. 149, 151
Jameson, Fredric 32, 101, 126–7
Jarman, Derek 72
Jaws 99
Jefferies, Richard 30
Jeffries, Lionel 23
Jenkins, Henry 157, 167, 188
Jericho 39
Joe 90 74–5, 77–8, 80–3, 85
Jones, Allen 77
Journal of Science Fiction Film and Television 5
Journey Into Space 41
Journey to the Far Side of the Sun 89
Journey's End 19
Jubilee 72
Judge Dredd 160
Juran, Nathan 23
Jurassic Park 25
Just Imagine 18
Just Like a Woman 61

Kael, Pauline 101
Karaoke 117, 119–21, 123
Karloff, Boris 19

Katz, Elihu 131
Keir, Andrew 57
Kenton, Erle C. 21
Kepler, Johannes 179
Kilmer, Val 24
King, Stephen 102
King Kong 20–1
The King Who Was a King 15
Kipling, Rudyard 14
Kipps (film adaptations) 11
Kneale, Nigel 2, 4, 7, 23, 44, 52–3, 57
Knight Without Armour 15
Knights of God 107
Koch, Howard 21
Koestler, Arthur 42, 44
Korda, Alexander 15–6
Korda, Michael 18–9
Korda, Vincent 15
Krauss, Rosalind 118
Kubrick, Stanley 4, 8, 56–8, 72, 88, 99–102, 138

Labour Party 2, 13, 189
Lady in a Cage 98
Lanchester, Elsa 15
Lang, Fritz 4, 69, 143
Langelaan, George 51
Lariat Boy 48
The Last House on the Left 98
The Last Man 30
The Last Man on Earth 161
The Last Train 36
Late Night Trains 98
Laughton, Charles 15, 21, 24
Lawrence, H.L. 55
The League of Extraordinary Gentlemen 146
Lean, David 11, 107
Leibes, Tamar 131
Leigh, Roberta 74
Lejeune, C.A. 18
Lenin 13
Lessing, Doris 36
Letts, Barry 24
Lewis, C.S. 105, 107
Lewis, Jon 100
Life on Mars 3
Lighthill, Brian 24
Listen with Mother 47
Logan, John 25
Lorre, Peter 77
Losey, Joseph 56, 96
Lost 3
Lovecraft, H.P. 184
Lugosi, Bela 135
Lyndon, Barré 22

MacDonald, Andrea 169
Mackintosh, Charles Rennie 69
Mad Max 36
Madame Butterfly 136
Making Sausages 4

The Maltese Falcon 77
Man at the End of Its Tether 12
The Man in the Moone 179
The Man in the White Suit 19
The Man Who Could Cheat Death 55
The Man Who Could Work Miracles 12, 15, 18–9
The Man Who Fell to Earth 4
Manson, Charles 87
Marsters, James 169, 172
The Martian Chronicles 180
The Martians and Us 5
Marx, Karl 13
Masefield, John 107
The Mask of Fu Manchu 20–1
Matheson, Richard 151
Matthews, Francis 77
Maxwell, Lois 77
Maxwell, Paul 77
McCoy, Sylvester 130
McDowell, Malcolm 97
McEwan, Ian 98
McGoohan, Patrick 3
McGown, Alistair 107, 115–6
McGuire, Bill 28
McHale, Brian 180
McTeigue, James 143, 147, 152–4
Méliès, Georges 14
Memoirs of a Survivor 36
Men in Black 188
Mendes, Lothar 18
Menzies, William Cameron 15–6, 18
Metro-Goldwyn-Mayer (MGM) 22, 75, 89–90
Metropolis 4, 69, 113, 143
MGM *see* Metro-Goldwyn-Mayer
Micromegas 179
The Midwich Cuckoos 160
Mille, Cecil B. 21
Miller, Catriona 121
Misfits 3
Mittell, Jason 40
A Modern Utopia 13
Modesty Blaise 72
Montagu, Ivor 15
The Moon Stallion 107
Moon Zero Two 50, 58
Moorcock, Michael 8, 60, 62–72
Moore, Alan 146, 148
More, Thomas 29
Morland, George 110, 112–4
Morley, David 137
Morrell, Andre 57
Munro, Rona 132
The Munsters 80
Murdoch, Rupert 117, 121, 124, 127
Murphy, Cillian 163
Murphy, Graham J. 108
Murphy, Stephen 101
Mystery Story 46

Naficy, Hamid 145, 206n6
The Naked Civil Servant 188

Nation, Terry 3, 35, 160–1, 196n26, 207n16
Neale, Steve 82, 200n25
Needham, Gary 187
New Maps of Hell 43, 197n13
New Worlds 62–3, 67, 198n8, 198n15, 199n23
New Worlds Quarterly 63
Newman, Kim 26, 65–6
Newsinger, John 109–10
Night of the Living Dead 99
Nightmare on Elm Street films 24
Nineteen Eighty-Four (book) 29, 42
Nineteen Eighty-Four (film) 112, 203n26
No Blade of Grass 23
No Heroics 3
Novello, Ivor 15
Numan, Gary 6
Number Three 46, 197n30
Nuovo Cinema Paradiso 147

The Omega Man 161
The Open Conspiracy 12
Operation Universe 55
Oranges Are Not the Only Fruit 188
Orwell, George 29, 42–3, 47–9, 53, 56, 112
Osgerby, Bill 86–7
The Outline of History 12
Owen, Clive 149, 154, 181, 183, 185, 187, 189

Pal, George 12, 21–2, 25–6
Paolozzi, Eduardo 63, 70, 198n15, 199n51
Parrinder, Patrick 190, 194n9, 196n22, 197n12
Parrish, James Robert 61
The Passionate Friends 11
Pater, Walter 64
Pathé, Charles 14
Paul, R.W. 14
Peace of Britain 17
Peeping Tom 100
Pennies from Heaven 119, 120, 203n3
The Penthouse 98
Performance 98
Périnal, Georges 15
The Phoenix and the Carpet 107
Pink Flamingos 99
Pirie, David 51–2, 55
Planet of the Apes 23, 36, 57, 195n48
Plato 29
Poe, Edgar Allan 62
Portman, Natalie 147
Potter, Dennis 7–9, 117–121, 123–7, 203n3, 203n4, 204n6–7, 204n9–10, 204n16
Powell, Michael 100
The Power Game 92
Pratchett, Terry 2
Predator 188
Priest, Christopher 35, 43
Pringle, David 42–3
The Prisoner 3, 74, 90, 93, 201n18
The Private Life of Henry VIII 15
The Protectors 81
Provis, Arthur 74

Psychomania 97
Puccini, Giacomo 136
Punch 147, 206*n*12
The Purple Comet 46
Pynchon, Thomas 180

Quantick, David 6
Quantum Leap 142, 169, 174
Quatermass (films) 50–8
Quatermass (1979) 189
Quatermass (TV serials) 4, 23, 44, 48, 50, 52, 157, 180, 189
Quatermass and the Pit 23, 57
The Quatermass Experiment (1953) 2, 44, 48, 52
The Quatermass Experiment (2005) 2
Quatermass II 47, 53, 56
The Quatermass Xperiment (1955) 52–4
Queer as Folk 178, 185, 188, 191
The Quiet Earth 162

Radio Times 2, 44–8
Rami, Sam 188
Ray, Robert 103
Red Dwarf 3, 121
Reefer Madness 96
Rembrandt 15
Reservoir Dogs 103
Resident Evil 159–60
Revelation, Book of 184
The Revenge of Frankenstein 55
The Revenge of the Stepford Wives 62
Riffaterre, Michael 135–6
Rigby, Jonathan 53–4, 57, 59
Rimmer, Shane 77
Roberts, Adam 105, 108
Roberts, Eric 135, 206*n*50
Robinson, Ann 22, 26
Robinson, Heath 22
The Rocky Horror Picture Show 140
Roddenberry, Gene 105
Roeg, Nicolas 4, 98
Romero, George A. 99, 158–60
Roosevelt, Franklin D. 13
Roosevelt, Theodore 13
Ross, Kristin 149
Rossini, Giachino 102
Runacre, Jenny 72
R.U.R. 40

The Saint 81
The Salvaging of Civilization 12
Sangster, Jimmy 51, 58
The Sarah Jane Adventures 191
Sarris, Andrew 101, 190
Saturday 98
Sax, Geoffrey 130, 136
The Scarlet Pimpernel 15
Schlesinger, Philip 146
Schneer, Charles H. 23
Scholes, Robert 180
The Science of Life 15
The Scientific Romances of H.G. Wells 41
Seaquest DSV 129
The Second Coming 178
The Secret Service 75, 200*n*1
Segal, Philip 128–34, 140–2, 205*n*35, 206*n*53
Sendall, Bernard 82
The Servant 98
Seven Famous Science Fiction Novels 41
Sewell, George 90
SFX 6
The Shape of Things to Come 11–3, 33
Sharma, Shailja 99
Shaw, George Bernard 15
Shelley, Mary 30, 54, 58, 157, 179
Sheriff, R.C. 19
Sheybal, Vladek 90
Siegler, Scott 141
The Silence of the Lambs 188
The Silver Sword 115
Silverberg, Robert 13
Simenon, Georges 42
"Singin' in the Rain" (song) 102–3
The Singing Detective 204*n*8
Skladanowksy brothers 14
Sleeper 23
Smith, Don G. 11, 26, 194*n*4–5
Smith, George Albert 4
Smith, Justin 97, 101
Smith, Matt 1, 171, 175–6, 208*n*7
Smith, Paul Julian 144
Sobchack, Vivian 102, 113–5
Solaris 4
Soldier Blue 100
Somnium 179
Sontag, Susan 29, 31–3, 60, 114, 199*n*21
Soylent Green 114
Space 1999 94
Spaced 158, 166
Spaceways 41, 52
Spielberg, Steven 25–6, 129, 195*n*46
Stableford, Brian 41
Stacey, Jackie 162
Staiger, Janet 96, 100
Stalin, Joseph 13
Stanley, Richard 36
The Star 30
Star au Psi de Cassiopée 179
Star Trek 105, 132, 135, 205*n*23, 205*n*29
Star Trek: The Next Generation 105, 140
Star Wars 115, 157
Stargate SG-1 158
The Stepford Wives 62
Stevenson, Robert Louis 157
Stingray 74–9, 82–3, 89
The Story of O 200*n*1
Strachey, John 15
Stranger from Space 47
Straw Dogs 98, 100–1
"Stuck in the Middle with You" (song) 103
Summer Scars 98
Supercar 73–4, 76–9, 81–3

Superman 48
Survivors 3, 35–6, 157, 161–2, 196n24, 207n16
Sweet, Matthew 96
Swift, Jonathan 42

TARDIS 1, 133–5, 138, 140, 175, 205n29, 206n45
Tarkovsky, Andrei 4
Taxi Driver 99
Tennant, David 2, 167–8, 170–8, 208n7
The Tenth Victim 72
The Terminator 137
Terminator 2: Judgement Day 188
The Texas Chain Saw Massacre 99
Thamm, Sylvia 74
Thatcher, Margaret 37, 105–6, 109, 111, 116–7, 118, 123–5, 127, 146
Them! 23
Theorem 98
The Thing 21
Things to Come 4, 11–3, 15–9, 26, 33, 39, 194n18
Threads 33–4, 38, 162
Thunderbirds 74–83, 85, 89, 200n1, 201n14
Time After Time 25, 195n48
The Time Machine (book) 12–4, 25, 30, 134, 180, 185, 195n48
The Time Machine (film) 12, 22–4, 25–6
Tomblin, David 90
El Topo 99
Torchwood 6, 8–9, 171, 176–7, 178–92, 207n1
Torchy the Battery Boy 74, 79
Trainspotting 153, 164
The Tripods (TV series) 8–9, 36, 104–16
Trodd, Ken 120–1, 203n3
Truffaut, François 4, 143
Truman, Harry S. 83
Tulloch, John 129, 167, 177, 188
The Tunnel 4, 18
TV Century 21 80
28 Days Later 3–4,7, 37–8, 143–4, 148–9, 151, 153–66
28 Weeks Later 37–8, 154, 207n22
24 190
Twilight series 169
2000 AD 6
2001: A Space Odyssey 57, 58

Universal Television 128, 204n2
Unwin, Stanley 75
Urban, Charles 14
U.S.S. *Enterprise* 132
Utopia 29

V 105
V for Vendetta 7, 121, 143–53, 55
Vadim, Roger 72
van Dyke, Willard 61
Verne, Jules 13–4, 41–2, 46, 179
The Village of the Damned 160–1
Virus/Fukkatsu no hi 162
Vogt, A.E. van 179

Voltaire 179
Le Voyage dans la lune/A Trip to the Moon 14
Voyage to the Bottom of the Sea 105

Wachowski, Andy 146–7
Wachowski, Larry 146–7
The War Game 4, 33–4
The War in the Air 13
The War of the Worlds (book) 12, 14, 21, 30, 38, 110, 114, 180, 195–6n48
The War of the Worlds (1953) 12, 21–2, 194n6, 194n8
War of the Worlds (2005) 12, 24–6, 195n46
The War of the Worlds (TV) 12, 194n6
Warhol, Andy 99–100, 199n50
Watchmen 146
Watkins, Peter 4, 33
Waugh, Evelyn 111
Wayne, John 124
Webber, Andrew Lloyd 25
Welles, Orson 21
Wells, H.G. 4, 6–8, 11–27, 30, 33, 38, 41–2, 46, 49, 51, 110, 114, 129, 134, 157, 179–80, 182, 185, 194n6, 195n43, 195–6n48
Wells, Simon 25, 56
Whale, James 12, 19–20, 26
The Wheels of Chance 11
When the Sleeper Wakes 13, 23
When the Tripods Came 115
When the Wind Blows 33–4
When Worlds Collide 21
The White Mountains 111
Whitney, Steven 61
The Wicker Man 98
The Wild Bunch 99–100
Williams, Keith 20
Williams, Linda Ruth 102, 112
Williams, Rebecca 169, 172
Wilmott, John 17
Wittgenstein, Ludwig 63
Wood, Robin 99
The Work, Wealth and Happiness of Mankind 12
The World Brain 13
The World Set Free (1914) 13, 196n7
Wright, Peter 5
The Writer's Tale 190
Wuthering Heights 61, 71
Wylie, Philip 21
Wyndham, John 3, 34, 42–3, 51, 106–8, 157, 160–2, 180

The X-Files 56, 87, 121, 140, 142, 169
The X-Ray Fiend 4
X the Unknown 52–3

The Year of the Sex Olympics 4
Youd, Sam *see* Christopher, John
Young, Roland 18

Zardoz 36–7
Žižek, Slavoj 153

www.ingramcontent.com/pod-product-compliance
Ingram Content Group UK Ltd.
Pitfield, Milton Keynes, MK11 3LW, UK
UKHW041946140426
5217IPUK00014B/678